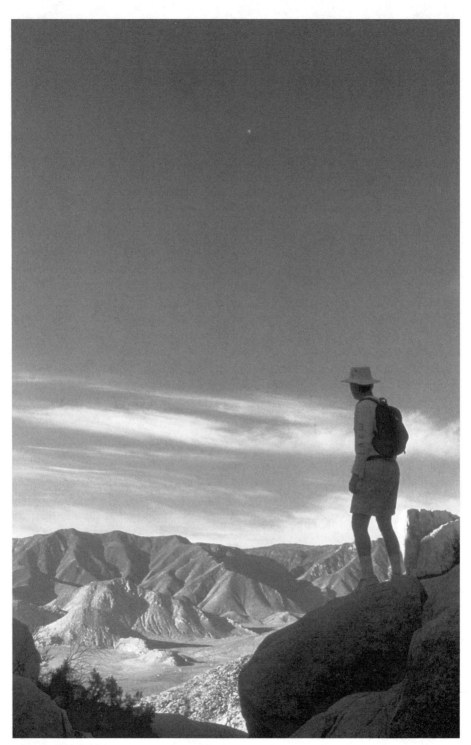

Smuggler Canyon overlook

AFOOT & AFIELD IN

San Diego County

Jerry Schad

 WILDERNESS PRESS · BERKELEY, CA

FIRST EDITION July 1986
SECOND EDITION November 1992
THIRD EDITION September 1998
Second printing July 1999
Third printing July 2000
Fourth printing February 2002
Fifth printing August 2002
Sixth printing August 2003
Seventh printing January 2004

Design by Thomas Winnett and Kathy Morey
Photos and maps by the author
Cover design by Larry B. Van Dyke

Library of Congress Card Catalog Number 98-17262
International Standard Book Number 0-89997-229-2
UPC 7-19609-97229-7

Manufactured in the United States of America
Published by **Wilderness Press**
　　　　　　　1200 Fifth Street
　　　　　　　Berkeley, CA 94710
　　　　　　　(800) 443-7227
　　　　　　　FAX (510) 558-1696
　　　　　　　info@wildernesspress.com

　　　　　　　Contact us for a free catalog
　　　　　　　Visit our Web site at **www.wildernesspress.com**

Cover photo (large): **View from Yucca point**
Cover photo (inset): **Sacred Datura—Jack Creek Meadow, Daley Ranch**

Library of Congress Cataloging-in-Publication Data

Schad, Jerry.
　　Afoot and afield in San Diego County / Jerry Schad. -- 3rd ed.
　　　　　p.　　　　cm.
　　Includes bibliographical references (p.　　) and index.
　　ISBN 0-89997-229-2 (alk. paper)
　　1. Hiking--California--San Diego County--Guidebooks. 2. Backpacking--California--San
Diego County--Guidebooks. 3. San Diego County (Calif.)--Guidebooks.　I. Title.
GV199.42.C22S2669　　1998
917.94'980453--dc21　　　　　　　　　　　　　　　　　　　　　98-17262
　　　　　　　　　　　　　　　　　　　　　　　　　　　　　　　　　　CIP

Acknowledgments

Many people have offered their time, talents, and knowledge during the various phases of producing this book. For the first edition, Mike Fry, Don Endicott, Nick Soroka, Bob and Sharon Hartman, Jane Rauch, Jim Sugg, Bill Becker, Gene Troxell, Janet Leavitt, Pete and Cinde Nowicki, and René Schad shared adventures with me on the trail, and/ or helped with transportation. George Leetch and Uel Fisk shared their knowledge of some of the more obscure parts of the county. Several people associated with local parks and public agencies were of assistance too; among them, Manfred Knaak, Paul Remeika, Torrey Lystra, Norm Machado, Greg Greenhoe, Susan Blankenbaker, George Kowatch, Jack Shu, and Russ Kaldenberg. Shannon O'Dunn, Mitch Beauchamp and Jeff Schaffer reviewed parts of the original manuscript, and Cathey Byrd prepared the symbols that appear at the top of every trip description.

During the period between the first publication of this book (1986) and the present year, I had the pleasure of re-hiking many familiar routes in San Diego County—and also exploring dozens of new trails in the county's newest parks and open-space preserves. This current, third edition features more than 50 trips added since the first edition. A host of people have shared these newer discoveries with me, or otherwise assisted in making this book as complete, up-to-date, and accurate as possible. In addition to the people mentioned above, I wish to thank Phillip R. Abbey, Marcelline Brogli, Steven Cowen, Jan Craven, Gaelen Daum, Beth Davis, Reena Deutsch, M.A. Durrin, Paul Freiman, Gail Hanna, Richard Hughes, Peter Jensen, Carl Johnson, Rob Langsdorf, Joan Lengyel, Norm Noyes, Alex Molnar, Dave Moser, Jack Pomeroy, Monta L. Pooley, Tom Schad, Bruce Silva, Sandie Stanton, James K. Sterrett, John Strauch, Gary Vogt, Bart Ward, Cal Williams, and Joan Wynn for help with the second and third editions.

Portions of the first edition of this book were derived from a series of articles I wrote for *San Diego Home/Garden* magazine between 1982 and 1991. Some of the new material in the second and third editions was derived from my writings in the now-defunct San Diego edition of the *Los Angeles Times*, and also from my current column, "Roam-O-Rama," which has appeared in the *San Diego Reader* weekly newspaper since 1992.

At Wilderness Press, Tom Winnett superbly edited both the first-edition manuscript and the extensive revisions and additions submitted for the second and third editions. Caroline Winnett has amply assisted in strategic planning for the product you now hold in your hands—the third edition. Paul Backhurst prepared the manuscript for typesetting, and Kathy Morey desktop-typeset it.

Jerry Schad
El Cajon, California
July 1998

Contents

Preface

Hiking and backpacking are just two of the many satisfying recreational pursuits enjoyed year-round by anyone fortunate enough to live in the sunny San Diego region. Not all hikers, however, realize how broad the spectrum of opportunity really is. On one end of this spectrum lie San Diego County's coastal canyons, foothills, and mountain parks, laced with well-marked hiking and bridle trails. The other end of the spectrum consists of vast stretches of undeveloped land in the county's public domain—including many new state and federal wilderness areas. There are few or no trails in these areas, but the potential for exploration of a rugged kind is almost unlimited.

Until the publication of *Afoot and Afield in San Diego County* in 1986, no single information source had attempted to exhaust even one end of the above-mentioned spectrum. By publishing this book, I hoped to bring into sharp focus almost every hike worth taking in the public lands of the county—hikes ranging in difficulty from short, self-guiding nature trails, to peak climbs and canyon treks that would challenge even the most skilled adventurer.

This third edition strives to do the exactly the same, except that now there is a comparatively greater emphasis on hikes in the county's western one-third, a region that until recently offered few hiking opportunities. Over the past decade the county and its coastal cities have been busy acquiring large and small tracts of federal and private land with significant biological and recreational value. These lands are now set aside as open space and parkland for all to use and enjoy. Parallel efforts in the mountain and desert regions have led to significant additions to Cleveland National Forest and Anza-Borrego Desert State Park. Overall, 56 new hikes, mostly in newly acquired areas, have been added to this book during its publishing history.

Astute readers of earlier editions and of this one will notice that a handful of trip descriptions, often of lengthy or obscure routes, have been deleted. This was done to save space or for other good reasons. Information about the missing trips, however, is sometimes incorporated into the revised trip descriptions in this edition. The overall result is a third edition containing far more information in a book of slightly larger size.

For years, mountain biking enthusiasts and pet owners have been asking to have their interests specifically addressed in this book. Therefore, I've added two new graphic symbols for the trip summaries: one denoting "suitable for mountain biking," the other indicating "OK for leashed dogs."

Others have asked for a rating indicating the quality of each hike, *à la* movie reviews. However, it is impossible to be remotely objective about this, as the quality of a hiker's experience in Southern California terrain is highly colored by the season, by the time of day, and by variable factors such as air quality and temperature. A sweaty trudge up, say, the chaparral-covered slope of Viejas Mountain on a hazy August day may fail to inspire one hiker, while another gets a fabulous summit view on a clear, crisp winter morning. Every hike in this book has been personally rewarding to me. Nonetheless, for anyone not familiar with San Diego area hiking, I have prepared a short list of recommended "Best Hikes" (Appendix 1) for various seasons and various personal interests.

The "Afoot and Afield" theme of this book emphasizes hikes of non-trivial length that are mostly removed from civilization. With a few exceptions, short "nature trails" in the smaller urban and suburban parks of San Diego County are not included. Some longer or technically difficult routes I've hiked in the county were rejected for inclusion as being too tedious or unacceptably hazardous. Absent, too, is a complete log of San Diego County's share (about 120 miles) of the Pacific Crest Trail. Since this information is adequately treated in other publications, I chose to highlight certain shorter trips on the most scenic parts of the PCT. In several of the trip descriptions, the PCT is used as a means to reach another trail or some interesting off-trail destination.

This book encompasses all public lands (and a few private lands on which the public is welcome) within San Diego County, with a few exceptions. Excluded are San Mateo Canyon Wilderness, a part of which intrudes into San Diego County north of Camp Pendleton, and San Onofre State Beach, just south of Orange County. These two areas are included in my book *Afoot and Afield in Orange County*. Certain public lands straddling the Riverside-San Diego county line, such as Bucksnort Mountain, were excluded because access from the San Diego side is awkward. On the other hand, a portion of the Jacumba Mountains, on the Imperial County border, was included because of its freeway-closeness to San Diego.

All hikes described in this book were hiked at least once by me at one time or another, and every effort has been made to ensure that the information contained herein is up-to-date. However, roads, trailheads, and trails can and do change every year. Recreational opportunities within the county will continue to expand during the next several years, especially as ongoing programs such as the Multiple Species Conservation Plan help to set limits on the spread of urban development and simultaneously provide for protection and public access to large tracts of open space.

I will continue to insert fresh updates in future printings of this edition, and a fourth edition will undoubtedly appear in the future. You can keep me apprised of recent developments and/or changes by writing me in care of Wilderness Press or by sending me an e-mail at schadj@worldnet.att.net. Your comments will be appreciated.

Read This

Hiking in the backcountry entails unavoidable risk that every hiker assumes and must be aware of and respect. The fact that a trail is described in this book is not a representation that it will be safe for you. Trails vary greatly in difficulty and in the degree of conditioning and agility one needs to enjoy them safely. On some hikes routes may have changed or conditions may have deteriorated since the descriptions were written. Also, trail conditions can change even from day to day, owing to weather and other factors. A trail that is safe on a dry day or for a highly conditioned, agile, properly equipped hiker may be completely unsafe for someone else or unsafe under adverse weather conditions.

You can minimize your risks on the trail by being knowledgeable, prepared, and alert. There is not space in this book for a general treatise on safety in the mountains, but there are a number of good books and public courses on the subject, and you should take advantage of them to increase your knowledge. Just as important, you should always be aware of your own limitations and of conditions existing when and where you are hiking. If conditions are dangerous, or if you are not prepared to deal with them safely, choose a different hike! It's better to have wasted a drive than to be the subject of a mountain rescue.

These warnings are not intended to scare you off the trails. Millions of people have safe and enjoyable hikes every year. However, one element of the beauty, freedom, and excitement of the wilderness is the presence of risks that do not confront us at home. When you hike you assume those risks. They can be met safely, but only if you exercise your own independent judgment and common sense.

Pine Valley Creek

Introducing
San Diego County

The San Diego region is special in that no simple description can ever hope to characterize it. Lacking any single, over-powering symbol (except, of course, the almost perpetually sunny weather), it revels instead in its remarkable diversity. The blue ocean, the tranquil bays, the sparkling beaches, the sun-splashed coastal mesas, and the rugged little coastal canyons that most San Diegans live with every day are but a small part of the whole. Beyond lies a beautiful and varied backcountry of boulder-strewn foothills, pine-clad mountains, and vast desert spaces.

For hikers, backpackers, and other explorers of the great outdoors, this diversity is good news. San Diego County offers a greater variety of experiences and more opportunities to practice an unconfined type of recreation than any other similar-sized area in the United States.

Of the county's 4255 square miles, more than one third, or a total of approximately 1550 square miles, is public land open to recreational use. Included in this total are several state parks (chiefly Anza-Borrego Desert State Park), more than 800 square miles; Cleveland National Forest, 438 square miles; land in the public domain administered by the federal Bureau of Land Management, about 250 square miles; and numerous county and city parks.

With the expenditure of less than two hours' driving time and one or two hours' walk, a San Diego urbanite can reach any of a dozen totally different natural environments, ranging from snowy mountain peaks and fern-bedecked streams to sculpted desert badlands. Nowhere else in America is such a broad range of natural environments so close and conveniently located, and so available year-round, to a large population.

In the next few pages, we'll examine some of the remarkable aspects of San Diego County's climate, landforms, and flora and fauna. Following that, you'll find some notes about safety and appropriate behavior on the trail, and some tips on how to use this book effectively. After perusing this material, you can dig into the heart of this book's descriptions of 220 hiking routes from the coast to the Anza-Borrego Desert. Happy reading and happy hiking!

Land of many climates

A succinct summary of San Diego County's climate might take the form of just two phrases: "warm and sunny," and "winter-wet, summer-dry." In the world-wide range of climates, this pattern is called a Mediterranean-type climate, typical of less than 3 percent of the world's landmass.

Actually a lot of variation exists, a fact readily apparent to anyone traveling east or west across the county. The distribution of San Diego's sub-climates is somewhat easy to picture geographically, since they tend to run in strips parallel to the county's coastline and its roofline, the Peninsular Ranges. Without resorting to technical classification schemes, let's divide the county into five climate zones:

The westernmost zone, extending inland several miles across the coastal plain, is greatly affected by the moderating influence of the Pacific Ocean. This zone is characterized by mild temperatures that are relatively unvarying, both daily and seasonally. Average Fahrenheit temperatures range from the mid-60s/mid-40s (daily highs/lows) in winter, to mid-70s/mid-60s in summer. Rainfall averages about 10 inches annually.

The next zone, about 20–40 miles wide, covers the inland valleys and the western foothills of the Peninsular Ranges. This area, which is only partly under the influence of moderating ocean breezes, experiences more extreme temperatures: low 70s/low 40s in winter and high 80s/high 50s in summer. Precipitation averages about 15 inches annually.

The next zone east, the coolest, encompasses the highest elevations of San Diego County—the forested heights of the Palomar, Cuyamaca, Laguna, and other mountains that form the backbone of the Peninsular Ranges. Winter temperatures average high 50s/low 30s, while summer temperatures average low 80s/high 50s. Precipitation, in the form of both rain and snow, averages about 30 inches annually.

Farther east, on the desert-facing slopes of the mountains, is a narrow strip characterized by a "high desert" climate. This zone also includes the tops of several eastern spurs of the Peninsular Ranges. Temperatures range from the low 60s/high 30s in winter to the high 90s/low 60s in summer. Precipitation averages about 10 inches per year.

The easternmost zone includes the "low desert" below about 3000 feet elevation. This area is almost completely cut off from the moderating influence of the ocean, and it experiences a relatively extreme "continental" type of climate. Temperatures range from the low 70s/low 40s in winter to 100-plus/high 60s in summer. Average precipitation is five inches or less.

No discussion of San Diego County climates would be complete without mention of some of the remarkable extremes of temperature and precipitation recorded within the county over the past century. The highest official temperature ever recorded in the county was 122°F at Borrego Springs (June 25, 1990). However, some low-desert areas near Borrego Springs regularly experience temperatures averaging five degrees higher than that. It's probable that shade temperatures above 125°F have occurred in those areas.

Even the coastal area can heat up to 100°F or more during a so-called Santa Ana condition. Santa Anas occur when dry air moves southwest from a high-pressure area in the interior toward San Diego County. As the air flows down mountain slopes, it compresses and becomes warmer at the rate of about 5°F per 1000 feet of descent. During strong Santa Ana conditions, which are common in early fall, San Diego or Imperial Beach or some other coastal weather station will sometimes record the highest temperature in the nation!

The lowest temperatures, and the only subzero temperatures, recorded in the

Lower Penasquitos Canyon

county to date, were -4°F and -1°F readings at Cuyamaca Rancho State Park.

Although San Diego County and all of Southern California lie in a belt of generally dry climate, both are susceptible to monster deluges from time to time. Annual precipitation measured at San Diego over the past 150 years has ranged from 3 inches to 26 inches. Palomar Mountain, the wettest spot in the county, once received a total of 82 inches. Occasionally, a *chubasco*, or tropical storm, from Mexico will move into the desert or mountains, resulting in intense, localized downpours. A century ago, one such storm dumped 16 inches of rain on the border town of Campo in 24 hours, 11.5 inches of that total in a single 80-minute-period! In 1976, another *chubasco*, Hurricane Kathleen, wreaked havoc in southeastern San Diego County, rearranging watercourses and destroying roads, a railroad line, and half a desert town.

Despite Nature's occasional temper tantrums, more than nine times out of ten your outings in San Diego County should coincide with dry weather and temperatures in a moderate register—for at least part of the day. Not many other places in the world can offer such good odds.

Reading the rocks

Some geographers think of San Diego County as being divided into three "geomorphic provinces." These provinces are not unique to San Diego County, but extend into neighboring counties and into Baja California.

The first, bounded by the curving shoreline of the Pacific Ocean and stretching no more than a few miles inland, is the Coast province. It has the form of a terraced plain, in places intricately dissected by steep-sided canyons and arroyos. This is the familiar "canyon-and-mesa" topography on which most of urban and suburban San Diego lies.

The second, the Peninsular Ranges province, consists of a series of discontinuous mountain ranges, some more than 6000 feet high. The ranges are generally parallel to one another, generally trend northwest-southeast, and are interspersed with high, sometimes narrow valleys. The bulk of San Diego County's land surface is included in this province, along with all the county's higher elevations. The province stretches north to include the San Jacinto Mountains in Riverside County and south to the tip of the Baja peninsula. The Peninsular Ranges and the Sierra Nevada range to the north are similar in topography: in rough form both are huge, tilted blocks of granitic rock, with steep east escarpments and more gradual west slopes.

The third province is called the Salton Trough. This large depression holds the Salton Sea, and most geologists would say it lies outside San Diego County. Geographers would say that some of the low-desert landscape of Anza-Borrego Desert State Park in the northeastern corner of the county belongs to this province.

The geomorphic provinces themselves are each very complex. Within even a single mountain range or coastal canyon or desert basin, there may exist a dazzling variety of small-scale landforms and underlying rock types. You might ask: how did San Diego County's surface get to be so convoluted; and what processes were responsible for the presence of so many different kinds of rock in the county today?

First, it's important to note that California, Oregon, Washington, British Columbia, and Alaska are composed largely of rock formations that were transported to their current locations from either the west or the south. This migration was accomplished by the formations riding "piggyback" atop large and small plates which, taken all together, form the earth's crust. Such grand-scale movements are still occurring today. For example, California's famous San Andreas Fault is just a boundary between two large plates that are gliding past each other. San Diego lies on the oceanic plate, which is drifting north with respect to the continental plate at a rate of a little more than 2 inches per year. If this rate continues, then in 14 million years, San Diego will have drifted far enough north to pass San Francisco, which lies on the continental plate. Future hikers—bring your overcoats!

With the above in mind, we begin a geologic story, as painted in broad brush strokes, back about 150 million years ago. At that time, most of present-day San Diego County, along with much of western North America, was below sea level. Over 2000 miles to the south or southwest, a mountain-building cycle began, as an arc of volcanic islands grew in the ocean. For 50 million years or so, the volcanoes spread lava and ash over a wide area. By the end of this volcanic episode, about 100 million years ago, the arc of volcanic islands had migrated close to the mainland, and the two were now separated by a narrowing, shallow sea. After the sediments of the shallow sea floor were uplifted, they were eroded away and deposited in deltas near the coast or offshore.

Erosion also carried away the debris from the island-arc volcanoes, exposing and attacking deeper layers that had been metamorphosed by heat and pressure generated as the volcanic islands slowly rammed into the mainland.

Still more debris arriving along the coast came from a volcanic area far inland that had evolved in response to the action of the oceanic plate carrying the island-arc volcanoes. The edge of this oceanic plate was diving beneath the mainland plate, and its rock melted when it reached a certain depth, creating magma. This magma rose within the crust, and parts of it solidified before reaching the surface, crystallizing to form granitic rock. But some magma broke through to the surface, and spewed lava and ash far and wide, constructing a volcanic landscape. (A similar process of volcanism, caused by an offshore, northward-migrating, diving plate, is occurring today in the Cascade Range of Washington, Oregon, and northern California.) Much of the debris from the mainland volcanic area was in the form of erosion-resistant rhyolitic rock. It seems that during one particular period lasting several million years, cobbles of this rhyolitic rock came to our area by way of a single large river, which once flowed west through today's state of Sonora, Mexico.

Erosive forces continued to nibble away at the volcanic landscape, finally exposing, after perhaps 20 million years (80 million years ago), the underlying granitic rock, which had originally solidified about three to nine miles below the earth's surface. In time, an increasing amount of the large granitic mass, or batholith, was exposed, and the landscape acquired a different look, perhaps like that of today's mostly granitic San Diego County. The vegetation, however, was very different, in part because plants back then were different, but more important, because this area was still well south of us, located in a tropical clime.

By about 40 million years ago the assemblage of volcanic rocks and granitic rocks plus sediments from both rock types had migrated far enough north to be located immediately west of the present-day state of Sonora, on the mainland of Mexico. Later, a "mere" 10 million years ago, the Gulf of California began to form as an inlet between mainland Mexico and the sliver of land that would become Baja California.

Today, San Diego County, riding on what is known as the Pacific Plate, continues to drift northwest relative to the "mainland" North American Plate. To the east and northeast is the boundary between the two plates, the great San Andreas Fault, running beneath the eastern side of the Salton Trough and under the Gulf of California. In the county's midsection, the granitic mass continues to rise, building up mountains faster than erosive forces are currently tearing them down.

We can now begin to understand the simplified geologic map and profile on page 6. The granitic rocks (which include diorite, granodiorite, and gabbro rock commonly found in San Diego County) encompass most of the Peninsular Ranges province (including what we generally call our foothills and mountains). Together all are part of the Southern California batholith— the vast mass of rock that crystallized deep beneath a tropical volcanic landscape about 100 million years ago.

Exposed on the western edge of the Peninsular Ranges province, and poking up in places through the coastal plain, is a belt of distinctly older metavolcanic rocks. This is a resistant remnant of the lava and ash that spewed out of the island volcanoes 150 million years ago, later to be metamorphosed when the islands collided with the mainland.

In the Coast province we find sedimentary deposits, both marine and nonmarine (river deposits) which were laid down in various periods from about 80 to 2 million years ago. The marine sediments are typically seen near the coast, the nonmarine sediments farther inland. In many locales you'll see exposures of sandstone, shale, and conglomerate. The rhyolitic cobbles so widely seen today on the beaches and in thick conglomerate beds through much of metropolitan San Diego were not formed where they lie today. They

GEOLOGICAL MAP OF SAN DIEGO COUNTY

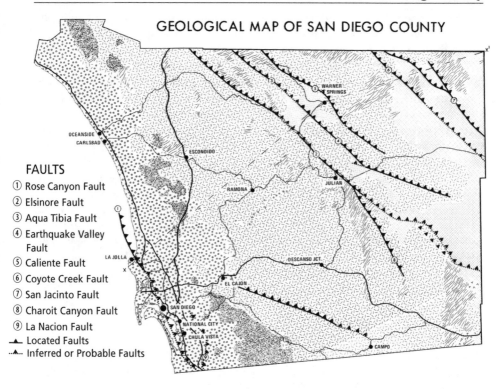

FAULTS

① Rose Canyon Fault
② Elsinore Fault
③ Aqua Tibia Fault
④ Earthquake Valley Fault
⑤ Caliente Fault
⑥ Coyote Creek Fault
⑦ San Jacinto Fault
⑧ Charoit Canyon Fault
⑨ La Nacion Fault
⊥ Located Faults
⋯▲⋯ Inferred or Probable Faults

KTQ	mv	Kgr	m	TQ	Tv
Cretaceous, Tertiary, and Quaternary marine and non-marine sedimentary deposits of the Coastal Province and western Peninsular Coastal Province	Metavolcanic and related hypabyssal intrusive rocks of Jurassic or Cretaceous (?) age	Cretaceous granite, dioritic, and gabbroic rocks of the batholith of Southern California; includes also hybrid (or "mixed") rocks	Metamorphic rocks of probable Cretaceous and older age; chiefly schist and gneiss, with minor limestone in eastern part of county; near Jacumba and other areas intruded by abundant granitic bodies	Tertiary and Quaternary marine and non-marine deposits on the Salton Trough and eastern Peninsular Range Province	Tertiary volcanic rocks of the Jacumba region

W. J. HERMISTON-75

Simplified geologic map and profile of San Diego County. Line XX' on the geologic map locates the cross section of the geologic profile. From *San Diego: An Introduction to the Region*, Philip Pryde, ed., © 1976, 1984 by Kendall/Hunt Publishing Company. Reprinted by permission of Kendall/Hunt Publishing Company.

GEOLOGICAL PROFILE OF SAN DIEGO COUNTY

KTQ	mv	Kgr	m	TQ
Cretaceous, Tertiary, and Quaternary marine and non-marine sedimentary deposits of the Coastal Province and western Peninsular Coastal Province	Metavolcanic and related hypabyssal intrusive rocks of Jurassic or Cretaceous (?) age	Cretaceous granite, dioritic, and gabbroic rocks of the batholith of Southern California; includes also hybrid (or "mixed") rocks	Metamorphic rocks of probable Cretaceous and older age; chiefly schist and gneiss, with minor limestone in eastern part of county; near Jacumba and other areas intruded by abundant granitic bodies	Tertiary and Quaternary marine and non-marine deposits on the Salton Trough and eastern Peninsular Range Province

are the water-worn pieces of volcanic rock delivered by the aforementioned large river.

The Coast province deposits are relatively soft and easily eroded. They exhibit a record of changing sea levels and gradual uplift in the form of wave-cut terraces. The terraces themselves are in many places deeply cut by drainage channels—the coastal canyons—which are fairly recent features.

The Salton Trough, an extension of the Gulf of California, lies buried in sediments as much as four miles thick, deposited in relatively recent times, the last few million years. These sediments have been carved into spectacular forms in the badland areas of Anza-Borrego Desert.

The geologic map shows two other less common general rock types: some volcanic rock exposures in the southeast corner of the county, and several much more

Toro Peak from Collins Valley

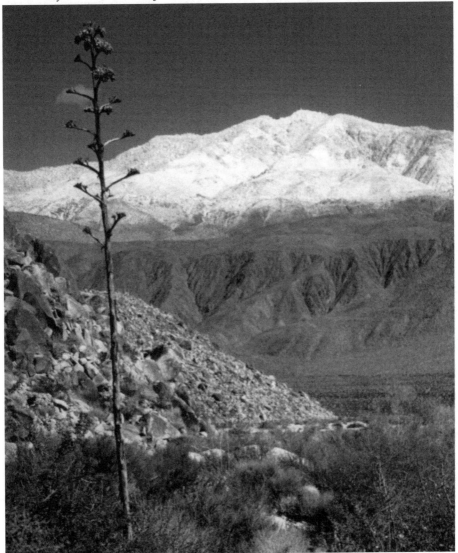

widespread bands of metamorphosed sedimentary rocks. The volcanic rocks are about 20 million years in age, and mark the only period of isolated volcanic activity in the county since the great batholith cooled. The metamorphosed sedimentary rocks, which may be 100 to 500 million years old, are the altered remnants of mud, lime, and sand layers deposited on a sea floor. This category includes the Julian schist, the presence of which is associated with pockets of ore containing gold and other valuable minerals.

Both the geologic map and the geologic profile show several sympathetic (splinter) faults associated with the San Andreas Fault. Because of these parallel rifts, the land surface of the county does not move as a solid unit toward the northwest, but rather creeps differentially. Vertical and horizontal movements along these faults have fractured the Peninsular Ranges province into a series of separate blocks (mountain ranges), most of them tilted in the characteristic west-dipping fashion.

More finely detailed—and colorful—geologic maps can give a more vivid picture of San Diego County's geological complexities. Refer to Appendix 2 for these and other sources of information about the county's fascinating geology.

Native gardens

About 2000 species of wild plants grow within the boundaries of San Diego County. As a single county, ours is thought to have the greatest botanical diversity of any county in the continental United States. About 10 percent of the 2000 are non-native (naturalized) plants from other places around the country and around the world.

There are two reasons for this plethora of plants. One reason has to do

with physical factors: topography, geology, soils, and climate. The sheer complexity of the interrelationships among these factors has produced a wide range of possible physical habitats.

The second reason is San Diego County's strategic location between two groups of flora: a southern group represented by drought-tolerant plants characteristic of Baja California, and a northern group represented by moisture-loving plants typical of the Sierra Nevada and California's north coastal ranges. As the climate has changed, seesawing from cool and wet to warm and dry over the past million years or so, species from both groups have alternately invaded the county. Once established, many of these species have remained in protected niches even as the climate turned unfavorable for them. Some have survived unchanged over the ages; others have evolved into unique forms. Many are present only in very specific habitats within the county.

Most of San Diego County's natural vegetation can be categorized into six general groups, which botanists often call plant communities or plant associations. In a broader sense, these are biological communities, which include animals as well as plants. The plant communities are briefly described below in the order you would encounter them if you were to drive east from the coast, over the crest of the highest mountains, and into the desert.

The *sage-scrub* (or coastal-sage-scrub) community lies mostly below 1500 feet elevation, and extends east from the coastline to the foothills and lower slopes of the mountains. The more-open sage-scrub community intermixes readily with the dense chaparral community, especially on north slopes and in canyons along the coastal strip. The dominant species are small shrubs, typically California sagebrush, white sage, black sage, and California buckwheat. Two larger shrubs often present are laurel sumac and lemonade berry, which, like poison oak, are members of the sumac family. Interspersed among the somewhat loosely distributed shrubs are a variety of grasses and wildflowers. The sage-scrub community in San Diego County is fast being displaced by housing tracts and industrial parks.

The *chaparral* community is commonly found between 1000 and 4500 feet elevation on the west slopes of the mountains, and between 3500 and 5000 feet on some of the east slopes. It also occurs in a few areas along the coast. Large areas of San Diego County are still carpeted by almost unbroken stretches of chaparral. The dominant species are chamise, ribbonwood, manzanita, scrub oak, and various forms of ceanothus ("wild lilac"). These species are tough, intricately branched shrubs with deep root systems that help the plants survive during the long, hot summers. Chaparral is sometimes referred to as an "elfin forest." Without the benefit of a trail, travel through mature chaparral, which is typically 5 to 15 feet high, is almost impossible.

The *southern oak woodland* community is found in scattered locations throughout San Diego County in areas from the foothills to just below the crests of the mountains . The indicator species are broadleaf trees such as black oaks and various live oaks. These are intermixed with abundant grasses and sometimes a sparse growth of chaparral shrubs. The southern oak woodland is very "park-like" in appearance, especially in the spring with the new growths of grass and wildflowers.

The *coniferous forest* (or ponderosa-pine forest) community exists only at the highest elevations of San Diego County—generally above 4500 feet. The common coniferous trees include the ponderosa, Jeffrey, Coulter, and sugar pines; white fir;

incense-cedar; and big-cone Douglas-fir. These are often intermixed with live and black oaks, various chaparral shrubs, grasses, and wildflowers. This is, of course, the type of plant community most people associate with "the mountains."

The *pinyon-juniper woodland* community covers parts of the east-facing slopes of the county's higher ranges, such as the Laguna Mountains. It also exists in the form of botanical "islands" on the crests of the arid Vallecito Mountains and the Santa Rosa Mountains (within San Diego County). The two principal species are rather stunted conifers, the one-leaf pinyon pine and the California juniper. Other plants belonging to this community have rather small, leathery or rigid leaves—a water-conservation feature necessary in the high desert.

The *desert shrub* (or creosote-bush scrub) community covers the desert floor and extends up the east slopes of the mountains to about 2000 feet in elevation. The indicator plant is the creosote bush, a plant not only abundant in our local Colorado Desert (a subdivision of the Sonoran Desert), but throughout the entire Sonoran and Mojave deserts. Ocotillo, many kinds of cacti, and a wide variety of drought-tolerant shrubs are also common. Displays of annual and ephemeral wildflowers are unpredictable but often spectacular within the desert shrub community.

Aside from the six fairly widespread communities above, there are others that are much more restricted in area: *rocky shore, coastal strand, coastal salt marsh, freshwater marsh, riparian woodland, mountain meadow, desert wash,* and *alkali sink.*

Of these plant communities, the riparian (streamside) woodland, covering less than one-fifth of one percent of San Diego County's land area, is considered the most valuable. Not only is this kind of environment essential for the continued sur-

Jeffrey pine forest in Laguna Mountains

vival of many kinds of birds and animals, it is also very appealing to the senses. Live oaks, sycamores, cottonwoods, and a screen of water-hugging willows are the hallmarks of the riparian woodland. The riparian woodland all over California has steadily declined as a result of urbanization and agricultural development, and the attendant exploitation of water resources.

San Diego County has more than its share of rare, endangered, unique, or otherwise unusual species of vegetation. Best known are the Torrey pine, the California fan palm, and two kinds of cypress.

Torrey pines are found in picturesque groves on the eroded bluffs overlooking the Pacific Ocean at Torrey Pines State Reserve, near Del Mar. These trees were widespread at one time, but an increase in aridity has caused their natural range to retreat to just this site and one other, the east end of Santa Rosa Island, which lies off the coast of Santa Barbara. Fog drip from the Torrey pine's long needles apparently provides the extra moisture it needs for survival.

California fan palms exist in a similarly narrow niche. According to one scenario, they are relicts from a time when today's desert was semitropical. Increasing aridity forced them to retreat to canyons and arroyos that have an uninterrupted supply of surface or subsurface water. Their range extends across the Colorado Desert (which includes the Anza-Borrego Desert) into the southern reaches of the Mojave Desert and into Baja California.

The cypresses also have retreated to "arboreal islands." The rare Cuyamaca cypress now is restricted to a small area of chaparral-covered slopes about one mile south of Cuyamaca Peak, while the range of the more widely distributed Tecate cypress includes three San Diego County locations (Otay Mountain, Tecate Peak-Potrero Creek, and Guatay Mountain), one Orange County location, and several sites in Baja California.

Late winter through early spring is the best time to appreciate the cornucopia of San Diego County's native plants. Many of the showiest species of spring wildflowers burgeon at this time, and other plants show fresh new growth. Peak periods for wildflowers vary according to elevation. The low desert blooms most profusely during a rather short period centered on late March; coastal areas and foothills are usually best in April; and the high mountains are best in late April and May. Irregular summer desert thunderstorms occasionally give rise to a second period of blooming during fall in the desert and along the eastern margins of the mountains.

For more information about the wildflowers, shrubs, trees, and other flora of San Diego County, see Appendix 2—Recommended Reading.

Creatures great and small

Your first sighting of a mountain lion, a bighorn sheep, a bald eagle, or any other seldom-seen form of wildlife is always a memorable experience. Because of the diversity and the generally broad extent of its habitats, San Diego County plays host to a great variety of indigenous creatures, including a number of rare or endangered species. If you're willing to stretch your legs a bit and spend some time in the areas favored by wild animals, then you'll eventually be rewarded by some kind of close visual contact.

The most numerous large creature in the county is the mule deer, with a population of several thousand. Unfortunately, the number of deer within the county has declined seriously in the past few decades, a circumstance widely blamed on loss of habitat and excessive hunting. The deer prefer areas of mixed forest and scattered chaparral, especially at the highest elevations in the county, but they can also be seen in the coastal canyons and on desert-facing slopes with moderate growths of vegetation. In places like Cuyamaca Rancho State Park, where the deer are protected from hunting, it is uncommon not to see any while out hiking the trails.

The mountain lion, or cougar, once hunted to near extinction in California, has made a comeback as a protected species. Perhaps more than a hundred mountain lions roam the county today. They inhabit virtually every natural habitat, and typically have a large territorial range (up to 100 square miles). Because of their wide-ranging travels, you may readily spot lion

Desert sunflowers in Borrego Valley

tracks and other signs if you look carefully for them. For the most part, the animals shy away from humans and human activities. In recent years, however, conflicts between mountain lions and humans have increased. In 1994 a woman was attacked and killed by a mountain lion while hiking near Cuyamaca Peak. This was the thirteenth known fatal attack by a cougar in the United States and Canada in this century. Experts are uncertain why the normally elusive mountain lions here and at other spots in California are becoming more aggressive. Precautions against mountain lion attacks are discussed in the next section.

The county's most interesting large mammal is the endangered peninsular (desert) bighorn sheep. Some 300 of these agile animals maintain a tenuous existence on the steep slopes and rocky crags of the Anza-Borrego Desert. Unlike mule deer, the bighorn sheep prefer open, rugged terrain, on which they are capable of escaping from almost any predator. They are also superbly adapted to surviving on meager supplies of water and coarse desert vegetation. Bighorn sheep tend to keep a safe distance from human activity, but sometimes seem possessed of a kind of curiosity about humans. Once accustomed to a hiker's presence, a sheep may approach quite closely and make a surprise appearance. After three or four seconds of eye contact, the animal turns and disappears.

The county's mammals also include the coyote, which has adapted to a broad range of habitats, including the margins of suburbia; the bobcat, a creature sometimes mistaken for a mountain lion, but smaller and more common; the gray fox of mountain habitats and the kit fox of desert habitats; the opossum; the skunk; the raccoon; and various rabbits, squirrels, woodrats, and mice.

Among the commonly seen reptiles are rattlesnakes, which we will discuss in the next section.

The variety of bird life in San Diego County is outstanding, not only because of the great diversity of habitats, but also because the county lies along the Pacific Flyway route of spring-fall bird migration and serves as an important wintering area for waterfowl. The San Diego chapter of the Audubon Society lists more than 480 species of birds within county borders—a figure that exceeds that of any other county in the nation.

The county's undeveloped areas support several species of rare or endangered birds, including the southern bald eagle, the peregrine falcon, the lightfooted clapper rail, the California least tern, and the least Bell's vireo. The diminutive California gnatcatcher, another endangered bird, has already played a pivotal role in the politics of urban development in San Diego County. Large tracts of sage-scrub habitat, on which the gnatcatcher depends, are now being set aside as open space or parkland (and declared off-limits to urban development) throughout coastal San Diego.

Mule deer, Cuyamaca Mountains

Health, safety, and courtesy

Good preparation is always important for any kind of recreational pursuit. Hiking the San Diego backcountry is no exception. Although few of the county's natural environments are ever hostile or dangerous to life and limb, some pitfalls are worth noting.

Preparation and equipment

An obvious safety requirement is being in good health. Some degree of physical conditioning is always desirable, even for the trips in this book designated as easy or moderate (rated ★ and ★★ in difficulty). The more challenging trips (rated ★★★, ★★★★, or ★★★★★) require increasing amounts of stamina and technical expertise. Running, bicycling, swimming, aerobic dancing, or any similar exercise that develops both the leg muscles and the aerobic capacity of the whole body are recommended as preparatory exercise.

For long trips over rough, cross-country terrain (there are several of these in this book) there is no really adequate way to prepare other than practicing the activity itself. Start with easy- or moderate-length cross-country trips first to accustom the leg muscles to the peculiar stresses involved in "boulder-hopping" or "non-technical climbing" (scrambling over steep terrain), and to acquire a good sense of balance. Sturdy hiking boots are recommended for such travel.

Since all hiking in San Diego County is below about 6500 feet elevation, serious health complications due to higher altitude are rare. Sea-level dwellers, of course, may find themselves breathing faster and tiring a little sooner.

Your choice of equipment and supplies on the longer hikes in this book can be critically important. The essentials you should carry with you at all times in the backcountry are the things that would allow you to survive, in a reasonably comfortable manner, one or two unscheduled nights out. It's important to note that no one ever plans these nights! No one plans to get lost, injured, stuck, or pinned down by the weather. Always do a "what if" analysis for a worst-case scenario, and plan accordingly. These essential items are your safety net; keep them with you on dayhikes, and take them with you in a small day pack if you leave your backpack and camping equipment behind at a campsite.

Chief among the essential items is **warm clothing**. Inland San Diego County is characterized by wide swings in day and night temperatures. In mountain valleys susceptible to cold-air drainage, for example, a midday temperature in the 70s or 80s is often followed by a subfreezing night. Carry light, inner layers of clothing consisting of polypropylene or wool (best for cool or cold weather), or cotton (adequate for warm or hot weather, but very poor for cold and damp weather). Include a thicker insulating layer of "pile" (polyester fiberpile), wool, or down to put on whenever needed, especially when you are not moving around and generating heat. Add to this a cap, gloves, and a waterproof or water-resistant shell (a large trash bag will do in a pinch)—and you'll be quite prepared for all but the most severe weather experienced in San Diego County.

In hot, sunny weather, sun-shielding

clothing may be another "essential." This would normally include a sun hat and a light-colored, long-sleeve top.

Water, and to a lesser extent **food**, are next in importance. If water isn't immediately available, carry a generous supply. In the arid San Diego backcountry, you'll need to drink up to a gallon of water during a full day's hike in 70° or 80° temperatures; and up to two or three gallons per day in summer desert conditions (hiking in these latter conditions is not recommended.) Food is needed to stave off hunger and keep energy stores up, but it is not as essential as water in a survival situation.

Down the list further, but still "essential," are a **map and compass, flashlight, fire-starting devices** (examples: waterproof matches or lighter, and candle), and **first-aid kit**.

Items not always essential, but potentially very useful and convenient, are sunglasses, pocket knife, whistle (or other signaling device), sunscreen, and toilet paper. High-tech apparatus such as cellular phones and Global Positioning System (GPS) navigation devices can be handy and fun, but don't rely on them for your survival. During an emergency your cell phone may fail to work or be out of range of an antenna relay. GPS receivers are a useful adjunct to navigation, but as yet they can't replace basic navigational skills and common sense.

The essential items mentioned above should be carried by every member of a hiking party, because individuals or splinter groups may end up separating from the party for one reason or another. If you plan to hike solo in the backcountry, being well-equipped is very important. If you hike alone, be sure to check in with a park ranger or leave your itinerary with a responsible person. In that way, if you do get stuck, help will probably come to the right place—eventually.

Taking children on hiking outings involves a special kind of responsibility. San Diego-based "Project Hug-a-Tree" (see Appendix 4) can provide you with information about training and outfitting a child to cope with the possibility of getting lost in the wilderness.

Special hazards

Other than getting lost or pinned down by a rare sudden storm, the five most common hazards found in the San Diego backcountry are loose or slick rocks and/ or steep terrain, spiny plants, rattlesnakes, ticks, and poison oak. A sixth hazard, uncommon though serious, is mountain lions. Each of these special hazards is described in turn below.

Cross-country hiking in the desert, and to a lesser extent in the mountains and the foothills, frequently involves travel over exposed rock on steep slopes. The erosive forces of flowing water, the freezing and melting of ice, and even brush fires tend to fracture the rock into chunks ranging from house-size to small pebbles. Middle-sized boulders, often poorly anchored, are probably the most dangerous. Before you step on a boulder or pull on it with your hands, try to judge its stability. Be very cautious, too, of water-worn slabs of rock near waterfalls and along canyon bottoms—especially if the rock is wet. A good many of the injuries suffered by hikers in San Diego County have been caused by slips and falls on slick rock surfaces.

Smaller pebbles that act like ball bearings underfoot are often a problem on desert slopes, especially where cacti and the desert agave grow. The agave plant (also known as century plant) consists of a rosette of fleshy leaves, each tipped with a rigid thorn containing a mild toxin. A headlong fall into either an agave or one of the more vicious kinds of cacti could easily make you swear off desert travel permanently. It's best to give these devilish plants as wide a berth as possible.

Most desert hikers will sooner or later suffer punctures by thorns or spines. This is most likely to happen during close encounters with the cholla ("jumping") cactus, whose spine clusters readily break off and attach firmly to your skin, clothes or boots. A comb can be used to gently pull away the spine clusters, and tweezers or lightweight pliers can be used to remove any individual embedded spines.

Rattlesnakes are common in all parts of San Diego County. Seldom seen in either cold or very hot weather, they favor temperatures in the 75–90°F range—spring and fall in the desert and coastal areas, and summer in the mountains. Most rattlesnakes are as interested in avoiding contact with you as you are with them. Watch carefully where you put your feet, and especially your hands, during the warmer months. In brushy or rocky areas where sight distance is short, try to make your presence known from afar. Tread with heavy footfalls, or use a stick to bang against rocks or bushes. Rattlesnakes will pick up the vibrations through their skin and will usually buzz (unmistakably) before you get too close for comfort. Most bad encounters between rattlesnakes and hikers occur in April and May, when snakes are irritable and hungry after a long hibernation period.

Ticks can sometimes be the scourge of overgrown trails in the sage-scrub and chaparral country, particularly during the first warm spells of the year, when they climb to the tips of shrub branches and lie in wait for warm-blooded hosts. If you can't avoid brushing against vegetation along the trail, be sure to check yourself for ticks frequently. Upon finding a host, a tick will usually crawl upward in search of a protected spot, where it will try to at-

Diamondback rattlesnake

tach itself. If you can be aware of the slightest irritation on your body, you'll usually intercept ticks long before they attempt to bite. Ticks would be of relatively minor concern here, except that tick-borne Lyme disease, which can have serious health effects, has now spread to San Diego County.

Poison oak grows profusely along many of the county's canyons below 5000 feet. It is often found on stream banks in the form of a bush or vine, and prefers the semi-shade of live and scrub oaks. Occasionally it is seen along well-used trails. Learn to recognize its distinctive three-leaved structure, and avoid touching it with skin or clothing. Since poison oak loses its leaves during the winter (usually January through March in San Diego County), but still retains some of the toxic oil in its stems, it can be extra hazardous at that time because it is harder to identify and avoid.

Some boulder-hopping trips in this book are routed directly down stream-courses where poison oak thickets are impossible to avoid. On these trips, you might consider taking along small garden clippers and gloves. Seldom is any major pruning necessary; just a snip here and there. Thick pants (jeans) and a long-sleeve shirt will serve as a fair barrier against the toxic oil of the poison-oak plant. Do, of course, remove these clothes as soon as the hike is over, and make sure they are washed carefully afterward.

For decades, encounters with mountain lions (cougars) were almost never reported in San Diego County. This began to change in the 1990s, due, in part certainly, to an increase in cougar population, a de-

Poison-oak leaves

crease in cougar habitat (especially in areas where suburban and rural housing development is increasing), and abnormal geographic concentrations of deer, a prime source of food for cougars.

Several incidents involving cougars stalking or menacing campers, hikers, and mountain bikers have occurred in the Julian and Cuyamaca Rancho State Park areas during recent years. In the worst such incident, a woman was attacked and killed by a cougar while hiking near Cuyamaca Peak. In these geographic areas, particularly, it pays to be acutely aware of the potential danger. The following precautions are urged for all persons entering cougar country, which may include virtually every non-urban San Diego County locale:

- Hike with one or more companions.
- Keep children close at hand.
- Never run from a cougar. This may trigger an instinct to attack.
- Make yourself "large," face the animal, maintain eye contact with it, shout, blow a whistle, and do not act fearful. Do anything to convince the animal that you are not its prey.

Here are a few more safety tips:

Most free-flowing water in San Diego should be regarded as unsafe for drinking without purification. This excludes, of course, developed water sources in state and county parks. Chemical (iodine or chlorine) treatment and filtering are the most convenient purification methods, but secondary in effectiveness to boiling. A bigger problem is the availability of any water at all. Most watercourses and many springs in San Diego County are intermittent. Even some streams shown as "permanent" on topographic maps occasionally dry up.

Deer-hunting season in San Diego County usually runs through the month of

October. Although conflicts between hunters and hikers are rare, you may want to confine your mid-autumn explorations to state and county parks, and wilderness areas where hunting is not permitted.

There is always some risk in leaving a vehicle unattended at a trailhead. It may be worthwhile to disable your car's ignition or attach an anti-theft device to your steering wheel. Never leave valuable property in an automobile. Report all theft and vandalism of personal property to the county sheriff, and report vandalism of public property to the appropriate park or forest agency.

Trail courtesy

Whenever you travel the backcountry, you take on a burden of responsibility—keeping the wilderness as you found it. Aside from common-sense prohibitions against littering, vandalism, and inappropriate campfires, some less obvious guidelines of which every hiker should be aware include:

Never cut trail switchbacks. This practice breaks down the trail tread and hastens erosion. Try to improve designated trails by removing branches, rocks, or other debris; but don't do this for unofficial trails or cross-country routes. Springtime growth can quite rapidly obscure pathways in the chaparral country, and funding for trail maintenance is often scarce—so try to do your part by joining a volunteer trail crew or by performing your own small maintenance tasks while walking the trails. Report any damage to trails or other facilities to the appropriate ranger office.

When off trail, resist the temptation to build cairns or ducks (rock piles) as route markers, except when absolutely necessary for route-finding. It is disappointing to follow a remote canyon or ridge, or a well-beaten trail, mindlessly littered with unnecessary markers. On the other hand, don't knock over cairns and ducks unless they are obviously recent and superfluous constructions. Many of the ancient Indian and early settlers' trails are marked by cairns and ducks of possible archaeological interest.

Be a "no trace" camper. Camp well away from streams and springs (there are a variety of reasons for this), and leave your campsite as you found it—or leave it in an even more natural condition. Because of the danger of wildfire, campfires are seldom allowed outside of developed campgrounds in San Diego County. Camping regulations vary considerably among the various parks and recreation lands, so be sure that you are aware of, and observe, the appropriate regulations. Look under "Agency" in the capsulized summary for each hike described in this book to find the appropriate park or agency. Phone numbers for these agencies are given in Appendix 4.

All animals, plants, and minerals are fully protected in state and county parks. National forest and Bureau of Land Management (BLM) regulations are a little more relaxed: hunting of certain animals and birds is permitted in season, for example. Rock collecting is allowed on most BLM lands.

Collecting archaeological artifacts anywhere is both ethically inappropriate and expressly forbidden by federal antiquities laws. Antiquities can include objects of rather recent origin, too, such as mining debris. Remember, never collect anything unless you've received permission from the governing agency.

It is impractical to review here all the specific rules associated with the use of the various public lands in San Diego County. You, as a visitor, are responsible for knowing them, however.

Using this book

Whether you wish to use this book as a reference tool or as a guide to be read cover to cover, do take the time to carefully read this section. Herein we explain the meaning of the special symbols and other bits of capsulized information which appear before each trip description, and describe the way in which trips are grouped together.

One way to expedite the process of finding a suitable trip, especially if you're unfamiliar with hiking opportunities in San Diego County, is to turn to Appendix 1, "Best Hikes." This is a cross-reference of several dozen highly recommended hikes described in this book.

Each of the 220 hiking trips has been assigned to one of 38 "areas." Each area has its own introductory text and map. The areas are coded according to "regions" within San Diego County. Areas B-1, B-2, B-3, etc., are in the **B**eaches and Bays region of the county. Areas C-1, C-2, etc., are in the **C**oastal Strip and Foothills region. Letter M in the area designation refers to the The **M**ountains region, and letter D refers to The **D**esert region.

The introductory text for each area includes any general information about the area's history, geology, plants, and wildlife not included in the trip descriptions. Important information about possible restrictions or special requirements (wilderness permits, for example) may appear there, too, so you should review this material before embarking on a hike in a particular area.

The beginning of each area section contains an area map. On most of these maps, more than one hiking route (trip) is plotted, the numbers in the squares corresponding to trip numbers in the text. These boxed numbers refer to the start/end points of out-and-back and loop trips. The point-to-point trips have two boxed numbers, indicating separate start and end points. For some hikes, the corresponding area map alone is complete enough and fully adequate for navigation; for other hikes, more detailed topographical or other maps are listed before each trip description. A legend for the area maps appears on page 23.

The following is an explanation of the small symbols and capsulized information appearing at the beginning of each trip description. If you are simply browsing through this book, these summaries alone can be used as a tool to eliminate from consideration hikes that are either too difficult, or perhaps too trivial, for your abilities.

Symbols

 Easy Terrain: roads, trails, and easy cross-country hiking

 Moderate Terrain: cross-country boulder hopping and easy scrambling

 Difficult Terrain: nontechnical climbing required (**WARNING:** THESE TRIPS SHOULD BE ATTEMPTED ONLY BY SUITABLY

EQUIPPED, EXPERIENCED HIKERS ADEPT AT TRAVELING OVER STEEP OR ROCKY TERRAIN REQUIRING THE USE OF THE HANDS AS WELL AS THE FEET.)

Only *one* of these three symbols appears for a given trip, indicating the general character of the terrain encountered. A trip almost entirely on roads and trails, but including a short section of boulder-hopping or perhaps nontechnical climbing, for example, will be rated as easy terrain, and the difficulties will be duly noted in the text. As the symbols suggest, light footwear (running shoes) is appropriate for easy terrain, while sturdy hiking boots are recommended for more difficult terrain.

Nontechnical climbing includes everything up to Class 3 on the rock-climber's scale. While ropes and climbing hardware are not normally required, a hiker should have a good sense of balance, and enough experience to recognize dangerous moves and situations. The safety and stability of heavy hiking boots are especially recommended for this kind of trip. Hazards may include loose or slippery rocks and rattlesnakes (don't put your hands in places you can't see clearly).

 Bushwhacking: cross-country travel through dense brush. This symbol is included for trips requiring a substantial amount of off-trail "bushwhacking." Wear long pants and be especially alert for ticks and rattlesnakes.

Only one of these two symbols appears:

 Marked Trails/Obvious Routes

 Navigation by Map and Compass Required (**WARNING**: THESE TRIPS SHOULD BE ATTEMPTED ONLY BY HIKERS SKILLED IN NAVIGATION TECHNIQUES.)

Unambiguous cross-country routes —up a canyon, for example—are included in the first category. The hiker, of course, should never be without a map, even if there are marked trails or the route seems obvious.

 Point-to Point Route

 Out-and-Back Route

 Loop Route

Only one of these three symbols appears, reflecting the trip as described. There is some flexibility, of course, in the way in which a hiker can actually follow the trip.

 Suitable for Backpacking

Many of the trips in this book are not. Some parks and trails are closed at night, others allow night hiking but prohibit camping. Sometimes, overnight camping is permitted at some spot off the route but nearby.

 Suitable for Mountain Biking

The trip, as described, is open to mountain biking as of this writing. Since regulations governing the use of mountain bikes on trails may change, it is a good idea to check with the agency having jurisdiction over the area.

 Leashed Dogs Allowed

When legally allowed, pets normally must be kept on a 6-foot or shorter leash. This symbol never appears for trips in areas unsuitable or dangerous (due to cactus or rough terrain) for most pets.

 Best for Kids

These trips are especially recommended for inquisitive children. They were chosen on the basis of their safety and ease of travel (at the time they were researched by the author), and their potential for entertaining the whole family.

Capsulized summaries

Distance: An estimate of total distance is given. Out-and-back trips show the sum of the distances of the out and back segments.

Total Elevation Gain/Loss: These are estimates of the sum of all the vertical gain segments and the sum of all the vertical loss segments along the total length of the route (both ways for out-and-back trips).

Hiking Time: This figure is for the average hiker, and includes only the time spent in motion. It *does not* include time spent for rest stops, lunch, etc. Fast walkers can complete the routes in perhaps 30% less time, and slower hikers may take 50% longer. The hiker is assumed to be traveling with a light day pack. (IMPORTANT NOTE: Several users of the first edition of this book got into trouble by misinterpreting this specification. To save future hikers from the grief or embarrassment of late arrival, let me emphasize that "hiking time" stated in this book is for time-in-motion only. Also, hikers carrying heavy packs could easily take nearly twice as long if they are traveling off-trail through difficult terrain. Remember, too, that the progress made by a group as a whole is limited by the pace of the slowest member or members. Hiking time on routes through canyons and along streams is very difficult to quantify. Delays can occur because of such factors as rain, snow, or high water.)

Optional/Recommended/Required Map(s): If no recommended map is given, then either the appropriate area map in this book or the optional map stated will suffice. Persons familiar with the terrain in a particular area may be able to do without a recommended map, as long as some other map is substituted. A required map

is one that is essential for the successful navigation of a particular trip route. Most maps, whether optional, recommended, or required, are US Geological Survey 7.5-minute series topographic maps. These are the most complete, accurate, and up-to-date maps of the physical features of San Diego County. In some cases, older 15-minute series maps may be substituted, but at a sacrifice in scale and detail. Even the most up-to-date topo maps (usually revised by aerial survey) often omit some well-established trails and other features, so it is important to compare them with the area maps given in this book. For a list of local sources of maps, see Appendix 4.

Best Times: Because of the extreme heat, the longer desert trips in this book should generally be avoided during any period except the one recommended here. Trips elsewhere in San Diego County are usually safe enough at other than "Best" times, but usually less rewarding.

Agency: These code letters refer to the agency, or office, that has jurisdiction or management over the area being hiked (for example, CNF/DD means Cleveland National Forest, Descanso District). You can contact the agency for more information. Full names, phone numbers, and some addresses (of larger agencies) are listed in Appendix 4.

Difficulty: The author's subjective, overall rating takes into account the length of the trip and the nature of the terrain. The following are general definitions of the five categories:

★ Easy. Suitable for every member of the family.

★★ Moderate. Suitable for all physically fit people.

★★★ Moderately Strenuous. Long length, substantial elevation gain, and/or difficult terrain. Recommended for experienced hikers only.

★★★★ Strenuous. Full day's hike (or backpack trip) over a long and/or challenging route. Suitable only for experienced hikers in excellent physical condition.

★★★★★ Very Strenuous. Long and rugged route in extremely remote area. Usually requires two days. Suitable only for experienced hikers/climbers in top physical condition.

Each higher level represents more or less a doubling of the difficulty. On average, ★★ trips are twice as hard as ★ trips, ★★★ trips are twice as hard as ★★ trips, and so on.

Final notes

In the trip descriptions, mileages along the highways (example: "mile 17.4") are keyed to the mile markers posted at frequent intervals along San Diego County's state and county highways. The mileage figures are sometimes stenciled on the roadside reflectors. In the descriptions of the hikes themselves, a phrase like "at 5.8 miles" means 5.8 miles from the beginning of the hike, not from the last intersection or point of interest.

In 1997 the national forests of Southern California (Angeles, Cleveland, Los Padres, and San Bernardino) collectively instituted a recreation fee program called the "National Forest Adventure Pass." Vehicles parked along roadsides and at trailheads are now required to display a National Forest Adventure Pass permit, or else risk being ticketed. The permit, which costs $5 daily or $30 yearly, can be purchased from any national forest office or ranger station, and from virtually every Southern California outdoor equipment and sports vendor. The permit is valid in all four of the national forests. In this book, most of the trips in "The Mountains" (Areas M-1 through M-9) lie within Cleveland National Forest and therefore require the adventure pass. Scan the introductory text for each specific mountain area in this book to determine whether or not you must display the permit for trips in that area.

The stated purpose of the national forest fee program is to provide funds for protecting natural habitat on national forest lands, and for campground and trail maintenance and improvement. At least 80 percent of the funds collected through the adventure pass program are to be applied to local projects. For more information about the National Forest Adventure Pass, call Cleveland National Forest, (619) 673-6180.

A similar fee program was initiated by Anza-Borrego Desert State Park in 1997. Any vehicle parked in areas off of the park's paved roadways and at trailheads requires a $5 daily pass, available for purchase at the entrances to Anza-Borrego Desert State Park campgrounds, at Anza-Borrego's visitor center in Borrego Springs, and at selected outdoor vendors in Southern California. A $50 annual sticker is available for advance purchase. Call (760) 767-5311 or (760) 767-4205 for more information.

Nearly all the trips included within "The Desert" section of this book are on Anza-Borrego Desert State Park land, and therefore require the pass or sticker.

MAP LEGEND

≈≈≈	Freeway
∿∿	State highway
⌢⌢	Secondary road
⌢	Minor paved road
⁼⁼⁼⁼⁼⁼	Unpaved road
- - - - -	Foot trail / abandoned road
· · · · · ·	Cross-country route
⁼⁼⁼⁼⁼⁼➤	Locked gate: no trespassing
⁼⁼⁼⁼⁼⁼➤	Gate: hikers OK
∿∿	Drainage (canyon, creek)
— — — —	County line
————	Wilderness boundary

5	Start/end point with trip number
6533 ▲	Peak (elevation in feet)
■	Point of interest
♦	Ranger station / fire station
▲	Campground
⅋	Picnic area
✕	Mine
▨	Lake / reservoir

Eroded granite near Mt. Gower

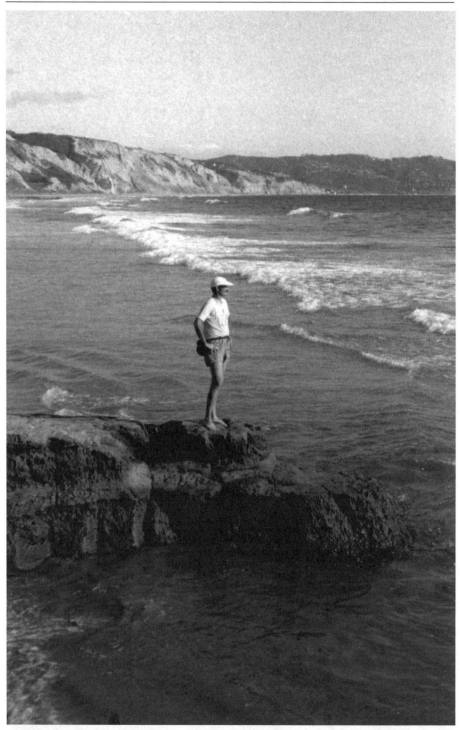

Torrey Pines Beach

Beaches and Bays

Area B-1: North County Coast

North County's almost unbroken line of beaches faces the Pacific along a gentle arc about 20 miles long. Just behind this is a string of cities and beach communities—Oceanside, Carlsbad, Leucadia, Encinitas, Cardiff, Solana Beach, and Del Mar. Compared to the more densely crowded coastal areas from La Jolla south, life is a bit slower in these communities. The locals take their beach-going and ocean-watching seriously. Some have chosen to live, at some peril, on the very brink of the cliffs overlooking the Pacific.

The popular term "North County" really refers to a middle segment of San Diego County's long coastal plain, not the northernmost part containing Camp Pendleton. Many of the beaches along the North County coast are included in state or county parks. Access to all is by way of the old coast highway (commonly known as Old Highway 101) wherever it runs next to the sand, and elsewhere by stairways that descend the bluffs from back streets.

Unfortunately for beach-goers, hikers, and coastal residents alike, the North County coastline is subject to some of the most rapid erosion anywhere along the California coast. Supplies of sand from formerly free-flowing streams are now blocked by dams. A jetty built to protect an artificial harbor north of Oceanside retards the natural flow of beach sand southward along the coast. Also, powerful win-

ter storms in past years have moved large amounts of sand to offshore sandbars, while the gentle summer waves return only a part of it to the shore. Since the beaches have shrunk in width, the bluffs right behind some of the beaches sometimes get the full brunt of wave action during high tides and storms. Housing development on top of the bluffs has disturbed

Area B-1: North County Coast

25

the normal drainage patterns and seems to be contributing to a faster rate of erosion.

Whether the destiny of the North County coastline is to become a series of broken cliffs and pocket beaches or a somewhat stable, continuous strand of sand is not known. For the moment, at any rate, hikers can still travel many miles—at low tide—without donning wet suits and fins.

Some of North County's coastal lagoons, or estuaries, have fared better than the coastline, even though urban development continues at a rapid rate around them. Two of these estuaries, Batiquitos Lagoon and San Elijo Lagoon, now have hiking trails along their shorelines.

Trip 1: South Carlsbad to Cardiff

Distance	5.5 miles
Hiking time	3 hours
Optional map	USGS 7.5-min *Encinitas*; or any street map
Best times	All year
Agency	CP/SDC
Difficulty	★★

The finest beaches, some of the nicest surf, and the most instructive vistas along the North County coastline are seen on this beach walk. Your visit should coincide with low tide—or at least an ebb tide. During high tide, passage is restricted in at least two places by the wash of the breakers.

If you plan to walk north to south, leave one car in or near the parking area at Cardiff State Beach (opposite San Elijo Lagoon), and take the other to the south end of South Carlsbad State Beach (0.1 mile north of La Costa Avenue), where roadside parking is available.

Start by walking south along the sandy or cobbled shore. Steep bluffs rise on the left. The bulk of these bluffs is a 50-million-year-old sandstone derived from lagoon and sandbar deposits. As the sandstone erodes away, cobbles embedded in it are released and deposited at the tide line by wave action. Most of the cobbles on this beach are metavolcanic rocks from distant sources, but some are granitic rocks apparently transported from the local Peninsular Ranges. All show the effects of prolonged tumbling and polishing.

In the next two miles you'll see many graphic illustrations of the fragility of the coastal cliffs. In winter, storm waves crash directly against the base of the cliffs, and tug at the lower underpinnings of the many private stairways that zigzag down to the beach. Some of these stairways have elaborate counterbalance mechanisms to raise and lower them to beach level. The cliffs are fluted with both old and fairly recent landslides, including one large semicircular feature perhaps 50 years old, now almost completely revegetated.

Blufftop property owners have used every strategy and tool imaginable to stabilize the cliff faces, including elaborate retaining walls and terraces, and flexible pipes to channel runoff. Some cliff faces are coated with gunite or other impervious materials, and others wear a coat of groundcover vegetation in the hope of holding things together. Overwatering is a constant problem: excess irrigation water constantly percolates into the porous sandstone, and oozes from the cliffs at beach level, weakening them.

Joggers enjoy a late afternoon run

At 2.8 miles from the starting point, the cliffs draw back and the sand widens. This is Moonlight Beach, a popular sunbathing beach complete with the usual amenities (water, restrooms, and a snack bar).

As you continue south, the strip of sand narrows again and you pass the "tightest" spot along this hike, an area just below the ornate Self Realization Fellowship building, known as "Swami's." During a winter storm in 1941, a section of cliff collapsed here, taking with it one of the temples above. The ocean bottom off Swami's gives rise to long combers that are renowned among local surfers.

South of Swami's the strip of sand widens. This is Sea Cliff County Park, accessible from above by a long, wooden stairway. The beach remains fairly wide as you continue past the San Elijo State Beach park, with its popular campground on the low bluffs. When these bluffs dwindle to nothing and you cross the inlet to San Elijo Lagoon, the parking area for Cardiff State Beach lies just beyond.

Trip 2: Batiquitos Lagoon

Distance	2.8 miles round trip
Hiking time	80 minutes (round trip)
Optional map	USGS 7.5-min *Encinitas*
Best times	All year
Agency	BL
Difficulty	★

Just beyond the placid north shoreline of Batiquitos Lagoon, white flecks of shell glint in the sunlight where the land begins to rise. Prior to two centuries ago, native Americans gathered and consumed shellfish here. As generations of Indians discarded the shell remains, their middens (refuse piles) grew in size. They remain in evidence today, assuming you keep a sharp eye out for them.

The Batiquitos Lagoon of prehistoric and early historic times lived up to its "lagoon" moniker. Seawater surged in and out on the tides, alternately bathing and uncovering the low-lying, salt-tolerant vegetation. Over the last century, however, vast loads of soil loosened by agricultural activity and urban development on the lagoon's watersheds were flushed downstream during winter floods. Much of this silt dropped out of suspension near the lagoon's mouth, forming a plug that interfered with normal tidal flows. As a result, Batiquitos Lagoon lost its permanent connection to the ocean and became a stagnating, fresh-water lake.

In a giant leap backward, or forward as the case may be, a massive dredging and lagoon restoration project was underway by the mid-1990s. Millions of cubic yards of sand were dredged from the lagoon's bottom and entrance channel and deposited on nearby beaches or piled up along the lagoon shoreline to provide nesting sites for least terns and western snow plovers. As of now the lagoon has been restored to a near-normal state, but it remains to be seen whether this condition can persist for long without expensive attention.

Now that the dredging project is finished, hikers, birdwatchers, and runners (no bikes or pets, though) are welcome to follow a path along the lagoon's north shoreline. This is a delightful walk during early morning or late evening—perfect for catching a bit of cool air during the warm summer months.

Starting from a small trailhead parking area on Gabbiano Lane (off Batiquitos Drive) in Carlsbad, the trail heads east, passing a tiny nature center housed in a trailer and regularly open on Saturdays. Beyond, the nearly level trail curls along the lagoon's north shore, where a number of elaborate interpretive panels have been installed. Traffic noise from Interstate 5, objectionable at first, fades as you continue east, passing several small eucalyptus copses. An iron fence separates a perfectly manicured golf course and upscale housing on your left from the wild assortment of native sage scrub vegetation and non-native palms, eucalyptus, mustard, and fennel on the shoreline strip you're walking through.

At a point 1.4 miles from the start, trail pulls left and goes under dense eucalyptus foliage. This is fine resting/picnic spot, and also a good place to turn around and return to the trailhead. Alternately, you may want to continue along the less interesting path ahead to as far as El Camino Real, some 2 miles farther. Various side trails branch north from this into Carlsbad's Aviara development, still being built as of this writing.

Trip 3: San Elijo Lagoon

Distance	1 to 3 miles out-and-back
Optional map	USGS 7.5-min *Encinitas*
Best times	All year
Agency	SEL
Difficulty	★

A great blue heron ambles on stilt-legs across the reed-fringed shallows, stabbing occasionally at subsurface morsels of food. Nearby, a willowy egret glides in for a perfect landing, scattering concentric ripples across the surface of the lagoon. Both birds seem oblivious to binocular-toting humans, who spy on them from a hillside a comfortable distance away.

A scene like this is repeated almost daily at San Elijo Lagoon, one of North County's most attractive coastal estuaries. Bisected by Interstate 5 and rimmed by expanding suburban development, the area has become the focus of considerable conservation effort. Local citizen groups, the San Diego County parks department, and California's Department of Fish and Game have teamed up to restore this long-neglected and formerly unappreciated resource.

West of I-5, high tides wash over mud flats and mats of salt-tolerant vegetation. Here, a dozen kinds of shorebirds can be seen on a typical day. A short trail near the site of the yet-to-be-built nature center off Manchester Avenue 0.5 mile west of I-5 gives direct access to the water.

From Old Highway 101, or from the north terminus of Rios Avenue in Solana Beach, you can gain access to other trails along the lagoon's beautiful south shore. These paths meander through coastal sage-scrub vegetation and copses of eucalyptus and other nonnative trees. Eroded sandstone bluffs half-hidden behind a screen of vegetation provide an impressive backdrop for the placid lagoon. Don't miss the spur trail leading south into secluded Holmwood Canyon. An abandoned apricot orchard lies tucked away halfway up the canyon's broad floor.

On the east side of I-5, runoff from Escondido Creek and La Orilla Creek supports a freshwater marsh—the East Basin. A quick access to that is by way of a flood-control dike just east of I-5. Park on the north side of Manchester Avenue, 0.3 mile east of I-5; cross Manchester (watch for fast traffic around the curves); and squeeze past a gate that keeps vehicles out. Walk past a second gate at the south end of the dike, and take the trail going left (east) toward El Camino Real. Before long the roar of traffic on the freeway fades, meadowlark songs fill the air, and your cares may disappear.

Egret at San Elijo Lagoon

Area B-2: Torrey Pines/La Jolla

Here's the San Diego coastline at its unspoiled best, with clean beaches, dramatic cliffs, and an unlikely forest of rare trees. Walking the wild stretch of beach from Del Mar to La Jolla Shores is more akin to adventuring than simply beachcombing. Exploring the caves at La Jolla Cove or looking out from the bluffs at Torrey Pines State Reserve is a sure way to forget that just inland lies the seventh largest city in America.

Try to avoid this area during summer afternoons, when tourists clog the beaches and coastal roads. Avoid by all means the traffic gridlock during weekday afternoon rush hour in the area between La Jolla and La Jolla Shores. If it's solitude you're looking for, you'll find it merely by venturing out at unconventional times—like early morning.

Torrey Pines Road, La Jolla Shores Drive, and North Torrey Pines Road are the major streets closest to the coast. Access to the beaches and coastline is frequent along these streets, except where cliffs intervene.

Trip 1: La Jolla Shores to Torrey Pines Beach

Distance	5.0 miles
Hiking time	2^1/$_2$ hours
Optional maps	USGS 7.5-min *La Jolla, Del Mar*; or a street map
Best times	All year
Agency	CP/SDC
Difficulty	★★

There are only a few places along the Southern California coastline where you can hike for miles in a single direction and not catch sight of a highway, railroad tracks, powerlines, houses, or other signs of civilization. The Torrey Pines beaches are one such place. Here, for a space of about three miles, sharp cliffs front the shoreline and cut off the sights and sounds of the world beyond.

Plan to do this beach walk at low tide. High tides—especially in winter—could force you to walk on cobbles at the base of the cliffs or oblige you to wade in the surf. Beach sand is often carried away by the scouring action of the winter waves, but is usually replenished by currents as summer approaches.

A good place to start from is Kellogg Park (La Jolla Shores Beach), where free parking is available when you can get it. If you're making this a one-way trip, leave a second car along North Torrey Pines Road, next to Torrey Pines State Beach, or in the adjacent Torrey Pines State Reserve—or have someone drop you off and later pick you up.

Walk north under Scripps Pier and on past the rocky tidepool area. Once beyond the last of the cobbles and wave-rounded boulders, you can slip off your shoes and enjoy the feel of the fine, clean sand underfoot.

Beyond the tide pools, you may notice that some beach-goers have doffed more than just shoes. You're now on Torrey Pines City Beach, also known as Black's Beach, San Diego's unofficial nude-bathing spot. The city rescinded a "clothing optional" policy for this beach in the late

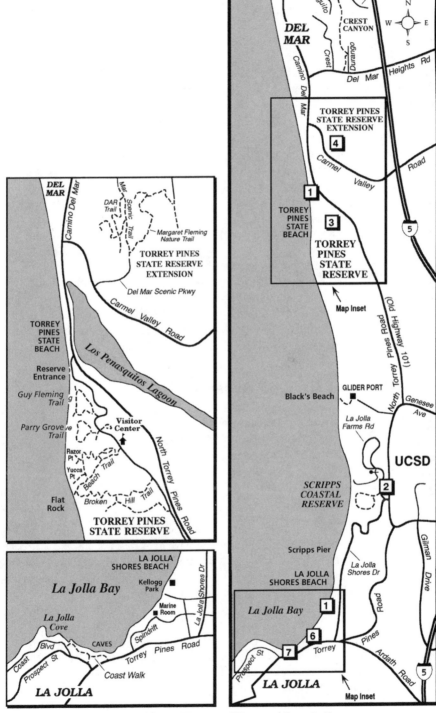

Area B-2: Torrey Pines / La Jolla

'70s, but old traditions have never died.

About a half mile past the tidepools, you'll see a paved road (closed to car traffic) going up through a small canyon. This is a good, safe way to reach (or exit from) the beach. There's a limited amount of 2-hour parking at the top along La Jolla Farms Road.

A bit farther ahead, where most Black's Beach users congregate, two precipitous trails ascend about 300 feet to the Glider Port, where hang-gliders launch their craft. Look up to see ant-like beachgoers lugging their gear up or down the zigzagging paths and hang-gliders soaring overhead. The southern of the two trails, improved and widened, is the safer one. There's plenty of free, all-day parking at the top if you want to start or end your beach walk there.

Lifeguards patrol some areas of Black's Beach during busy periods, so you can feel fairly safe about jumping into the water, which may reach a temperature warmer than 70° July through September. Elsewhere you swim at your own risk—

watch out for rip currents.

At about 4 miles from Kellogg Park, you reach Flat Rock, where a protruding sandstone wall blocks easy passage. Follow the narrow path cut into the wall. From a low shelf on the far side, Beach Trail begins its ascent to Torrey Pines State Reserve's visitor center.

In the fifth and last mile, the narrow beach is squeezed between sculpted sedimentary cliffs on one side and crashing surf on the other. These are the tallest cliffs in western San Diego County. A close look at the faces reveals a slice of geologic history: the greenish siltstone on the bottom, called the Del Mar Formation, is older than the buff or rust-colored Torrey Sandstone above it. Higher still is a thin cap of reddish sandstone, not easily seen from the beach—the Linda Vista Formation.

In the end, the beach widens, the cliffs fall back, and you arrive at Torrey Pines State Reserve's entrance along North Torrey Pines Road.

Trip 2: Scripps Coastal Reserve

Distance	0.6 mile
Hiking time	20 minutes
Optional maps	USGS 7.5-min *Del Mar, La Jolla*
Best times	All year
Difficulty	★

The Scripps Coastal Reserve, managed by the University of California Natural Reserve System, includes a small, undeveloped mesa overlooking the ocean, canyon slopes to either side of the bluff, and an underwater preserve beneath Scripps Pier. No visit to the La Jolla area is complete without a walk on the self-guiding Biodiversity Trail, which takes you along the very brink of the sea cliffs.

You'll find the trailhead on La Jolla Farms Road, 0.1 mile west of its intersection with La Jolla Shores Drive. There's limited curbside parking nearby. The short

trail circles the rim of the mesa, and lets you gaze over miles of spectacular coastline both north and south. So commanding is the view that gun emplacements were set up here during World War II to defend San Diego from enemy attack by sea.

At the trailhead you can borrow a self-guiding booklet that has a lot to say about the reserve's diverse array of indigenous plants and animals. Over 200 different kinds of plants, nearly 100 birds, and a dozen mammals have been identified within the boundaries of this small reserve.

Trip 3: Torrey Pines State Reserve

Distance	0.5- to 1.0-mile loops
Optional map	USGS 7.5-min *Del Mar*
Best times	All year
Agency	TPSR
Difficulty	★ to ★★

The rare and beautiful Torrey pines atop the coastal bluffs south of Del Mar are as much a symbol of the Golden State as are the famed Monterey cypress trees native to central California's coast. Torrey pines grow naturally in only two places on earth: in and around Torrey Pines State Reserve and on Santa Rosa Island, off Santa Barbara. Of the estimated 6000 or fewer native Torrey pines, more than half grow within the boundaries of the main reserve and its detached extension area.

Torrey Pines State Reserve would be botanically noteworthy even without its pines; more than 330 species of plants have been identified there so far. Sage-scrub, chaparral, and salt marsh plant communities are present in various parts of the reserve.

If you're interested in identifying plants and wildflowers typical of the coast and coastal strip, the reserve is simply the best single place to go in San Diego County. Excellent interpretive facilities at the reserve's museum make this an easy task. Besides the exhibits, you can browse through several notebooks full of captioned photographs of common and rare plants within the reserve. You can also visit the native plant gardens surrounding the museum building and at the head of the Parry Grove Trail.

If you visit the reserve a number of times during February through June, you'll be able to follow the succession of flowering as the spring season progresses. Wildflower maps, updated monthly, are often available.

A network of well-trodden trails over the eroded bluffs will take you nearly everywhere in the reserve, except into most canyon bottoms. It's important that you stick to these trails and eschew shortcuts and cross-country travel. The thin soils are easily eroded without the protection of healthy vegetation. As you'll plainly see, there are already enough instances of erosion here, both natural and man-made.

The entrance to the reserve is on North Torrey Pines Road (old Highway 101) at the bottom of the long grade up Torrey Pines Mesa. Past the entrance a paved road goes up to a parking lot adjacent to the reserve office and museum. From there, you can walk to the beginning of any of the trails in 10 minutes or less. If the lot is full, you'll have to leave your car in the lower parking lot down near the entrance, or along the highway shoulder nearby.

The reserve has a carrying capacity of about 400 people. When this level is reached, as on certain weekends, further entry may be restricted.

After a stop at the museum for a bit of educational browsing, you might first explore nearby High Point, where your gaze encompasses the intriguing but currently off-limits section of the reserve known as East Grove. East Grove experienced a wildfire in 1972, and young Torrey pines are establishing a foothold on the bluffs and canyons below.

Next you might head south on the concrete roadbed of the "old" old coast highway (closed to traffic) and pick up the Broken Hill Trail. The two east branches of this trail wind through thick chamise chaparral and connect with a spur trail leading to Broken Hill Overlook. You'll be

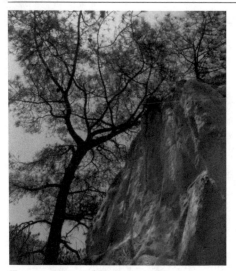

Torrey pines and Torrey sandstone

able to step out (very carefully) onto a precipitous fin of sandstone and peer over to see what, except for a few Torrey pine trees here and there, looks like desert badlands. A third (west) branch of the Broken Hill Trail winds down a slope festooned with wildflowers and joins the Beach Trail at a point just above where the latter drops sharply to the beach.

The popular Beach Trail originates at the parking lot near the museum and intersects with trails to Yucca Point and Razor Point. Fenced viewpoints along both of these trails offer views straight down to the sandy beach and surf.

The Parry Grove and Guy Fleming loop trails wind among the largest and thickest groves of Torrey pines. Unfortunately, the prolonged dry spell of the late '80s killed many of the large trees—mainly on account of the susceptibility of Torrey pines to attack by bark beetles during drought. Seedlings have been planted here and there in an effort to restore these groves to their former glory.

The Guy Fleming Trail is mostly flat, while the Parry Grove Trail starts with a steep descent on stair steps. In spring, the sunny slopes along the Guy Fleming Trail come alive with phantasmagoric wildflower displays. Fluttering in the sea breeze, the flowers put on quite a show as several different vivid shades of color dynamically intermix with the more muted tones of earth, sea, and sky.

The Torrey Pines trails can be enjoyed the year round, but they're open only during daylight hours. Ranger-led walks are featured on weekends. You can't picnic in the reserve, but after you do your hiking, you can use the tables or the beach down near the entrance. Do take water along on the trails if it's a hot day. Also bring binoculars: the soaring ravens and the red-tailed and sparrow hawks are interesting to watch, as are the hang-gliding humans you'll sometimes see.

Trip 4: Torrey Pines Extension

Distance	Up to 3 miles (all trails)
Optional map	USGS 7.5-min *Del Mar*
Best times	All year
Agency	TPSR
Difficulty	★★

Thanks to public donations for land acquisition, an area of natural bluffs and Torrey pine groves south and east of Del Mar is now merely surrounded—not over-

whelmed—by housing developments. This is the Torrey Pines State Reserve Extension.

The extension area is farther removed from the ocean than the main reserve, but in many respects is equally interesting. The gnarled and twisted Torrey pines clinging to stark, eroded sandstone walls here seemed to have escaped the ravages of the last drought. The extension area's narrow, less-maintained pathways offer a sense of peacefulness and isolation you can't get along the main reserve's well-beaten trails.

Of the extension area's many entrances, the dead-end of Del Mar Scenic Parkway (off Carmel Valley Road, 1.1 mile west of Interstate 5) is perhaps the easiest to find. Park near the end of the cul-de-sac and choose either the Margaret Fleming Nature Trail to the right, which goes up a sage-filled basin sparsely dotted with Torrey pine trees, or the Mar Scenic Trail to the left, which leads to the superb D.A.R.

(Daughters of the American Revolution) Trail. The latter trail slants up and then along a linear ridge to the west. From the Torrey-pine-shaded south brow of this ridge, you can look across Los Penasquitos Lagoon to the bluffs of the main reserve, and out to the ocean horizon. West of this ridge, a spur trail descends into an intimate little hollow with picturesque sandstone walls and gnarled Torrey pines.

On the Margaret Fleming Nature Trail you eventually climb toward a ridge capped with reddish rock. This cap is part of the familiar Linda Vista Formation, which is well represented on top of San Diego's coastal mesas.

A recently reopened stretch of this trail descends southwest to join Mar Scenic Trail.

Trip 5: Crest Canyon

Distance	1 to 2 miles
Optional map	USGS 7.5-min *Del Mar*; or a street map
Best times	All year
Agency	SDOS
Difficulty	★

Crest Canyon, a City of San Diego open-space park, fills a bowl-shaped valley that slopes down from Del Mar Heights Road on the south to San Dieguito Lagoon on the north. On the canyon floor, native sage-scrub and chaparral vegetation mixes with African daisy, ice-plant, saltbush, and other hardy plants that were introduced years ago to solve an erosion problem. Young Torrey pines are being introduced as well, hopefully to join the handful of century-old pines that thrive higher up on the canyon's side walls.

A good place to begin is along Racetrack View Road, not far from Jimmy Durante Boulevard and the Del Mar race track. From there, an initially wide, sandy path swings uphill along the canyon's broad floor. About two-thirds of the way up the canyon (0.7 mile), the narrowing path swings left toward Durango Drive on the canyon rim and thereafter stays high, roughly paralleling Durango, until it reaches Del Mar Heights Road. By crossing the latter street and following Mar Scenic Drive two blocks south, you can reach the upper end of the Mar Scenic Trail in Torrey Pines State Reserve Extension.

If you plan to poke around off the beaten trail in Crest Canyon, keep in mind a couple of caveats: The outcrops of sandstone, especially on the east side, are interesting to look at (from afar), but unstable and potentially hazardous. Watch out for rattlesnakes, too, particularly in the spring and summer.

In the Torrey Pines Extension

Trip 6: La Jolla Caves

Distance	1.0 mile round trip
Hiking time	1 hour (round trip)
Optional map	USGS 7.5-min *La Jolla*; or a street map
Best times	Extreme low tides during any time of year
Difficulty	★★

As you walk south from La Jolla Shores Beach, the wide strip of sand is soon replaced by cobbles and wave-washed cliffs. Just offshore, a major submarine canyon, La Jolla Canyon, swallows the sand that normally would migrate down the coast. This is the main reason why sandy beaches are the exception rather than the rule from La Jolla to Pacific Beach.

La Jolla lies on a step-like terrace at the foot of Soledad Mountain, an uplifted block of erosion-resistant sandstone. The precipitous north flank of this terrace faces the usually calm and deep waters of La Jolla Bay. Here, wave action from infrequent storms has gouged out a series of sea grottos, known as the La Jolla Caves.

The westernmost cave, at Goldfish Point, is well-known among tourists and natives alike; it can be reached from above by a long stairway that begins inside a gift shop called the Cave Store and passes through a man-made tunnel. The half-dozen or so other grottos in the series are usually accessible only by water. Extreme low tides (minus 1 foot or less), however, can bring some of these within easy reach of hikers. Extreme low tides typically occur on several afternoon occasions monthly from October through March. From April through September, the extreme lows tend to occur a few times a month as well, but nearly always at or near dawn.

Check tide tables for the most favorable low tides, and begin your hike about 30 minutes before predicted low. Start from the south end of La Jolla Shores Beach, or from the public beach access alongside the Marine Room restaurant on Spindrift Drive.

Work your way south over the cliff-hugging cobbles, or across the newly exposed tidepools, taking care not to step on the slippery, green rocks. The tidepool areas in particular show much evidence of "biological erosion"—that is, the breakdown of the structure of the rock itself by the chemical secretions of urchins, barnacles, and other sea creatures. As you walk along, you'll hear rasping noises as crabs, startled by your approach, retreat hastily into crevices. Occasionally you can find an octopus in one of the deeper pools.

The biggest grotto is enormous—about 50 feet high—at its entrance, but it pinches in toward the rear. The sandstone walls are stained with a rainbow of colors: red and orange from iron oxide, greens and grays from plant life, and purple from iodine in kelp. In the back of the cave is a low passage leading to an adjacent grotto. Enjoy, but don't forget about the incoming tide!

Trip 7: La Jolla Coast Walk

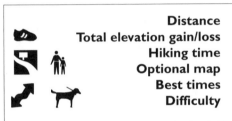

Distance	0.5 mile round trip (to Goldfish Point)
Total elevation gain/loss	100'/100'
Hiking time	20 minutes (round trip)
Optional map	USGS 7.5-min *La Jolla*; or a street map
Best times	All year
Difficulty	★

You get a stunning perspective of La Jolla Bay and the sparkling La Jolla Shores coastline on this short walk along the clifftops. You'll be walking directly above the La Jolla Caves, on or near the very brink of a 100-foot drop to the bay's calm surface.

An interesting if obscure place to begin is the small parking area (room for two cars only) at the east end of Coast Walk. This is reached by a short spur street, signed COAST WALK, that intersects Torrey Pines Road at a point 200 yards east of the traffic signal at Prospect Place.

From the tiny parking area, a cliff-hugging dirt path guides you just below the back yards of several palatial houses. A footbridge and steps span a ravine plunging directly to the blue-green waters below. Just beyond that ravine, a short spur path goes up some steps to the intersection of Prospect Place and Park Row. Keep straight. In about 200 yards you arrive at a grove of graceful Torrey pines on Goldfish Point. Although these trees grow naturally just up the coast at Torrey Pines State Reserve, they were planted here.

La Jolla Caves

The path ends just beyond the pine grove, next to the Cave Store. Some walkers like to continue by following the paved sidewalk past the pocket beach of La Jolla Cove and around the periphery of Scripps Park. Goldfish Point itself is a good place to sit and relax. You can watch the swimmers, snorkelers, and divers below as they float or glide through the often-glassy water. If you climb down to the edge of the water, you can look across the face of the cliffs to the east and make out the openings to several of the caves.

Evening strolls along Coast Walk are always interesting, especially during rare periods when the "red tide" (plankton) blooms and produces bioluminescence in the churning water below. Watch your step, though, night or day. Most of the cliff edges are not protected by fencing.

Brown pelicans at La Jolla Bay

Area B-3: Point Loma

The long, south-pointing peninsula of Point Loma and the spectacular curving shoreline of San Diego Bay are two of the principal elements responsible for San Diego's legendary beauty. The peninsula itself is an elongated block of sandstone uplifted about 400 feet above sea level by fault action. It serves as a natural breakwater for the once-shallow (now dredged) bay behind it.

Most of the south half of the Point Loma peninsula is reserved for military uses. Perched on its end, centered on the highest promontory, is one of America's smallest (144 acres) national monuments—Cabrillo National Monument. Because of its location adjacent to the tourist-happy city of San Diego, Cabrillo is consistently ranked as one of the two busiest national monuments in the country.

Whether you're a tourist or not, the view alone is worth the almost obligatory visit here. On the clearest winter days, you can see all the way to San Clemente Island, 70 miles offshore, and to the snow-capped summits of the San Bernardino Mountains, 100 miles north. Other attractions are the whale-watching overlook, the old and new lighthouses, the visitor center with its panoramic vista of the bay and cityscape, and a tidepool area located on the west (Pacific) shore. The one real hiking path in the monument—the Bayside Trail—is described below.

Because the access road into Cabrillo National Monument passes through a military reservation, visiting time is limited to the daylight hours, generally after 9 A.M. A parking fee is levied at the monument entrance; a lesser fee applies to those arriving by foot or bike.

A second patch of parkland lies on Point Loma's north end—Sunset Cliffs Natural Park, dedicated in 1983. Although the park remains little-known today, we profile its small network of trails in this section as well.

Area B-3: Point Loma

Trip 1: Bayside Trail

Distance	2.0 miles round trip
Total elevation gain/loss	320'/320'
Hiking time	70 minutes (round trip)
Optional map	USGS 7.5-min *Point Loma*
Best times	All year
Agency	CNM
Difficulty	★

Coastal sage scrub and chaparral vegetation are highlighted along this trail, but it's more worth taking for the wonderful, unobstructed views of San Diego Bay, the Silver Strand, and San Diego's flashy skyline. You'll double your pleasure if you walk this trail on a crystal-clear day, typical of the period December through March. Note that you must be off the trail well before the time of Cabrillo National Monument's closing, typically around dusk.

The trail begins just east of the old lighthouse, not far from the visitor center. Large metal interpretive plaques have been installed along the length of the trail, detailing the natural history of the area. The trail is simply an old asphalt road, now coated with gravel, that descends gradually in a rough semicircular arc to a point about 300 feet below and east of the visitor center lookouts.

Point Loma's bay slope is honeycombed with the ruins of a World War II defense system of mortars, observation bunkers, generators, and searchlights. You will see some of these remains along the trail. At the point where the trail ends (or rather runs into off-limits Navy property), you'll still be about 90 feet above the water surface. This is a good place to observe the sailboats and ships maneuvering in and

Point Loma tidepools

out of the bay's narrow entrance. There are also aerial acrobatics to watch, courtesy of gulls, terns, and pelicans—plus aircraft taking off and landing at the North Island Naval Air Station across the bay.

Return to the lighthouse the same way you came. Tempting as they may be, don't take shortcuts—the vegetation is easily trampled and the soil eroded by one footprint too many. Besides, off-trail exploration is strictly forbidden within the national monument.

Trip 2: Sunset Cliffs Park

Distance	0.5 to 1.0 mile
Optional map	USGS 7.5-min Point Loma
Best times	All year
Agency	SDOS
Difficulty	★

Stretching 1.5 miles along the Pacific shoreline, Sunset Cliffs Natural Park encompasses one of the county's more impressive stretches of coastline. The northern part covers just the cliffs that separate Sunset Cliffs Boulevard from the ocean. As is the case in North County, beach-cliff erosion is very rapid here, and elaborate retaining walls that dissipate wave energy have been installed to keep the road from being undermined. The remainder of the park includes a half mile of coastline plus some hillsides that slope upward toward the campus of Point Loma Nazarene College.

Currently there is controversy over erosion problems within the park, and encroachment on park land by playing fields and parking lots used by the college. A master plan for the park has been drawn up which recommends restoring the park to a more natural condition.

As of this writing, you can enjoy following the small, informal network of trails starting at Ladera Street and Cornish Drive. These take you up and down the hillsides and out to the tops of the low cliffs, just above where the ocean waves crash against water-worn boulders. Near sunset on clear days, a golden glow settles across the ocean and cliff faces, and Sunset Cliffs Park becomes one of the best places to toast the day's end. At nearby Cabrillo National Monument you can't usually do this, since the monument closes too early during most of the year.

During extremely low tides, which tend to occur on several afternoons each month from October through March, you can descend the steep steps at Sunset Cliffs Boulevard and Ladera Street to reach the intertidal zone below. The tidepools here contain little marine life, but it's fun to pick your way along the rocky shoreline beneath the banded cliffs.

Sunset Cliffs Park is great for kids, but little ones much be watched carefully. Most of the cliff edges are unfenced, and it's possible to slip on the hard-packed, eroded soil.

Below Sunset Cliffs at low tide

Area B-4: The Border Coast

Four square miles of marshes, tidal creeks, and sage- and chaparral-covered hillsides in and around the Tijuana River Estuary now enjoy federal protection as the Tijuana River National Estuarine Research Reserve. Included within this area is Border Field State Park, fronting the international border, and undeveloped tracts of land adjacent to the communities of Imperial Beach and San Ysidro.

For a long time now, sewage overflows from Tijuana, Mexico, have coursed through the Tijuana River and polluted parts of the estuary and beaches. Governments on both sides of the border continue to attack this problem, which grows more serious every year as Tijuana's population continues to explode.

Despite the problems with sewage, the estuary probably remains the county's richest habitat for birds. Birds congregate by the thousands here on a typical day, and over 340 bird species have been recorded to date. The reserve's best-known endangered inhabitants are the light-footed clapper rail and the California least tern. Visiting birds include ospreys, golden eagles, and peregrine falcons.

Since the salt marsh surrounding the tidal creeks of the estuary receives both fresh water (from river flows and local runoff) and salt water (from tidal flows), plant life exists in tenuous balance. Plants must be able to survive in an environment that ranges from wet to dry, and from fresh to saline.

As you walk from higher elevations (a few feet above sea level), where nonnative grasses, cattails, and typical shrubs native to the coastal uplands flourish, toward lower areas along the tidal creeks, you'll notice a succession of plants tending toward greater salt tolerance: pickleweed, sea blite, sea lavender, and finally cordgrass. At the lowest levels, the soft sediment of the mudflats supports al-

Area B-4: The Border Coast

gal films, and houses worms, crabs, snails, and other small creatures which are food for the shorebirds.

When you're out exploring the reserve, stick to the designated trails to avoid trampling any vegetation. Depending on the season, you may encounter sticky mud, so its wise to wear an old pair of shoes. Parts of the beach may be closed in spring and summer to protect nesting birds such as the least tern.

Recreational opportunities are increasing in the border and south San Diego Bay regions. Some 1100 acres of wetlands and former farmland, east of the national estuarine reserve, are being purchased by the county for inclusion in the future Tijuana River Valley Regional Park. Plans for a similar regional park are afoot for the Otay River Valley, inland from Chula Vista.

Several miles north of the border, on the east shore of San Diego Bay, Sweetwater Marsh National Wildlife Refuge has been established on formerly degraded wetlands at the mouth of the Sweetwater River. An interpretive facility called the Chula Vista Nature Center has been established here, and a new 1.2-mile trail guides visitors through the surrounding brackish marsh. Visitors park at the foot of E Street in Chula Vista, and from there ride a trolley to the nature center (open 10 A.M. to 5 P.M. most days).

Birdwatchers and advocates of ecotourism regard the coastal border region as a potentially major draw for tourists from all over the world. The first few steps toward realizing this dream have already been taken, though much effort remains.

Trip 1: Tijuana River Estuary

Distance	1 to 3 miles
Optional map	USGS 7.5-min Imperial Beach
Best times	All year
Agency	TEVC, CP/SDC
Difficulty	★

It's best to begin your exploration of the Tijuana River estuary and marsh with a stop at the reserve's new visitor center at 3rd Street and Caspian Way in Imperial Beach. In addition to interactive exhibits inside, a demonstration garden outside shows off about 100 species of the typical, but fast disappearing coastal sage-scrub vegetation that once blanketed San Diego's coastal mesas and hills.

From the visitor center, a trail runs south across the flat, green marsh land to the edge of a tidal pond. You can also start at 5th Street and Iris Avenue, and explore a larger network of trails going as far as the bank of the Tijuana River. Explorations

on Sunday are far more rewarding; otherwise you must endure the almost-constant noise of helicopter landings and takeoffs being practiced by pilots at the adjacent naval air station.

Another fine walk is the stretch of beach going south from the south end of Seacoast Drive. After 1 mile you arrive at the mouth of the Tijuana River. When storm runoff courses down the river, it's fascinating to watch the outrushing turbid freshwater mixing with the incoming bluegreen ocean waves. In winter, gulls set up shop here, feeding in the water and wheeling overhead in great flocks.

Also worth a possible visit is Border

Field State Park, which lies within the reserve boundaries. There, a picnic area atop a low coastal terrace offers a superb view of the Coronado Islands, Point Loma, and the downtown San Diego skyline, which is bisected by the Coronado Bridge. Nearby, an old stone monument, placed in 1851, commemorates the first point at which the boundary of the United States and Mexico was staked, following the 1848 Treaty of Guadalupe Hidalgo. The monument marks the extreme southwest corner of the conterminous United States, a place as significant from the standpoint of geographical trivia as Cape Flattery, Washington; Key Largo, Florida; and Madawaska, Maine.

As of this writing, the facilities at Border Field and the access road into it are in sorry shape. Plans for rebuilding and straightening the road are afoot, and it is hoped that the park will again become a pleasant place to visit.

Egret, Tijuana River Estuary

Coastal Strip and Foothills

Area C-1: Oceanside/Fallbrook

Aside from North County's beaches, not many public spaces for pleasant walking can be found in Oceanside or in the suburban communities that lie inland from it. This is changing, somewhat, as open space and agricultural land continue to be gobbled up by subdivisions, and activists respond by trying to preserve what they can of the region's formerly serene and gracious character. Unlike other areas of the county, there are no large blocks of publicly owned land here.

Here we feature the 557-acre Guajome Regional Park, off Highway 76 in east Oceanside; the 670-acre Wilderness Gardens Preserve east of Pala; and the 43-acre Los Jilgueros Preserve in Fallbrook. More significantly, we include a walk along the "wild" Santa Margarita River north of Fallbrook. As yet, the river is untouched by urban development, and no dam has constricted its flow—though various dam-building proposals have floated about for decades. Nearly all of the land along the Santa Margarita River is owned by public utilities, the state of California, The Nature Conservancy, or the military (Camp Pendleton). The chances are good that the river will remain wild, serving as a corridor of wildlife habitat and open-space parkland, into the far future.

Trip 1: Santa Margarita River

Distance	5.2 miles round trip
Total elevation gain/loss	400'/400'
Hiking time	2^1/$_2$ hours (round trip)
Optional map	USGS 7.5-min *Temecula*
Best times	October through June
Agency	FLC
Difficulty	★★

A wild and scenic section of the Santa Margarita River, a part of the last undammed major watercourse in San Diego County, is at last open to visitation by self-propelled explorers. A new recreational trail incorporates fragments of earlier roads and paths and wends its way along the semi-shaded south bank of the river, north of Fallbrook.

During all but the driest spells, water slides down the silty, willow-fringed riverbed and gurgles its way around obstacle courses of rounded granitic boulders. Winter floods periodically tear out the older willows, paving the way for dense growths of young willows, which is the kind of habitat the least Bell's vireo (an endangered bird) prefers.

To find the trailhead, drive north from Mission Road (in downtown Fallbrook) on Pico Avenue, which quickly becomes De Luz Road. After negotiating a

46

Area C-1: Oceanside/Fallbrook

short, twisty downgrade, turn right on Sandia Creek Road. Proceed 1.2 miles to a large dirt trailhead parking area on the right. There's a trail register here; please sign in.

In the first half mile of walking you negotiate two slippery stretches where the trail, squeezed by the river, presses close against a steep slope. Side paths lead down to the river, some crossing it to meander aimlessly amid the dense growths of willow saplings on the floodplain. Stay on the main south-side path, where all around you filigrees of wild grape and poison oak climb the trunks and limbs of sturdy live oaks and many-trunked California sycamores. In June, the ripened purple fruit of elderberry trees hangs over the trail, ready for the taking and eating.

The serene, almost pristine scene around you belies the state of affairs over a century ago, when trains following the tracks of the short-lived California Southern Railroad rumbled through here, probably on some of the flat-bedded pieces of trail you yourself travel on. Completed in 1882, ripped apart by winter flooding in 1884, rebuilt, and finally destroyed and abandoned for good in 1891, the Oceanside-to-Temecula section of this railroad was San Diego County's first connection to the nation's transcontinental rail network.

At 1.4 miles, the main path veers right up a hill, briefly joining a dirt road, ascending and later descending about 100 feet in order to bypass a boulder-strewn, curving section of the riverbed. At 2.5 miles, there's a fork in the trail. The left fork, signed Wil-

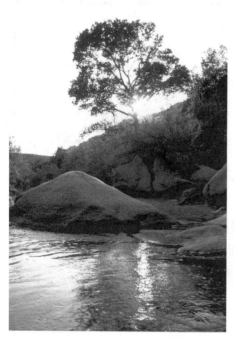

low Glen Trail, continues a level 0.3 mile to a gate. Instead, follow the trail on the right, Rainbow Creek Trail, for about 200 yards, until you find yourself in one of the most densely shaded hollows in San Diego County—dark and gloomy even at noon. This is the turnaround point for a 5.2-mile out-and-back hike. Pause here and let the coolness and quiet soak in, before returning the way you came.

If you prefer a 3.5-mile point-to-point hike, the Rainbow Creek Trail meanders on for another 0.9 mile to a bridge on Willow Glen Road, 1.3 miles north of Mission Road. You can leave or meet a vehicle here.

Santa Margarita River

Rainbow Creek

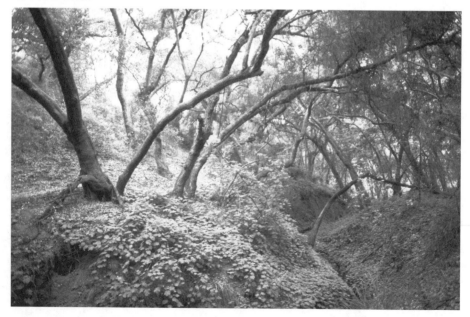

Trip 2: Los Jilgueros Preserve

Distance	1.0 mile
Hiking time	30 minutes
Optional map	USGS 7.5-min *Bonsall*
Best times	All year
Agency	FLC
Difficulty	★

Flanked by avocado orchards and newer suburban housing, the 43-acre Los Jilgueros Preserve (*jilgueros* means finches) stands as a quiet oasis of tranquillity in booming Fallbrook. Endowed with two good-sized ponds and patches of freshwater marsh, this former ranch property has been enhanced by extensive plantings of native oak, sycamores, ash, and cottonwood trees, plus a variety of native shrubs.

Sunday morning is a good time to visit if you enjoy quiet; otherwise, the traffic noise from busy Mission Road can be annoying.

Out of the network of old roads and paths in the preserve, you can fashion a 1-mile loop around its perimeter. Start at the preserve's south parking area, off Mission Road 0.3 mile north of Stage Coach Lane. Start by walking north on a curving, wood-planked bridge. At the preserve's north end, you'll find benches and a kiosk with interpretive information. From there, another plank footbridge leads to the shoulder of Mission Road. Spend a moment on the bridge and let the sensations soak in: Water vapor and moist odors transpire from the cattails, bulrushes, and yerba mansa thriving in the black mud a foot or two below. A breeze tinged with the dank odor of avocado and the sweetness of citrus ruffles the slender leaves of the willow branches spreading above, and caresses your exposed skin. White and yellow butterflies scintillate in shifting beams of sunlight.

On your way back to the parking lot, you can visit the "firescape garden," which exhibits fire-resistant plants for landscaping, and also swing by the larger of the two ponds.

Trip 3: Guajome Regional Park

	Distance	1 to 3 miles
	Optional map	USGS 7.5-min *San Luis Rey*
	Best times	All year
	Agency	SDCP
	Difficulty	★

Oceanside's Guajome Regional Park has a nice mix of wild and civilized features. There's cattail-fringed Guajome Lake for fishing, two picnic grounds, a large campground, and a grassy knoll that serves as a wedding site. Guajome's 4-mile trail system encircles Guajome Lake and visits a small pond hidden in a secluded back corner of the park. The park's topography is gentle, making almost all of its trails ideal for jogging as well as walking.

The westernmost trail in the park skirts a fresh-water marsh that oozes with water much of the year. Flanked by willows and cottonwoods and overgrown with cattails and volunteer palms, this marshy area exudes a complex mixture of damp odors that you can't often experience around most parts of arid San Diego County. For more exercise, head east toward the upper pond.

Guajome Park's coastal valley location and mild climate make it suitable for hiking nearly any day and any time. On summer days a cooling ocean breeze sweeps up the San Luis Rey Valley and provides natural air conditioning.

Trip 4: Wilderness Gardens Preserve

Distance	1 to 4 miles
Optional map	USGS 7.5-min *Pala*
Best times	November through May
Agency	SDCP
Difficulty	★ to ★★

Wilderness Gardens Preserve isn't a true wilderness, but rather the grounds of an old ranch—once the showplace of Manchester Boddy, owner of a Los Angeles newspaper and developer of the renowned Descanso Gardens in Pasadena. Today the ranch is managed for wildlife habitat and for recreation (walk-in only) and has largely reverted back to a wilderness character. Closed intermittently during the mid-1990s, Wilderness Gardens again welcomes day users, but now only on Fridays, Saturdays, and Sundays, 9:30 A.M. to 4:30 P.M. The former walk-in camping opportunity has been phased out, but picnic facilities remain. Wilderness Gardens is located 10 miles east of Interstate 15 on Highway 76 (if you cross the bridge over Agua Tibia Creek, you've missed the turnoff).

Down the middle of the preserve runs a wide strip of oak woodland along the San Luis Rey River. Intermixed with the oaks and sycamores are remnants of exotic plants such as silver-dollar eucalyptus, camellias, roses, shiny-leafed holly, bottlebrush, pyracantha, and oleander. A tough, fast-growing mixture of native chaparral and sage-scrub vegetation clothes the hillsides.

There are at least three distinct hikes you can make in Wilderness Gardens once you arrive at the entrance. Northwest of the parking area, a short trail loops around the sunny north bank of the San Luis Rey River, passing through a sparse cover of drought-resistant, desertlike vegetation.

By following the main road into the

preserve, you'll stay mainly under cover of spreading oaks, many festooned with wild grape vines. Ahead, you'll find several ponds (some may be dry) on the south bank of the river. These are fed partly by rainwater and partly by water pumped up from the water table, which lies just below the ground surface. The larger ponds are fringed by cattails and serve as a mecca for wildlife—over 140 species of birds have been seen here and in the surrounding area.

A third hike is the Meadows Trail, which rises on the slope of Pala Mountain to the south. After crossing over the San Luis Rey River on your way into the preserve, bear left on the Meadows Trail. This follows a boulder-strewn, dry channel before climbing a brush- and tree-covered slope overlooking a cluster of old buildings. Down below are the ranger's residence, an old barn remodeled as a conference center, a former chicken coop, and the

remains of San Diego County's
first grist mill, built more than
a century ago.

A little higher, you'll
pass the lower meadow, a
soft carpet of green dotted
with wildflowers in late winter and early spring. After
curving around the usually
dry bed of an old reservoir,
the trail dips and continues
toward the ponds below. If
you can find and follow it, an
old roadbed, now reverted to
a narrow trail, branches left
and ascends on switchbacks up the lower
slope of Pala Mountain.

Fungus on a decaying log

*Oak woodland along
San Luis Rey River*

Area C-2: Escondido

Fifteen years ago, hardly any designated hiking trails existed within 10 miles of Escondido. Now, as Escondido's population pushes 150,000 and that of inland North County approaches half a million, hiking opportunities have exploded. In 1991, Elfin Forest Recreational Reserve (initially named Mount Israel Recreation Area) was set aside in a secluded area southwest of Escondido. Part of the reserve is the site

of a water-storage reservoir, under construction as of this writing. The site includes 15 miles of trail, and more may be constructed in the future.

In 1997, the last remaining large section of natural habitat within Escondido city limits, the 3058-acre Daley Ranch, was opened to public use. The previous year, the fate of the area was decided when the city of Escondido decided to purchase the

Area C-2: Escondido

53

entire ranch and maintain it as permanent open space, rather than allow massive sub-urban development, which would other-wise have taken place there. Today the Daley Ranch's 20+ mile network of dirt access roads, transformed into hiking and biking trails, draws hundreds of visitors on most weekends.

Since the late 1980s, a major effort to create a 55-mile-long open-space park, cen-tered on Escondido, has been underway. When and if it is completed as envi-sioned—perhaps well after the turn of the century—the San Dieguito River Park will stretch from the ocean at Del Mar to the summits of the Volcan Mountains, north of Julian. The sometimes-narrow and sometimes-wide swath of the park is de-signed to protect the scenic and natural integrity of the San Dieguito River and its principal tributary, Santa Ysabel Creek.

The San Dieguito River Park Joint Powers Authority, a consortium of county and city governments, is acquiring pub-licly and privately owned parcels of land so as to stitch together the proposed 66,000-

acre linear park. In the mid-1990s these efforts ran afoul of certain private land-owners and interests within the proposed park planning area. That turn of events has slowed efforts to fill in gaps needed to complete the park.

The San Dieguito River Park JPA wastes no time in providing facilities for potential users of the parkland it has succeeded in acquiring so far. Since 1990, about 20 miles of new trails have been constructed. Many more miles of existing roads and trails within the park area are open for public use.

On the drawing boards, and already in place in a couple of spots, is the Coast to Crest Trail, which will eventually serve as the backbone for a network of existing and future lateral trails. When completed the Coast to Crest Trail will proceed from San Dieguito Lagoon in Del Mar past Rancho Santa Fe to Lake Hodges, near Escondido. An existing section already runs along the north shore of Lake Hodges and crosses under Interstate 15 to connect with Via Rancho Parkway. From there the trail will continue up through San Pasqual Valley and onto Cleveland National Forest lands near Ramona. Following the gorge of Santa Ysabel Creek, the trail will skirt Sutherland Reservoir, head east across Santa Ysabel Valley, and finally climb to the headwaters of Santa Ysabel Creek in the Volcan Mountains. A proposed extension of the Coast to Crest Trail would descend east into the arid San Felipe Valley and link up with the segment of the Pacific Crest Trail that passes through Anza-Borrego Desert State Park.

Trip I: Dixon Lake Recreation Area

Distance	2.5 miles
Total elevation gain/loss	350'/350'
Hiking time	80 minutes
Optional map	USGS 7.5-min *Valley Center*
Best times	November through May
Agency	DLRA
Difficulty	★★

Perched several hundred feet up in the hills just north of Escondido, Dixon Lake stores drinking water and serves as a recreational resource as well. Camping facilities, picnic grounds, playgrounds, boat rentals, and the opportunity to fish along most of the lake's shoreline are enough to draw a steady stream of visitors 7 days a week.

Out of the tight little network of trails along and above the lakeshore, you can fashion a route that loops upward to a high point overlooking the lake. There, on crystal-clear days, you may discern San Clemente Island and Santa Catalina Island in the far west, and trace the southern coastline down past San Diego and into Baja California.

To get to the lake, follow El Norte Parkway 3 miles east from Interstate 15. Turn left (north) on La Honda Drive and follow it 1 mile uphill to the recreation area's entry station.

Just beyond the entry station, you should spot the large, wooden sign marking the start of the Jack Creek Nature Trail. This half-mile-long, sometimes-steep ramble down to the lake shore and back includes 15 numbered stops keyed to a self-guiding booklet you can borrow from the ranger station. Along the way you'll become acquainted with several of the common native plants of the area—buckwheat, manzanita, chamise, California sagebrush, black sage, ceanothus, laurel sumac, toyon, willow, and live oak—and some non-native (planted) acacia and eucalyptus trees. Blue-flowered ceanothus shrubs fill the hillsides with color in March and April, while delicate, red monkeyflower plants bloom dependably from spring into summer. With jungle-like growths of acacia, jagged rock outcrops, and rugged little stair-step inclines, toddlers will find the place fascinating—but they'll likely need some hand-in-hand guidance over several rough spots.

For the 2.5-mile loop hike profiled here, observe the following directions: Just beyond the entry station, turn left onto the paved road that leads toward two fishing piers on the north shore of the lake. Less than a hundred yards down, pull off and park in the dirt turnout on the left. From the far corner of this turnout, start walking on the narrow trail (the Chaparral Trail) that cuts east, parallel to the road, through jungle-like growths of chaparral. You descend slightly, traverse a patch of riparian bottomland along trickling Jack Creek, and then climb easily through more chaparral. After 0.5 mile, the trail splits. Veer right, climb, and in moments you reach the edge of a dirt road. Turn right, walk downhill about 100 yards on the road, and pick up the narrow Lake View Trail slanting up the slope on the left.

A short, steep climb through a veritable tunnel of tall chaparral takes you to the brow of a ridge offering a view of the lake, part of Escondido, and hopefully the ocean. An equally steep, and rugged and rocky, descent lies ahead. At the bottom you come to another dirt road.

Go right and follow the road about 300 yards down toward the lake shore, near the dam, which is off-limits to hikers. Leave the road and head downhill to join the Shoreline Trail. Stay on the Shoreline Trail, heading generally west for the next mile, and ignore several side trails to parking areas above.

Leave the Shoreline Trail when you reach a narrow cove just beyond the second fishing pier, where the Jack Creek Nature Trail ascends. Climb either branch of that trail to the paved road above, and turn right to return to your parked car.

Along the Jack Creek Nature Trail

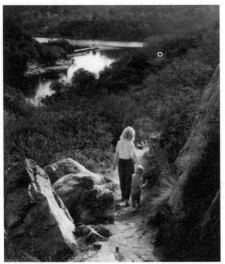

Trip 2: Daley Ranch—Tour of the Ponds

Distance	3.5 miles
Total elevation gain/loss	600'/600'
Hiking time	1^1/2 hours
Optional map	USGS 7.5-min *Valley Center*
Best times	All year
Agency	DR
Difficulty	★★

With more than 20 miles of trails for self-propelled travelers, the 3058-acre Daley Ranch, a former cattle spread and dairy, offers far more than any casual visitor should try in a single day. The following introductory hike, consisting of the Ranch House Loop trail plus a bit more, will give you a taste of the new park and probably whet your appetite for more. Get an early-morning start, so as to take advantage of the best bird watching and listening, the solitude, and the cool comfort of the morning air.

Start at the Daley Ranch main trailhead, right next to Dixon Lake, 1 mile up La Honda Drive from El Norte Parkway in Escondido. Park in the large lot on the left, just short of the Dixon Lake entrance. Step around the Daley Ranch gate and walk uphill, rather steeply, on pavement. At 0.4 mile the roadway starts descending into live-oak woods and you get a glimpse of the largest of several stock ponds on the ranch, its shoreline guarded by tall cattails.

After 1.2 miles, pavement on the access road ends and the quaint redwood Daley ranch house (closed to the public for the time being) lies to the left. Descendants of Robert Daley, who settled in this valley in 1869, erected the house in 1928. The pioneering Daley family continues to control large tracts of land around rural San Diego County, and also is prominent in the construction industry.

Continue north another 200 yards past various outbuildings to the beginning of the dirt-road route signed "Jack Creek Meadow." Take the road to the right, walk 200 yards, and then turn right on the steeply ascending Chaparral Loop Trail. After 0.4 mile you reach a secluded upper pond. Walk out along the dam (west edge of the pond) and look down on the valley of Jack Creek, dimpled with the two other ponds you'll visit on your return route.

From the upper pond, return to the ranch house, but from there, take the Ranch House Loop trail southeast, between the

Stock pond, Daley Ranch

two ponds. Be still, and your ears may catch the comical, deep-throated groans of a bullfrog, the buzz of a hummingbird's wings, or the warbling song of a redwing blackbird.

On foot, beyond the ponds, you can circle about south and west on the Ranch House Loop to return to your car—encountering along the way a couple of short, but very steep and slippery sections. If you're on a mountain bike, however, you may want to avoid that stretch by going back to the ranch house and exiting on the entrance road.

Trip 3: Daley Ranch—Jack Creek Meadow

Distance	5.6 miles
Total elevation gain/loss	500'/500'
Hiking time	2 1/2 hours
Optional map	USGS 7.5-min *Valley Center*
Best times	All year
Agency	DR
Difficulty	★★

The nearly flat ramble along sunny Jack Creek Meadow is fine anytime during the cooler months, and is even comfortably suitable during the summer provided you travel in the early morning or late afternoon. If you live or work in inland North County, consider this route for a bit of quick and intense exercise: a speed-walk of perhaps 90 minutes, a 60-minute jog, or a 40-minute mountain-bike ride.

As in Trip 2 above, head 1.3 miles up the paved Daley Ranch access road to the Jack Creek Meadow Loop Trail. The elongated loop you follow ahead takes you around the margins of a linear meadow, so narrow and so straight that it suggests some underlying, probably ancient fault structure. The meadow, lined with a dark green row of coast live oaks and backed up by steep

Jack Creek Meadow Loop Trail

slopes shaggy with mature chaparral, looks impressive when seen in early-morning or late-afternoon light. Close at hand you pass several gnarled specimens of Engelmann oak, with gray-green leaves and light-colored bark. The meadow grasses are almost entirely nonnative, typically of an emerald green color for about three months in the winter, and bleached yellow-brown after a month of two of springtime sun and prolonged drought.

After completing the loop around the meadow, return to your car the way you came.

Trip 4: Daley Ranch—Boulder Loop

Distance	4.0 miles
Total elevation gain/loss	750'/750'
Hiking time	2 hours
Optional map	USGS 7.5-min *Valley Center*
Best times	October through June
Agency	DR
Difficulty	★★

The aptly named Boulder Loop Trail traverses a ridge dotted with gleaming, creamy white granitic boulders. Each boulder has been sculpted into its own unique, often fanciful shape, a product of tens of thousands of years of weathering and erosion. Much of inland San Diego County is underlain by crystalline rocks such as these, which were the result of magma cooling and crystallizing deep underground some 100 million years ago.

To reach the Boulder Loop Trail, park at the Dixon Lake trailhead and head north on foot into Daley Ranch, using the paved Daley Ranch access road. You pass over a summit at 0.4 mile and then descend into oak woods where, at 0.7 mile, you find the south leg of the Boulder Loop Trail on the left. On this steep, slippery old bulldozer track hewn into decomposed-granite soil, you quickly gain 250 feet of elevation. Look behind you for an agreeable view of the pond-dotted valley below. To the south and southwest spreads the quintessentially suburban city of Escondido, and beyond that (on crystal clear Santa-Ana days at least) lies the San Diego and Baja coast, and the blue arc of the Pacific.

One mile into your hike, you reach a gently rolling plateau averaging about 1600 feet in elevation. Proceed west for a while on a narrowing path. Swing north at 1.5 miles, and go up and over a low saddle. At 1.9 miles stay right, joining a wider dirt road. A virtual boulder garden lies hereabouts, with tooth-like specimens of coarse-grained bedrock jutting upward from the ground. Many of the outcrops and boulders exhibit the effects of spheroidal weathering, a process of micro-erosion that eats away at the surface of a rock and rounds its shape by removing mineral grains from the sharp edges one at a time.

Heading east now, you pass the unimaginatively named Central Valley Loop Trail on the left. Keep straight and descend back to the paved Daley Ranch access road (3.2 miles). Retrace your earlier steps on pavement back to your car, 0.8 mile away.

Weathered boulders

Trip 5: Daley Ranch—Engelmann Oak Loop

Distance	5.1 miles
Total elevation gain/loss	800'/800'
Hiking time	$2^1/_2$ hours
Optional map	USGS 7.5-min *Valley Center*
Best times	October through June
Agency	DR
Difficulty	★★

This trail highlights the Engelmann oak (or mesa oak)—a somewhat rare evergreen oak tree found only in parts of interior Southern California. Along the way you'll also see the ubiquitous coast live oak, with its characteristic dense and dark green foliage. Engelmanns, with sparser foliage and grayish-green leaves, tolerate dryness better and tend to thrive on high, as well as low, ground. In the ravine bottoms, where subsurface water gathers, the thirstier coast live gather thickly and often succeed in excluding other trees.

The quickest way to access the Engelmann Oak Trail is by way of a back en-

trance to Daley Ranch off the northern extension of Broadway. From Escondido, drive north about 5 miles on Broadway, then follow graded Cougar Pass Road 1.4 miles east and north to a gated access road on the right. Limited roadside parking is available.

On foot, on the access road, you traverse a grassy flat and soon plunge into coast live oak woods, where perpetual twilight reigns. A small stream trickles through here during the wetter half of the year. At 0.7 mile ignore the first road on left, signed Engelmann Oak Loop Trail (that leg of the trail can be skipped on the return in favor of the nicer "alternate trail"). At 0.9 mile stay right, avoiding the lesser trail on the left, the "alternate trail." You climb more briskly now, attaining a saddle. Stay on the main road, which angles east upward along a ridge, and negotiate your way over a steep section with loose rocks underfoot. Most of Escondido lies in view; you can see how "Hidden Valley" (the English translation of the Spanish *Escondido*) is nestled in a bowl surrounded by rounded hills whose summits rise about 1000 feet.

At the next junction, 1.5 miles, bear left. Continue climbing and don't miss the beautiful old stock pond on the right, brimming with water after winter rains. Continue through a park-like spread of coast live oaks—where, on a warm spring day, sweet, toasty aromas rise from the drying grass and oak leaf litter.

Next, you skirt the south base of Burnt Mountain, a rounded, boulder-studded promontory guarded by thick chaparral. At 2.3 miles, stay straight as the Central Valley loop trail veers right. As you curve left shortly ahead, there's a view northeast of the rolling mesa occupied by the rural community of Valley Center. At 3.3 miles (0.3 mile past a large, blue water tank on the right), in a grassy vale, turn left on the narrow trail designated "Alternate Trail" on park maps.

A delightful one-mile descent down a shallow ravine ensues, first through swaying grass, then amid fragrant chaparral, then under densely clustered live oaks whose intertwining limbs nearly blot out the sky. Nowhere along this passage can you see any sign of unnatural disturbance, save for the trail tread itself.

When you reach the next trail fork, bear right, and return to the road you came in on.

Stock pond off Engelmann Oak loop

Trip 6: Lake Wohlford

Distance	1.0 mile
Hiking time	$^1/_2$ hour
Optional map	USGS 7.5-min *Rodriguez Mtn.*
Best times	All year
Agency	LW
Difficulty	★

This short piece of trail, primarily used for fishing access at Lake Wohlford's shoreline, winds for about half a mile amid dense growths of chaparral and coast live oak. Leafy curtains of poison oak drape the oak limbs, lending a Tolkienesque flair to the scene. It's tranquil here on weekdays, but a bit noisy on weekends with boat traffic on the lake and car traffic along the far shore. You can sit on benches or lie on a large rock slab by the shore, all the while observing the rippling lake surface or the activities of birds (I witnessed several hawks exploding into flight over the crown of an oak tree).

To reach Lake Wohlford, drive 1.9 miles up Lake Wohlford Road from Valley Center Road and turn right on Oakvale Road. Drive 0.7 mile to a gated dirt access

road on the left, open during the daylight, which leads to the shore of the lake. One segment of the shoreline trail goes 0.2 mile west, while the other segment winds north for about 0.3 mile.

Trip 7: Hellhole Canyon Open Space Preserve

Distance	5.0 miles round trip
Total elevation gain/loss	700'/700'
Hiking time	$2^1/_2$ hours
Optional map	USGS 7.5-min *Rodriguez Mtn.*
Best times	November through May
Agency	SDCP
Difficulty	★★

A wide-ranging system of trails is now open in the county's new and still obscure, 1712-acre Hellhole Canyon Open Space Preserve, east of Valley Center. The county acquired this and other parcels of surplus Bureau of Land Management (public-domain) land in North County when the BLM sought to dispose of them in the 1980s.

To reach the starting point, take Paradise Mountain Road 3.3 miles east from Lake Wohlford Road to Kiavo Drive, where you bear left (north). Continue another 0.5 mile north on Kiavo to the preserve's well-marked entrance and parking lot.

From the edge of the parking lot, a trail leads down along a scruffy ridgeline. The boulder-studded west rampart of 3886-foot Rodriguez Mountain lies to the east; on humid days the mountain sometimes creates its own cloud cap. Perhaps you'll see a slice of ocean horizon in the northwest if the weather's clear and dry.

You then round a switchback and descend more quickly, passing a wooden bench on the right. At 0.8 mile, you come down to a secluded spot along Hell Creek that can only be described as enchanting. During winter and early spring, water happily spills over smooth boulders under a canopy of spreading live oaks and twisted sycamores. Downstream from here, a century ago, travelers sometimes had a "hell" of a time getting their wagons across the rain-swollen creek while on the Escondido to Palomar road—hence the stream's colorful name. Curiously, there's no connection between the names of Hell Creek and the nearby upland area called Paradise Mountain. The latter was apparently christened by a couple of hot and thirsty prospectors after they discovered a cold spring there.

Just ahead, the trail joins an old, rock-lined canal bed and passes through one of the most charming oak glens in the whole county. Succulent live-forevers cling to the crumbling canal walls. For another 0.5 mile, the trail sticks with the old canal, which contours (or rather rises at the imperceptible rate of 10 vertical feet per mile) across a sunny, chaparral-covered slope.

At 1.3 miles, the trail veers uphill, leaving the old canal. Stay left at the trail fork 100 yards ahead. (The right branch climbs to the mountainous, east part of the preserve, and loops back down to join the trail ahead. Using this you can piece together a loop hike, adding some 5 miles, that traverses the view-rich, northwest shoulder of Rodriguez Mountain. It's a tedious climb and descent—worthwhile only for the view, assuming the air is very clear.)

On the lower trail, you traverse a grassy slope dotted with redolent wild onions. You then start descending back to the canal bed, join it for a short while, and descend further to reach Hell Creek right

Hell Creek

at the point where a large metal pipe crosses over. The pipe—an "inverted siphon"—short-cuts the path of the original canal you were walking along earlier. The purpose of this canal is to shunt water from the San Luis Rey River over to Lake Wohlford, which lies on the Escondido

Creek watershed.

You've now traveled 2.5 miles from the parking lot, and this is a good place to turn back and return the same way. If time and energy allow, then you can keep going on the dead-end trail ahead for another 1.5 miles.

Trip 8: Elfin Forest Recreational Reserve

Distance	1 to 8 miles
Optional map	USGS 7.5-min *Rancho Santa Fe*
Best times	All year
Agency	EFRR
Difficulty	★ to ★★★

The nearly 800 acres of open space at the Elfin Forest Recreational Reserve (formerly Mt. Israel Recreation Area), southwest of Escondido, were opened to the public in December 1992 as a cooperative effort between the Olivenhain Municipal Water District and the US Bureau of Land Management. The BLM owned the land, whereas the water district wished to build a small reservoir on the south edge of the property and open the rest to recreational use by hikers, equestrians, and mountain bikers.

Today, construction on the reservoir has started, and 13 miles of the original 17 miles of recreational trails remain open outside the construction area. More trails may be added when the reservoir is completed.

There's something for everyone here. For small kids there are short, nearly flat trails down near the entrance, where Escondido Creek murmurs and splashes over boulders. Ambitious hikers and bikers must travel upward. They can fashion a number of wide-ranging loops, several miles in length, out of the intricate network of old roads and trails atop Mt. Israel—the ridge looming south of the reserve's entrance.

You'll find the well-marked entrance and trailhead parking area near mile 6 on

Harmony Grove Road, 3 miles west of the outskirts of Escondido. From there, the wide path dubbed "The Way Up Trail" crosses Escondido Creek and begins a crooked ascent of a canyon wall studded with tooth-like rock outcrops and dripping with thick, almost jungle-like growths of chaparral. The community of Elfin Forest below and to the west takes its name from chaparral's lyrical nickname. Until late in the spring, this cool, north-facing canyon wall retains its spring-green grass and exhibits showy clusters of red monkeyflower and nightshade. Look north to the other side of the canyon and notice the sparsely vegetated slopes there. They were swept by wildfire during the 8600-acre Harmony

Escondido Creek

Grove Fire in October 1996.

The shadeless Ridge Top Picnic Area comes into view after 1.5 miles, and about 700 feet of climbing. Of the manifold possibilities for pressing on from this point, here's one recommendation: From the west side of the picnic area, climb to Elfin Forest Overlook, at the top of the ridge to the southwest. The parallel trails along the ridge are segregated according to the type of user (hiker, biker, horse). On clear days, you can look down the valley of Escondido Creek to San Elijo Lagoon and the ocean, 9 miles away.

Next, head south down the Tyke's Hike Trail to the Valley Access Trail, which skirts the reservoir construction area. Climb east to Lake Hodges Overlook for a really amazing view of that sprawling reservoir. Circle north and west, returning to Ridge Top Picnic Area, and from there The Way Up Trail will take you back down to your car.

The Elfin Forest Recreational Reserve is open from 8 A.M. to dusk daily, with interpretive hikes given on the weekends.

Trip 9: North Shore Lake Hodges

Distance	6.0 miles round trip
Total elevation gain/loss	250'/250'
Hiking time	2^1/$_2$ hours (round trip)
Optional map	USGS 7.5-min *Escondido*
Best times	All year
Agency	SDRP
Difficulty	★★

Lake Hodges is destined to become one of the key units in the sprawling San

Dieguito River Park, now taking form along 55 miles of river valley from the coast at Del Mar to the Volcan Mountains near Julian. Already some designated trails are in place around the lake's shoreline, most notably the Coast to Crest Trail which follows the north shore. Like all of the county's reservoirs, Hodges serves two purposes besides recreation: water storage and flood control. At various seasons and during various years the water level may stand anywhere from brimming full to unattractively low.

To get to the starting point of this particular scenic stretch of the Coast to Crest Trail, drive to the north end of the woodsy community of Del Dios (south of the intersection of Del Dios Highway and Via Rancho Parkway) and follow a paved access road south to the boat launch concession on the shore of Lake Hodges. Park in the huge lot here, and head east on the Coast to Crest Trail, a dirt road at this point. In the next 2 miles, you curl around the base of massive Bernardo Mountain, contouring some distance above the water level. Look for hawks and ravens patrolling the scrubby slopes above, and for snow-white egrets parasailing over the wind-rippled surface of the lake below.

At 1.8 miles you cross a tiny stream where oaks, sycamores, palms, and other water-loving vegetation thrive. Thereafter, the narrowing trail follows the shoreline somewhat more closely and approaches Interstate 15, where a new and elaborate concrete walkway cuts under the busy lanes of traffic, just above the highest level of the lake. The trail continues ahead for another half mile, joining Sunset Drive opposite the North County Fair shopping center. Unless you've planned for a one-way trip, the I-15 undercrossing (about 3 miles from your starting point) is a good turnaround spot.

Trip 10: Piedras Pintadas Trail

Distance	3.8 miles round trip
Total elevation gain/loss	250'/250'
Hiking time	2 hours (round trip)
Optional map	USGS 7.5-min *Escondido*
Best times	All year
Agency	SDRP
Difficulty	★★

Just south of today's Escondido a lazy river once ran, fed by tentacle-like tributaries that drew water from as far away as the desert-bordering mountains to the east. On the banks of this river dozens of kinds of wild plants grew, providing the prehistoric Kumeyaay people with food, fiber, and medicine.

Some of these plants were deliberately cultivated; others were suppressed through controlled burns and other means. Many were simply left undisturbed to thrive or to fail under the pressures of natural selection. Small game was hunted and captured amid the rocky hills. Fine-grained, river-bottom soil was collected for use in making clay pottery. Pigments fashioned from soluble minerals, wild seeds, and insects were carefully applied to the surfaces of large hillside boulders. The geometrical, abstract designs of the resulting pictographs expressed in some way the ritual and ceremonial practices of the Kumeyaay.

Fast-forward several hundred years to the present, and place yourself on the high point of the Peidras Pintadas ("painted rocks") interpretive trail. Down below, where willows once swayed on the soggy banks of the river and smoke from cooking fires rose, you now see Lake Hodges, a smooth, spreading sheet of water. Distant cars hum along Interstate 15, and a discontinuous carpet of homes creeps over the hills and dales of Escondido and Rancho Bernardo. Above, on boulder-studded slopes guarded by tough chaparral, a collection of pictographs fades from view under the imperceptibly slow onslaught of solar radiation, acidic rainfall, and drying winds.

Although the Kumeyaay rock-art site is officially off-limits to visitation, you can walk along the nearby interpretive trail, getting the equivalent of a small book's worth of historical, cultural, and botanical information from the many plaques spaced along it.

To get to the starting point, drive 0.5 mile south from Interstate 15 on West Bernardo Drive. A large dirt parking lot lies to the west—the trailhead for the Piedras Pintadas Trail and also the site of a proposed visitor center for San Dieguito River

Wild cucumber fruit

Park. From there, follow the well-marked trail around Bernardo Bay (the south arm of the lake), passing a small waterfall which splashes happily during the wet season. Farther on you come to a terminal loop in the trail, where you swing up along a rocky ridge and behold the lake and its surroundings.

Trip 11: Highland Valley Trail

Distance	4.8 miles round trip
Total elevation gain/loss	150'/150'
Hiking time	2 hours (round trip)
Optional map	USGS 7.5-min *Escondido*
Best times	All year
Agency	SDRP
Difficulty	★★

The Highland Valley Trail runs parallel to Highland Valley Road on oak-dotted slopes overlooking the shallow (and sometimes dry), easternmost arm of Lake Hodges. It presently ends after more than 2 miles at Sycamore Creek Road, though its future south extension will tie into the elaborate trail system being developed within the city of Poway. You can spend an easy-going couple of hours rambling out and back along this trail, alternately in warm sunshine amid the chaparral or in cool dampness beneath the overspreading live oaks.

In early spring, the Highland Valley Trail appears at its freshest, with radiant greenery covering everything on the ground except for the thick brown accumulations of oak-leaf litter.

The trail originates at a small dirt

parking lot on Highland Valley Road, just west of Pomerado Road. After only 0.3 mile on the trail, there's a bridged passage over a deep, densely wooded ravine—an impressive destination for small kids first testing their hiking legs. About halfway down the length of the trail, look for the *morteros*, or grinding holes, on a sloping slab of granitic rock to the left. Here, Kumeyaay women rhythmically pounded acorns into meal using heavy *manos*, or hand stones—a scene repeated here and at many hundreds of other sites around the county two centuries or more ago.

Trip 12: Battle Monument Trail

Distance	1.0 mile round trip (to the ramada)
Total elevation gain/loss	240'/240'
Hiking time	30 minutes (round trip)
Optional map	USGS 7.5-min *San Pasqual*
Best times	All year
Agency	SPBSP
Difficulty	★

San Pasqual Battlefield State Historic Park recently gained a very handsome visitor center, which undoubtedly helps to snag a few of the millions of people who visit the nearby San Diego Wild Animal Park. The center features some fine interpretive displays on the 1846 Battle of San Pasqual (part of the Mexican-American War) and on the use of the valley by Native Americans and later settlers.

You'll find the visitor center along Highway 78, 1.4 miles east of the Wild Animal Park entrance. Our recommended hike starts with the short, self-guiding nature trail on the slope just behind the visitor center. After about 0.2 mile on this, you can continue west on the Battle Monument Trail across dry slopes toward a hilltop ramada and bench. Thickets of prickly-pear cactus dot the slope, their ripe red fruits bulging by the hundreds during the fall season.

From the ramada the broad, flat San

Trailside view of upper San Pasqual Valley

Pasqual Valley spreads before you. Most of the valley is a designated agricultural preserve within the city limits of San Diego—which is why it is not filled with subdivisions. In the opposite direction you can spot parts of the Wild Animal Park, and often some of the large animals that roam

more-or-less-free there.

After you've had an eyeful, and perhaps lunch, at the ramada, you can head east back to your starting point. The Battle Monument Trail itself continues west down the hill to reach a state historical monument alongside Highway 78.

Trip 13: San Pasqual Hiking Trails

Distance	up to 25 miles (whole network)
Optional map	USGS 7.5-min *San Pasqual*
Best times	November through May
Agency	SDRP
Difficulty	★ to ★★★

Two of the newer additions to the emerging San Dieguito River Park are undeveloped parcels of former BLM land lying north and south of Highway 78, just east of San Pasqual Valley. Thanks to a summer's worth of labor by San Diego Urban Corps members, a 13-mile network of hiking trails was opened here in fall 1991.

Like any low-elevation route in the county's arid, warm interior, the San Pasqual hiking trails (a.k.a. Clevenger Canyon trails) are best explored during the cooler months. If you go on an unusually clear day, the coast-to-mountain views on these trails can be truly stunning.

The trails are divided into two networks, each with its own trailhead. To explore the easier, south trail system, start from the parking lot on the south side of Highway 78, 5.3 miles east of the San Diego Wild Animal Park entrance. You start by zigzagging 0.6 mile to the first marked trail junction. Choose the right branch for a relatively easy climb to a 1550-foot knoll. From this vantage, there's often a rather good ocean view.

The left branch of the trail—a more rugged alternative—begins with a short passage through a spooky ravine, replete

with live oaks, mosses, and fungi. On the other side, you tackle switchbacks leading toward a prominent, monolithic boulder on a high ridge to the east. After passing within of few yards of the boulder, there's a side trail on the right leading to a 1755-foot viewpoint—good for another view to the west. Keep straight to continue toward a 1635-foot bump on a ridge half a mile northeast (you join a dirt road briefly, and resume travel on a foot trail branching left toward the high point). That's where you get a really stupendous view of upper San Pasqual Valley, a slice of ocean horizon in the west, and the distant, blue-tinted mountains in the east. Almost straight down a thousand feet, you'll see toylike cars making their way along the sinuous gray ribbon of Highway 78.

By tracing all branches of south trail network and returning, you cover about 7 miles with a 1900-foot total elevation gain, and the same loss.

The maze-like, north trail system involves some strenuous uphill and downhill walking—more than you might expect for any trail so close to the urban area. You start from a parking lot on the north side of Highway 78, 5.6 miles east of the San Diego Wild Animal Park. If you're coming from Escondido, the turnoff comes unexpectedly; note that it is 0.3 mile beyond the parking lot for the south trails.

Exhausting the possibilities of the north trail network in a single day is just that—exhausting. You'd have to walk 18 miles with a total elevation gain (and loss) of 4500 feet. There's something for everyone here, though—even small kids. Beautiful Santa Ysabel Creek lies only 200 feet below, 0.3 mile away by trail. There you can sit for a spell amid beautiful oaks and

sycamores. Water may or may not be careening off the boulders, depending on recent rains. Don't try to cross the creek if the water level is dangerously high. The trees with gray-green leaves hereabouts are Engelmann oaks, a relatively rare variety whose endangered habitat centers on northern San Diego County.

The steeply ascending trail ahead, which has been difficult to maintain over the past several years and therefore may be in poor shape, is for peripatetic hikers only. Dozens of switchbacks take you to a trail junction 1300 feet higher and 2.5 miles farther. At the trail fork there, decide where you want to go—right toward any of three marked viewpoints, or left toward any of six marked viewpoints.

My favorite viewpoints on the north trail maze are the 1847-foot knoll west of Tims Canyon, and the big boulder pile at 1762 feet. Both feature virtually aerial views down the length of San Pasqual Valley. Unpack your lunch at either one and enjoy a view probably superior to that from any hilltop mansion in North County.

Trip 14: Boden Canyon

Distance	11 miles round trip
Total elevation gain/loss	500'/500'
Hiking time	4½ hours (round trip)
Optional maps	USGS 7.5-min *San Pasqual, Rodriguez Mtn*
Best times	October through June
Agency	CDFG
Difficulty	★★★

Comely Boden Canyon, rich with live-oak woodland and nestled between baked hillsides redolent with the sweet fragrance of sage, has become a part of San Diego County's newest parcel of protected open space. The Boden Canyon Ecological Reserve, west of Ramona, contains 2068 acres administered by the California De-

partment of Fish and Game, and the city and county of San Diego.

With dirt roads of varying width featuring gentle ascents and descents, the reserve is a perfect place for casual hiking and jogging. Mountain bikes, horses, and all forms of motorized transport are prohibited.

The as-yet unmarked trailhead (a dirt-road intersection) is located on the north side of Highway 78, 7 miles east of the San Diego Wild Animal Park and 5 miles west of the Highway 78/67 intersection in Ramona. Park on the dirt road so as not to block access to other vehicles, and walk downhill, passing a locked vehicle gate. Just beyond is a small bulletin board with a box of maps.

Continue descending to a hairpin turn, where the road swings around the bottom of Clevenger Canyon. The sycamores and oaks in the canyon bottom, draped with poison oak and wild grape, give a foretaste of much more of the same kind of scenery to come. At 1.7 miles, you cross Santa Ysabel Creek on a concrete ford. There could be anywhere from a torrent of water at this crossing to nothing, depending on the recency of heavy rainfall. A little before this river crossing, the Lower Santa Ysabel Road branches to the right, but it is so little traveled that you won't likely go astray.

Your course is now steadfastly north, with little wiggles here and there, as you make your way up the wide crease in the landscape known as Boden Canyon. Extravagant growths of coast live oak cast dense pools of shade upon the trail at frequent intervals. You'll also spot scattered Engelmann oaks, with gray-green foliage, and sycamores of all sizes, some with trunks twisted into fanciful shapes. Eucalyptus grows at two spots, probably the location of former ranch dwellings. At 5.5 miles into your hike or run, you come to the turnaround point, a locked gate with private land beyond. An old, tumbledown corrugated metal shack hides in the foliage nearly.

The Fish and Game department has established an interim hunting zone in the northernmost accessible part of the canyon, encompassing the last mile of the trail. Be aware that hunting for various game animals may take place in this zone at intervals during the year.

Oak woodland in Boden Canyon

Area C-3: Poway

Much of the area east and northeast of Poway, extending to the outskirts of Ramona, has been earmarked as permanent open space. This includes Woodson Mountain, one of the county's most picturesque promontories, and a swath of land to the south of it.

The upper and middle slopes of Woodson Mountain were declared open space by the City of San Diego in 1978. In the area to the south, an administrative transfer of public domain land from the BLM to the City of Poway has allowed that city to build a riding and hiking trail system stretching from Lake Poway across Woodson Mountain to Iron Mountain. This system now ties into an intricate network of recreational trails being developed throughout the semirural neighborhoods of Poway.

Lake Poway serves as a kind of central staging area for trails that run in several directions. A nice complement of recreational facilities has been developed along the shoreline of the lake to serve the local residents—and also non-Poway residents, who must pay a fee for parking and day use. Visitors can picnic; play horseshoes, volleyball, or softball; rent boats to fish or cruise about on the 60-acre surface of the reservoir; camp at a primitive campground accessible only by foot or horseback; and, of course, hike or ride the trails. Hours for the recreation area are sunrise to sunset, 7 days a week (the lake itself is open Wednesday through Sunday).

A scenic section of riparian bottomland below Lake Poway's dam was added to the region's protected open space in 1989 with the purchase of the 410-acre Blue Sky Ranch. The California Department of Fish and Game now runs the area as a wildlife preserve.

Sycamore Canyon Open Space Preserve, southeast of Poway, opened in 1988, and the adjacent Goodan Ranch, once slated for housing development, was added to it in 1993. As the years go by, this block of open space will serve as a buffer between the growing cities of Poway and Santee.

Ultimately Poway's trail system will tie into a countywide network of trails. One such regional trail, the Trans-County Trail (distinct from the Coast to Crest Trail described previously in this book) is on the drawing boards now. It will originate near Del Mar, travel up Los Penasquitos Canyon, traverse Poway, pass through Sycamore Canyon Open Space Preserve, climb up and over El Cajon Mountain, run up through Cleveland National Forest lands toward Cuyamaca Rancho State Park, and finally descend into the Anza-Borrego Desert. The Trans-County Trail has been imaginatively nicknamed the "Pines to Spines Trail," in reference to the Torrey pines on the coast and the bristling cacti of the desert.

Area C-3: Poway

Trip 1: Lake Poway Loop

Distance	2.5 miles
Total elevation gain/loss	400'/400'
Hiking time	1¹/₂ hours
Optional map	USGS 7.5-min *Escondido*
Best times	All year
Agency	LPRA
Difficulty	★★

This loop trail around Lake Poway serves two purposes. It's an excellent exercise trail for runners and walkers, with a good mixture of flats, gentle hills, and a few fairly steep switchbacks. It is also an interpretive trail, with a leaflet (available at the lake entrance) keyed to numbered posts along way. On the trail, you'll pass through four distinct plant communities: sage scrub, chaparral, oak woodland, and riparian woodland.

Pick up the trail just beyond the lake entrance on the left (north) side of the developed area. The trail follows the west shoreline to a point beyond the dam, then drops well below the rock-fill base of the dam to cross the creek. When you reach the dirt road below the dam, you can make a short side trip, if you wish, to visit a small campground. It's used mostly by horse riders, but backpackers are welcome too. Tables at vacant sites can be used for picnicking. The Blue Sky Reserve lies right below the campground; you can enter it this way if you want.

The loop trail resumes on the east side of the dirt road. Climbing by way of a long switchback segment, you gain a slope above the east end of the dam. Continue winding around the east and south shoreline, at some distance above the water, until you reach the edge of the developed area.

Trip 2: Blue Sky Ecological Reserve

Distance	2.5 miles round trip
Total elevation gain/loss	100'/100'
Hiking time	1¹/₂ hours
Optional map	USGS 7.5-min *Escondido*
Best times	All year
Agency	BSER
Difficulty	★

Now that the California Department of Fish and Game has purchased the former Blue Sky Ranch along Green Valley Truck Trail, one of the finest examples of riparian woodland remaining in San Diego County will be fully preserved and protected. Never a ranch—just property held for investment—the 470 acres include typical sage-scrub/chaparral hillside vegetation and more than a mile's worth of lushly shaded canyon bottom.

After a wet winter, the whole place acquires an almost unbelievable sheen of green. Mosses, ferns, annual grasses, and fresh new shrub growth coats everything, even the rocks. Wildflowers appear in great numbers by about April, and start to fade by June. More than 100 kinds of wildflowers have been identified here in a single year.

You'll find the entrance along the east side of Espola Road, just south of its big bend toward Rancho Bernardo and 0.6 mile north of Lake Poway Road. On foot, follow the unpaved truck trail down along the south bank of the creek. Traffic noise disappears, and frogs entertain you with their guttural serenades. Live oaks spread overhead, casting plenty of welcome shade, while willows, sycamores, and lush thickets of poison oak cluster along the creek itself. Here and there, paths diverge toward the creek, where you can spot tadpoles, frogs, and perhaps other amphibious creatures.

At 1.0 mile, a side road goes south toward the Lake Poway wilderness campground. One-quarter mile farther, where powerlines pass overhead, the road splits three ways. The right branch goes up-slope to a house foundation amid a eucalyptus grove. The road straight ahead heads toward a hillside water tank. The left branch (Green Valley Truck Trail) goes across the creek and starts climbing a sunny slope

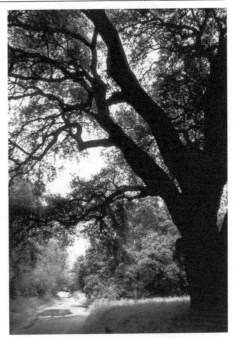

Oak woodland, Blue Sky Ecological Reserve

toward the Ramona Reservoir. This split in the road is the end of the line for casual hiking. If you want a lot more exercise, just keep walking—all the way up to the Ramona Reservoir dam, 1.3 miles away.

Trip 3: Mount Woodson Trail

Distance	4.5 miles
Total elevation gain/loss	1600'/850'
Hiking time	$2^{1}/_{2}$ hours
Optional maps	USGS 7.5-min *Escondido, San Pasqual, San Vicente Reservoir*
Best times	October through June
Agency	LPRA
Difficulty	★★★

The Mt. Woodson Trail starts at Lake Poway, traverses the rugged south slopes of Woodson Mountain, and ends just below Highway 67, south of Ramona. Hand tools and human labor were used to forge the eastern part of this trail. Huge boulders and a massive tangle of chaparral presented constant route-finding and construction difficulties. There are sudden turns, steep up and down stretches, and, in some places, a thick canopy of ground-hugging vegetation which blots out all views. It's a real adventure to walk this trail—but only if the following caveats are observed:

Pick a cool day. (My first experience on the trail coincided with a September sizzler, with air temperatures on the sunny slopes as high as 112°F!) Also allow plenty of time to negotiate the almost constant ups and downs. Although you'll be on good trail tread all the way, there are a few very steep stretches. Wear shoes with good traction.

If you can swing a ride at the east end (or set up a car shuttle), a good way to do this trail is point-to-point, as we suggest in this description. Begin at the grassy picnic area on southwest shore of Lake Poway, and follow either of two wide trails southeast (these join together after 0.4 mile. After skirting the south shore and dipping to cross Warren Canyon, you come to a trail junction at 0.8 mile. Turn right on the signed Mt. Woodson Trail and climb east on a steep grade through sage scrub and chaparral. The white-flowering ceanothus, occurring in dense patches, comes into full bloom hereabouts around March.

You'll pass another junction, with a beautiful pond on the left (filled with water in winter and spring) at 1.2 miles. Stay left and continue east. At 1.6 miles, stay left and continue east again. At the next trail junction, 1.8 miles, a newly cut trail up Woodson Mountain's west ridge branches left. Stay right and ascend to a 1690-foot saddle. An older trail up Woodson's west ridge joins at this point; however, it is being phased out in favor of the newer and smoother path you passed earlier.

Now, with Woodson Mountain's boulder-peppered south flank in view ahead, you begin a rollercoasterlike descent through thick brush and around huge boulders. You'll pass two picnic sites under spreading oak trees along the way. These are great spots for a break, especially in the heat. After about 2 miles' further travel (4 miles from the start) eastward, the trail turns abruptly south and descends to a point at the foot of a fill slope created several years ago by the widening of Highway 67. Clamber up the fill slope on a path worn into it and step over the guard rail to reach the shoulder of the highway. There's a parking turnout just west of here on the far side of the highway, at a point 1.7 miles north of Poway Road. There is no marked pedestrian crossing, so be extremely careful when crossing the busy road.

Eventually, a trail will be constructed parallel to the highway which will connect the east end of the Mt. Woodson Trail to the Iron Mountain Trail at Ellie Lane.

Trip 4: Woodson Mountain—East Approach

Distance	3.6 miles round trip
Total elevation gain/loss	1200'/1200'
Hiking time	2 hours (round trip)
Optional map	USGS 7.5-min *San Pasqual*
Best times	October through June
Agency	SDOS
Difficulty	★★

Indians called it "Mountain of Moonlit Rocks," an appropriate name for a landmark visible, even at night, over great distances. Early white settlers dubbed it "Cobbleback Peak," a name utterly descriptive of its rugged, boulder-

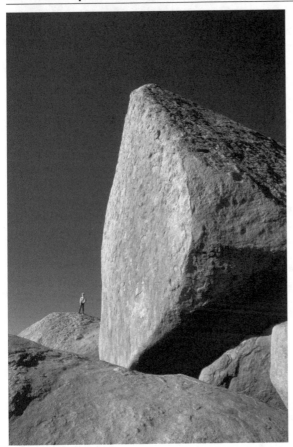

Granodiorite boulders on
Woodson Mountain

less face behind. It's no wonder that local rock climbers consider Woodson Mountain (or "Mt. Woodson," as it is popularly called) to be the best place in the county for bouldering practice.

The mountain's upper and middle slopes are publicly owned open space managed by the City of San Diego. This open space surrounds a 15-acre parcel on the summit ridge reserved for communications antennae. Hikers and climbers have easy access to the slopes via a paved service road (closed to vehicular traffic) serving the antenna site at the summit.

Park on the wide shoulder of the east side of Highway 67, 3 miles north of Poway Road, opposite the entrance to the California Division of Forestry fire station. Carefully cross the four lanes of the highway (there's no crosswalk, though pedestrians scoot across here frequently), and follow a well-beaten path south past the fire station to where it hooks up with the paved service road. The road underfoot is at times very steep, but offers good traction.

On most weekends, the sounds of nature will be accompanied by the clink of aluminum hardware, plus the shouts of "On belay!" and other phrases in climbers' parlance. Even if you don't see climbers, chalk marks (from gymnast's chalk) on boulders by the roadside mark their favorite routes.

Near the top of the mountain, the road passes narrowly between immense, egg-shaped boulders and split-boulder faces 20 to 30 feet high—some, perhaps, unclimbable by "ethical" means.

strewn slopes. For the past 100 years, however, it has appeared on maps simply as "Woodson Mountain," in honor of a Dr. Woodson who homesteaded some property nearby well over a century ago.

The light-colored bedrock of Woodson Mountain and several of its neighboring peaks is a type geologists call "Woodson Mountain granodiorite." When exposed at the surface, it weathers into huge spherical or ellipsoidal boulders with smooth surfaces. The largest boulders have a tendency to cleave apart along remarkably flat planes, forming "chimneys" from several inches to several feet wide. Sometimes, one half of a split boulder will roll away, leaving a vertical and almost seam-

When you reach the top of the mountain, you'll be amid an antenna farm. Prior to 1990 a metal fire lookout tower stood here. This was a replacement for an older structure destroyed by wildfire in 1967. That fire, which eventually burned as far west as today's Interstate 15, leaped on raging Santa Ana winds from its point of origin in Ramona to the top of Woodson in just 90 minutes. With the tremendous growth in the population of the area, and the proliferation of communication systems (exemplified by the towering antenna structures here), fire lookouts are fast becoming a distant memory.

Just east of the easternmost antenna is a disused cubical water tank with a peaked roof perched on a large boulder. On the surface of the boulder are bench marks indicating the highest (natural) point on the mountain.

Walk west along the narrow summit ridge, passing various antenna towers, to reach a vantage point overlooking Poway, the North County coastal region, and the great blue expanse of the Pacific Ocean. Santa Catalina and San Clemente islands are visible on the clearest days. Nearby you'll spot an amazing cantilevered "potato-chip" flake of rock, the result of exfoliation and weathering. This spot, 1.8 miles from the start, is a good spot to turn back and return the way you came.

Alternately, from the end of the service road, you can follow a narrow path down the boulder-punctuated west ridge to reach a new network of trails hacked into the mountainside by local activist Mike Fry and other Poway volunteers. By swinging around toward the northeast on the shortest route, you can descend to a point near the intersection of Highway 67 and Archie Moore Road, and circle back to your car by walking on the shoulder of Highway 67. This longer, rougher loop route measures 5.5 miles and involves an elevation gain and loss of 1500 feet each.

Trip 5: Woodson Mountain—West Approach

Distance	7.2 miles round trip
Total elevation gain/loss	2300'/2300'
Hiking time	4¹/₂ hours (round trip)
Optional maps	USGS 7.5-min *Escondido, San Pasqual*
Best times	November through May
Agency	LPRA
Difficulty	★★★

This superior, but twice-as-difficult hike to Woodson Mountain's summit (compared to the standard, east approach—Trip 4) takes you through a veritable obstacle course of gigantic boulders. The variety of shapes is amazing, from smooth and rounded, to angular or shattered.

Begin, as in Trip 3 above, by hiking the Mt. Woodson Trail to the junction of the new trail up to Woodson's west ridge, 1.8 miles. A vigorous climb ensues as the trail crookedly ascends the sunbathed, south-facing flank of the ridge, curving around boulders and twisting amid the low-growing chaparral. The ever-widening view across the lowlands to the south and west duly compensates for the effort.

At 2.5 miles the trail reaches Woodson's sharply defined summit ridge and turns east toward the antenna towers. Turn right and stay on the ridge, ignoring side trails slanting left. A final narrow and rough link of trail runs on to meet the end of the service road atop Woodson's summit, 3.4 miles, just short of the summit; this last link lies just outside Poway city limits and therefore receives little or no maintenance. Don't miss the remarkable, razor-sharp boulder flake on the left. Continue another 0.2 mile to reach Woodson's high point.

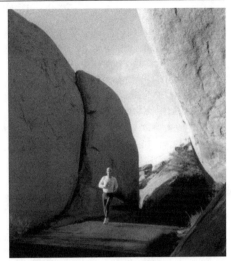

Nearing summit on Mt. Woodson road

Trip 6: Iron Mountain

Distance	9.0 miles
Total elevation gain/loss	1600'/1600'
Hiking time	5 hours
Optional map	USGS 7.5-min *San Vicente Reservoir*
Best times	November through May
Agency	LPRA
Difficulty	★★★

After five years of piecemeal construction by California Conservation Corps crews, the Iron Mountain Trail was finally dedicated and fully opened to the public in 1991. Hiking this trail on a clear, crisp late-autumn or early winter day is one of my favorite local experiences. Because it is part of Poway's multiuse trail system, the trail has become popular among equestrians and mountain bikers as well as hikers.

Iron Mountain's conical summit rises to nearly 2700 feet. You may start at either of two trailheads some 1000 feet below the summit. For the easiest way up (and then back the same way), you can start from the road shoulder of Highway 67, just south of Poway Road, where limited parking is available. The route, first a dirt road and then a trail, proceeds directly

east for 1.5 miles to join the main Iron Mountain Trail. The summit lies 1.7 trail miles south of that junction. The resulting hike is 6.2 miles round trip.

I prefer the longer, tougher, and more rewarding loop route starting from the main Ellie Lane trailhead (it's the one whose data appear in the capsulized summary above):

Begin at Highway 67 and Ellie Lane (0.7 mile north of Poway Road). The trail takes off from the edge of a fenced equestrian staging area just east of the highway. In the next 1.5 miles, you'll climb through tall growths of chaparral and practically rub shoulders with boulders the size of small trucks. The boulders, which often look like oversize jelly beans or jelly-bean fragments, are the same "Woodson Mountain granodiorite" seen on nearby Woodson Mountain. The chaparral includes a lot of ceanothus, or "wild lilac," which bursts into fragrant bloom sometime around March. You'll also detect the ineffable sweetness of Cleveland sage, which permeates the air in many places along the trail almost year-round.

A large live oak spreads a pool of shade across the trail at 0.9 mile. At 1.4 miles, you bend around another large oak and soon pass Table Rock, a curious mushroom-like balanced slab of rock. From there, you'll get your first glimpse of Iron Mountain's summit, poking up over lesser ridges in the south.

Ahead, the occasionally very steep trail meanders down to cross a small ravine, and then zigzags sharply up along the side of a ridge. You'll catch your breath just in time to start an equally steep switchback descent into another ravine. Like Sisyphus, you must tackle yet another set of uphill switchbacks, this time alongside the bottom of the ravine.

Salvation lies at the saddle ahead (2.4 miles), with a glorious view of mile upon mile of olive-green mountains, culminating at the dark-blue wall of the Cuyamacas. Watch for an easy-to-miss switchback turn ahead—a false trail goes straight and continues for some distance, while the real trail makes a hairpin turn to the left and descends a dry, east-facing slope. At 2.8 miles, a side trail branches east and follows a ridgeline to a high spot offering a good view of the Ramona valley.

The main trail descends moderately south and swings west to reach a signed trail junction, 3.5 miles from Ellie Lane. Iron Mountain's summit—despite the posted 2 miles—is really a bit less than 1.7 miles away. The wide, well-graded trail zigzags up the mountain's north flank, offering an ever-widening view of the coastal strip and the mountains to the east. Early

On the Iron Mountain Trail

on many springtime mornings there's no view along this stretch, as you're in the midst of the coastal stratus clouds. Just after this trail was completed, I'd invariably collect a dozen dew-drop-laden spider webs on my shirt on the way up. This no longer happened after a while; the orb-weaving spiders apparently learned to construct their webs so that the lowermost supporting strand lay just above the heads of passersby. A 1995 wildfire swept Iron Mountain, reducing all vegetation to blackened sticks and ash, so it will be a while before the spiders return in force.

When you reach the summit, you can sign your name on the visitor's register, and sometimes admire a true panorama of the Pacific Ocean, glistening beyond the sparkle of rooftops and cars in the distant suburbs below.

Retrace your steps 1.7 miles back to the trail junction, turn left (west), and start the descent down along a ravine toward the south trailhead near Poway Road. At a point 50 yards past where you cross the ravine bottom, a side trail goes north almost straight up a hill (gaining 200 feet) to a small pit where iron ore was once mined. Dark, dense chunks of the ore lie strewn about—bring along a magnet to confirm their identity.

Close the loop by turning right on a connector trail going north. You pass by two beautiful ponds—the first on public land, the second behind a fence on private property. Both brim after the winter rains, and reflect the green-mantled, bouldered mountainsides east and north. You end up joining the trail running west from the Ellie Lane parking lot, your starting point.

Trip 7: Sycamore Canyon Open Space Preserve

Distance	4.7 miles
Total elevation gain/loss	500'/500'
Hiking time	2 hours
Optional map	USGS 7.5-min *San Vicente Reservoir*
Best times	All year
Agency	SDCP
Difficulty	★★

Sycamore Canyon Open Space Preserve, along with its recent addition, the Goodan Ranch, sprawls across more than 2000 acres of granite-ribbed mountains southeast of Poway. About 10 miles of old ranch roads, fire roads, and new trails presently lace through the area.

The preserve has two entrances: one (open weekends only) along Highway 67, 0.7 mile south of Scripps Poway Parkway, and the other (open 7 days) at the terminus of Sycamore Canyon Road. The latter entrance, accessible from Poway by way of Garden Road, is the starting point for the loop route described just below and referred to in the capsulized summary above. Note that although Scripps Poway Parkway (a limited-access expressway) passes over Sycamore Canyon Road, there are no access ramps connecting the two.

Limited parking is available at the east end of Sycamore Canyon Road. There you'll find an informational bulletin board and the start of a narrow trail contouring across the slope to the left. In the first half mile this trail cuts across hillsides densely covered with a mixture of chaparral and sage-scrub vegetation. Look for wild peony, its inconspicuous reddish-brown flowers nodding circumspectly by the trailside. To the south, in a gently sloping bowl, lies the Goodan Ranch, with its smattering of buildings amid the oaks.

After a short, steep descent, you cross a ravine bottom shaded by overarching oaks. Ahead a short distance is the Martha Harville Memorial Oak Grove (0.7 mile), with wooden benches thoughtfully provided. It's hard to believe peaceful places like this still exist so close to the city and suburbs. The Kumeyaay Indians appreciated this spot as well. Centuries ago they processed acorn meal in the deep *morteros* and shallow grinding slicks indenting the surfaces of nearby rock outcrops. Watch out for poison oak, which grows large and thick here. In vine form it has embraced some of the larger oaks, forming a mock tree-canopy of foliage.

Continue following the trail down along the woodsy ravine. You soon reach a sloping meadow, reverberating with chirping crickets. At 1.7 miles, this trail crosses a dirt road. Just beyond a side trail branches right toward the Olive Grove Picnic Area, nestled into an small grove of olive trees on the Goodan Ranch. This is a spot to visit now, or else later, for a breather and a bite to eat. Continue south past the picnic area, go up a little rise, then curve down and west toward a barn and a dirt road following Sycamore Canyon. Turn left here and head south paralleling the trickling (in season) Sycamore Canyon stream for another 0.4 mile. At that point, take the trail to the right which connects to a narrow, paralleling footpath. Double back on this parallel trail, going north past scattered oaks and skirting the ranch buildings. Farther on, on the same trail, you arrive at an intersection of dirt roads out in the open and north of the ranch. From there, the remaining 0.9 mile of the hike is unremarkable and perhaps tedious as you head north (uphill) on the Goodan Ranch access road to return to your car.

The other significant loop hike in the Sycamore Canyon preserve is best begun at a parking lot on Sycamore Park Drive (the dirt-surfaced entryway off Highway 67 which is open to vehicles on weekends only). From there, a ridge-running trail descends into Sycamore Canyon, losing some 500 feet of elevation over about 2 miles. You can then circle back via Goodan Ranch, gaining back the same elevation.

Child-packing at Sycamore Canyon Open Space Preserve

Area C-4: Penasquitos

About a third of San Diego's total share of acreage set aside as open space lies within the city's fast-developing northern sector. This area includes the suburban communities of Mira Mesa, Rancho Penasquitos, and Carmel Valley. When the urban fabric of San Diego and its northern suburbs joins together as a tightly woven tapestry in a decade or two, the wisdom of preserving these, and hopefully other, parcels of natural landscape will be very much appreciated.

One patch of open space lies on the chaparral-clad slopes of Black Mountain, the dominant topographic feature in the Rancho Penasquitos area. Hike to the summit of this peak, and you'll experience a bird's-eye view of the city, the ocean, and the mountains to the east.

A much bigger patch of open space comprises the 6-mile-long, 3000-acre Los Penasquitos Canyon Preserve, already being referred to as an "oasis amid urban sprawl." Stretching between Interstate 5 and Interstate 15, it includes both Los Penasquitos Canyon—a major east-west drainage—and a tributary, Lopez Canyon. Riparian woodland, chaparral, and grassland habitats are superbly represented in various parts of the preserve.

Most acreage in the preserve centers along the canyon bottoms and steeper canyon walls and excludes the tops of the ridges. That exclusion is how a high-speed road, Sorrento Valley Boulevard, and other major streets were pushed across the heart of the preserve in the early 1990s. In just a few years, thousands of houses popped up on the slopes north of Los Penasquitos Can-

yon. The next several years may see the construction of rows of condominiums along the south wall of Los Penasquitos Canyon.

Over 130 kinds of birds, 26 mammals, 22 amphibians, and 90 different plants have been identified within the preserve. Currently a herd of about 35 mule deer roam the preserve, and bobcats and mountain lions were spotted in recent years. It is not certain how the larger animals will fare after the ultimate "build-out" of the surrounding area. Another factor impacting the wildlife of the region will be the imminent construction of the Highway 56 freeway across lands north the preserve.

Visitor facilities at the preserve include parking/equestrian staging areas off Black Mountain Road on the east side, and next to Sorrento Valley Boulevard on the west side. Near the east entry stands the Johnson-Taylor ranch house, now the preserve's headquarters, dating from 1862. In 1991, archaeologists announced the discovery that part of the ranch house is a surviving remnant of a house built in 1824 for Captain Francisco Maria Ruiz. Ruiz was commandant of the Presidio of San Diego, and the recipient of the county's first Spanish land grant. The crumbling remnants of another adobe structure, also owned by Ruiz, stand under a protective roof at the west entrance to the preserve.

Human activity within the preserve centers along the 6-mile-long dirt road through Los Penasquitos Canyon. This is a multiuse trail for hikers, horse riders, and mountain bikers. Elsewhere, the other trails (which are closed to mountain bikes) are informal and usually unmaintained.

Area C-4: Penasquitos

Trip 1: Black Mountain

Distance	3.5 miles
Total elevation gain/loss	1000'/1000'
Hiking time	2 hours
Optional map	USGS 7.5-min *Poway*
Best times	October through June
Agency	SDOS
Difficulty	★★

On a really clear day atop Black Mountain your gaze encompasses a stretch of coastline from Dana Point in Orange County to Playas de Tijuana just south of the border. Mexico's Islas de Los Coronados poke up sharply beyond Point Loma to the south, while San Clemente Island and Santa Catalina Island float like mirages above low-lying coastal haze to the west. Quite often in winter you can spot the snowy summit of Old Baldy (Mt. San Antonio) in the San Gabriel Mountains to the north.

For years, local residents have been climbing Black Mountain by means of whatever old dirt road or firebreak seemed most convenient. In the early 1990s, however, about two miles of new hiking trail were constructed in the City of San Diego's Black Mountain Open Space park, which covers the north slope.

On this hike, you'll follow a 2.5-mile loop around the mountain's thickly chaparraled lower slopes. By tacking on an extra, steep, 1.0-mile round-trip climb, you include the top of the mountain and the wonderful view.

From the Black Mountain Road/Carmel Mountain Road intersection in Rancho Penasquitos, drive 1.4 miles north of Black Mountain Road to Emden Road. From there, turn east on the old, poorly maintained Black Mountain Road (construction of Carmel Valley Road will change this access by 2002 or 2003). After

1.2 miles on this dirt road, look on the right for a paved road with a gate open during daylight hours. Follow this entrance road uphill to a large parking lot on a knoll overlooking a large spread of rolling hills to the north, now being overrun by the 4S Ranch housing development.

From the parking lot, follow an old road, marked by trail signs, east. Ignore the first marked trail (old road) coming down the mountain from the right; continue on to the narrow path that swings south up a ridge. Follow the path, generally uphill, passing three side trails—each one leading about 100 yards to an overlook. Benches have been thoughtfully placed at the second and third overlooks.

Onward past the overlooks, the trail at first sets a course for the microwave-antenna structures atop the mountain, but then it unexpectedly curves away and descends west. When you come to the next junction, an old firebreak, turn left to start the rocky, arduous 0.5-mile climb to the mountain's summit.

Even though you can't enjoy a full, 360° view from the summit in one stance,

Author jogging in Los Penasquitos Canyon in the early morning

all you have to do is walk half-way around the fenced antenna structures to get the whole picture. The unique perspective afforded by Black Mountain tells a lot about San Diego's topography. To the south, overlain by seemingly endless rooftops, is a mesa-like platform called the Linda Vista Terrace. This is actually the middle level of three successive marine terraces evident in the area. A few remnants of the oldest and highest terrace, the Poway Terrace, can be glimpsed in the southeast and east. Imagine how this landscape looked sometime in the Pleistocene Epoch—with ocean waves rolling in over today's Rancho Penasquitos, Mira Mesa, and Kearny Mesa, and breakers crashing against a shoreline somewhere east of Interstate 15.

Trip 2: Los Penasquitos Canyon—East Approach

	Distance	6.4 miles round trip to falls
	Total elevation gain/loss	300'/300'
	Hiking time	3 hours (round trip)
	Optional map	USGS 7.5-min *Del Mar*
	Best times	All year
	Agency	LPCP
	Difficulty	★★

Take along a picnic lunch and a blanket on this hike. There are many fine places—sunny meadows, oak-shaded flats, and the sycamore-fringed streamside—to stop for an hour's relaxation. A good turn-around point is a small set of waterfalls and pools in the canyon bottom. This is about three miles out, midway through the Los Penasquitos preserve.

You begin at the large parking and equestrian staging area on the west side of Black Mountain Road, opposite Mercy Road. Head west on the wide dirt trail. In the first mile this hugs Los Penasquitos Canyon's south wall, a steep, chaparral-covered hillside (*Los Penasquitos* means "the little cliffs").

As you pass near the Johnson-Taylor ranch (screened from view by willows and dense vegetation along the creek), you'll notice several non-native plants—eucalyptus, fan palms, and fennel, for example—introduced into this area over the past century. Next you enter a long and beautiful canopy of intertwined live oaks,

accompanied by a lush understory of mostly poison oak.

Mile posts along the roadside help you gauge your progress. At mile 2 the trail winds out of the dense cover of oaks and continues through grassland dotted with a few small elderberry trees. Wildflowers such as wild radish, mustard, California poppies, bush mallow, and violets put on quite a show here in March and April. Look, too, for the fuchsia-flowered gooseberry, quite unmistakable when in bloom.

Soon after mile 2, an old road intersects and goes north across the creek to connect with a trail going along the north side of the canyon. You could follow this when you return from the falls.

At the 3-mile marker the road winds up onto a chaparral slope in order to detour a narrow, rocky section of the canyon. Near the top there's a wide spot, with racks for securing bikes, and a foot trail descending north to the falls area, where the stream has carved a narrow constriction into the bedrock. At times during the winter and early spring, a voluminous cascade of water tumbles through here. Polished rock 10 feet up on either side testifies to its maximum depth. By fall, the flow slows to a trickle, and the pools and potholes in the bedrock may be filled with stagnant, odiferous water. The outcroppings of greenish-grey rock, just in this one small area, are a type called Santiago Peak volcanics; they're typical of the metavolcanic rock on Santiago Peak in the Santa Ana Mountains.

Trip 3: Los Penasquitos Canyon—West Approach

Distance	5.5 miles round trip to falls
Total elevation gain/loss	200'/200'
Hiking time	2 hours
Optional map	USGS 7.5-min *Del Mar*
Best times	All year
Agency	LPCP
Difficulty	★★

As in the previous trip, the destination of this hike is the waterfall at the midpoint of Los Penasquitos Canyon. This time you approach from the west trailhead, just east of an industrial complex along Sorrento Valley Boulevard. Take the Sorrento Valley Road exit from either Interstate 5 or Interstate 805, follow frontage roads to Sorrento Valley Boulevard, and go north.

You'll enjoy the characteristic openness of this end of the canyon best if you come here on a cool day; the main dirt road stays well away from the stream most of the time, and is fully exposed to the sun. Try this hike sometime on a summer evening: plan to reach the falls by sunset, and return by the light of the moon.

Follow the trail going west under Sorrento Valley Boulevard and up broad Los Penasquitos Canyon. Sometimes fine springtime displays of lupine and owl's clover cover the steep, grassy slopes on the right. Wild radish, a plant introduced from Europe, often paints the lower slopes with shades of blue, white, and purple.

At about 0.7 mile (near the 5-mile marker, measured from the east end of the canyon) the road comes close to the creek, and it's tempting to cross and explore the far bank. Do this only if the foliage along the creek is leafed out, so you can see and identify the poison oak that flourishes there.

Next, the road climbs a small hill and then descends to more grassland, dotted with small trees and shrubs such as elder-

Yerba mansa blossom in Los Penasquitos Canyon

berry, live oak, laurel sumac, toyon, and gooseberry. Large sycamores and cottonwoods flank the creek. At a point well past mile marker 4, the road starts curving up a chaparral-covered slope. At the bottom of the next dip take one of the several small pathways leading to the waterfall area in the canyon bottom.

Trip 4: Lopez Canyon

Distance	3.5 miles
Total elevation gain/loss	120'/120'
Hiking time	1^1/$_2$ hours
Optional map	USGS 7.5-min *Del Mar*
Best times	All year
Agency	LPCP
Difficulty	★★

As "little brother" to Los Penasquitos Canyon, Lopez Canyon gets relatively little use, yet it could stand alone on its merit as a place worth saving. Lopez is dry most of the year, but the sights and smells of sage and chaparral and the stately sycamores down along the creekbed create a sense of a time long past when vaqueros herded cattle through this and many other coastal canyons. Cattle were

Sycamores in Lopez Canyon

grazed in both canyons until the late 1980s, a tradition that stretched back to the Spanish and Mexican periods.

Begin at Los Penasquitos Canyon's west trailhead (see Trip 3 above), and walk east on the remnants of a dirt road up along Lopez Canyon's bottom. On the scenic stretch ahead, you'll spot an enormous, multitrunked sycamore tree on the right covering an area about 100 feet across.

At 0.5 mile, the Old Lopez Road (now a trail) comes down the south slope from Pacific Center Boulevard. The Lopez family homesteaded this canyon early this century and built a cabin on a little flat just north of the canyon stream. You can look for the cabin's remains next to an old pepper tree. Farther up the slope is a concrete cistern with the inscription RAMONA LOPEZ, OCT. 25, 1947.

After traveling about 1.7 miles up the canyon, you'll reach the last of the trees— just short of the towering Camino Santa Fe concrete bridge. This is a good place to turn around. Beyond lies a cobble-strewn, open stretch. By pressing on, you could reach Montongo Street, which crosses the canyon about 4 miles from the trailhead.

Area C-5: Clairemont/University City

Aerial views of the Clairemont and University City neighborhoods of San Diego make one thing perfectly obvious: here is San Diego's "mesa and canyon" topography at its highest level of development. Geologists know this landform as an ancient marine terrace (the Linda Vista Terrace) incised by stream channels and their tributaries.

A strange kind of co-existence between unspoiled nature and full-speed-ahead development is apparent here: The mesa tops continue to fill up with a grid of housing developments and high-rise office buildings, while no more than a half mile away, a stream trickles through a canopy of oaks or a grove of sycamores in a canyon.

These once-ignored canyons, and their tributaries, or "finger canyons," have been the focus of many a fight between land developers and local homeowners. People have come to realize that canyons are valuable for their natural, educational, and recreational value. Thanks to the establishment of open space parks in the three largest major canyons of this area—Rose, San Clemente, and Tecolote—it looks as if the natural scenery will never be fully overwhelmed.

In recent years the canyons have become very popular among hikers, runners, and mountain bikers. If you live in Clairemont or University City, consider yourself lucky. If not, just hop on the freeway, or bicycle over on the surface streets, and you'll reach any of these canyons within minutes from most places around San Diego.

Area C-5:
Clairemont / University City

Trip I: Rose Canyon

Distance	3.5 miles round trip
Total elevation gain/loss	100'/100'
Hiking time	1¹/₂ hours
Optional map	USGS 7.5-min *La Jolla*
Best times	All year
Agency	SDOS
Difficulty	★

From its outlet at Mission Bay, Rose Canyon extends north past the east brow of Soledad Mountain, and curves east toward the flat mesas of Miramar Naval Air Station. About 200,000 people unwittingly follow part of its course every day: Interstate 5 parallels the lower canyon's stream channel for about three miles, and the Santa Fe tracks (the main rail link to Los Angeles) stick with it for more than six miles. There's a proposal afoot to run San Diego Trolley tracks through here as well.

Luckily, the most picturesque and undisturbed section of Rose Canyon has been declared an open-space park by the city of San Diego. Lying only a scant mile from the Golden Triangle's high rises and traffic snarls, the park offers up a fine, smooth pathway perfect for walking, jogging, or lazy mountain-biking. Except for the Coaster commuter trains gliding through every hour or so, the canyon resonates more with the sounds of woodpeckers, meadowlarks, and crickets than with the din of auto traffic.

A convenient place to pick up the trail is along Genesee Avenue, across from University City High School. (There's no parking allowed on Genesee, but you'll find curbside parking space along Decoro Street, 0.2 mile north of the trail.) A large sign marks the beginning of the wide path, which follows the south side of the canyon. Dense clumps of willow and sycamore line the streambed and occasionally shade the path.

After about 1.5 miles, you'll come abreast of La Jolla Colony Drive, next to where Gilman Drive meets Interstate 5. This is a good spot to turn back and retrace your steps.

Trip 2: San Clemente Canyon

Distance	1- to 4-mile hikes (out and back)
Optional map	USGS 7.5-min *La Jolla*, or street map
Best times	All year
Agency	MBP
Difficulty	★ to ★★

Eastbound in the right lane of Highway 52, the San Clemente Canyon Freeway, you can look down upon a long, slender, almost unbroken swath of natural vegetation: massive sycamores, stately live oaks, climbing vines, and tangled shrubs. This is one of San Diego County's best examples of riparian, or stream-loving, vegetation. (Recall that less than 0.2% of the county's land area consists of this type of vegetation.) The decision to divert the freeway well above the canyon bottom and spare the trees, at slightly added cost, was a happy one indeed.

Much of San Clemente Canyon and several of its steep finger canyons are now included within the boundaries of Marian Bear Park, an area set aside by the city of San Diego as natural open space. Facilities include parking areas, picnic tables and rest rooms off Regents Road and Genesee Avenue, and benches elsewhere.

Missing, of course, is the important element of silence. If you come here early on a Sunday morning, however, noise from the adjacent freeway is not particularly objectionable.

The easiest hiking is along the old roadbed which runs through the canopy of trees along the canyon's seasonal stream. The path stretches about three miles, is almost flat, and crosses the stream bed four times. In summer these crossings simply mean walking across cobblestones, but in winter some wading may be necessary.

The east end of the park (between Genesee Avenue and Interstate 805) offers the prettiest vegetation, the densest shade, and the biggest infestations of poison oak—which lie mostly away from the path in great tangled masses among the trees. Beginning about October, the leaves of the poison oak turn bright red in pleasing complement to the evergreen live oaks and the yellows and oranges of the sycamores and willows.

There are several back entrances into Marian Bear Park. With the help of a city street map, you might incorporate these into a longer hike. For example:

From the west end of the main path, you can cross Rose Canyon's creek and the railroad tracks to reach the bike path paralleling Interstate 5; you can then go north to connect with Rose Canyon (Trip 1 above) or south to connect with frontage roads along Interstate 5. From a point between Regents Road and Genesee Avenue, a 0.5-mile-long trail goes north under Highway

52, follows a sage-scented ravine, zigzags through a hidden eucalyptus grove, and tops out at Standley Park in University City.

On the south side of San Clemente Canyon, an obscure pathway goes up to Cobb Drive on the mesa above. Another path follows high-voltage powerlines up toward Kroc Junior High School. These trails could be used in connection with residential streets in Clairemont to reach Tecolote Canyon Natural Park (see next trip).

Old live oak in San Clemente Canyon

Trip 3: Tecolote Canyon

	Distance	6.0 miles
	Total elevation gain/loss	1000'/700'
	Hiking time	3^1/2 hours
	Recommended map	San Diego street map
	Optional map	USGS 7.5-min *La Jolla*
	Best times	All year
	Agency	TCNP
	Difficulty	★★★

Rustic signs along some of Clairemont's major streets call attention to one of the most valuable canyon habitats in San Diego's urban core: the 900-acre Tecolote Canyon Natural Park. On the park's patchwork of old roads and trails it's possible to poke into just about every nook and cranny. By day you're sure to spot a hawk soaring on the thermals or perching high on the crown of a dead oak tree. By night you might hear the yapping of a coyote or the plaintive hoot of an owl, the creature for which this canyon was named.

The title "Natural Park" refers in part to the native vegetation. The dominant plant communities are sage scrub (California sagebrush, white sage, black sage, lemonade berry, laurel sumac, monkeyflower) and chaparral (chamise, toyon, scrub oak, hollyleaf cherry, redberry). Live oaks, willows, and sycamores grow along the stream channel in places where water is more plentiful. Since Tecolote Canyon has been completely surrounded by an urbanized environment for about 30 years, it's not surprising to find invading non-native plants here too. The worst "offenders" are tumbleweed, wild chrysanthemum, mustard, fennel, pampas grass, and ice plant.

For all but the most cursory exploration of this canyon, you should wear hiking boots, or at least a pair of running shoes designed for off-road traction. Parts of the canyon are rough, but even small kids will like it—though perhaps not if they are forced to go too far. Be forewarned that winter rains can turn the clay soils into sticky mud. Take along a city street map to assist in general orientation. Most of these maps show the park's boundary.

Begin at the east terminus of Tecolote Road, opposite Interstate 5 from Mission Bay. Tecolote Park and Recreation Center lies to the south, while a small but superb new visitor center for Tecolote Canyon Natural Park lies at the trailhead east and straight ahead. Begin by walking up the smooth, dirt roadway. This lower-canyon path is fine for casual walking, or jogging, or even mountain biking at first.

Ahead, as you approach the perimeter of the Tecolote Canyon Golf Course, you'll start struggling up and down some steep hillsides. Don't miss the narrow side path on the left that continues contouring above the golf course, not far above the perimeter fence. It bends east on the slope overlooking the club house and descends to a tributary (which harbors a small stream in season) entering from the east. The side trip up along this fine, oak- and sycamore-dotted ravine to Genesee Avenue is well worth it in itself, and if you reverse your steps upon reaching Genesee and return to the starting point, then your round-trip hike measures about 5.5 miles.

Our one-way route, however, continues by following large powerlines upward to Via Bello. Go left on Via Bello for one block, then use the shoulder of Mt. Acadia Boulevard to get back to the bottom of Tecolote Canyon. Someday, the construction of a trail skirting the golf course may make this awkward detour unnecessary.

Go up the canyon now on the well-beaten path along Tecolote creek's east bank. There are good picnic spots here and there among the oaks—but watch out for poison oak!

Balboa Avenue, next, is somewhat of an obstacle. You can cross underneath the roadway in the tunnel (if reasonably dry) that carries the floodwaters of the creek, or climb the embankment and attempt to scoot across the busy lanes and over the concrete center divider—a dangerous maneuver at best. On the safe side, you could walk up the south shoulder of Balboa Avenue, cross at the traffic light on Clairemont Drive, then walk back on the north shoulder.

North of Balboa Avenue you have two choices: go up the eastern tributary to Mt. Etna Park, or thread your way up the main canyon on a well beaten path to either Genesee Avenue or North Clairemont Park. Either results in a roughly 6-mile, one-way hike.

Southern oak woodland at Tecolote Canyon

Area C-6: Center City

Hiking opportunities in the city of San Diego extend right into its urban core, where Balboa Park sprawls across 1400 acres of mesa tops and shallow canyons adjacent to downtown's north edge. Apart from the manicured paths of the park's west side, the zoo, and the museum quarter, the park's eastern section contains undeveloped Florida Canyon and its small network of multiuse nature trails.

The older neighborhoods of San Diego, north of downtown, also feature some of the finest historic walks found anywhere in the city. Although it may be an anomaly in a book of this sort, I've included the nicest of these walks, in Banker's Hill, just west of the park. The walk features two architectural gems from the past—a wood-trestle footbridge crossing one canyon and a suspension footbridge spanning another canyon.

Trip 1: Florida Canyon

Distance	loops of 1 to 3 miles
Optional map	USGS 7.5-min *Point Loma*
Best times	All year
Agency	BP
Difficulty	★

For years a network of informal trails existed in Florida Canyon, a part of Balboa

Park's eastern sector. Volunteer docents from the San Diego Natural History Mu-

Area C-6: Center City

seum led interpretive walks here by day, while by night transients and homeless people bedded down in whatever shelter they could find amid the sage and chaparral. Starting in 1993 efforts were made to realign the trails, solve erosion problems, and replant scarred areas with native species of vegetation. These efforts culminated in June 1997 with a grand reopening of the Florida Canyon trail system. With increased security patrols, these trails are now being touted as perfect for hikers and mountain bikers of all ages.

Do realize that at first glance the natural vegetation of Florida Canyon is bound to appear scruffy and desiccated by comparison with the lushly (but artificially) landscaped acres of Balboa Park's west side.

The aesthetic differences between the two are minimized in late winter and early spring when new growth burgeons, the sage and other aromatic plants emit ineffable fragrances, and wildflowers carpet the ground.

The principal starting point for the trail system lies just west of the Morley Field athletic complex in the northeast corner of Balboa Park. At the trailhead parking lot you'll find a native plant demonstration garden, with a short trail looping through it. South of this, the Florida Canyon trails cling to both sides of a ravine, the floor of which is traversed by Florida Drive. That street may someday be permanently closed to automobile traffic at its northern end, an improvement for hikers and bikers to be sure.

Trip 2: Banker's Hill

Distance	1.5 miles
Hiking time	1 hour
Optional map	USGS 7.5-min *Point Loma*
Best times	All year
Difficulty	★

With two steep ravines spanned by quaint footbridges, scores of well-kept, historically significant homes, and mature landscaping, Banker's Hill is a monument to the elegance of the past. The work of turn-of-the-century architect Irving Gill, recognized today as one of the trend-setters in modern building design, is well represented here. So is the work of his partner, William Hebbard, and several of Gill's proteges including Richard Requa and Frank Mead.

Park on Spruce Street at First or Second Avenue, and start by walking east on Spruce Street toward Balboa Park. Past Third Avenue, on the right side, is a low building originally designed as a store by William Hebbard in 1913. The style was apparently borrowed from the bottom floor of the powerhouse for the old San Diego Cable Railway, which at that time stood next door along

Fourth Avenue. The cable car line went into operation in 1889, carrying passengers from downtown to Hillcrest, and on to a landscaped park on Adams Avenue.

Walk south on Fourth (there's a sidewalk on the east side only) until you reach the Quince Street footbridge (1905), built across one of the two deep ravines penetrating Banker's Hill. Walk across the wooden planks and admire the sliver of view of San Diego Bay and Point Loma.

From Quince, turn right at Second Avenue. At the northeast corner of Second and Quince, and again at the northwest corner of Second and Redwood, compare classic revival styles. The residence across Second Avenue at 136 Redwood is one of the earliest (1898) results of the partnership of William Hebbard and Irving Gill. The camphor tree on the corner is one of the largest in the city of San Diego.

A left on Redwood to First brings you opposite Irving Gill's Bishop's Day School (1908), today occupied by the Self-Realization Fellowship. The Gill-designed wing wraps around an older Tudor structure, and epitomizes Gill's philosophy of simplicity and—using his own phrase — "monastic severity."

Now head north on First, go left on Spruce, and go left again on Front Street, a dead-end. The fine old houses here, some designed by Richard Requa, have a view over the canyon edge, but that view is screened at street level by tall trees.

Go back to Spruce and head west to walk across the suspension footbridge, one of San Diego's hidden treasures. Built in 1912 to give access to the streetcars on Fourth Avenue, it has recently undergone repairs. Stand in the middle of the swaying bridge, 70 feet above the canyon floor, and admire the eucalyptus, pepper, and palm trees, and the carpet of nasturtiums below.

On solid ground again, turn left on Brant Street, another dead end. The house at the end (3100 Brant), was designed by Hebbard in 1907 after his partnership with Gill ended, but retains some of Gill's influence. Back on Spruce, at the southeast corner of Spruce and Curlew, is a 1914 design by Requa and Frank Mead influenced by Mediterranean and North African imagery. To the north a half block, at 3226 Curlew, you'll find a 1912 Edwardian house designed by Hebbard.

Across the street, at the southeast corner of Curlew and Thorn, is an interesting Palladian-style mansion, dating from 1927. To poke fun at passersby, the plaque here reads "ON THIS SITE IN 1897 NOTHING HAPPENED." Zigzag east on Thorn, north on Brant, east on Upas, and north on Albatross. On the east side of Albatross are some of the Gill "canyon houses," dating from 1912-13. Perched on the canyon edge, these simple cottages were designed to blend harmoniously with the natural landscape.

Around the corner, at the west end of Walnut Avenue, is a seemingly out-of-place Queen Anne Victorian house. Built in 1892 at Fourth and Walnut, it was moved to this site in 1911. To conclude your walk, go east on Walnut to either First or Second and head south back to your starting point. Second Avenue is preferred, as it is the quieter of the two streets.

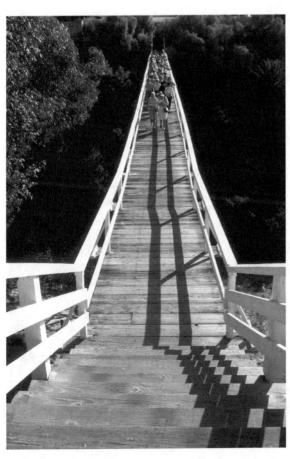

Quince Street footbridge

Area C-7: Mission Trails Regional Park

Touted as one of the largest urban parks in the country, Mission Trails Regional Park preserves some of the last remaining open space lying close to the heart of San Diego.

The concept of a new park on the east edge of San Diego was formalized in 1960, following the transfer of surplus former military reservation land to the jurisdiction of the City of San Diego. By the late '70s, the City and County of San Diego had cooperated in the purchase of 2000 acres on Cowles Mountain for preservation as open space, and a broader concept emerged—that of a 5800-acre regional park serving the diverse needs of residents throughout the entire county.

The last decade has seen the estab-

lishment of a first-class visitor center in Mission Gorge, parking and interpretive facilities at several trailheads and points of interest, and extensive development of a system of marked trails—now totaling about 50 miles. Subdivision development has crept up to the park boundary on three sides, and the Highway 52 freeway was extended around the north perimeter of the park in 1993, thus hemming in the park on nearly every side. Mission Trails is rapidly becoming an urban park, rather than an outlying rural preserve—and serves the recreational needs of thousands of local citizens.

Mission Gorge along with Fortuna Mountain comprise the nucleus of the original park proposed in 1960. The visi-

Area C-7: Mission Trails Regional Park

tor area overlooking the Old Mission Dam (a national historical landmark) has recently been rehabilitated, and a new campground at Kumeyaay Lake, east of the dam, has just opened. Father Junipero Serra Trail, the original road through Mission Gorge, has been reconfigured with a divider down the middle: one side is for one-way car traffic going northeast, while the other side has become a two-way paved path used by bicyclists, pedestrians, and skaters. One of San Diego's best rock-climbing sites lies a mile southwest of the Old Mission Dam. There, climbers practice moves on several near-vertical granite walls overlooking the gorge and the San Diego River. North and east of the gorge, a maze of old truck trails and fire roads has been transformed into a coherent system of designated hiking and biking trails.

Cowles Mountain, centerpiece of the regional park, stands 1591 feet above sea level, the highest point within San Diego's city limits. Hundreds of people walk the main south trail to its summit daily. Several newer trails have been laid out on the east and north slopes of the mountain, so now hikers can choose among several summit routes.

The southern end of the regional park includes a golf course and Lake Murray, a city reservoir open to recreational uses such as walking, bicycling, picnicking, fishing, and boating.

The following descriptions are suggestions for ten interesting trips in the Mission Trails Regional Park area. After a look at the park map, you'll doubtless be able to invent a few more.

Trip 1: Cowles Mountain—South Approach

Distance	3.0 miles round trip
Total elevation gain/loss	950'/950'
Hiking time	2 hours (round trip)
Optional map	USGS 7.5-min *La Mesa*
Best times	October through June
Agency	MTRP
Difficulty	★★

Starting from a parking lot and trailhead at Navajo Road and Golfcrest Drive, this popular switchbacking trail ascends the sunny south side of Cowles Mountain, consistently offering a vista stretching from the Pacific Ocean to Mexico. The predominant chaparral and sage scrub growth rarely exceeds shoulder height, so views are unobstructed from nearly every point on the trail.

Short spur trails branch from the main trail and lead to secluded overlooks—nice places to relax and enjoy the view, or have a picnic.

The trail was cut on mostly decom-

posed granite, so it is quite susceptible to erosion wherever the slope gets steep. Please don't shortcut the switchbacks, tempting as it may be on the way up or down, as this aggravates the erosion problem.

At a point 0.9 mile from the start, the main trail bends sharply left, while a side trail continues straight to a flat spot on the mountain's south shoulder. At the flat spot, there once existed a circular array of stones crossed by an "arrow" of rocks pointing southeast to the rising point of winter-solstice (December 20 or 21) sun. When it first appears on that occasion, just after 6:50 A.M., the sun's upper rim is initially split by a large boulder pile perched on a far-off ridge to the southeast. Within a few seconds, the dual image fuses into one brilliant point of light. According to local archeologists, the prehistoric Kumeyaay Indians kept dawn vigils here yearly and witnessed the same event.

At 1.0 mile from the start, another trail branches right and eventually descends the east slope. Stay left and continue up the slope on the series of long switchbacks leading to the rocky summit of the mountain. A concrete monument marks the high point, and two large interpretive panels stand nearby, with the names and directions of major features visible on the horizon.

A blocky building bristling with microwave dishes obstructs the northward view somewhat, but otherwise the panorama is complete. With binoculars and a street map, you could spend a lot of time identifying features on the urban landscape. In the rift between the coastal terrace to the west, there's a good view of Mission Valley and the tangle of freeways that pass over and through it. Southwest, the towers of downtown San Diego stand against Point Loma, Coronado, and the sparkling bay. Lake Murray shimmers to the south. The chain of Santee Lakes contrasts darkly with pale hills to the north. In all directions, you can get a sense of how urbanized the region has become. More than four million people (on both sides of the border) now live within a 35-mile radius centered on the mountain.

On clear winter days, the view expands to include most of the higher peaks of San Diego County. Southward into Baja, you can see the flat-topped "Table Mountain" behind Tijuana, and the Coronado Islands offshore. During absolutely crystalline weather, look for the profiles of Santa Catalina and San Clemente islands, to the northwest and west respectively.

Here's a suggestion for romantics and adventurers who don't mind descending the trail by flashlight: Catch the sunset from Cowles' summit when the moon is full. After the sun slides into the Pacific, turn around and enjoy the moonrise over the El Cajon valley!

View of San Diego from the slopes of Cowles Mountain

Trip 2: Cowles Mountain—East Approach

Distance	3.0 miles
Total elevation gain/loss	1000'/1000'
Hiking time	2 hours
Optional map	USGS 7.5-min *La Mesa*
Best times	October through June
Agency	MTRP
Difficulty	★★

If you tire of the hordes of Cowles Mountain regulars on the popular south trail, try this loop on the east slope instead. Partly on a service road (open only to maintenance vehicles) and partly on a narrow foot trail, the route draws relatively few travelers. Since I live close to the mountain and use it as a training ground, you'll often find me jogging up either the road or trail by the light of dawn. When early-morning fog hugs the ground, most commonly in the fall, a quick trip up the slope allows me to punch through the cloud layer and witness a scene every bit equal to the famous sunrises over the cloud-wreathed crater of Haleakala on Maui.

Begin near the west terminus of Boulder Lake Avenue (at Barker Way), one block west of Cowles Mountain Boulevard, where curbside parking is plentiful. Step past the vehicle gate and start climbing up the service road. Footwear with good traction will help on the sometimes steep and slippery, hard-packed dirt roadway. Two level stretches relieve the uphill grind, then six short, very steep switchback legs lead to the summit.

Return to your starting point by descending the upper 0.5 mile of the main,

Sunset from Cowles Mountain

south trail. Then veer left (east) on the lesser-traveled east trail, which is signed "Barker Way." You bend northeast around the mountain and soon start descending on many tight switchbacks. They'll take you down to the lower end of the service road, near where you started.

Trip 3: Cowles Mountain—Northeast Approach

Distance	4.8 miles
Total elevation gain/loss	1400'/1400'
Hiking time	3 hours
Optional map	USGS 7.5-min *La Mesa*
Best times	October through June
Agency	MTRP
Difficulty	★★★

This most difficult approach to Cowles' summit is also the most beautiful—especially in the early spring when blooming chaparral, ground-hugging wildflowers, and bright-green grass freshen the landscape.

The meandering roads and ugly paths cut into the mountain's northeast slope long ago by bulldozers and motorcycles have been replaced in recent years by well-engineered hiking trails, complete with water bars and other features designed to divert runoff and prevent erosion. Please stay on the designated paths so as to let the scarred areas of the mountain return to a natural state.

Big Rock Park (corner of Mesa Road and Prospect Avenue), Santee's most attractive city park, is a good starting point for the northeast trek to the summit. Follow the park's perimeter fence to a trail running south and parallel to small watercourse we'll call Big Rock Creek. After passing the west end of Rancho Fanita Drive, you go up along a hillside, gradually heading away from the creek and a row of houses to the west. At 0.5 mile a trail merges from the right—it leads back down to Big Rock Creek and hooks up with the end of Big Rock Road.

Work your way sharply uphill through dense, aromatic chaparral, passing a trail to the left (your return route), and reach a junction with the Cowles Mountain service road at 1.4 miles from the start. From there, use the road to climb 0.8 mile farther to the summit.

On the way back, retrace your steps 0.8 mile to the top of the northeast trail, descend the northeast trail for 0.5 mile, and

Owl's clover in Mission Trails Regional Park

turn right on the trail going east across the flank of the mountain. After another 0.7 mile of mostly downhill travel you reach a wide, graded dirt road (the future Mesa Road extension that will one day link up with Lake Murray Boulevard). Follow this road down past a rock outcrop on the left— a beautiful mini-waterfall after lots of rain—and return to Big Rock Park.

Trip 4: Cowles Mountain—Northwest Approach

Distance	3.2 miles round trip
Total elevation gain/loss	1400'/1400'
Hiking time	2 hours (round trip)
Optional map	USGS 7.5-min *La Mesa*
Best times	October through June
Agency	MTRP
Difficulty	★★★

The short but challenging ascent of Cowles Mountain by way of its northwest ridge begins with a steep, informal trail best suited for hikers wearing sturdy footwear. Once past the initial rough and rocky section, a newer well-graded trail, high on the west slope, takes you more or less directly to the summit. This is a great improvement over the primitive ridgeline path previously followed by hikers.

You begin along the shoulder of Mission Gorge Road, just around the corner from (east of) Golfcrest Drive. Find the narrow trail that wastes no time in going straight up the ridge ahead. One half mile (and 600 vertical feet) later, you come upon a wider, maintained section of trail. Continue climbing on an easier gradient and pass a side trail going northeast up to the rocky summit of Pyles Peak.

Nearing a saddle just south of Pyles Peak, the trail veers right and maintains a steadily rising, gently curving course high on the west side of the ridge leading to Cowles Mountain. Chaparral-clad slopes fall away on your right to the curving streets and toylike houses of suburbia, which seem to lap at the foot of the mountain. On mornings when a low-elevation marine layer blankets the lowland and the suburban sprawl disappears, the distant, rumbling roar of traffic floats up and reminds you of your place amid the city.

When you reach the summit you can either retrace your steps, 3.2 miles for the round trip; or instead, for a longer, roundabout return, follow the main trail down Cowles' south side and then the sidewalk along Golfcrest Drive.

Trip 5: Visitor Center Loop

Distance	2.1 miles
Total elevation gain/loss	200'/200'
Hiking time	1 hour
Optional map	USGS 7.5-min *La Mesa*
Best times	All year
Agency	MTRP
Difficulty	★

A new parking lot/trailhead at the foot of Jackson Drive and Mission Gorge Road is a convenient starting point for this easy ramble past the Mission Trails Regional Park Visitor Center and down along the San Diego River.

Head east on the Visitor Center Loop Trail, traversing a dry slope overlooking Mission Gorge Road, and arrive shortly at the visitor center entryway. Sooner or later you should explore the center, which features a unique auditory experience as you approach the front door. Inside there are video displays, archaeological exhibits, a library, and bay-window views of Mission Gorge and neighboring peaks.

Your hike, however, goes east across the paved road (Father Junipero Serra Trail), where you pick up the Oak Grove Loop. On it, you circle about for 0.7 mile, dipping at one point into a shady ravine graced by overarching oaks and a trickling brook (in season). Elsewhere along this loop, volunteer naturalists have planted oak saplings and other native vegetation.

Back at the entrance to the visitor center, take the Visitor Center Loop Trail north and later west (downhill) toward the San Diego River. A short spur trail on the right leads down to some bedrock *morteros*, or grinding holes, near the river. Two more minor paths access the willow- and oak-lined riverbank later on. The river surges exuberantly during and after heavy winter rains, but becomes sluggish and clogged with mats of algae by late summer.

The trail passes through an old quarry, from which large quantities of andesitic metavolcanic rock were once taken—a practice that continues today downstream, outside the park limits. For decades the native vegetation has been trying to stage a slow comeback on the torn hillsides. At 0.8 mile from the visitor center, you come to a wide, bulldozed path ascending left. Turn left and return to the foot of Jackson Drive.

Trip 6: Kwaay Paay Peak

Distance	2.5 miles round trip
Total elevation gain/loss	900'/900'
Hiking time	1^1/2 hours (round trip)
Optional map	USGS 7.5-min *La Mesa*
Best times	November through May
Agency	MTRP
Difficulty	★★

Flanked by steep walls on all sides but one, Kwaay Paay peak's platform-like top stands quite aloof from all else around it. The summit offers a unique vantage for

View east from Kwaay Paay Peak

tracing the lower San Diego River's course. To the east you'll see the river's willow-lined flood plain, which cuts through the flat carpet of houses and shopping centers that increasingly fill the city of Santee. In the west and southwest you'll see how the river's mighty flow (in Pleistocene times, at least) carved the granite walls of Mission Gorge.

A well-defined but sometimes steep old road/trail ascends the peak's north ridge, starting from the east vehicle gate (closed nightly) along Father Junipero Serra Trail, between Mission Gorge Road and the Old Mission Dam. The trail goes up and down a bit before settling into a steady grind up along the north ridge.

There's not much to find in the way of comfortable sitting spots on the summit, but you can wander east over to the top of the rock outcrops overlooking Mission Gorge Road for lunch and a great view of Santee. There are rock outcrops on the west and south sides as well. You should avoid scrambling down to the outcrops on west, so as not to dislodge rocks that could roll and injure the climbers who practice on the sheer rock faces below.

Trip 7: Oak Canyon

Distance	3.0 miles round trip
Total elevation gain/loss	200'/200'
Hiking time	2 hours (round trip)
Optional map	USGS 7.5-min *La Mesa*
Best times	October through June
Agency	MTRP
Difficulty	★★

Oak Canyon, a sycamore- and oak-lined ravine winding north from the Old Mission Dam, is a perfect place to celebrate the return of spring in San Diego. Heavy rains never fail to revive the canyon's intermittent stream and transform the hillside vegetation from dormant brown to festive green. By March, annual wildflowers pop up amid the tender new blades of grass, blooming ceanothus colors the slopes, and the sweet-pungent smell of sage floats on the warm breeze.

Start at the Old Mission Dam parking area, along the paved Father Junipero Serra Trail, 0.8 mile west of Mission Gorge Road in Santee. (Vehicle gates on both ends of Father Junipero Serra Trail swing shut between sunset and sunrise, so don't get caught with your car inside.) The dam was built between 1807 and 1816 under the direction of the San Diego Mission, and was considered a major engineering feat of its day. A 6-mile-long flume carried water from the dam to the mission located at the east end of Mission Valley.

From the parking area, walk west (downstream) on a wide, smooth path past the old dam and across the turbid waters of the San Diego River by way of an iron footbridge. Once across the river, double back east for 0.1 mile. Curve left across a hillside and down to the bottom of Oak Canyon. In the next 1.2 miles you'll wend your way upstream along the banks of the trickling creek, passing small cascades and rock-bound pools (in season, of course). Small kids will need a hand in places, and they should be kept well away from the sheer drops here and there along the banks.

All will enjoy the scamperings of cottontail rabbits through the brush, and with some luck, you might flush a covey of quail. Coyotes patrol these spaces, but unless the hour is either very early or very

Falls in Oak Canyon tributary

late you'll likely see no more than tracks and scat.

At 1.2 miles the path intersects a dirt powerline access road. Turn left, follow the road about 100 yards, and go right on a path that continues up Oak Canyon. About 0.3 mile farther you'll come to a picturesque mini-chasm of water-polished rock, with a deep, narrow pool. This is about as far as it's worth going. Highway 52 passes over the canyon just ahead on twin high bridges, and off-limits Marine Corps land lies beyond.

Trip 8: South Fortuna Mountain

Distance	4.6 miles round trip
Total elevation gain/loss	900'/900'
Hiking time	3 hours (round trip)
Optional map	USGS 7.5-min *La Mesa*
Best times	November through May
Agency	MTRP
Difficulty	★★★

Unlike the view from Cowles Mountain, Fortuna Mountain's expansive vantage encompasses a good deal of still-undeveloped country. Mission Trails Regional Park maps now refer to the original 1291-foot Fortuna Mountain as North Fortuna Mountain. A 1094-foot subsidiary peak to the southeast is now unimaginatively dubbed South Fortuna Mountain. From either summit, you can look farther southeast to 1194-foot Kwaay Paay peak, 1379-foot Pyles Peak, and finally 1591-foot Cowles Mountain. It's easy to see why this linear range of mountains is called "Long Mountain" on century-old maps.

This hike starts at the Old Mission Dam and takes you to Fortuna's south summit, but a side trip up to the north summit can be added as well. Trip 9 below describes a route up North Fortuna from the southwest (Tierrasanta) side of the park.

You begin exactly as in Trip 7 above by following the course of Oak Canyon north from the Old Mission Dam. At 1.2 miles turn left on a dirt road built to service the power lines passing overhead. Continue 0.5 mile west, up a steep ravine to a 910-foot saddle. (Just short of that saddle, the road becomes so steep it's difficult to keep from slipping in the dirt.) Bear left at the saddle, and follow a wide, rocky path up the broad ridge to the southeast. When you reach the summit, 2.3 miles from the start, you can either turn back there, or forge ahead another 0.2 mile to where the ridge becomes narrower and the views, on all sides but north, become more panoramic and dramatic.

Trip 9: North Fortuna Mountain

Distance	4.8 miles round trip
Total elevation gain/loss	1300'/1300'
Hiking time	3 hours (round trip)
Optional map	USGS 7.5-min *La Mesa*
Best times	November through May
Agency	MTRP
Difficulty	★★★

This is an alternate, though no easier way to reach the saddle between the two Fortuna Mountain summits. As described here, the route heads to the higher north summit; however, you can visit the south summit in addition to (or instead of) the north summit.

You begin at the southeast edge of

Tierrasanta, a residential community north of Interstate 8 and east of Interstate 15. Start at the main trailhead there, which is 0.3 mile east of Rueda Drive on Calle de Vida. Colina Dorada meets Calle de Vida at this spot. Head northeast along the wide trail, and at 0.5 mile pass a deep road cut (accompanied by a trail) on the right where Clairemont Mesa Boulevard may someday cut east toward a proposed Jackson-Drive-to-Highway-52 extension. These on-again, off-again road building proposals have been tabled for the foreseeable future, to the relief of park proponents who wish to keep the west side of Mission Trails park quiet and serene.

Continue straight (northeast) along the west side of a hill to a wide intersection of trails on a 730-foot saddle at 0.8 mile. The cylindrical structures nearby are ventilators for the Second San Diego Aqueduct. Continue straight, dropping sharply northeast toward the bowl-like valley west of Fortuna Mountain. This secluded valley, its oak-lined, intermittent stream dubbed Suycott Wash, still hosts mule deer and coyotes—despite its isola-

tion by the Highway 52 extension. Mitigation efforts for the freeway included a tunnel underneath for wildlife migrating north into Miramar Marine Corps Air Station lands and south into Mission Trails park.

Let the northeast-trending powerlines be your guide as you continue across the bottom of the valley, cross Suycott Wash (1.3 miles), and climb to the 910-foot saddle of Fortuna Mountain (2.0 miles). The last 300 yards to the saddle are extremely steep and slippery. Bear left at the intersection on top, and proceed 0.4 mile northwest up a steep, eroded firebreak to North Fortuna's 1291-foot summit, which is marked by an outcrop of granitic boulders.

If you're looking for a cool resting or picnic spot on the way back, then Suycott Wash is the place. Follow the narrow trail downstream from the Suycott Wash ford you crossed earlier. A strip of oak woodland extends from about 0.3 to 0.8 mile south. In places the creek trickles over boulders, and oak limbs arch overhead in an intricate tangle. Be aware of the abundant poison oak in the area.

Trip 10: Rim Trail

Distance	4.0 miles
Total elevation gain/loss	550'/550'
Hiking time	2 hours
Optional map	USGS 7.5-min *La Mesa*
Best times	October through June
Agency	MTRP
Difficulty	★★

Worthwhile primarily for the view, which can be wide-ranging and spectacular on the clearest days, the Rim Trail rambles along a sparsely vegetated ridgeline overlooking much of metropolitan San Diego to the south and west. To the east, Fortuna Mountain rises like a scruffy hog's

back, and below, at its foot, lies the pristine and spring-green valley of Suycott Wash.

Start, as in Trip 9 above, at the corner of Calle de Vida and Colina Dorada in Tierrasanta. Proceed to the 730-foot saddle at 0.8 mile, but this time veer left on the signed Rim Trail. Some 2.4 miles later you will return to this saddle, after looping counterclockwise on a route that is popular with mountain bikers as well as hikers. There are many intersections along the way, with directional signs that are easier to spot if you follow the route counterclockwise. Keep in mind that the Rim Trail is just that—it stays high on the ridges and does not descend very far into ravines. When you get back to the 730-foot saddle, return to the trailhead the way you came.

Indian paintbrush, Rim Trail

Area C-8: Lakeside/Ramona

Several newly opened parks and open-space preserves in the foothills between Lakeside and Ramona now beckon hikers and nature lovers. All are county-managed facilities, except for the oldest one—the Audubon Society's Silverwood Wildlife Sanctuary. All offer the city-dwelling public an opportunity to study and enjoy the chaparral, oak woodland, and riparian vegetation that is fast disappearing on San Diego County's urban fringes.

Most of the parks and preserves lie along Wildcat Canyon Road, which climbs steeply into the foothills north of Lakeside and continues through the scenic Barona Indian Reservation toward Ramona and San Diego Country Estates. To reach Wildcat Canyon Road, take Highway 67 to Mapleview Street in Lakeside, go east for 0.3 mile, then north on Ashwood Street. Ashwood becomes Wildcat Canyon Road after one mile. From Ramona, you can reach the north end of Wildcat Canyon Road by way of San Vicente Road, which is the south extension of 10th Street in Ramona.

This can be mighty hot and dry country in summer—but cool and invigorating in the "dead" of winter, and green, moist, and inviting during the magical months of March and April. When the right morning comes along, go ahead and "seize the moment." Make your getaway for a couple of hours or a half day of great hiking close to the city.

Trip 1: Stelzer County Park

Distance	1 to 2 miles
Optional map	USGS 7.5-min *San Vicente Reservoir*
Best times	All year
Agency	SDCP
Difficulty	★ to ★★

Stelzer County Park features 314 acres of trails, campsites, and picnic areas, and a small interpretive area. The park was specially designed to attract handicapped persons, though nonhandicapped visitors and hikers are welcome as well. You'll find the park's well-marked entrance on Wildcat Canyon Road, 2 miles up from Mapleview Street in Lakeside.

Of interest to hikers are two trails of quite different character. The Riparian Trail parallels the stream bottom of Wildcat Canyon for about 0.5 mile, ending at a secluded picnic site. It is shaded throughout by a stream-hugging canopy of live oaks, some draped with filigrees of wild-grape and poison-oak vines.

The Stelzer Ridge Trail, on the other

Area C-8: Lakeside / Ramona

hand, zigzags 0.6 mile toward the ridge-line south and east of Wildcat Canyon. This wide, gradually ascending trail up along a chaparral slope was designed to accommodate wheelchairs, though the efficacy of that use depends on the trail condition.

At the top of the Stelzer Ridge Trail, there are two choices for those who wish a better view: you can go 0.3 mile southwest on a powerline access road to reach "Kumeyaay Promontory," or go 0.5 mile northeast up a steep ridge to "Stelzer

Summit."

From Stelzer Summit, you can climb toward the rock pile atop the nearby hill, and discover a hidden boulder cave with an opening that overlooks a rural stretch of the San Diego River Valley. On a summer day, when the sea breeze blows up the valley, this cave becomes a pleasantly cool spot to rest a while. Off in the distance, down the valley toward the west, sprawl the suburbs of Lakeside and Santee.

Trip 2: Oak Oasis Open Space Preserve

Distance	2.4 miles
Total elevation gain/loss	300'/300'
Hiking time	$1^1/2$ hours
Optional map	USGS 7.5-min *San Vicente Reservoir*
Best times	All year
Agency	SDCP
Difficulty	★★

Serene Oak Oasis Open Space Preserve covers 397 acres of oak woodland, boulder-studded hillsides, and mature stands of chaparral. Try visiting during March, when almost every living thing in the plant kingdom is green and the sweet fragrance of both blue- and white-flowering wild lilac (ceanothus) floats on the sun-warmed breeze.

At mile 4.2 on Wildcat Canyon Road (4.2 miles from Mapleview Street in Lakeside), turn west onto a narrow paved road leading 0.1 mile to a trailhead parking lot—a staging area for the future east-west, 110-mile-long Trans-County Trail. On foot, continue west on a gravel road for 200 yards, then veer right on a narrow, signed trail that goes down a north-facing hillside clad in impenetrable chaparral. At 0.4 mile from the start you strike a disused dirt road following the bottom of a shallow ravine. Turn left (west) on this road, and for the next 0.3 mile enjoy the cool, oasis-like effect of walk-

ing under closely spaced coast live oaks whose opaque, overarching foliage blots out all but tiny glimmers of sunlight.

At the west end of this oak oasis, 0.7 mile from the start, you come upon a sagging cabin constructed of split logs in 1936. Continue west and northwest on the old roadbed (or you can opt for an alternate route up and over a hillside to the north). Very soon you catch sight of the sparkling surface of San Vicente Reservoir, a mile to the west and some 800 feet below. Ahead, at 0.9 mile, there's a better view of the lake on a left-branching spur trail.

Next, you go up and over a saddle, traverse a grassy vale, drop into a minor ravine, and go gradually uphill to a flat area at the top of that ravine—all the while circling right. By 1.8 miles, you're curving right into the oak-oasis ravine you visited earlier. When you strike the old roadbed again, cross it and retrace your earlier steps up to the gravel road and back to your car.

Trip 3: El Capitan Open Space Preserve

Distance	10.0 miles
Total elevation gain/loss	4000'/4000'
Hiking time	6 hours
Optional maps	USGS 7.5-min *San Vicente Reservoir, El Cajon Mtn.*
Best times	November through April
Agency	SDCP
Difficulty	★★★★

As you walk along the granite-ribbed ridgeline down the middle of the El Capitan Open Space Preserve, a binational panorama of ocean, islands, and innumerable mountain peaks lies in view. The broad San Diego River valley below curves beneath the sheer south face of El Cajon Mountain—the landmark informally known as "El Capitan."

The 2800-acre preserve was pieced together out of former BLM lands adjacent to the Cleveland National Forest. If you have the determination to tackle some really severe uphills and downhills, try following the main ridge-running trail—actually an old road bulldozed by miners years ago. It twists and turns over a scrubby, boulder-punctuated landscape that in spring comes alive with a blue frosting of ceanothus blossoms.

If you follow the old road to its end, 5 miles out, you'll reach a 3367-foot peak subordinate only to the slightly higher summit of El Cajon Mountain nearby. This strenuous effort involves a surprising gain and loss of 4000 vertical feet (because of various ups and downs) over the entire round trip. Still, a nice vista of the surrounding mountains can be yours even if you hike less than a mile to reach the first of the five trailside rest stops along the way.

Park in the gravel trailhead lot on the east side of Wildcat Canyon Road (at mile 4.2), opposite and just north of the entrance to Oak Oasis Open Space Preserve. From the lot, walk east 0.4 mile on a graded dirt road, then past some houses, to where the trail starts a steep, zigzag ascent up a cool, north-facing slope. You soon hook up with the old mining road, and the going gets easier for a while. Once you're past a small summit, the round top and sheer south brow of El Cajon Mountain become visible in the middle distance. Closer, on the left, rises the impressive Silverdome peak (in the Silverwood Wildlife Sanctuary), believed to be the largest granite monolith in San Diego County. As you start descending, a narrow trail forks right—this leading south 1.5 miles to a deadend (so far) at the preserve's south boundary. This side trail will eventually connect with Stelzer Park's trail system.

A very steep pitch, starting at 2.6 miles, will turn you back if you're not se-

Old mining road in El Capitan Preserve

rious about this hike. A proposed trail will veer south from here and follow a south ridge down to El Monte Park, 1500 feet below.

At 4.0 miles, a rock-lined spring on the left, brimming with iron-rich water, serves horses (not people) that can make it this far. At 4.8 miles, the road arrives on a saddle between El Cajon Mountain's summit dome on the left and a smaller 3367-foot peak on the right (west). Turn right on the spur road going west to reach the latter summit, which offers a 270° view of distant horizons.

At the saddle, a sign indicates private property ahead (to the south). As an option on this hike, you can bag El Cajon Mountain's summit, which has a climber's register, by going due east. You'll soon pick up the brushy summit trail, worn in by hikers, that goes through national forest land to the summit. The Forest Service is considering building a trail east over El Cajon Mountain, down the other side, northwest around El Capitan Reservoir, and thence toward Cuyamaca Rancho State Park. This would be a link in the 110-mile Trans-County Trail which could one day guide hikers from Del Mar on the coast to Borrego Valley in the desert.

Trip 4: Silverwood Wildlife Sanctuary

Distance	1- to 4-mile loops
Recommended map	Silverwood trail map (available at entrance)
Optional maps	USGS 7.5-min *San Vicente Reservoir, El Cajon Mtn.*
Best times	October through June
Agency	SWS
Difficulty	★ to ★★★

Silverwood. The name comes from the glittering effect of sunlight upon the leaves of the coast live oak. Scores of these trees, some of them 200-year-old giants scarred by fire, shade the canyon floor at the entrance to the Silverwood Wildlife Sanctuary and Nature Education Center. Owned and managed by the San Diego Audubon Society, the sanctuary preserves 700 acres of flora and fauna indigenous to the foothill region.

Silverwood is open to the public every Sunday (except in August) between 9 A.M. and 4 P.M. You'll find the entrance on the east side of Wildcat Canyon Road at mile 4.8. For your first visit, plan to attend the guided nature walk (at 10 and 1:30) to familiarize yourself with the area's natural history. Topics include plant identification, chaparral ecology, geology, bird watching, and identification of animal tracks and scats.

Several miles of hiking trails lace the area. A short and easy stroll from the parking lot to the director's house will introduce you to a cool, moist environment in the shade of the spreading oaks. Half a dozen kinds of fungi can be found clinging to fallen limbs or pushing through the leaf litter. Just beyond the house is a small *cienaga*, or soggy meadow, adorned in spring with blue-eyed grass and paintbrush blossoms.

The outlying trails of Silverwood are narrow, rugged, easily overgrown, and not always maintained. Some of these climb, like spokes in a wheel, to Circuit Trail, a loop trail following the rugged, chaparral-clad ridges that overlook the oak-filled valley. A single eucalyptus tree, planted next to the director's house, stands head and shoulders above all else in the valley and marks the direction of return for confused hikers.

On the relatively short (2 miles) but difficult hike around the Circuit Trail, the springtime blossoms of ceanothus, sage, coast spice bush, manzanita, and a dozen other flowering plants scent the air with sweet fragrances. Take lots of water and be sure you can get back before closing time.

From Circuit Trail you can spot, in the near distance to the east, a rounded granitic dome about 500 feet high, believed to be the largest granite monolith in San Diego County. Ecologists have done a study of the biological "successional islands" on the exposed, exfoliating surface of the dome. Lichens are the first colonizers; then come certain hardy mosses—but only in crevices and depressed areas where surface flows of rainwater are concentrated, yet not too erosive. If the mosses trap dust particles and debris to form a layer of soil, succulent live-forevers (specifically a type descriptively called "lady fingers") establish a foothold on the rock. The live-forevers act as a further trap for soil, which leads to colonization of many more species, including ferns, grasses, and flowering plants. Some of the richer islands on the dome exhibit, in concentric zones, the full range of succession. In other places, succession has been halted, and only lichens and mosses survive, often in mazelike patterns on the rock.

Trip 5: Mount Gower Open Space Preserve

Distance	4- to 11-mile hikes
Optional map	USGS 7.5-min *Ramona*
Best times	November through April
Agency	SDCP
Difficulty	★★ to ★★★

The 1574-acre Mount Gower preserve is one of several parcels of surplus federal land that have been transferred from the BLM to San Diego County jurisdiction. The preserve is being managed primarily for protection of the natural vegetation and wildlife, but public use is mandated as well. Eight miles of trail have been completed within the Mount Gower preserve so far.

To reach the preserve from Ramona, take San Vicente Road 6 miles south and east to Gunn Stage Road. Turn left (north), and continue 1.8 miles to the preserve entrance. Drive another 0.2 mile on a graded dirt road to the fenced lot on the right. An informational kiosk marks the start of the trail system at the far end of the lot.

The trail system has two main branches. The meandering west trail, 2.0 miles long, leads to a 2300-foot viewpoint on top of a barren ridge. This is worth the climb on clear days, when you can take advantage of a view that includes the Coronado Islands, Point Loma, Mt. San Antonio in Los Angeles County, and a long roster of San Diego County high points.

The more difficult, rambling trail to the south, east, and finally southwest extends nearly 6 miles. At 1.2 miles along this trail you reach a pleasant rest area overlooking oak-lined Swartz Canyon. From there you can follow a short spur trail up to a 1976-foot peaklet perched strategically over San Diego Country Estates and San Vicente Valley. Onward on the main trail, a series of Sisyphian ascents and descents takes you across a small stream in Swartz Canyon and up along an undulating ridgeline.

At about 3.5 miles, as reckoned by the wooden mileposts, you can leave the trail and scramble due east over granite bedrock slabs to reach the northernmost of Mt. Gower's three highest summits. (All three have nearly identical elevations—just over 3100 feet.) From atop a large boulder on the north summit, you can look down upon the secluded EA Ranch, with its quarter-mile thoroughbred track. Mt. Gower's two other summits are guarded by dense, prickly thickets of brush and are hard to reach.

The remainder of the main trail is unremarkable. If you follow it you eventually arrive at a vantage point overlooking the sprawling San Diego Country Estates subdivision.

Trip 6: Conejos Creek

Distance	9.6 miles round trip
Total elevation gain/loss	700'/700'
Hiking time	5 hours (round trip)
Recommended maps	USGS 7.5-min *Alpine, El Cajon Mtn.*
Best times	November through April
Agency	SDCL
Difficulty	★★★

Little remains of the century-old, redwood-planked flume that once brought the waters of the Cuyamaca Mountains to a reservoir at Grossmont Summit in La Mesa. Much of the flume's 36-mile-long grade is hard to identify, since no fill-dirt was used to maintain the waterway's uniform fall of 4 feet, 8 inches to the mile. Instead, workers employed numerous cuts, several tunnels, and more than 300 trestles. The 9 million board-feet of lumber used for both the flume itself and the trestles have long since been scavenged.

Today, thanks to the ongoing efforts of volunteers, you can walk a section of the flume's grade along the east shore of El Capitan Reservoir. The completion of this very reservoir in the 1930s put an end to the flume's usefulness and signaled its demise.

The old flume bed can be approached by way of the south end of the former Anderson Truck Trail, which is now washed out in many places and closed to vehicles. The old truck trail (now a foot and mountain-bike trail) intersects paved Peutz Valley Road, 0.9 mile north of Alpine Boulevard. Parking space off the narrow pavement of Peutz Valley Road is very limited.

Descend on the old truck trail for 1.0 mile, passing enroute (at 0.8 mile) a charming little waterfall along the creek descending from Peutz Valley. At the 1.0 mile mark, slant left on a lateral trail that steadily descends to the southeast shore of El Capitan Reservoir. Not far above the high-water mark, the trail levels out and you continue, more or less on a level course, along the shoreline. For the next 3 miles you will be either on, or very near, the original flume grade. Depending on the level of recent maintenance and/or the rate of springtime growth, the trail may or may not be choked with grass and weedy vegetation.

Nearing Conejos Creek, along the Conejos (east) arm of the reservoir, you'll scramble up and down in places to avoid washed-out sections of the flume grade. Finally, at 4.8 miles from the start, where Conejos Creek enters the reservoir, you'll come upon a sublime, sylvan scene, with water darting over and around boulders and century-old masonry associated with the flume.

Area C-9: Alpine/Jamul

A kind of low-density suburbia has been creeping across the rugged foothills and valleys east of San Diego as more and more people who work in the city seek a quiet, pseudo-rural lifestyle. Still, opportunities for hiking in the areas around Alpine and Jamul have actually increased in recent years.

After falling into disuse in the '70s and '80s, the California Riding and Hiking Trail, which passes near Alpine and Jamul, is once again coming to life—thanks mainly to the efforts of groups such as the San Diego Trails Council (an equestrian organization). One of the biggest obstacles has been legal access to the route. The original trail was routed in many places over private property, so it was necessary to obtain easement rights from various property owners before the trail could be signed and reopened to public use.

Much of the current California Riding and Hiking Trail is routed on existing roads open to auto traffic, which makes it a bit tedious for walking—though good enough for horseback riding and mountain biking. In this section I will highlight a stretch of the trail, closed to motor traffic, that descends into scenic Sloan Canyon.

Another worthwhile part of the trail you might want to try goes between Japatul Road and Via Dieguenos in the Palo Verde (southeast) part of Alpine.

Just east of Alpine, in the Cleveland National Forest, the Sweetwater River cuts through a rugged little gorge ending at Palo Verde Lake. Someday the Forest Service may construct a trail through here, and perhaps another to the nearby granite-ribbed summit of Bell Bluff, which also lies in the national forest. Northeast of Alpine, massive Viejas Mountain rises to a summit of over 4000 feet. Its summit can be reached by an obscure trail described below.

Another hike described in this section focuses on McGinty Mountain, just outside Jamul, which is notable for the extraordinary number of rare plants found there. The Nature Conservancy picked up most of the McGinty land from the Bureau of Land Management in 1983, when the BLM sought to dispose of isolated lands it could not properly manage. Additional purchases of private land in the late '80s increased the preserve's size to its present 800 acres and made it possible to construct a public access trail.

Trip 1: Viejas Mountain

Distance	3.5 miles round trip
Total elevation gain/loss	1600'/1600'
Hiking time	2¹/₂ hours (round trip)
Recommended map	USGS 7.5-min *Viejas Mountain*
Best times	November through April
Agency	CNF/DD
Difficulty	★★★

Undistinguished by either its moderate height or its rather squat shape, Viejas Mountain is nonetheless a fairly prominent topographic feature. Standing aloof from nearby peaks, it can be seen from many parts of metropolitan San Diego as a dusky,

Area C-9: Alpine / Jamul

obtusely triangular feature along the eastern horizon. A faint, partially overgrown trail up the west slope offers the only straightforward passage to the summit, a trek that is well worth the effort during crystal-clear weather.

Many San Diegans can drive to the trailhead in as little as 30 minutes. Exit Interstate 8 at Tavern Road, go south 0.1 mile, then go east on Alpine Boulevard through the town of Alpine. After 1.5 miles, turn left (north) on East Victoria Drive, passing under I-8. Proceed 1.1 miles north to Anderson Road. Turn right and continue northeast 0.5 mile to a large water tank and gate (which may or may not block motor traffic). Park just short of the gate. You'll need a National Forest Adventure Pass if you park on the dirt truck trail ahead.

From the water tank, walk 0.3 mile uphill to a point just before where the road becomes level. To your right (east) look for the unmarked beginning of the informal trail up the brushy slope of Viejas Mountain.

The ascent is straight up the mountain at first, then slightly winding as you near the summit. You'll be in waist-to-shoulder-high chaparral the whole way. The occasional passage of hikers and coyotes is apparently all that keeps the rock-strewn path barely open. Scattered among the tangled web of chamise, scrub oak, manzanita, ceanothus, and yucca are a few open areas with fair displays of spring wildflowers—woolly blue curls, prickly phlox, wild onion, and cow parsnip.

Years ago there existed on the summit of Viejas Mountain an arrangement of stones interpreted by local anthropologists to be a winter-solstice marker, used for ceremonial purposes by the Indians. The marker was a **T**-shaped array of stones that pointed precisely to a small peak on the southeastern horizon about 16 miles away. At winter solstice (December 20 or 21) the sun comes up directly behind this peak. On topographic maps, this peak is identified as "Buckman" peak, elevation 4641 feet, located south of Pine Valley. Unfortunately the marker was thoughtlessly destroyed by campers in the mid-1970s. In its place is a wall of stones evidently built as a windbreak.

On exceptionally clear days the view from the Viejas summit can be stupendous—all the way from Mexico to Orange County, with the blue Pacific Ocean spread wide before you. You never quite get the feeling of being "away from it all," however, since the wide gash of Interstate 8 and the fast-spreading suburban sprawl of Alpine lie in the foreground.

Trip 2: Loveland Reservoir

Distance	1.0 mile or less
Optional map	USGS 7.5-min *Alpine*
Best times	All year
Agency	CNF/DD
Difficulty	★

In 1997 Cleveland National Forest, in cooperation with the Sweetwater Authority (a water utility serving south San Diego County), opened a new fishing-access trail to Loveland Reservoir, thereby replacing an earlier (and now closed) trail that was featured in some earlier versions of this book.

The new trail descends from a trailhead parking lot on Japatul Road, 0.7 mile east of Tavern Road. After just 0.2 mile of descent, you reach the high-water level of the reservoir, whereupon you can work your way right or left along the lake shore for some distance. Loveland's storage of water fluctuates considerably, so that at certain times its easternmost, shallow arm turns into a soggy meadow. For fishing enthusiasts, a low lake level is a blessing, because it concentrates fish (especially bass) into smaller areas where they can be easily caught. When full, Loveland's surface shimmers beautifully, cupped amid the shaggy, chaparral-clad walls formed by the canyon of the Sweetwater River.

Trip 3: Sloan Canyon

Distance	4.0 miles round trip
Total elevation gain/loss	900'/900'
Hiking time	2 hours
Optional map	USGS 7.5-min *Alpine*
Best times	November through May
Difficulty	★★

This short stretch of the California Riding and Hiking Trail takes you down a south-facing slope into beautiful Sloan Canyon, where a riparian strip of vegetation accompanies the winding Sweetwater River. Try this hike early on a cold winter morning, when beams of light from the rising sun scatter amid the dew droplets or ice crystals.

From Japatul Road, 0.3 mile east of Tavern Road, turn south on the newly paved Sequan Truck Trail. The California Riding and Hiking Trail soon joins from the east, and runs west along the road shoulder for the next 3 miles. After 2.8 miles (from Japatul Road), pavement ends. Continue 0.2 mile to a sharp right bend in the road and park off the pavement, where there's space for 3 or 4 cars.

Walk south on the road for 0.25 mile past some houses, then follow the signed California Riding and Hiking Trail as it diverges to the left and descends sharply. South across Sloan Canyon the broad, north slope of Sycuan Peak (pronounced "Sequan") rears into the sky. Uncut by roads, this flank of the mountain wears its thick chaparral naturally, like a shaggy variegated carpet. The rocky summits of Lyons, Lawson, and Gaskill peaks poke up in the southeast.

After 1.3 mile, the trail joins a spur road. A messy collection of rural houses lies to the left, down below in Sloan Canyon. You go right and pass above an intriguing (but privately owned) little gorge where the Sweetwater River

Rock jumble at Loveland Reservoir

has cut its way through exfoliated granite slabs. At 2.0 miles you reach the Sweetwater River and the site of an old bridge, now gone. Beyond this, across the normally sluggish river, the California Riding and Hiking Trail continues on Sloan Canyon Road. This oak- and willow-shaded spot is great for watching birds and other wildlife. Rest before you reverse your steps back up the ridge to the starting point.

In 1992 The Nature Conservancy and California Department of Fish and Game purchased 496 acres of the nearby Sloan Ranch. The ranch includes riparian woodland on the Sweetwater River and on Lawson Creek. This sensitive habitat supports several rare or endangered plants and animals, including the least Bell's vireo.

Trip 4: McGinty Mountain

Distance	5.0 miles
Total elevation gain/loss	1400'/1400'
Hiking time	3^1/$_2$ hours
Optional maps	USGS 7.5-min *Dulzura, Alpine*
Best times	November through May
Agency	MMP
Difficulty	★★★

Rising like a scruffy whaleback above a sea of new luxury homes, McGinty Mountain hosts a rich but circumspect treasure of botanical oddities. Several rare and endangered plant species make their home here on soils derived from a relatively uncommon form of bedrock called gabbro. Over half of California's remaining specimens of Dehesa beargrass cling to the mountain's rocky spine. The endemic San Diego thornmint, its habitat reduced by 90% over the last century by urbanization, survives here, as does San Miguel savory, Perry's tetracoccus, and Gander's butterweed. Some of these plants are believed to be relict species, once common but now almost squeezed out of existence by gradual climate changes occurring over the past 10,000 years or more.

To reach the starting point for the access trail into the McGinty Mountain preserve, follow Lyons Valley Road 0.8 mile north from Highway 94 at Jamul, turn left on Jamul Drive, and proceed 0.4 mile to the gated entrance. Park on the shoulder of Jamul Drive and walk in.

Follow the dirt road north and up, along a shallow draw. After 0.4 mile, turn right on a switchback trail that quickly rises to McGinty Mountain's long south ridge. Trained eyes might pick out some of the rarer plants, but mostly you'll notice the typical sage-scrub and chaparral vegetation—attractively green and very aromatic if moistened by winter rains. Look for the somewhat unusual coast spice bush (a member of the citrus family) and the Lord's Candle yucca, whose tall flower stalks bear white blossom clusters in the early spring.

At 1.0 mile, you meet an old dirt road on top of the ridge. Turn left (north) to set a course for McGinty Mountain's rounded, 2183-foot summit, another 1.5 miles away. You'll be returning on the same route, so take note of any intersecting roads that might cause confusion on your way back. In a few places, this road is very steep and rocky.

Clumps of Dehesa beargrass dot the ridgeline, looking somewhat like poor cousins of the common yuccas. They can be identified by their diminutive stature and fibrous, pale green, ribbon-like leaves. As you climb up the ridge, the fragrance of Cleveland sage—probably the most pleasantly aromatic plant in the county—is almost overpowering, especially in springtime.

The panoramic view expands as you get higher, easily encompassing most of the border-region peaks from Tecate Peak to San Miguel Mountain. Off to the west, beyond Mount Helix and Cowles Mountain, you can sometimes spot the ocean—dark blue or glistening with sun glare, depending on the time of day.

Live oak near Alpine

Area C-10: Bonita

From headwaters in the Cuyamaca Mountains, the Sweetwater River flows through foothills south of Descanso, pools up in Loveland Reservoir near Alpine, and flows again through the Dehesa Valley past El Cajon and Spring Valley. After being detained by the Sweetwater Reservoir, whatever is left of the water continues 7 miles through Bonita and Chula Vista to the river's mouth at south San Diego Bay.

Urban development has yet to catch up with the rolling country south and east of Sweetwater Reservoir. It's still a place where wild oats and foxtails chafe in the afternoon breeze, hawks glide overhead, and coyotes and other small animals flourish.

Although the entire surface and shoreline of the reservoir are closed to the public, the Sweetwater River Trail, for horses and hikers, traverses the hills to the south and east. Someday it may tie into the California Riding and Hiking Trail near

Alpine or into future trails north of Interstate 8, thereby establishing a trail link between the South Bay suburbs and Cuyamaca Rancho State Park high in the mountains.

Area C-10: Bonita

Trip 1: Sweetwater River Trail

Distance	7.5 miles round trip (to hilltop view)
Total elevation gain/loss	1100'/1100'
Hiking time	3 hours (round trip)
Optional maps	USGS 7.5-min *National City, Jamul Mtns*
Best times	October through June
Agency	SDCP
Difficulty	★★★

The most scenic segment of the Sweetwater River Trail begins in the Bonita area, east of the main Sweetwater County Park and Chula Vista Golf Course. Take the Bonita Road exit from Interstate 805 and

drive 4 miles to the point where Bonita Road swings left to cross the Sweetwater River on a long, narrow bridge. Park off the pavement beside Bonita Road, or on any nearby residential street.

Pick up the narrow trail underneath the bridge and follow it east along the perimeter of the Bonita Golf Club course. After 0.7 mile the trail starts zigzagging up a grassy hillside. The view of Bonita and the lower Sweetwater River valley widens, with a slice of the ocean in the distance. At 1.4 miles, you skirt the county's new Sweetwater Summit equestrian campground and soon catch a first glimpse of the reservoir. Stay on the trail—the shoreline is strictly off limits to everyone.

The trail, which is following dirt roads at this point, meanders east and north over rolling grassland, staying well back from the shoreline of the reservoir. At 2.3 miles the route starts going north along a wide dirt road. After another 150 yards it becomes a narrow path that veers east up a grassy hillside alongside a wire fence. Then it descends sharply, goes up a few switchbacks, drops again, and goes up to a grove of pepper trees on a hillside. It drops once more, goes through a pipe gate, contours across a scrubby hillside, and finally begins a switchbacking ascent of a prominent hill.

The top of this hill offers the best view of the lake and surrounding mountains. To the east rises 2565-foot San Miguel Mountain, its summit bewhiskered by several spiky radio and TV broadcast antennas. Across the lake to the north and west is the unkempt suburban sprawl of Spring Valley and the huge Pointe Resort development now taking form. Right around you you'll notice some good examples of the fairly rare native coast cholla and coast barrel cactus, along with some common prickly pear cacti.

The hilltop is a good turnaround point. If you want, you can continue exploring the trail ahead. About a mile farther ahead, it reaches a dirt road that parallels the Sweetwater River upstream from the reservoir. Much of the land ahead has recently been purchased by public agencies for open space and wildlife habitat, and the next several years will probably see the development of recreational trails there.

On the Sweetwater River Trail

The Mountains

Area M-1: Agua Tibia

The 18,000-acre Agua Tibia Wilderness lies northwest of Palomar Mountain, straddling the San Diego-Riverside county line in Cleveland National Forest. Until 1984, Agua Tibia was the only officially designated wilderness area in San Diego County. Now it is joined by three others within the Cleveland forest—Pine Creek, Hauser, and San Mateo Canyon—and by several other state wilderness areas within Cuyamaca Rancho and Anza-Borrego Desert state parks.

Agua Tibia Mountain, one of the three distinct mountain blocks of the Palomar range, is the centerpiece of the wilderness that bears its name. Forests of Coulter pine, bigcone Douglas-fir (a.k.a. bigcone spruce), incense cedar, live oak, and black oak cover the highest elevations, while the lower slopes are scrub-covered and fluted by many steep canyons holding intermittent streams. The wilderness was named after one of these streams, Agua Tibia ("warm water") Creek.

The 16,000-acre Vail Fire of 1989 burned the north slopes of Agua Tibia Mountain to a crisp, and spared only part of the oak and conifer forest atop the highest ridges. Several ensuing wet seasons triggered a vigorous new growth of vegetation, which has proven problematical for the trail system. For several years in the 1990s, most of the trails in Agua Tibia Wilderness were severely overgrown. The uppermost trail, an old fire road called Magee-Palomar Trail, was rendered completely impassable due to innumerable fallen trees and a tangle of shrubby vegetation. Since then trail crews have been busy clearing away the undergrowth, and as of 2001 all Agua Tibia trails were open.

Wild creatures were plentiful before the fire, and they have gradually returned to the burned-over areas. In addition to the usual deer, squirrels, rabbits and common birds of chaparral and pine-oak forest habitats, bobcats, mountain lions, wild pigs, prairie falcons, and bald and golden eagles have been noted here.

There is only one easy entry into the Agua Tibia Wilderness—Dripping Springs Campground, located 10 miles east of Interstate 15 on Highway 79 in Riverside County. Trip 1 below begins and ends there. Trip 2, which begins on Palomar's remote northeast slope, requires several miles of dirt-road driving.

All federal and state wilderness areas in the county are subject to stringently protective management rules. These rules permit free access to anyone on foot or horseback, but prohibit any wheeled devices—bicycles and carts included. You must also be in possession of a wilderness permit in order to enter Agua Tibia Wilderness. Permits for the Agua Tibia Wil-

Area M-1: Agua Tibia

derness are available at the Dripping Springs Fire Station (open approximately April through November). Better yet, call or visit the Palomar ranger district office well in advance of your visit to obtain the permit and to inquire about the current condition of the trails.

Trip 1: Dripping Springs Trail

Distance	13.6 miles round trip
Total elevation gain/loss	2900'/2900'
Hiking time	8 hours (round trip)
Recommended maps	Cleveland National Forest recreation map; USGS 7.5-min *Vail Lake*
Best times	November through May
Agency	CNF/PD
Difficulty	★★★★

Make this an all-day hike to and from the summit ridge, or an overnight backpack, or set your sights on an intermediate destination. In any case, there is only one direct way up to the forested heights of Agua Tibia Mountain: the Dripping Springs Trail. In cool weather this is a fine hike for your well-conditioned dog, but be sure you take plenty of extra water along for it.

You start from the trailhead parking area at the south end of Dripping Springs

Campground, 0.4 mile south of the fire station on Highway 79. (The campground may be seasonally closed; if so you must park outside and walk in.) Just beyond the trailhead, ford Arroyo Seco Creek and begin a switchbacking ascent through sage scrub and chaparral vegetation, liberally sprinkled with annual wildflowers in March through May. After 0.1 mile, the Wild Horse Trail branches left. (Its twisting course ascends along the slopes south and west of Arroyo Seco Creek and after about 7 tedious miles reaches the Crosley Trail). Keep straight on the Dripping Springs Trail.

At about 1.0 mile, Dripping Springs Trail gains the top of a nearly flat ridge and proceeds south. After another mile, you start a series of switchback segments criss-crossing an old firebreak (stay on the gradually ascending trail—don't make short cuts). Vail Lake and Southern California's highest mountains—Mount San Antonio, San Gorgonio, and San Jacinto—are visible in the north. On a clear winter day, these snow-covered summits etched against the blue sky are a memorable sight.

At about 3.5 miles (3100'), the trail crosses the head of a small creek, where the chamise- and ceanothus-dominated cover begins to yield to manzanita and ribbonwood (red shanks) shrubs. The smooth, bronzed limbs and branches of the manzanita support dark green, leathery leaves that turn edge-on to the sun on hot days, thus conserving moisture. Ribbonwood has a per-

petually peeling reddish bark and feathery, light green foliage. Starting in February, the manzanita shows off myriads of tiny white or pinkish blossoms shaped like hanging lanterns. Later in the year, red berries (*manzanita* is Spanish for "little apple") appear. When ripe, these edible berries taste a lot like a pippin apple.

At about 4 miles (3300') you'll pass what little remains of the truly giant specimens of manzanita and ribbonwood that stood here until the 1989 fire. The century-old shrubs that grew here, up to 20 feet high, represented the equivalent of a "climax forest" consisting entirely of chaparral. The loss of this mature patch of veg-

Arroyo Seco Creek

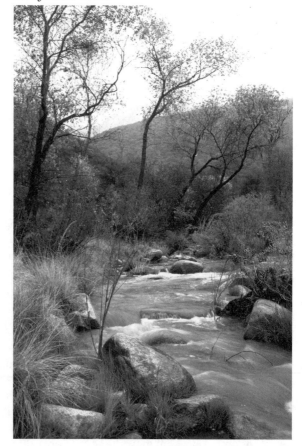

etation was tragic, but it must be remembered that without the effect of fire-suppression measures enacted over the past century, the natural cycle of growth and incineration by natural causes (roughly every decade) would probably never have allowed so mature a stand of chaparral to develop.

At about 4.5 miles, the trail descends a little and crosses an area of poor soil. A view opens up to the southeast. The white dome of the Hale Telescope at Palomar Observatory gleams on a ridge about 9 miles away. After crossing a ravine, you resume climbing on switchbacks, passing the

burned-out hulks of several large Coulter pines, plus their fledgling offspring. A patch of unburned live-oak forest heralds your arrival (6.8 miles) at the main ridge of Agua Tibia Mountain and a remnant of the Magee-Palomar fire road. If you're backpacking, this is a good spot to bed down for the night. If you work your way a short distance south or west from the top of the trail, you'll get a fine view of the coastal valleys and hills to the west and south. On many a spring morning, you can look down on the top of the marine layer, which looks like a flat, white ocean of mist.

Trip 2: Eagle Crag

Distance	16.2 miles round trip
Total elevation gain/loss	3800'/3800'
Hiking time	10 hours (round trip)
Recommended maps	Cleveland National Forest recreation map; USGS 7.5-min *Aguanga, Vail Lake*
Best times	November through May
Agency	CNF/PD
Difficulty	★★★★

This out-and-back route across Cleveland National Forest lands on Palomar's north slopes traverses some wild and lonely country—in fact, some of the most remote territory found anywhere in Southern California. The destination is Eagle Crag, a granite outcrop upon which you can sit with dangling legs and contemplate the sheer drop of 1000 or more feet below you.

On the way you'll cross a number of small streams that flow in winter and spring. Remember that this water must be purified for drinking purposes. Ask about trail conditions and the availability of water when you obtain your wilderness permit. You'll also need to have a National Forest Adventure Pass for parking at the

trailhead.

To reach the trailhead, turn south from Highway 79 (just east of Aguanga) on the paved access road toward the Thousand Trails campground. From the campground entrance, continue south on the graded-dirt High Point Road (8S05) 5 miles south to the signed Cutca Trail on the right.

Start off by descending sharply on Cutca Trail into the shady depths of Cottonwood Creek, 0.5 mile. Climb to a saddle at 1.2 miles, then descend slightly to the Aguanga Trail junction at 2.1 miles. (The poorly maintained Aguanga Trail, which goes north, runs into private property near the Riverside County line.)

Continue over rolling terrain, through chaparral and oaks, crossing Long

Canyon and two of its tributaries. These streambeds usually have water until early summer. Nearing Cutca Valley you strike Cutca Road at 5.0 miles. Walk 0.4 mile north on the dirt road into Cutca Valley, then resume westward travel on the Cutca Trail. The valley, with its flat, open spaces, is a good spot to spend the night if you're backpacking.

Rise out of the valley, cross the Agua Tibia Wilderness boundary, and follow a shady ravine with a seasonal, trickling brook. Sword ferns on the bank flutter in the cool and languid breeze. Switchbacks take you up to a junction with the Magee-Palomar Trail (7.6 miles), which is the old roadbed following the Palomar-Agua Tibia crest. From this junction, or from another point 0.2 mile west, you may make your bid for Eagle Crag. This involves a short, steep, cross-country climb through post-fire scrub vegetation. The rock pile at the apex of Eagle Crag's sheer south face offers a dramatic platform for a vista unparalleled at any other site in the Palomar mountains.

Eagle Crag

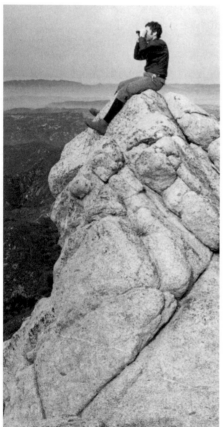

Area M-2: Palomar Mountain

Without a doubt, the rolling high country of Palomar Mountain contains San Diego County's most picture-perfect mountain scenery. Palomar's uplands, covered with thick forests of pine, oak, fir, and cedar, and its gentle valleys, laced with sparkling streams, bring to mind landscapes more commonly seen in mountain ranges far to the north. With an average annual precipitation of more than 40 inches, snowfalls of up to 3 feet in winter, and vibrant spring and fall color, this is San Diego County's best answer to those who might complain about the lack of four seasons in Southern California.

Palomar Mountain is the middle of three distinctively named promontories forming the 25-mile-long range often known as Palomar. Agua Tibia Mountain anchors the range to the northwest, while Aguanga Mountain stretches to the southeast. Several faults pass through the area, including the Elsinore Fault which parallels Highway 76 and the San Luis Rey River at the foot of Palomar Mountain.

The amount of public acreage on Palomar Mountain itself is not large. Palomar Mountain State Park spreads across 3 square miles of the finest wooded area on the mountain. The national forest is checkered with private inholdings, including a big piece of property owned by Palomar Observatory. Nonetheless, there are enough trails in both the state park and national forest to keep hikers busy for a while.

Public campgrounds are located within Palomar Mountain State Park (open year-round), at Palomar Mountain County Park (open year-round), and in the national forest (open seasonally) along the road to Palomar Observatory. Backpacking is not permitted in Palomar Mountain State Park. Backpacking and remote camping is encouraged in such areas as Agua Tibia (Area M-1) and Barker Valley (Trip 11 below). Trips 5, 6, 7, 9, 10, and 11 below require a National Forest Adventure Pass, as their trailheads lie on national forest land.

Palomar Mountain is served by two paved highways that climb up from State Highway 76. South Grade Road (County Highway S-6) is steep and winding; while East Grade Road (County Highway S-7) offers a longer, more gradual ascent. Both provide spectacular views and fine roadside scenery. At the junction of South Grade and East Grade roads on the Palomar Mountain crest, you can turn west toward Palomar Mountain State Park (Trips 1–4 below), or north toward the national-forest campgrounds (Trips 5–7) and Palomar Observatory. The observatory houses the famous 200-inch Hale Telescope, now far from the largest in the world, but still a marvel to behold. Visitors are welcome to view the telescope and visit a nearby museum from 9 A.M. to 4 P.M. daily.

At the foot of Palomar Mountain along Highway 76, the La Jolla Indian Reservation welcomes campers to its busy campground on the San Luis Rey River. Hikers and backpackers can follow the shady river bank downstream some distance from the main camping area (Trip 8).

On the dry and warm south and east slopes of Palomar Mountain and Aguanga Mountain, elfin forests of chaparral and parklike oak woodlands predominate. From East Grade Road near Lake Henshaw you can descend into oak-filled Love Valley (Trip 9). From Oak Grove on Highway 79, you can tackle Palomar's "High Point" the hard way via the Oak Grove Trail (Trip 10). Oak Grove also features a national-forest campground.

Probably the most intriguing trip below Palomar's high plateau is the descent into Barker Valley (Trip 11). This oak-dotted swale, caressed by the San Luis Rey River's West Fork, is perhaps the most isolated nonwilderness area in San Diego County.

Area M-2: Palomar Mountain

Trip 1: Scott's Cabin/Boucher Hill Loop

Distance	3.0 miles
Total elevation gain/loss	800'/800'
Hiking time	1$^{1}/_{2}$ hours
Recommended map	Palomar Mountain State Park map/ brochure
Optional map	USGS 7.5-min *Boucher Hill*
Best times	All year
Agency	PMSP
Difficulty	★★

Like most hikes on Palomar Mountain, this one is at its very best during spring and fall, especially April–May and October–November. The route begins along an open ridge dotted with black oaks, and these trees undergo rapid color changes in both seasons.

Park at the Silver Crest Picnic Area, just beyond the state park's entrance. Walk back to the paved road and go west toward a junction of five roads. Now continue west up the ridgeline between the two roads to the left (these roads are a one-way loop around the summit of Boucher Hill), following a narrow, unmarked trail through the grass and bracken ferns. Black oaks crown the ridgeline, their gnarled limbs bare in winter, but alive with fluttering leaves during the remainder of the year. A few white firs appear as you approach the fire tower and microwave structure on Boucher Hill. From the parking area at Boucher Hill, there's a good view west down to Pauma Valley, but it's often too hazy to spot the Pacific Ocean.

Now find the Boucher Trail, which descends on a stretch of old fire road to the north. Beyond more black oaks, bracken ferns, and a meadow dotted with baby-blue-eyes, the trail swings right to traverse a north slope, entering a dense, almost gloomy forest of white fir. Upon reaching Nate Harrison Road, cross and pick up the

Adams Trail on the other side. You're in mixed forest now, with a few bigcone Douglas-fir trees whose wandlike limbs tower head and shoulders above all else. Winding around a sunlight-flooded ravine, you'll see beautiful specimens of dogwood and ceanothus, in bloom during April and May. In early summer, Humboldt lilies brighten up the shady areas.

When you arrive at Cedar Grove Group Campground, walk out to the entrance, where you can pick up the trail to Scott's Cabin. A steep climb through mostly white fir forest takes you to the modest remains of the cabin, built by an early homesteader. Complete the circle by bearing right at the next junction, taking the trail that ends up opposite the Silver Crest Picnic Area.

Palomar Inset

Trip 2: Thunder Spring/Chimney Flats Loop

Distance	4.0 miles
Total elevation gain/loss	900'/900'
Hiking time	2 hours
Recommended map	Palomar Mountain State Park map/ brochure
Optional map	USGS 7.5-min *Boucher Hill*
Best times	All year
Agency	PMSP
Difficulty	★★

This loop has a little of everything—a walk along a stream-edged meadow; a passage through a canopy of western azaleas (relatively rare in San Diego County); a stroll through a century-old apple orchard; a visit to an old grave; the best views in the entire park; and a visit (once more, if you've already taken Trip 1) to the old ruins of Scott's Cabin.

The parking lot at Doane Pond—the lowest elevation on this hike—is a good place to begin. Tiny Doane Pond is stocked with trout and is very popular, especially with youngsters. The buildings just east belong to San Diego's Palomar school camp. This camp, along with Camp Cuyamaca in Cuyamaca Rancho State Park, provides elementary-school students with an opportunity to experience a week of adventure and learning in lieu of regular class attendance.

Walk around the lake, then go southeast up the Thunder Spring Trail (or, if it's one of those frosty days of winter, you can gravitate toward the Upper Doane Trail, the parallel dirt road on the sunny side of the valley). The Thunder Spring Trail skirts a patch of skunk cabbage, then plunges into a dark forest of oaks and conifers. Alder-fringed Doane Creek on the left appears luminescent in the sunlight. A side path on the right leads to Thunder Spring, framed by four-foot-long fronds of chain fern in a shady ravine.

At the end of the valley, commence a steep climb on an informal trail up along Chimney Creek. Azalea grows thickly through here, displaying hundreds of white blossoms in mid-spring. Near the top there's a small seasonal waterfall in the tiny creek.

Next you reach Chimney Flats, an oak-fringed, bracken-filled meadow. Bear right (west) on the Chimney Flats Trail, an old fire road. Climb through the forest to another flat, this one filled with the remains of a century-old apple orchard believed to have been tended by the man who built Scott's Cabin. At the entrance to this flat, turn left on the service road from the reservoir, cross East Grade Road, and pick up the Silver Crest Trail. On the left is "Big Willy's grave," the resting place of William Pearson, an early settler, killed by a falling tree. According to the inscription, Willy was "AGED 66 Y'S 1 MO. 16 D'S." The Silver Crest Trail meanders along the edge of a steep ridge affording spectacular wintertime views of the San Luis Rey River valley and the distant Pacific Ocean. Up ahead is Silver Crest Picnic Area, where water is available.

From the picnic area head east across the road and pick up Scott's Cabin Trail. Follow this past the cabin, down through the white-fir forest, then go right (east) on the Cedar-Doane Trail—formerly known as the "Slide Trail" because of its steepness.

Chimney Creek

This passes through mixed forest and emerges at the shoreline of Doane Pond, your starting point. There's quite a lot of poison oak in the shade of the oaks along this narrow trail. If it's winter, avoid brushing against any twigs poking up; the twigs of poison oak contain some of the same skin-irritating oil found in the leaves.

Trip 3: Doane Valley Nature Trail

Distance	1.0 mile
Total elevation gain/loss	150'/150'
Hiking time	30 minutes
Recommended map	Palomar Mountain State Park map/ brochure
Optional map	USGS 7.5-min *Boucher Hill*
Best times	All year
Agency	PMSP
Difficulty	★

This is a trail for inspiration. Here is the Palomar forest at its best, complete with a trickling stream that seems out of place amid the generally arid mountain ranges of far-southern California.

The brochure available at the trailhead is excellent in its descriptions and sketches of trees and shrubs seen along the route. Among the more interesting species: box elder (a tree rare in San Diego County), creek dogwood, wild strawberry, mountain currant, and Sierra gooseberry. At one point, the brochure calls attention to a massive incense-cedar towering 150 feet.

If you weren't educated to its true identity, you might think it was a giant (sequoia) redwood.

You'll find the trailhead at the Doane Pond parking lot. The trail goes downhill along Doane Creek for about 0.3 mile, then curves and climbs around a hill to connect with Doane Valley Campground. Walk through the campground and down the road toward Doane Pond to close the loop.

Doane Pond

Trip 4: Lower Doane Valley/Lower French Valley

Distance	2.5 miles round trip
Total elevation gain/loss	300'/300'
Hiking time	1^1/2 hours
Recommended map	Palomar Mountain State Park map/brochure
Optional map	USGS 7.5-min *Boucher Hill*
Best times	All year
Agency	PMSP
Difficulty	★★

Unquestionably, the best time of day to make this hike is during the first two hours of daylight. At midday the landscape is bathed in a harsh, flat light. Afterward, lowland haze may blow in, diluting the purity of the light. In early morning light, however, magic is wrought. Long shadows from the treetops stab across the pillowy meadows, then recede quickly as the sun gains altitude. Subtle shades of color come alive in the foliage as light from the blue sky mixes with golden-white sunlight. Silver dewdrops glisten on the blades of grass.

As in Trip 3 above start hiking on the Doane Valley Nature Trail, but bear left at the trail fork after 0.3 mile. This is the Lower Doane Trail, following Doane Creek through stately groves of white fir and incense-cedar. Walk all the way down to the weir at the end of the trail, and admire the stone-and-mortar structure above it. This small dam and gauging station were used in the late 1920s to test the hydroelectric potential of the stream. The tests proved there was not enough flow to justify construction of a power plant. Today, the silted-in dam holds barely enough water to soak your feet in.

Some fishermen and hikers are familiar with the rugged and beautiful stretch of Pauma Creek below the weir. You can scramble down the creek to the park boundary about 0.2 mile away, but beyond this point lies Pala Indian Reservation land and access is forbidden. Several years ago rangers rediscovered banana slugs crawling along this creek, which was surprising since many people thought they were native only to California's central coast range and points farther north. The local subspecies is dull olive in color, not yellow like their northern cousins. Like some the relict plant species around San Diego County, these creatures are probably holdovers from the Pleistocene epoch, when the climate here was cooler and wetter.

From the weir, backtrack 0.2 mile and take the short connecting trail across Lower Doane Valley to the Lower French Valley Trail. Go left (north), passing into Lower French Valley. The setting is idyllic: rolling grasslands dotted with statuesque pines, surrounded by hillsides clothed in

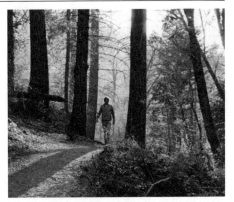

On the Doane Valley Nature Trail

oaks and tall conifers.

Several of the pines are riddled with holes—some plugged with acorns. This is the handiwork of the acorn woodpecker, who uses the holes to store acorns filled with larvae. The birds retrieve these acorns and the grubs in leaner times. Listen for the repetitive, guttural call of this bird, and observe the distinctive red patch on its head and the white wing patch when in flight.

You can hike up as far as the bank of French Creek, then return along the same trail, staying left to finish the hike on the Lower French Valley Trail.

Trip 5: Observatory Trail

Distance	2.2 miles
Total elevation gain/loss	100'/750'
Hiking time	1 hour
Optional maps	Cleveland National Forest recreation map; USGS 7.5-min *Palomar Observatory, Boucher Hill*
Best times	All year
Agency	CNF/PD
Difficulty	★

The Observatory Trail has won kudos as one of only four National Recreation trails in San Diego County. Since the trail roughly parallels Highway S-6 (Canfield Road), it can be walked one-way, either uphill or downhill. For the easier trip, start at the upper trailhead, just below Palomar Observatory's entrance gate, and have someone drive around to meet you at the trail's lower end at Observatory Campground. A car-shuttle arrangement works well, too, since there's only 2 miles of highway distance in between the trailheads.

From the upper trailhead, walk first through a thicket of dense chaparral, then past pines, oaks, and incense-cedars. In the sunny clearings between the trees, wildflowers dot the grassy slopes and bracken ferns spread like a lacy carpet at waist level.

About halfway down, the trail bends around a ravine, alive with the sound of a trickling stream until summer's heat and drought silences it. Soon after, you come to a wooden platform on the left overlooking

Mendenhall Valley—one of several large meadows tucked into Palomar's rolling flanks. Mendenhall Valley sheds water into the San Luis Rey River's West Fork. The water flows east through Barker Valley, circles around to Lake Henshaw at Palomar Mountain's southeastern tip, rushes down along Highway 76, tumbles through a deep canyon on the La Jolla Indian Reservation, and emerges upon the sloping alluvial plain between Rincon and Pauma Valley.

After meandering some more under a leafy canopy, you descend to the east edge of Observatory Campground.

Trip 6: Fry Creek Trail

	Distance	1.5 miles
	Total elevation gain/loss	300'/300'
	Hiking time	1 hour
	Optional maps	Cleveland National Forest recreation map; USGS 7.5-min *Boucher Hill*
	Best times	All year
	Agency	CNF/PD
	Difficulty	★

This beautiful trail circles the head of Fry Creek, visiting a "Penny Pines"

(planted) grove of Coulter pines atop a saddle. You'll find the signed trailhead just

Mendenhall Valley overlook

inside the entrance to the campground, 2 miles below Palomar Observatory and 2.7 miles north of the South Grade/East Grade road junction. Although the trail receives a fair amount of use, you may find that it is ill-maintained and a bit hard to follow.

The trail winds up along the slope north of the creek, crosses a dirt road, and continues on to the Penny Pines. You pass live and black oaks, pines, and scattered underbrush. This mix of vegetation is well adapted to the sunny, somewhat dry south-facing slopes. October and November are the most glorious months: the black oak in full autumn color delights the eye, and the sporadic pitter-patter of falling acorns pleases the ear—if not the top of the head.

In late April and early May there's a curious kind of pseudo-autumn color in these forests. When the black oak leaves first emerge from buds, they're reddish in color. They gradually acquire a shade of green as they unfold. Wherever the oaks are exposed to varying conditions of elevation and sun exposure, bands of color ranging from reddish-brown to green can be seen on the mountainsides. You can see this effect near the Penny Pines, where springtime pseudo-autumn color contrasts with the green palette of white firs, live oaks, and Coulter pines.

Look for common birds such as Steller's jays, chicadees, and acorn woodpeckers. I've seen mule deer here—and once, at twilight, a striped skunk.

After you reach the Penny Pines, don't take the road to the east (a shortcut to the campground) if you want to complete the whole trail. Instead, find and follow the continuation of the Fry Creek Trail which angles down the slope south of the creek. You thread your way amid closely spaced incense-cedar, white fir, and live oak tree trunks. Very few black oaks and no Coulter pines grow here—they seem to prefer the sunnier slopes on the other side of the creek.

Trip 7: Fry Creek to Doane Valley

Distance	1.5 miles
Total elevation gain/loss	300'/550'
Hiking time	1¹/₂ hours
Recommended maps	Cleveland National Forest recreation map; USGS 7.5-min *Boucher Hill*
Best times	All year
Agency	CNF/PD
Difficulty	★★

This short, cross-country route serves as the only convenient connection (for hikers) between the Fry Creek/Observatory campground area in Cleveland National Forest, and Palomar Mountain State Park. The distance from start to end point via roads is almost seven miles.

From the entrance to Fry Creek Campground, walk up either branch of the Fry Creek Trail (see Trip 6) to the Penny Pines plantation. Several roads and trails diverge there. You go west down a narrow ravine on a trail worn in by the footsteps of many hikers. All other paths go up, or back down toward Fry Creek. In the ravine you may have to dodge fallen trees and, depending on the amount of recent use, you may have to push through scratchy brush as well.

Near the bottom of the ravine, you'll be boulder hopping over outcrops of gray metasedimentary rock. Back along Fry Creek, the rock is granitic. You're on one of several wedges of pre-Cretaceous metasedimentary rock that alternate with younger granitic rock exposures along the summit of Palomar Mountain.

At the bottom you come out behind the buildings of the Palomar School Camp. The parking lot at Doane Pond lies a short distance away.

Trip 8: La Jolla Indian Reservation

Distance	3.0 miles round trip (to San Luis Rey River narrows)
Total elevation gain/loss	150'/150'
Hiking time	3 hours (round trip)
Optional map	USGS 7.5-min *Palomar Observatory, Boucher Hill*
Best times	All year
Agency	LJIR
Difficulty	★★

In the heat of summer, the La Jolla Indian Reservation draws plenty of visitors to its campground and water slide. On the hot days, "tubing" down the lazily flowing San Luis Rey River (on giant inner tubes) is very popular as well. If it's peaceful and quiet hiking you're looking for, though, you'd best come during late fall through early spring when the place is practically deserted.

The campground turnoff is located at mile 41.7 on Highway 76, about 25 miles east of Interstate 15. The day-use or camping fee you pay at the campground entrance entitles you to a "trespass permit" for hiking or backpacking on the reservation.

The best hiking is downstream from the campground. The river here is graced with a dense riparian strip of willows, sycamores, cottonwoods, and live oaks, nourished by steady releases of water from Lake Henshaw upstream.

Drive to the farthest camping area on the downstream side, and begin hiking along the right (northwest) bank of the river. You'll be on a fairly well defined trail beaten down by tubing enthusiasts who must cart their tubes upriver after floating down. Poison oak appears here and there. In places you may have to scramble over rock outcrops if you don't want to get your feet wet.

Shady camp spots are available back from the bank. You won't want to drink the often-murky river water, even after purification, so bring all you need.

At about 1.5 miles down the river, the canyon walls become steep and close in. This is a good spot for the average person to turn back. The more adventurous can continue by making a long traverse over steep rock slabs on the right bank, or by staggering right through the river itself, which is usually about mid-thigh depth. You'll be lucky if you don't fall in, since you can't always see the bottom.

Over the next 2 miles, the canyon swings around a gooseneck and tumbles over several waterfalls two to four feet high. Beyond this stretch, a diversion dam takes virtually all the water and sends it through the Escondido Canal to Lake Wohlford, often leaving a bone-dry creekbed below.

San Luis Rey River

Trip 9: Love Valley

Distance	2.0 miles
Total elevation gain/loss	300'/300'
Hiking time	1¹/₂ hours
Optional map	USGS 7.5-min *Palomar Observatory*
Best times	November through June
Agency	CNF/PD
Difficulty	★

After a wet winter, the ponds in Love Valley hold the shimmering, upside-down image of a classic California landscape: a weathered barn nestled at the far end of an Ireland-colored meadow, rounded foothills studded with oaks, and white cumulus billowing over the dark, conifer-draped Palomar crest. By April or May, the shallow ponds in the valley bottom start shrinking, leaving in their wake an eye-popping display of yellow tidy tips.

This little-known, day-use destination near the foot of Palomar Mountain is perfect for a picnic—at least in the cooler months, when fresh daytime breezes and cold nighttime temperatures keep crawl-ing and flying insects at bay. The starting point is easy to find, mile 3.3 on East Grade Road (3.3 miles north of Highway 76). Park in the large turnout on the south side of the road, walk around the locked vehicle gate, and continue over a low rise on the dirt road ahead.

As you descend, watch for three kinds of oak trees—black, coast, and Engelmann oaks. The 3600-foot elevation here is a bit too low for coniferous trees. As you curve south, Lake Henshaw comes into view, tucked into a corner of the large Valle de San Jose—which is a down-dropped basin along the Elsinore Fault.

When you reach the edge of Love

Valley at 0.8 mile, you can walk straight to the old barn (which, upon closer inspection, is made of unromantic and rusty corrugated metal), or veer left toward the two

ephemeral ponds on the valley floor. Choose your picnic site on the open meadow, or beneath one of the oaks. There are no facilities out there, so you must pack out whatever you pack in.

Trip 10: Oak Grove to High Point

Distance	13 miles round trip
Total elevation gain/loss	3600'/3600'
Hiking time	7 hours (round trip)
Recommended map	Cleveland National Forest recreation map
Optional maps	USGS 7.5-min *Aguanga, Palomar Observatory*
Best times	October through May
Agency	CNF/PD
Difficulty	★★★★

How's this for a climb of Palomar Mountain from bottom to top? Start at Oak Grove, along the east base of the mountain, and climb steadily up 6.5 miles of foot trail and fire road to reach High Point, the highest mountain within a radius of 14 miles. Of course, with the right kind of vehicle it's usually possible to drive to High Point—but you'd miss the exercise that way. There's no water along this route, so plan accordingly.

The tiny community of Oak Grove is 14 miles north of Warner Springs by way of Highway 79. Begin at the fire station at mile 49.1 on Highway 79. Follow the "Oak Grove Trail" signs directing you over dirt roads and footpaths behind the station. After crossing a small stream just behind the station, the trail meanders up to a ridgeline and begins cutting back and forth across an old firebreak.

You're now in the usual chaparral community of the mid-elevation moun-

Love Valley in spring

tains, where chamise, ribbonwood, scrub oak, and manzanita thrive. A few conifers cluster below in the ravines on either side of the ridge. Sunny exposures along the trail support a fair springtime growth of annual wildflowers, including wild canterbury bells, chia, monkeyflower, and aster. A view opens to the north toward the summits of San Gorgonio Mountain and San Jacinto Peak.

At about 1.8 miles you reach Oak Grove Road, which is closed to public travel below this point. Go uphill (west) on the road and continue toward an intersection with High Point Road at 3.4 miles. Turn left and continue uphill through chaparral and oak forest to Palomar Divide Road at 5.2 miles. Go right and head west around the north flank of High Point through a cool, shady forest of oaks and pines. At 6.2 miles you veer left on the steep road to the summit.

The 67-foot-high fire tower is one of the remaining few in San Diego County. It may be possible to climb up the first few flights of steps for a better view of the surroundings. The list of peaks visible— including the one you're on—reads like a roster of the highest points in Southern California. Combs Peak, whose summit is right about eye level if you stand on the tower, is the nearest rival, 14 miles to the east. Parts of the Santa Rosa, San Ysidro, and Vallecito mountains in the Anza-Borrego Desert are visible, along with the Laguna and Cuyamaca mountains farther to the southeast. In the north are the real giants—Old Baldy, San Gorgonio, and San Jacinto. On very clear days, several of the Channel Islands are visible far out in the Pacific. A lookout here once reported a fire burning in Santa Barbara County, almost two hundred miles away.

As an alternative to the long climb up, you could have someone drop you off at the top (High Point is often accessible to sturdy vehicles via the Palomar Divide Road or High Point Road) and do this hike one-way downhill to Oak Grove. But then you'd miss the fun of coming up. Right?

Trip 11: Barker Valley

Distance	6.2 miles round trip (to foot of trail)
Total elevation gain/loss	1000'/1000'
Hiking time	4 hours (round trip)
Recommended map	Cleveland National Forest recreation map
Optional map	USGS 7.5-min *Palomar Observatory*
Best times	October through July
Agency	CNF/PD
Difficulty	★★★

A cool current caressed my feet, erasing the memory of several long, hot miles on the trail. Sunlight scattered among a thousand fluttering leaves, and a tiny sliver of new moon glowed softly in a blue wedge of sky overhead. Water skaters flitted nervously on the rippled surface of the pool, casting fleeting shadows on a trio of small fish feeding on the bottom. Even in the warm month of July, with the creek ebbing, Barker Valley could still be delightful.

Barker Valley perches squarely in one of the more remote corners of Palomar Mountain, 3 miles by dusty foot trail and 8 miles by bone-shaking dirt road from the nearest paved road, Highway 79. At the least, you'll need a sturdy, high-clearance passenger car or truck to reach the trailhead.

(Check first to see if the road is open; storms can render it temporarily unusable.)

Turn west from Highway 79 at a point 6.5 miles northwest of Warner Springs (mile 41.9) and continue up the unpaved Palomar Divide Road for 7.8 miles to the Barker Valley Spur trailhead on the left (west) side.

Park off the roadway and head down the trail (an old roadbed). On the way down, keep an eye out for bald eagles in the sky. A number of these raptors roost in old snags on the shore of nearby Lake Henshaw during the winter.

Hike for 1.7 miles on a gradual descent until the old roadbed switches back sharply. Continue around the U-curve, and within 0.1 mile veer to the right on a newer trail that lazily zigzags down a dry slope and into oak-rimmed Barker Valley. If you're looking for a campsite, they're abundant around here. Just remember to select one at least 100 feet away from the nearest water—in this case, the West Fork San Luis Rey River. A second trail descends into Barker Valley from Deer Flats—from the direction of the metal look-out tower on High Point.

Barker Valley is notorious for cold air drainage at night. I had the interesting experience of sweating out an 85° July day, and awakening next morning to find frost along the stream.

A rugged set of falls and pools awaits adventurous hikers a mile downstream from the foot of the Barker Spur Trail. These occur just below an old stone weir and gauging station. By following rough paths traversing the steep, brushy, north canyon wall, it's possible to reach hidden swimming holes worn in the water-polished rock. Wild trout can be found in the pools below the first falls. Don't attempt to explore this area unless you're adept at scrambling over steep terrain and across potentially slippery, water-polished rock. An ill-timed slip in a couple of places could result in a deadly, 50-foot plunge down a cascade.

When it's time to return, go back the same way. The consistently gradual trail is not in itself challenging, but it may prove difficult after many hours of exposure to the warm sun.

Cascade and pool below Barker Valley

Area M-3: Warner Springs

Some of the loftiest—and least visited—mountain country in San Diego County surrounds the resort community of Warner Springs. Hot Springs Mountain, on the Los Coyotes Indian Reservation to the east, is recognized as the county's highest point. At 6533 feet, it beats the better-known, 6512-foot Cuyamaca Peak by a whisker.

Northeast, a rather remote section of the Cleveland National Forest spreads into an even more remote corner of the immense Anza-Borrego Desert State Park. The roadless, eastern section of the national forest parcel, the so-called Caliente Wilderness Study Area, was one of two national-forest WSA's in San Diego County that did not make the cut for wilderness designation in 1984. The other is the Sill Hill WSA adjoining Cuyamaca Rancho State Park. These two WSA's remain "unroaded" and could at some future time be included in the National Wilderness Preservation System. The Pacific Crest Trail passes near Warner Springs, and two of its most scenic segments (within the county) are profiled in the trip descriptions below.

Hikers and backpackers are in on a little secret when they discover the Los Coyotes Indian Reservation. This is the largest (25,000 acres) of the 17 reservations on San Diego County, yet one of the least populated. Visitors can make use of developed camping facilities there, as well as explore the undeveloped parts on a network of graded dirt roads, 4-wheel-drive roads, and trails. Motorcycles are prohibited on the reservation and the vehicle traffic is light on the roads, so you're quite likely to find this a pleasant place to go hiking. With its network of roads and trails that seem to go everywhere, the reservation has also become popular among mountain bikers. Out of many possible hikes on the reservation, I've chosen two (Trips 1 and 2 below) that are well suited for a bit of challenging foot travel. Another trip in this book (Area D-2, Trip 3) starts in the reservation and ends down in the desert at Borrego Springs.

To reach the Los Coyotes reservation, turn east on Camino San Ignacio from Highway 79 (mile 35.0) at Warner Springs. After 0.6 mile, bear right on Los Tules Road and continue 4.5 miles to the reservation gate. There you pay a fee for an entrance permit and pick up a sketch map of the roads and trails. The main campground (where water is available) lies another 2.7 miles on via paved and dirt road. Los Coyotes is open year-round on the weekends and holidays, weather and road conditions permitting. Call first if you plan to visit on a weekday.

Trip 1: Hot Springs Mountain

Distance	5.5 miles round trip
Total elevation gain/loss	1250'/1250'
Hiking time	3^1/2 hours (round trip)
Recommended map	USGS 7.5-min *Hot Springs Mtn.*
Best times	March through November
Agency	LCIR
Difficulty	★★★

In the mist, the ghostly, abandoned fire lookout tower appeared. We climbed the steps and reached the observation deck. Suddenly there was a radiant heat

Area M-3: Warner Springs

around us and a flood of light from above. A residue of tiny water droplets floated in the blue glare, and a dozen mountain peaks were unveiled—the glistening summits of San Jacinto and San Gorgonio in the north, the somber Santa Rosas to the east, the dark Lagunas and Cuyamacas southward, and more. In the chasm of Agua Caliente Creek to the northwest, a tenuous rainbow rode a billowing cloud.

That's what it's often like in winter or early spring up on Hot Springs Mountain—uncertain weather, but clear as a bell if and when the clouds part. Summer days, on the other hand, are usually sunny and warm, but often quite hazy. Santa Ana days near the end of the year can be just about right, especially when the autumn leaves of the black oaks are falling.

Some people like to drive, hike, or mountain bike up along the 7-mile dirt road

going up the mountain's south slope, but the northern approach described here is cooler, more interesting, and much shorter. This approach, however, may be blocked by snowfall during part of the winter.

Drive up Los Coyotes' main road, past the developed campground, to an intersection of roads in a valley near the top of Middle Fork Borrego Palm Canyon (6.1 miles past the entrance gate). Turn left (west) and drive up the valley on a sandy road to reach a saddle above the valley, 2.2 miles farther. Just beyond this saddle, on the left (west) side of the road, is Nelson's Camp, with campsites nestled in a shallow bowl shaded by live oak, pine, and cedar trees. Picnic tables, fire rings and privies are here. (Los Coyotes permits open fires in campgrounds, but bring your own wood and make sure you observe safe campfire practices.)

Park at the camp and begin hiking

southwest up along a small tributary stream that flows north and west into Agua Caliente Creek. You'll follow an old jeep trail up this drainage, still used by daring 4-wheel drivers, gaining more than 500 feet in just over a mile. At the top, you'll meet a better road that runs up the south slope to Hot Springs Mountain. Turn right (west) on this road and climb another 1.6 miles along the ridgeline to the tower. You'll pass through dense forests of black oak, Coulter pine, and white fir, and across sunny meadows dotted in late spring with wildflowers.

The lookout tower, dilapidated and seemingly on its last legs, sits on the west shoulder of the mountain. You can go a bit higher on the ridge by following a faint trail through thick brush and around boulders to the true summit. A flat concrete platform, the foundation of an old radio antenna, caps the summit block.

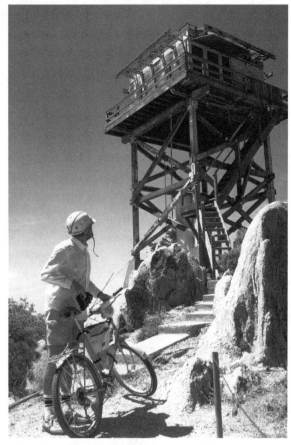

Abandoned fire lookout, Hot Springs Mountain

You may use Nelson's Camp as a base for at least two other interesting trips in the northern part of the reservation. You can go north and east to explore the uppermost reaches of Cougar Canyon. Or you can go north and west down the tributary of Agua Caliente Creek to some pleasant backpacker's campsites about a mile away.

Trip 2: Upper Cougar Canyon

Distance	6.0 miles round trip (to old mines)
Total elevation gain/loss	1400'/1400'
Hiking time	4 hours (round trip)
Recommended map	USGS 7.5-min *Hot Springs Mtn.*
Best times	October though May
Agency	LCIR
Difficulty	★★★

Several challenging mountain-to-desert routes will become apparent if you spend much time exploring the northeastern corner of the Los Coyotes reservation. One such route, still marked as a trail on the *Hot Springs Mtn.* and *Borrego Palm Canyon* topographic maps, descends from upper Cougar Canyon into Indian Canyon and thence into Coyote Canyon. That route, colorfully described in Joseph Smeaton Chase's 1919 book *California Desert Trails*, was worn into a steep mountainside by generations of Native Americans. Other routes to the desert floor—all steep and extremely difficult—are possible via the south ridge of Cougar Canyon, and down tributaries of both Sheep Canyon and Borrego Palm Canyon. The more modest, and still interesting, goal of this trip is to explore a somewhat gentle, but overgrown section of upper Cougar Canyon.

Drive to the intersection in the valley above Middle Fork Borrego Palm Canyon (called San Ignacio on older maps), 6.1 miles past the entrance gate. Find a parking spot nearby off the road. Begin hiking northeast 0.3 mile over a low saddle, where a view opens up of the northern Santa Rosa Mountains and San Jacinto Peak. Descend moderately on eroded jeep tracks, past some springs at 4650 feet, to a 4534-foot knob, 1.5 miles from the start. Continue sharply downhill to a usually wet, south tributary of Cougar Canyon, shaded by live oaks, sycamores, and alders.

The road peters out, but continue north down this tributary, pushing through willow and alder thickets. Occasionally there's a snippet of road above the washed-out bank. When you reach the confluence of Cougar Canyon, you'll find a delightful grove of tall live oaks flanked by bracken and chain ferns. You can make camp on any flat spot nearby (be sure to find a fire-safe place to operate your camp stove).

Downstream about 300 yards, near more live oaks and a few Coulter pines, are the remains of mining equipment including a sluice box. Beyond this point the bottom of Cougar Canyon gets quite steep and rugged, so this is a good place to turn back.

The mine can be the starting point for at least two very rugged trips down to the desert floor:

The first is by way of lower Cougar Canyon. From the mine, go down along Cougar's south wall, detouring around a rocky section with small waterfalls, until you can drop into the canyon bottom at 3400 feet. An easy section follows. Below the 3080-foot contour, the canyon becomes impassable without technical climbing equipment. You must climb south out of the canyon and make a long traverse over a rocky ridge before dropping down to the lower canyon floor. Area D-1, Trip 4 has further details.

The second is by way of an old and mostly overgrown jeep trail from the mine to a 4490-foot peak (not labeled on the topo map) north of the reservation boundary. The pinyon-pine-dotted peak offers up an extraordinary panorama of perhaps a hundred square miles of mountains and desert—with no visible signs of the works of human beings, save an almost imperceptible microwave tower on distant Toro Peak. From there a determined hiker could push toward South Fork Sheep Canyon and descend through that steep and rugged canyon. See Area D-1, Trip 3 for further details.

Horned lizard in Upper Cougar Canyon

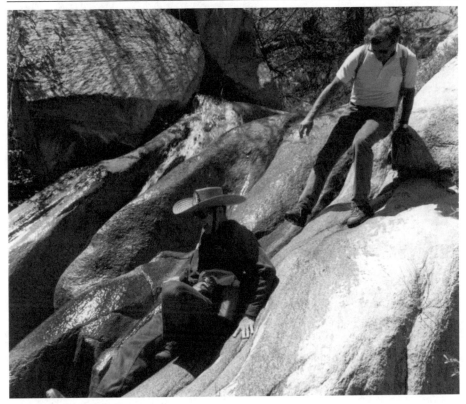

Cougar Canyon below mine

Trip 3: Indian Flats

Distance	0.6 mile round trip
Optional map	USGS 7.5-min *Warner Springs*
Best times	November through July
Agency	CNF/PD
Difficulty	★

What better way to pique a toddler's interest in nature than to introduce him or her to a shallow, lazily flowing river, full of tadpoles and frogs? At Indian Flats Campground, you get to the river in a matter of minutes, and also make use of the usual conveniences of developed campgrounds—such as drinking water, restrooms (no showers), and fire rings—that are nice during a overnight campout with small kids.

This no-reservation campground fills up on most weekends, so it's a good idea to either get there early on a Friday afternoon, or come up on a weekday. From the turnoff along Highway 79, 1.6 miles west of Warner Springs, drive 6.5 miles north on the newly paved Lost Valley Road (formerly Indian Flats Road) to the campground.

From the far end of the campground, simply head downhill over rock slabs and decomposed granite to the bank of the East Fork San Luis Rey River. By turning upstream, you'll very quickly reach a spot where the water twists and turns through an obstacle course of boulders. Since the river doesn't have much drainage up-stream, it seldom flows at a dangerous rate. Rattlesnakes are a more immediate hazard, but only when the weather is warm enough for them to be out and about.

Trip 4: Agua Caliente Creek

Distance	8.0 miles round trip
Total elevation gain/loss	900'/900'
Hiking time	4 hours (round trip)
Recommended map	Cleveland National Forest recreation map
Optional maps	USGS 7.5-min *Warner Springs, Hot Springs Mtn.*
Best times	November though May
Agency	CNF/PD
Difficulty	★★★

Until about two decades ago, the middle reaches of Agua Caliente Creek seldom saw the intrusion of humans. After the Pacific Crest Trail was routed through, it became a favorite resting spot for hikers heading north or south. This is one of only four places in San Diego County where the PCT dips to cross a fairly dependable stream, and the only place where the trail closely follows water for a fair distance. The stream—if not perennial every year—is at least alive from the first rains of fall into early summer.

Begin at the Agua Caliente Creek bridge at mile 36.6 on Highway 79. There's a turnout for parking just west (mile 36.7) and a dirt road slanting over to where the PCT crosses under the highway. Proceed upstream along the cottonwood-shaded creek, first on the left (north) bank, then on the right. In this first mile, the trail goes through Warner Ranch resort property on an easement. Near the Cleveland National Forest boundary (camping allowed past this point), water flows or trickles from a canyon mouth. The trail detours this canyon by swinging to the east and climbing moderately onto gentle, ribbonwood-clothed slopes. After almost 2 miles of somewhat tedious twisting and turning in the chaparral you join the creek again at the 3200-foot contour.

Now the gorgeous scenery begins. In the next mile the trail crosses the stream several times and passes a number of appealing small campsites well up on the bank. Live oaks, sycamores, willows, and alders line the creek. The canyon walls soar several hundred feet on either side—clad in dense chaparral on the southeast side, dotted with sage and yucca on the northwest.

After a final crossing of the creek, the trail doubles back and begins a switchbacking (and not too scenic) ascent northwest toward Lost Valley Road. This is a good place to turn around.

If you want to explore farther upstream, you can do it by boulderhopping and wading. With prior permission to enter Los Coyotes reservation property, starting about a mile ahead, you could go all the way to Nelson's Camp. That would involve some serious scrambling around small waterfalls, possibly swimming across one pool, and doing battle with the ever-present alder branches.

Trip 5: Caliente Wilderness

Distance	12 miles round trip
Total elevation gain/loss	1700'/1700'
Hiking time	7 hours (round trip)
Recommended map	Cleveland National Forest recreation map
Optional maps	USGS 7.5-min *Warner Springs, Hot Springs Mtn.*
Best times	November though May
Agency	CNF/PD
Difficulty	★★★

This section of the Pacific Crest Trail through the Caliente WSA winds along boulder-strewn ridges dotted with Coulter pine, and through small ravines shaded by mini-groves of live oak. In the upper reaches, there's no noise other than the wind, and no signs of man other than the trail itself. Even the skies are quiet; the area seems to be removed from the flight paths of aircraft.

Running the PCT

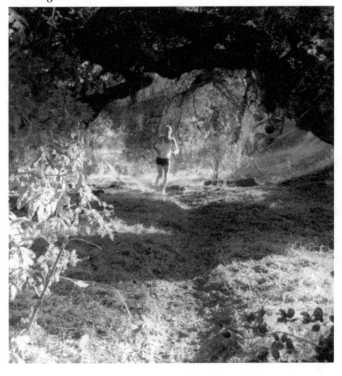

To reach the starting point, drive north on Lost Valley Road from mile 37.0 on Highway 79. After 4.6 miles of winding road, you'll come to a road summit and the intersection of a gated, abandoned dirt road. Park in the limited space provided, and walk up this abandoned road 0.5 mile to the point where the PCT joins from the right. Continue uphill on the old roadbed, somewhat monotonously, a mile farther to the point where the PCT tread diverges right. Make the right turn (by staying left you would descend to a seasonal spring).

The scenery improves with every step now. You wind up through scattered Coulter pines and picturesque granitic outcrops, with nice views of Lake Henshaw and the grasslands surrounding it. You lose that view as you pass north of peak 5212 and contour around the head of a ravine.

The trail continues to climb moderately and winds around another ravine, this just south of a knob also labeled 5212 feet. It then descends slightly to cross a saddle and resumes climbing on the south side of a hill. From this hill there's a wonderful vista into Agua Caliente Creek and across to the north slope of Hot Springs Mountain. From nearly every vantage point but this, Hot Springs Mountain looks like an inconspicuous bump on a ridge, but from here it looks decidedly massive. Black oaks cluster along the small drainages along its flank, flashing gold in the fall season.

Next the trail bends north and contours, with small ups and downs, along the east side of the ridge containing peak 5412. In late April and early May, these slopes are tinted pink with the blossoms of manzanita, and blue and white with blooming ceanothus. A dozen exotic fragrances scent the air. The Coulter pines are joined by live oaks and an occasional black oak.

At a point east of peak 5412, you'll see below and to the east a grassy flat, filled with Coulter pines and black oaks, along an upper tributary of Agua Caliente Creek. This is a perfect place for a midday picnic, and even better for an overnight stay. Leave the trail at any point where the brush thins, and descend cross-country about 0.2 mile, losing 150 feet, to the seasonal creek. Water trickles through here until about June after a normal wet season.

Farther north, the Pacific Crest Trail winds over a stretch of less interesting chaparral country. This hidden glade, then, is a good place to turn around.

Boulders and Coulter pines beside the Pacific Crest Trail

Area M-4 Santa Ysabel Creek

Arising on the west slope of the Volcan Mountains, Santa Ysabel Creek slides through Santa Ysabel Valley and soon enters the Lake Sutherland reservoir, northeast of Ramona. Once below the dam, water in the creek trickles or tumbles (depending on the season) down a steep, rocky, 5-mile-long gorge, and emerges upon the flatter terrain of Pamo Valley.

The following two hikes, on Cleveland National Forest lands, explore this pristine and isolated region. Save for the graded Black Canyon and Sutherland Dam roads, and a couple of primitive old truck trails, there's not a single dwelling to be seen in the Santa Ysabel gorge and its principal tributary, Black Canyon.

Fifteen or twenty years ago, this lightly patrolled area was a haven for rowdy, gun-slinging alcoholics, but a prohibition on target shooting helped put an end to that. In time, management of the area may fall under the auspices of the San Dieguito River Park and perhaps visitor facilities will be built. For now, it is national forest land, and you'll need to display a National Forest Adventure Pass if you park your car here.

Area M-4: Santa Ysabel Creek

Trip 1: Black Canyon

Distance	2.0 miles
Total elevation gain/loss	200'/200'
Hiking time	1¹/₂ hours
Optional map	USGS 7.5-min *Ramona, Mesa Grande*
Best times	November through June
Agency	CNF/PD
Difficulty	★★

In Black Canyon water has amply illustrated its mindless yet artistic ability to sculpt stone. Every once in a great while, a gush of sediment-laden water tears through the canyon bottom, carving and polishing the bedrock slabs, drilling potholes ever deeper, toppling trees, and pushing rounded boulders downstream. In a normal winter or spring season, the stream of water in Black Canyon is quite placid: it happily splashes over small waterfalls, pauses in pools, slides along inclined slabs, and finds hidden passages beneath immense boulders.

This short little ramble up along

Black Canyon's lower end is consistently enchanting, but it is no mere stroll. Rock scrambling is required. Although kids are often adept at such moves, they must be watched carefully and perhaps helped at a couple of spots. The most serious hazard is the slippery surfaces of rocks at or near the stream.

To reach the starting point, drive east from Ramona on Highway 78 and turn north on Magnolia Avenue. Magnolia soon becomes Black Canyon Road, and later becomes a narrow, twisting, graded dirt road. At 7.3 miles from Highway 78, just short of an old metal bridge over Santa Ysabel

Black Canyon cascade

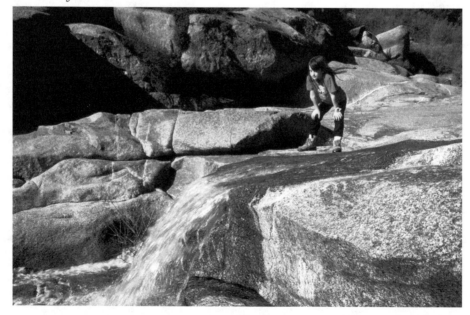

Creek, you meet the road coming down from Sutherland Dam. (This road, which is rough and rocky for 1 mile between here and Sutherland Dam and paved south of there, connects to Highway 78. This is an alternate route for your drive into or out of the area.)

Turn left over the bridge and continue 200 yards on Black Canyon Road to a junction with a gated, descending road—the Santa Ysabel Truck Trail. Park at the top, along the road shoulder.

Walk 0.3 mile down the deteriorating macadam surface of the descending road. This once was the entrance to the Black Canyon Campground, closed nearly two decades ago. At the bottom, the road fords Black Canyon and doubles back to contour along the north slope of the Santa Ysabel gorge, heading circuitously toward Pamo Valley. Don't cross the ford but stay right, following the oak-shaded floodplain on the south side of Black Canyon's creek.

Noting traces of the old campground facilities, continue another 0.3 mile to where the canyon narrows and scrambling begins. Perhaps 20 to 40 minutes later, depending on how much time you wish to dawdle amid the fine scenery, you'll come to a wide, shallow pool fed by a 20-foot waterfall. Black Canyon Road lies on the slope immediately above. Climb up to it and return to your car by walking along the road.

Trip 2: Black Canyon to Pamo Valley

Distance	4.9 miles	
Total elevation gain/loss	450'/1200'	
Hiking time	2^1/$_2$ hours	
Optional maps	USGS 7.5-min *Ramona, Mesa Grande*	
Best times	November through April	
Agencies	CNF/PD, SDRP	
Difficulty	★★	

This easy-going, mostly downhill walk on the Santa Ysabel Truck Trail is fine for a cool day, but a potentially hot and sweaty affair during the warmer half of the year. You follow the course of the future Coast to Crest Trail, meandering downhill and sometimes uphill on shadeless south- and west-facing slopes blanketed in chamise and other drought-resistant forms of chaparral. The truck trail may or may not be open to the 4-wheel-drive vehicles—if so it carries only an occasional vehicle.

Set up a car shuttle in advance by leaving one car at the finish, along Pamo Road, 1.5 mile north of its crossing over Santa Ysabel Creek. Take the other vehicle to the trailhead described in Trip 1 above. Or, with a willing driver, you can arrange to be a dropped off and later picked up. The San Dieguito River Park has sponsored hikes along this route (starting from Lake Sutherland) that involve a shuttle by charter bus.

As in Trip 1, start at Black Canyon Road and descend into Black Canyon. Step over or wade across the Black Canyon stream by way of the concrete ford (but not if the water is too deep and swift). Gradual ups and downs and many twists and turns on the truck trail take you farther and farther away from Santa Ysabel Creek. At 3.3 miles, a live-oak shaded ravine spreads a dense pool of shade across the trail. Shortly thereafter, on a ridgeline at 3.5 miles, a road comes down-ridge from the right. It leads upward toward Black Mountain, a former fire-lookout site, nearly 6 miles away. Your course continues downhill to Pamo Road, a crooked 1.4 miles away.

Santa Ysabel Creek at Pamo Valley

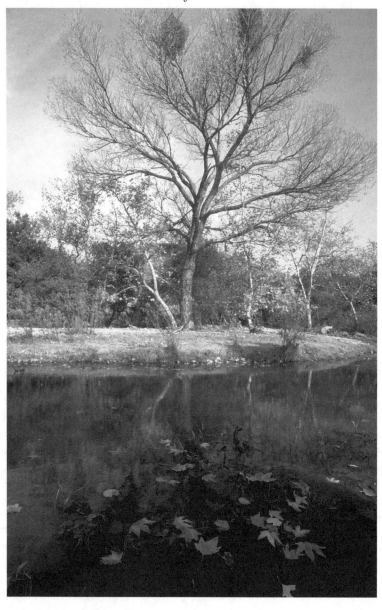

Area M-5: Upper San Diego River

The San Diego River and its upper tributaries drain the pastoral valleys and forested hillsides around Julian, and the rugged western slopes of the Cuyamaca Mountains. The water flows generally southwest through V-shaped canyons, and eventually reaches El Capitan Reservoir, not far from the East County suburbs. Quite frequently in the higher country, the water encounters resistant layers in the underlying igneous and metamorphic rocks. In several places it tumbles over cataracts up to a hundred feet high. The grinding of stones trapped in pockets below these falls has created deep pools, or "punchbowls."

Highways and paved roads bypass most of the upper San Diego River area, making it seem more remote that it really is. There are plenty of unpaved roads—but some, with locked gates, cross private land with no public easement. Cleveland National Forest encompasses most of the area, but several large private properties, or inholdings, exist within the forest boundaries.

Because of the mix of public and private ownership, access to some of the more interesting spots in the canyons can be problematical. As a general guide to where you can and can't go, consult the Cleveland National Forest recreation map. Green tinted areas are national forest lands open to the public, while the white areas are private lands. You are allowed to drive or hike any public road going through private property, as long as you don't stray from the road. Aside from public easements like this, don't trespass on private land (unless you've obtained the landowner's permission first).

The following field-tested trips will take you to some of San Diego County's most spectacular and hidden spots—by legal routes. If you're planning to stay out overnight, either car-camping or backpacking, you'll need a remote camping permit. Obtain one in advance from any forest service office or fire station.

Trip 1: Inaja Trail

Distance	0.5 mile
Total elevation gain/loss	100'/100'
Hiking time	20 minutes
Optional map	USGS 7.5-min *Santa Ysabel*
Best times	All year
Agency	CNF/PD
Difficulty	★

The Inaja Trail, one of four trails in San Diego County to have earned the appellation "National Recreation Trail," begins at the Inaja Picnic Area along State Highway 78/79, just 1 mile east of Santa Ysabel and 6 miles west of Julian. The picnic area memorializes 11 firefighters who lost their lives in the San Diego River can-

157

Area M-5: Upper San Diego River

yon while battling the 60,000-acre Inaja Fire in 1956.

An excellent trail brochure, available at the trailhead, gives information about the typical live oak-chaparral vegetation seen here and elsewhere in the upper foothills of San Diego County. An overlook at midpoint in the trail gives a good view down the linear canyon of the San Diego River. At 3440 feet elevation, this overlook is often just above a temperature inversion layer that traps cooler, moist air below. On some mornings, you'll find the canyon hidden by a cottony blanket of fog, while neighboring peaks and ridges stand like islands in clear air.

Out along the north side of the trail your gaze takes in the fertile Santa Ysabel Valley, the rolling hills of Mesa Grande, and the dark, brooding Volcan Mountains.

Trip 2: San Diego River

Distance	1.0 to 6.4 miles round trip
Total elevation gain/loss	1300'/1300' (maximum)
Hiking time	Up to 8 hours
Recommended maps	Cleveland National Forest recreation map; USGS 7.5-min *Santa Ysabel*
Best times	November through May
Agency	CNF/PD
Difficulty	★★ to ★★★★

A trip down the upper San Diego River canyon in early spring is a true adventure. Runoff from winter storms fills the riverbed with a silvery band of water. New leaves and gaily colored wildflowers brighten the banks as well as the slopes. The stream drops abruptly several times over rock precipices as much as a hundred feet high.

Bedrock *morteros* and *metates* along the river, especially near groves of oaks, attest to frequent use of the canyon by Native Americans for hundreds of years. Contemporary human usage pales by comparison; only an occasional hiker, backpacker, or hunter penetrates these canyon depths today.

Sturdy boots and a patient, cautious attitude are essential for this trip. By April or May, when hungry and irritable rattlesnakes emerge from their wintertime burrows, you'll have to be extra vigilant. Long pants are recommended, as are small clippers to prune back the branches of poison oak in a few tight spots. If you're traveling with a heavy or awkward pack, bring a 30-foot length of cord to assist in lowering it over rock faces as you detour around the waterfalls. Avoid the canyon after intense storms, when high water levels may make stream crossings difficult or dangerous. Get an early start if you are planning to thoroughly explore the canyon.

You begin at Inaja Picnic Area, where you descend a precipitous slope south of the restrooms into the canyon's oak-shaded floor, a short distance below. Turn down-canyon, and at 0.5 mile arrive at the first falls, a set of two, each about 50 feet high. To get by, you'll probably need to traverse through brush and over tilted rock slabs on the right (west) side. If you don't like this dicey maneuver, go no further and turn back. You will encounter nothing but long stretches of boulder hopping and bush dodging ahead.

After a total of 3.2 miles and much effort, you'll come upon the lip of a 100-

foot-high waterfall (1950-foot elevation)— the highest falls on the San Diego River. The water tumbles over a rock face and collects in a shallow pool perhaps 60 feet across. This destination is about as far as it is prudent to go in a full day. Remember that the trip back is all uphill and will almost certainly take longer than the trip down.

More falls and pools lie along the river below the highest waterfall. These can be visited by means of a point-to-point traverse of the canyon, ending near Cedar Creek Falls or San Diego Country Estates. Details on this "five-star" hike are given in previous editions of this book.

The San Diego River canyon

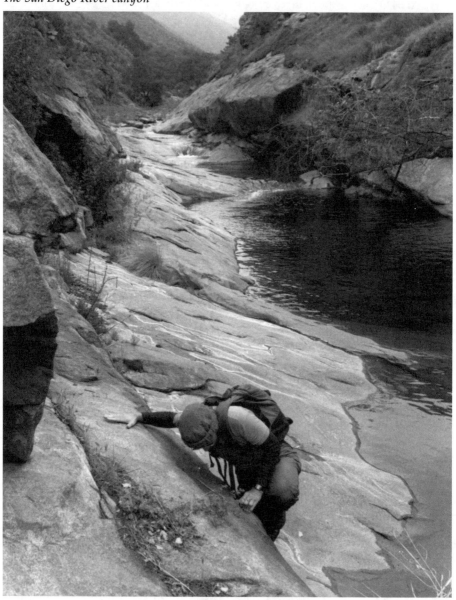

Trip 3: Cedar Creek Falls

Distance	4.5 miles round trip
Total elevation gain/loss	1200'/1200'
Hiking time	2^1/2 hours (round trip)
Recommended map	Cleveland National Forest recreation map
Optional maps	USGS 7.5-min *Santa Ysabel, Tule Springs*
Best times	November through June
Agency	CNF/PD
Difficulty	★★

Here's one of San Diego County's hidden treasures, tucked back in a tributary of the upper San Diego River, and accessible (legally) only by a circuitous drive down a long dirt road and a hike on an abandoned road. Before the construction of El Capitan Dam in the early '30s, the falls were a popular destination for Sunday outings, and could be reached relatively easily on an auto road up the San Diego River valley from Lakeside.

From the coast, drive east through Ramona toward Santa Ysabel and Julian. Six miles east of Santa Ysabel and 1 mile short of (west of) Julian, turn south on Pine Hills Road. After 1.5 miles, bear right on Eagle Peak Road. After 1.4 more miles, veer right again, staying on Eagle Peak Road. Now you face 8.2 miles of progressively poorer road, parts of which could become slippery and muddy in wet weather. In the end, you'll come to a 4-way junction of roads (called "Saddleback" on the topo map) and a forest-service sign announcing the old road—now a riding and hiking trail—toward the falls.

As you head downhill on foot, look up the canyon in the north to see Mildred Falls, arguably San Diego County's highest at more than 100 feet. Unfortunately, it's often little more than a dark stain on an orange-tinted cliff. In flood, however, it is truly an awesome sight.

The road winds farther west, offering a splendid view of the upper San Diego River canyon, then turns south on a long descent to the river bed. At 1.4 miles (1270'), take the spur road that goes left (southeast) over a low saddle into the Cedar Creek drainage. Descend to the bank of the creek and continue following the old road and trail down to the shallow, reflecting pool at the brink of the falls. Be extremely cautious here, as the rock is very slippery. Long-time San Diego hiker Uel Fisk remembers quite vividly watching one of his classmates fall to her death from this brink in 1926.

From a ridge on the right side, it's possible to admire the 90-foot-high cascade and the cottonwood-framed punchbowl at the bottom—some 50 feet across and 20 feet deep. After heavy rains, water thunders over the precipice, but by late summer the falls merely whisper. Many people obviously make the steep traverse down to the pool at the bottom, though Forest Service personnel advise against it.

There are other routes to the falls via the mouth of Cedar Creek canyon, but they necessitate crossing property owned by the Helix Water District (land below the 995-foot contour in the San Diego River drainage.) The Forest Service says that permission must be obtained from the landowner to cross this land.

Cedar Creek Falls

When you've had your fill of the almost overwhelming natural beauty, return to your starting point the same way. If the spirit moves you, you can try this more adventurous, difficult route on the return: From the top of the falls, walk east along the north bank of Cedar Creek about 0.5 mile until the canyon walls close in. There you'll be forced into the creekbed. After about two hours (about 1.2 miles) of boulder-hopping, bushwhacking, and wading through a beautiful and isolated stretch of canyon, Cedar Creek Road will lie above you on the left. Climb north up the slope to Cedar Creek Road and follow it a short distance up to Saddleback, your starting point.

Trip 4: Three Sisters Waterfalls

Distance	4.0 miles round trip
Total elevation gain/loss	1000'/1000'
Hiking time	3 hours (round trip)
Recommended maps	Cleveland National Forest recreation map; USGS 7.5-min *Tule Springs*
Best times	November through June
Agency	CNF/PD
Difficulty	★★★

This triple set of waterfalls in Boulder Creek, dubbed the "Three Sisters," is an amazing San Diego County feature not many have seen. In full flood these cascades put on a show reminiscent of Yosemite's show stoppers—except at a reduced scale. Since some of the upstream drainage of Boulder Creek comes from

Cuyamaca Reservoir, regulation of water there can affect the flow over the falls. During late summer and early fall, there may be almost none.

Previous editions of this book described a rough route chosen to avoid a section of private land that offered an easier way. Now, that awkward approach is unnecessary. In 1997 the Forest Service purchased 922 acres east of Eagle Peak from the Rutherford family, who had used this land for decades for cattle grazing. The approach to the falls over this formerly posted land is easier, but the final plunge down to the falls (and subsequent ascent) remains difficult.

The starting point is reached most easily via Pine Hills Road, Eagle Peak Road, and Boulder Creek Road near Julian (see Trip 3 above). At the point where Eagle Peak Road forks to the right a second time, stay left (south). At the next intersection make a sharp right on Boulder Creek Road. Go south on Boulder Creek Road for 8 miles (pavement ends in 3 miles) to a hairpin turn where Cedar Creek Road joins from the west. Park there, taking care not to block traffic. You can also reach this intersection by driving 13.0 miles north on Boulder Creek Road (less than half paved) from Oak Grove Drive in Descanso.

From the intersection, follow the remains of an old ranch road (not Cedar Creek Road) due west for 0.7 mile to a saddle, where an old mining road on the left slants southeast and descends into Sheep Camp Creek. (Just beyond this saddle, a large and isolated Engelmann oak casts semishade upon an inviting patch of spring-green grass—a beautiful, airy spot for a picnic. When the falls are in flood, you can easily hear them from here.)

Descend southwest on the mining road for 0.4 mile, cross Sheep Camp Creek, and switch back onto a narrow path cut into the south slope. After about 0.3 mile, the trail veers sharply left and passes over a saddle in the divide between Sheep Camp Creek and Boulder Creek. Down below, in the **V**-shaped gorge of Boulder Creek, you'll both see and hear the falls. If you're backpacking, this saddle makes a good campsite, especially if you can't handle packing your gear down the precipitous slope ahead.

Next, you negotiate an abrupt drop of 500 vertical feet on a primitive trail cut by hikers' footsteps into the dense, low-growing chaparral. At the bottom you can either forge a path through the brush along the left side of the creek, or rock hop and wade toward the falls. Great masses of poison oak, intermixed with wild grape vines, lie along the banks. Be very cautious of slippery rocks.

When you reach the base of the waterfalls, all the previous trouble will have been worth it. The "middle sister" is impressive, with water sliding 50 feet down a smooth channel worn in the bedrock into a kidney-shaped pool about 80 feet long and at least 10 feet deep. Watch your footing—it's deceptively easy to slip on the smooth rock and perhaps be seriously injured. It's difficult and dangerous to climb up to the uppermost fall, although if you're agile it's possible to reach it by climbing a narrow path on the right side.

A circular feature worn in the bed of Boulder Creek called the Devils Punch Bowl lies 0.6 mile upstream from the falls. You can work your way toward it on public land, but the punchbowl itself lies on private property.

Trip 5: Eagle Peak

Distance	4.2 miles (round trip)
Total elevation gain/loss	1200'/1200'
Hiking time	3 hours (round trip)
Recommended maps	Cleveland National Forest recreation map; USGS 7.5-min *Tule Springs*
Best times	November through May
Agency	CNF/PD
Difficulty	★★★

Standing tall amid lesser bumps on the west slope of the Cuyamaca Mountains, Eagle Peak presides over a panoramic view of the island-dimpled ocean, scattered parts of urban and suburban San Diego, and the wall of mountains—dominated by Cuyamaca Peak—in the east. Hawks and golden eagles can sometimes be seen soaring on updrafts overhead.

Start, as in Trip 4 above, by walking due west from Boulder Creek Road on the old dirt road through former Rutherford ranch property. Pass over the saddle with the solitary Engelmann oak at 0.7 mile, climb along a brushy hillside for another 0.5 mile, then start descending, still heading west, into a vale shaded by live oaks. After 0.4 mile of descent on an increasingly poor old road/trail, you'll notice a shallow, shady draw to the left (on ahead lies an old stock pond, and possible sites for trail camping). Leave the trail at this point and work your way southwest, through brush and trees and over boulders, to the ridge some 300 vertical feet above. Once atop the boulder-strewn ridgeline, take note of the heart-stopping dropoff to the south. Peering over the edge, you look down upon a silvery thread of water making its way amid the tree-lined gorge of Boulder Creek.

Eagle Peak's true summit, with a hiker's register on it, lies about 0.2 mile farther up the ridge, beyond a couple of false summits. After you've had your fill of the view, return the same way.

Area M-6: Julian

The town of Julian enjoys a reputation far wider than its modest size would seem to call for. Tourists come in droves to this gold-mining-boom-town-turned-apple-growing-center to tour its quaint museums, buy an apple pie, bend an elbow at the soda fountain, and, of course, to walk in the pine-scented woods. Actually there isn't too much woods-walking available close to town. Beyond the little grid of streets, east of town, you can find the path leading to the site of the old Washington Mine; otherwise the land all around is private.

Hiking opportunities multiply if you drive some distance out of town. Cuyamaca Rancho State Park and the Laguna Mountain Recreation Area (Areas M-7 and M-8 in this book) offer a plethora of trails. Somewhat closer is William Heise County Park, with its small network of trails in a superb forested setting; the Ban-

ner Toll Road, a historic wagon road going through a parcel of BLM land; and the Volcan Mountain Wilderness Preserve, a new San Diego County open-space park. All of these are profiled in the trips below.

Some years hence, a greatly expanded Volcan Mountain Preserve should stretch across much of the Volcan Mountains north of Julian, encompassing the uppermost reaches of the Santa Ysabel Creek watershed. This area will be a key acquisition for the emerging San Dieguito River Park, which will ultimately consist of a series of linked parks and greenways stretching 50 miles from the mouth of the San Dieguito River at Del Mar to the Volcan Mountains. Considered one of the most ambitious and innovative land-use projects in the country, the park will comprise a significant fraction of the entire watershed of the San Dieguito River and its main tributary, Santa Ysabel Creek.

Trip 1: William Heise County Park

Distance	1- to 3-mile hikes
Recommended map	William Heise County Park map/brochure
Optional map	USGS 7.5-min *Julian*
Best times	All year
Agency	SDCP
Difficulty	★ to ★★

At Heise Park you can find your quintessential walk in the pine woods. The park is located in one of the most beautiful and unspoiled pockets of undeveloped land around Julian, and is just large

enough to contain a significant network of footpaths.

About one-tenth of the park is devoted to meticulously maintained camping and picnic areas. These lie along the

Area M-6: Julian

thickly wooded bottomlands of Cedar Creek and its upper tributaries. The surrounding area is a virtual wilderness laced with about 7 miles of loop trails. Heise Park is also the northern terminus of the outstanding Kelly Ditch Trail, which leads into Cuyamaca Rancho State Park (Area M-7, Trip 1).

The Cedar Trail and the self-guiding Nature Trail, each a mile in length, stay beneath a shady canopy of oaks, pines, and cedars. The Manzanita and Canyon Oak trails, on the other hand, climb up along steep slopes clothed with dense chaparral; in some places, the manzanita grows to 10 feet or more in height, enclosing you in a tangled net of limbs and leaves.

Glenn's View lies on a windswept ridgeline in the northeast corner of the park. The view here is similar to, but more inclusive than, that enjoyed by motorists at Inspiration Point, a half mile below on Highway 79. To the south you can look over a rolling expanse of timbered hills toward the summits of the Cuyamaca and Laguna mountains. Eastward, the Anza-Borrego Desert and the Salton Sea shimmer in the distance. On late-summer after-

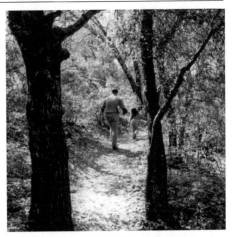

Oak-shaded trail in Heise Park

noons, when conditions are propitious, you can watch massive thunderheads roil in as moist air flowing across the desert from the Gulf of California rises over the mountains.

The well-marked turnoff to Heise Park is one mile west of Julian on Highway 78/79. Signs direct you south on Pine Hills Road to Frisius Drive, then east on Frisius to the park entrance.

Trip 2: Old Banner Toll Road

Distance	2.5 miles round trip
Total elevation gain/loss	700'/700'
Hiking time	1¹/₂ hours
Optional map	USGS 7.5-min *Julian*
Best times	October through June
Agency	BLM/EC
Difficulty	★★

Honeycombed hillsides and bits and pieces of rusted equipment—that is the legacy left behind by Julian's gold-mining heyday over a century ago. Although a few mines continue to be worked sporadically today, most have long been abandoned. For a look at one of the first mines to be

discovered (1870) and one of the last to be extensively worked, try this short hike down the Old Banner Toll Road.

Drive 1 mile east of Julian on Highway 78, then turn right at Whispering Pines Road. Immediately after, make a sharp right, then a left to connect with

Woodland Road. After 0.4 mile on Wood-land Road, go left at a fork (the right fork leads to a locked gate) and proceed another 0.1 mile to the end of the pavement. Park here, off the roadway.

On foot now, take the dirt road that curves steeply downward to the left (gen-erally east). This is one of the two roads down Banner Canyon from Julian to Ban-ner shown on a circa-1910 topographic map of the area. Nature has not been kind to this old road in recent years. Violent storms over the past several winters have caused deep washouts across its bed. As tracks show, only foot travelers, horses, coyotes, and a few intrepid motorcyclists come this way today.

Below you is the modern road through Banner Canyon—Highway 78. It appears only slightly less twisting than the road you're on, but offers a more gradual—if longer—descent to the town of Banner. Below Highway 78, near the very bottom of the canyon, there once existed even ear-lier routes of travel between Julian and Banner. The earliest was a "skid road" so steep that a driver descending it would have to drag an uprooted tree behind his wagon to provide enough braking power.

The linear shape of Banner Canyon is due to repeated ruptures along the Elsinore Fault. This splinter fault of the San Andreas is the most extensive fault system in San Diego County, and is believed ca-pable of causing a major earthquake. Look across the canyon to see the fault's surface trace, which cuts low across the north wall, and also notice how some of the ravines exhibit a dogleg or offset pattern due to horizontal movements.

Old mine shafts pierce the earth on the steep slopes above and below you, but most are concealed by thick chaparral. At about 1 mile, the Warlock Mine, with its processing mill, comes into view.

The mine suspended operations in 1957 and lies in a state of advanced dilapi-dation. It's worth a look around though. You'll find a relatively intact ball mill, the superintendent's formerly cozy cottage with its fine view, and other buildings in a state of collapse. In 1962 the mine's shafts were declared a radioactive fallout shelter for 222 people by the Civil Defense Com-mission and stocked accordingly with emergency provisions. A cave-in two years later ended its usefulness in that regard. Tread carefully among the ruins, and don't enter the mine openings.

Beyond the Warlock Mine, Old Ban-ner Toll Road runs into private property, so it's best to turn back after visiting the mine.

Trip 3: Volcan Mountain

Distance	3.2 miles round trip (to gate)
Total elevation gain/loss	800'/800'
Hiking time	2 hours (round trip)
Optional map	USGS 7.5-min *Julian*
Best times	October through June
Agency	SDCP
Difficulty	★★

Named by early Spanish or Mexican travelers for its dubious resemblance to a volcano, Volcan Mountain (called the "Volcan Mountains" on topographic maps) is really a fault-block mountain range, es-sentially no different from any other ma-jor component of the Peninsular Ranges. Two faults—the Elsinore and the Earthquake Valley—bracket the range on the southwest and northeast sides respectively.

Crowned with magnificent forests of oak, pine and cedar, the mountain has been privately owned and off-limits to public access for more than a century. In the early 1990s the county acquired approximately 800 acres on the southwest slope, and more recent acquisitions have brought the total up to 2325 acres. Perhaps soon (pending completion of a county management plan for the area) it will be possible to walk all the way up to "Volcan" peak, the southernmost of several knolls along the crest of the range. Already it's possible to do that, but only if you participate in one of the hikes led by San Diego County Parks rangers or docents.

A single trail (old jeep road) leads from the edge of the apple orchards north of Julian to the top. Park alongside Farmer Road, 200 yards north of Wynola Road, and walk east along a dirt road marked by a sign indicating the Volcan Mountain Wilderness Preserve. After 0.2 mile, you'll pass a carved entry designed by noted Julian artist James Hubbell, and stonework including an open-air "kiva" for use during interpretive programs. The Elsinore Fault, a major splinter of the San Andreas, passes almost directly under this spot.

On the old jeep road now, you swing north, round a horseshoe bend, and continue climbing in earnest along a rounded ridgeline leading toward Volcan peak. Along the ridge, wind-rippled expanses of grassland alternate with dense copses of live oak, and the view expands to include the townsite of Julian, its "suburb" of Whispering Pines, and the dusky Cuyamaca Mountains to the south.

At 1.4 miles beyond the Volcan Mountain Preserve gateway, you come to a locked gate and must turn back. Before heading back, enjoy watching birds of prey soaring over the grassy slopes hereabouts, and admire the view in the northwest of rolling hills and wooded hollows on the upper Santa Ysabel Creek drainage.

Area M-7: Cuyamaca Mountains

Who among those unfamiliar with Southern California would believe that such beautiful forests could exist less than 40 miles from San Diego Bay? Who would believe the intensity of the fall and spring color? Who would believe that snow can blanket the Cuyamaca Mountains, while at the same time the coastal area bakes in subtropical sunshine?

This knowledge is not lost among San Diego hikers. The Cuyamaca Mountains are probably the most popular place to hike in San Diego County. Cuyamaca Rancho State Park, one of California's largest state parks, has over 100 miles of trails and old fire roads for hiking. Anyone in San Diego willing to spend barely an hour driving up there can easily escape the pressures of the city.

The Cuyamacas have attracted humans for at least 7000 years. Until the arrival of Europeans, bands of Native Americans migrated to higher elevations such as these every summer. Then, as now, game and certain basic vegetable foodstuffs, such as acorns, were plentiful. The Indians called the area *Ah-ha-Kwe-ah-mac*, variously translated as "the place where it rains," and "rain yonder," in reference to the relatively wet climate at higher elevations—about 35 inches of precipitation a year. Dozens of archaeological sites have been identified within the park. As you explore, you'll probably discover some of the many bedrock milling sites (mortars or *morteros*) that were a common feature around springs and resting areas.

In 1845 the area became a Mexican land grant, Rancho Cuyamaca. The promise of harvesting timber from the rancho was never fulfilled, and it was not until 1855 that the first non-Indian, James Lassator, settled here.

Gold was discovered in the hills around Julian and along the north edge of the Cuyamacas in the 1860s, and within a few years the influx of prospectors and miners had displaced the remaining native people. A prospect near the shoreline of today's Cuyamaca Reservoir eventually became southern California's most productive gold mine, the Stonewall Mine.

After the gold boom, the old rancho property changed hands several times until it was purchased by the state in 1933 for use as a park. With subsequent additions, today's Cuyamaca Rancho State Park now includes nearly 30,000 acres, of which about 13,000 acres have been set aside as state wilderness.

The backbone of the Cuyamaca Mountains consists of a chain of forested peaks—North, Middle, and Cuyamaca—that runs north to south. Most of North Peak is in private ownership, while Middle Peak and Cuyamaca Peak lie along the state park's west boundary. Lower and drier, chaparral-covered peaks—like Stonewall and Oakzanita—lie along the park's eastern edge.

The highest ridges are crowned with forests of live and black oak, incense-cedar, white fir, and four varieties of pine—Coulter, sugar, ponderosa, and Jeffrey. Below that are broad, treeless mesas and valley bottoms, awash in tall grasses. Sycamore, alder, and willow cling to the major watercourses. Still lower are boulder-strewn foothills densely covered with chaparral.

For better and for worse, the park is split asunder by a rather heavily trafficked (on weekends, at least) road—Highway 79. This route permits fast access from either Interstate 8 on the south or from the Julian area on the north. Since many of the trails depart from turnouts along the highway and head directly into park's back areas, you can quickly get away from traffic noise—and most people, too.

Area M-7: Cuyamaca Mountains

The park's camping and picnic areas include Green Valley and Paso Picacho, popular among families; and Los Caballos and Los Vaqueros, which cater to equestrians. You'll find interpretive displays at Paso Picacho and in the Indian Museum next to park headquarters. The Stonewall Mine site features some old relics of the mining days. Ranger-led walks, and lectures on the geology, wildlife, and history of the area are offered on most weekends.

Backpacking within the park is rewarding, but somewhat limited. Only two trail campgrounds in the park serve hikers (and also horse riders): Arroyo Seco and Granite Spring. Both are available on a first-come-first-served basis by pre-registration at the park headquarters, Green Valley, or Paso Picacho. Some "environmental" (walk-in) sites are also available near Paso Picacho. Outside of these designated spots trail camping is not allowed; however, the state park shares its east and west borders with Cleveland National Forest, where remote camping (by permit) is allowed.

Pure water gushes from several springs in the park, but most have never undergone the necessary, expensive tests that would certify them as officially "potable."

Check with the rangers first, or plan on carrying your own water while on the trails.

The 17 trips described below hardly exhaust all possibilities. One possible trip intentionally not described in this book is a visit to the Cuyamaca cypress groves. The Cuyamaca cypress, recognized as one of the rarest trees in the world, has retreated to a small area straddling the park boundary. The park rangers may be able to help you find these trees if you express an interest in seeing them.

The Cuyamaca Mountains offer special opportunities for two other modes of travel: mountain bicycling and cross-country skiing. You can mountain bike any of the park's qualifying fire roads, but none of the trails. Qualifying roads are marked on the current Cuyamaca Rancho State Park map and brochure. The hiking trips below that are also entirely suitable for mountain biking are duly noted with a bike-wheel icon. Ski touring is possible on several roads and wide trails at higher elevations, but good conditions are fairly rare. When the cold, wet storms of winter strike—perhaps two or three times a year—don't hesitate to grab your skis and take off at the first sign of clearing skies.

Trip 1: Kelly Ditch Trail

Distance	5.5 miles
Total elevation gain/loss	1000'/1600'
Hiking time	4 hours
Recommended map	Cuyamaca Rancho State Park map/brochure
Optional maps	USGS 7.5-min *Cuyamaca Peak, Julian*
Best times	All year
Agency	CRSP
Difficulty	★★★

The Kelly Ditch Trail, completed in 1985, is perhaps the most beautiful pathway yet built in the Cuyamaca-Julian area. This hiking/horse trail is routed partly along a century-old diversion ditch. You'll

also tread over dim traces of "skid roads" where freshly-cut logs were slid down off the mountain ridges to serve as lumber and fuel for the mines and boom towns of Julian's gold rush era.

Hiking the trail is rewarding in any season, but it's hard to beat the fall-color season which reaches its peak around late October. By then the black oaks exhibit full crowns of crispy, golden leaves, and fat, glossy acorns litter the ground. Crimson squaw bush and poison oak leaves show their stuff amid the glades of russet-colored bracken fern.

The Kelly Ditch Trail is best hiked one-way, with the aid of a car shuttle or a drop-off-and-pick-up arrangement. The easier (mostly downhill) direction is south to north—Cuyamaca Reservoir to William Heise County Park. The starting point is on Highway 79, 8.3 miles south of Julian, near the intersection of Engineers Road and Highway 79. The trail ends at a parking lot just inside William Heise County Park (see Area M-6, Trip 1 for driving directions).

Pick up the trail west of Engineers Road and just north of where Highway 79 crosses the low dam impounding the waters of Cuyamaca Reservoir. In the first mile you'll travel in, or on the rim of, the remnant Kelly Ditch, constructed by pick and shovel labor more than a century ago. Its purpose was to divert runoff from the south slope of North Peak into the then-new reservoir. Poison oak grows alongside the trail—take care to avoid contact with it.

After one mile the trail climbs abruptly out of the ditch, veers north through a sun-struck patch of chaparral, and then crosses paved Engineers Road. You pass a spring-fed horse trough, and continue a short distance to join a disused dirt road. Turn right and follow the road's gentle uphill course around the west slope of North Peak. You'll stroll past a few ancient sugar pines, and enter a delightful, parklike meadow, dotted with black oaks and carpeted by bracken ferns. On the clearest days, blue sky meets the blue Pacific horizon more than a hundred miles to the west.

At the next fork (about 2.5 miles from the start), you're directed left across a sunny bowl, and then up to a low ridge shaded by live oaks, black oaks, Coulter pines, incense cedars, and white firs. From

Ranger-led bird watch in Cuyamaca Rancho State Park

this point, the highest elevation of the hike, a long series of switchbacks leads you steadily downward (and north) to a small stream—a tributary of Cedar Creek—fringed with ferns and wild berries.

Past the creek, the trail goes up a steep ravine evidently cut deeply by some agent other than running water. This is the remnant of one of the skid roads. After a 120-foot gain, the trail tops a saddle and joins a dirt road. You descend to a second creek (the main fork of Cedar Creek), cross a meadow beyond, and pick up the last link of trail that leads to the Heise Park entrance.

Trip 2: Middle Peak

Distance	5.7 miles
Total elevation gain/loss	1100'/1100'
Hiking time	3 hours
Recommended map	Cuyamaca Rancho State Park map/brochure
Optional map	USGS 7.5-min *Cuyamaca Peak*
Best times	All year
Agency	CRSP
Difficulty	★★

If you like big trees, Middle Peak is the place to go. Middle Peak's cone-shaped bulk is crowned with the largest conifers in the Cuyamaca Mountains—and possibly in all of San Diego County.

The old fire trails that encircle Middle Peak have long been popular hiking routes. This trip description, however, introduces a variation: along with one of the older loop trails, it includes the new Sugar Pine Trail, which goes through an area added to the park in the early '80s.

Begin at the parking area just south of Cuyamaca Reservoir, mile 10.7 on Highway 79. Walk across the highway and pick up the Minshall Trail going north along the roadside. At about 0.7 mile, the trail pulls away from the highway, turns westward behind several cabins, and joins a dirt road. Continue 0.2 mile on this dirt road, then go left on the marked Sugar Pine Trail (an old roadbed) toward Middle Peak.

You climb moderately through dense forests of black oak, white fir, and incense-cedar, reversing direction twice. After the second switchback (hairpin turn), ponderosa pines appear along with patches of bracken fern. A little higher, you come upon the first sugar pines; notice the long, narrow cones on the tips of the drooping branches. Some of the sugar pines on Middle Peak have diameters over six feet. Both sugar-pine and ponderosa-pine trunks exhibit "puzzle patterns" in their bark, but ponderosas are distinguished by smaller cones and shorter branches.

At 2.5 miles the road passes the foundation of an old cabin and then curves southwest to join Middle Peak Fire Road. Keep left at the intersection, go 50 yards, and then turn left, staying on Middle Peak Fire Road.

The summit of Middle Peak now lies south and about 200 feet above you. (You can make the trailless scramble to the top easily enough as a side trip, but views in all directions are screened by brush and trees.) Continue east, then south around the upper flank of Middle Peak, keeping straight on the Black Oak Trail as Middle Peak Fire Road veers left and begins a sharp switchbacking descent toward the starting point.

In another mile you'll come to a 5-

way intersection of roads and trails on the saddle between Middle and Cuyamaca peaks. Double back (left, east) on Milk Ranch Road to complete the hike. As you walk along Milk Ranch Road, you'll be treated to some superb parklike vistas of broad, rolling meadows and distant, thickly forested slopes. When the leaves of the black oaks flush a bright yellow around late October and early November, these vistas are reminiscent of Appalachian landscapes.

Trip 3: Sill Hill Waterfall

Distance	6.5 miles round trip
Total elevation gain/loss	1400'/1400'
Hiking time	4^1/$_2$ hours (round trip)
Required map	USGS 7.5-min *Cuyamaca Peak*
Recommended map	Cleveland National Forest recreation map
Best times	November through June
Agency	CRSP, CNF/PD
Difficulty	★★★

This hidden grotto and 30-foot waterfall lie within Cleveland National Forest, just outside the west boundary of Cuyamaca Rancho State Park. It is a part of the Sill Hill Wilderness Study Area, one of two national forest WSA's in San Diego County that have so far failed to win official wilderness designation.

Finding the waterfall and grotto may be challenging, as the informal trail down to it is sketchy. The last few hundred yards involve a bit of rock hopping and bushwhacking. In addition, you must take care not to enter an island of private land lying between the national forest and the state park.

Begin at the parking turnout (day use only) at mile 10.7 on Highway 79. (Overnighters can inquire about parking at the resort area near Cuyamaca Dam or at Paso Picacho Campground). From the parking turnout, cross the highway and go up Milk Ranch Road. After climbing gradually around the southeast flank of Middle Peak, you come to a saddle and a 5-way intersection of fire roads and trails. Continue straight (west) for 0.4 mile, then bear right (north) on Middle Peak Fire Road.

Climb for 0.7 mile through oak and pine forest until you come abreast of a barbed-wire fence on the left (west) side of the trail, precisely at the 5160-foot contour. Step over the fence, entering Cleveland National Forest, and descend west and northwest along a faint path through the oak forest.

You'll soon come upon a beautiful hillside meadow, with views stretching to the coastline. The south-pointing finger of Point Loma is visible along with much of the suburban sprawl of the coastal strip and inland valleys. This meadow is one of several conspicuous bald spots on Middle Peak that can be seen from San Diego on crystal-clear days.

Since the meadow is on national-forest land outside the state park, an overnight stay (with remote camping permit from the Forest Service) is permitted.

From the southwest edge of the meadow, work your way south-southwest along the oak- and brush-covered slopes, skirting the corner of the fenceline that defines the island of private land. You lose elevation gradually, while avoiding thickets of poison oak. Within 0.3 mile of the meadow, you'll hear the sound of falling

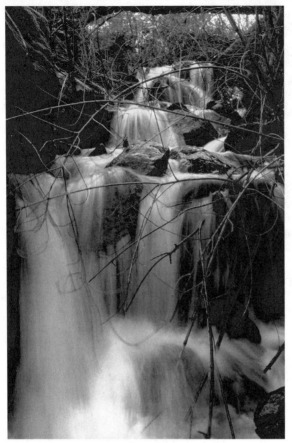

water. The waterfall is located at about 4500 feet elevation along the perennial stream that arises from La Puerta Springs near the aforementioned 5-way intersection of roads and trails.

The water makes an abrupt leap over a dark cliff into a grotto shaded by oak and alder trees. It's tough to take a photo that does justice to the scene, because the sunlight never seems to fall at the right angle.

The surrounding area isn't suitable for camping, but the rocks at the base of the falls are fine for lounging or having lunch. (Safety reminder: resist the temptation to approach the lip of the falls; fallen leaves conceal a slippery rock surface.) With much effort and caution, you can explore downstream and come upon more falls sculpted into the bed of the canyon.

Cascades below Sill Hill Waterfall

Trip 4: Paso Nature Trail

Distance	0.4 mile
Total elevation gain/loss	50'/50'
Hiking time	15 minutes
Optional map	Cuyamaca Rancho State Park map/brochure
Best times	All year
Agency	CRSP
Difficulty	★

This short, self-guiding nature trail highlights some of the native trees and shrubs of the Cuyamaca Mountains. Look for it at the north end of the picnic area at Paso Picacho. There are 12 stations along the trail, keyed to a leaflet available at the entrance station. If you aren't familiar with the local flora and fauna, visit the small interpretive center just outside the entrance to the campground as well.

Trip 5: West Side Trail (to *Morteros*)

	Distance	0.7 mile round trip
	Total elevation gain/loss	50'/50'
	Hiking time	20 minutes (round trip)
	Optional maps	Cuyamaca Rancho State Park map/brochure; USGS 7.5-min *Cuyamaca Peak*
	Best times	All year
	Agency	CRSP
	Difficulty	★

At least a dozen major Indian villages existed in the Cuyamaca Mountains prior to about 130 years ago. These were the mountain villages or summer camps of the Kumeyaay Indians, who divided their time between the mountains and the desert. Many of these sites, identified by the presence of bedrock *morteros*, are today occupied by modern campgrounds. Other sites have remained more isolated, reachable only by trail. One such place, marked by a large cluster of *morteros* on a granite slab, lies a short distance from Paso Picacho Campground by way of the West Side Trail.

The easiest way to reach the West Side Trail is by way of the paved Cuyamaca Peak Fire Road (Lookout Road) beginning behind the fire station just outside the campground entrance. Beyond the gate that blocks vehicle traffic on the fire road, a sign marks the beginning of the West Side Trail—a trail that parallels Highway 79 all the way to Green Valley Campground.

After about 0.2 mile on the West Side Trail, you emerge from the forest cover and skirt the north edge of a meadow. Look for a complex of about 30 *morteros* near the trail. Others are nearby.

With a modest leap of imagination, it's not too difficult to picture a typical scene on a summer's day two hundred years ago: Indian women grinding acorn meal, children squalling nearby, men off hunting small game, or perhaps fashioning stone tools or arrowheads. Unfortunately, collectors long ago carried off all the arrowheads and tools, but the well-worn pits in the granite remain as reminders of an age not far removed in time from our own.

Morteros, *West Side Trail*

Trip 6: Azalea Glen Trail

Distance	3.0 miles
Total elevation gain/loss	550'/550'
Hiking time	1¹/₂ hours
Recommended map	Cuyamaca Rancho State Park map/brochure
Optional maps	USGS 7.5-min *Cuyamaca Peak*
Best times	All year
Agency	CRSP
Difficulty	★★

Of all the trails in Cuyamaca Rancho State Park, this one is my favorite for a leisurely walk. Dense forests, a sunny meadow, a trickling brook, Indian *morteros*, and a refreshing spring are all in one delightful 3-mile loop.

You begin across from the Paso Picacho picnic area, not far from the restrooms. Follow the trail 0.2 mile west to a split. Take the right fork to hike the trail counterclockwise—the way I'll describe it.

Contour through the mixed forest of oaks, pines, firs, and cedars, crossing three small ravines. At 0.6 mile from the split, you emerge from the shade into a cheerful, bracken-fringed meadow. It's hard to miss the fine collection of *morteros* on the nearby granite slabs. Leaving the meadow, you plunge into the dark forest again, and descend to the bank of a small brook, informally called Azalea Creek. Here, western azalea, thimbleberry, and other moisture-loving plants form a delicate understory of greenery under dense stands of white fir and incense-cedar. Come in May or June to see the azaleas in bloom.

Our route joins the California Riding and Hiking Trail and turns steeply uphill through white fir forest, then through thickets of manzanita and other brush forms. After about 0.5 mile of climbing, the trail tops out, joining Azalea Spring Fire Road in a clearing. Azalea Spring is nearby, a popular resting place and water stop for hikers and horses. A giant pine, with a trunk perhaps 6 feet in diameter, stands on the slope just south of the spring.

From Azalea Spring, it's back into the forest again as you descend moderately on the last leg of the Azalea Glen Trail. Let gravity pay its debt, but don't rush through: watch and listen for gray squirrels, chipmunks, chickadees, acorn woodpeckers, and the ubiquitous Steller's jays.

Trip 7: Cuyamaca Peak

Distance	5.5 miles round trip
Total elevation gain/loss	1650'/1650'
Hiking time	3 hours (round trip)
Recommended map	Cuyamaca Rancho State Park map/brochure
Optional map	USGS 7.5-min *Cuyamaca Peak*
Best times	All year
Agency	CRSP
Difficulty	★★★

Cuyamaca Peak, San Diego County's second highest summit, lies only a few miles from the county's geographical center. Its unique position and height make it the best land-based vantage point for studying the topography of our county. The view from ground level on the peak is somewhat less than a continuous 360° due to the presence of some antenna structures and a few trees, but you can still take in the complete panorama in increments by simply moving around a bit.

The one-lane, paved Lookout Road ("Cuyamaca Peak Fire Road" on many maps) is closed to public vehicles, but provides a very straightforward passage to the top of the peak for self-propelled travelers—be they hikers, runners, bicyclists, or cross-country skiers. You can pick up the road at its intersection with Highway 79 just south of the Interpretive Center, or you can wend your way through Paso Picacho Campground and pick it up just beyond the southernmost campsites. It's an uphill grind all the way, moderate at first, then steep beyond the intersection of the California Riding and Hiking Trail.

After 1.5 miles the road grade becomes flat for a short stretch and you pass Deer Spring, for years a dependable source of potable water for hikers on their way up the mountain. Sadly, the pipe that used to dispense cold water is gone and no water is available.

Views improve as you continue beyond the spring into an area finally recovering from forest fires that swept through in 1950 and 1970. Some tall snags poke above the smaller trees, serving as perches for a variety of birds. The now tree-screened vista to the north and east includes Cuyamaca Reservoir and some of the desert mountain ranges.

In the final steep stretch, you go climb past some mature timber that survived the fires and suddenly arrive at the flat, antenna-cluttered summit of the peak. A fire-lookout structure stood here until the late '80s, when it was removed for lack of use.

During a Santa Ana condition in fall or winter, and after the passage of major winter storms, Cuyamaca Peak becomes a grandstand seat for views stretching into at least five counties and one foreign state. To name some of the features visible within San Diego County: the Palomar Mountains (look for the tiny white speck on the summit ridge—the Hale Telescope dome) northwest more than 30 miles away; Hot Springs Mountain, 26 miles almost due north over the summit of nearby Middle Peak; Granite Mountain, 11 miles to the northeast; the south end of the Santa Rosa Mountains, 40 miles northeast; and Whale Peak and the Vallecito Mountains, 18 miles east-northeast.

Close in, just 10 or so miles to the southeast, are the conifer-covered Laguna Mountains. South and southwest along the international border are Tecate Peak and Otay Mountain, 25–30 miles away. The Pacific Ocean gleams in the west, with Point Loma, the Silver Strand, San Diego Bay, and Mission Bay visible at distances of about 35–40 miles. Along an arc from west to southwest, you'll spot coastal peaks like Black Mountain, Soledad Mountain, Fortuna Mountain, Cowles Mountain, Mount Helix, and San Miguel Mountain. Along a west-to-south arc, but closer in, you'll see El Cajon Mountain, Viejas Mountain, Lyons Peak, and Corte Madera Mountain.

You'll enhance the pleasure of your stay on the peak if you bring along a good county map and binoculars.

Trip 8: Stonewall Peak

Distance	4.5 miles round trip
Total elevation gain/loss	850'/850'
Hiking time	2^1/$_2$ hours (round trip)
Recommended map	Cuyamaca Rancho State Park map/brochure
Optional map	USGS 7.5-min *Cuyamaca Peak*
Best times	All year
Agency	CRSP
Difficulty	★★

Stonewall Peak's angular summit of white granite is a conspicuous landmark throughout Cuyamaca Rancho State Park. Although Stonewall stands some 800 feet lower than nearby Cuyamaca Peak, its unique position and steep, south exposure provide a more inclusive view of the park area itself.

Beginning across the highway from the entrance to Paso Picacho Campground, the trail climbs steadily and moderately on a set of well-engineered switchbacks up the west slope of Stonewall Peak. Thick groves of live and black oaks keep you in semi-shade most of the way.

About halfway up the trail, a view

opens to the north and east. Cuyamaca Reservoir lies to the north, its level and its extent variable according to the season and the year's precipitation. When it is full, its surface covers nearly 1000 acres.

When you reach the top of the switchbacks, turn right (south) toward the summit of the peak. (The trail to the left descends sharply to Los Caballos Camp; if you prefer, this can be used as an alternate, but substantially longer, return route.) Follow the trail through chaparral and scattered trees to the base of the exposed granite cap. A series of steps hewn in the rock and a guardrail are provided in the last hundred feet or so. Small children will certainly need assistance here.

On top, you won't see any ocean views (the main Cuyamaca massif stands tall in the west), but the foreground panorama of the park's rolling topography is impressive enough. Patches of meadow along the streamcourses and the bald

Dandelion, Cuyamaca Mountains

grassland areas on East Mesa and West Mesa change color with the seasons: green in spring, yellow in summer, brown or gray in fall, and occasionally white with fallen snow in winter. The forested slopes appear as a tapestry of color, the light green or yellow-tinted black oaks playing counterpoint to the rather dark hues of the conifers and live oaks. Direction-finders on the summit assist in the identification of major peaks in the middle and far distance.

Swallows or swifts practically rake the summit during their high-speed maneuvers, and larger birds—ravens, hawks, and even bald eagles may cruise by. Eagles, along with egrets, herons, and ospreys, are sometimes attracted to the shoreline of nearby Cuyamaca Reservoir, especially in winter.

Trip 9: Stonewall Creek/Soapstone Grade Loop

Distance	8.2 miles
Total elevation gain/loss	1050'/1050'
Hiking time	4 hours
Recommended map	Cuyamaca Rancho State Park map/brochure
Optional map	USGS 7.5-min *Cuyamaca Peak*
Best times	September through June
Agency	CRSP
Difficulty	★★★

This is probably the flattest of any of the longer hikes possible within Cuyamaca Rancho State Park. Instead of climbing a mountain or a mesa, the route follows, for the most part, the gentle valleys of Stonewall Creek and the upper Sweetwater River. Most of the elevation gain takes place in the first 3 miles.

(The loop portion of the route described below is allowable for mountain bikers, but only if they begin and return to the Camp Cuyamaca school camp near park headquarters, staying on fire roads the entire trip. Cold Spring Trail is off-limits to mountain bikers.)

Begin at the parking turnout on the east side of Highway 79 at mile 7.3. Cross the creek (Cold Stream), and go east about 100 feet to join the Cold Stream Trail. Go left (north) and continue about 200 yards to Cold Spring. From the spring, bear right on the Cold Spring Trail and follow it northeast 1.2 miles, up and over a chaparral- and oak-covered ridge. On the far side of the ridge you'll cross Stonewall Creek,

whose flow becomes sluggish after the rainy season, but pools up in shallow bedrock basins until about June. Turn left (north) at the next intersection—Stonewall Creek Fire Road.

The fire road meanders along the east bank of Stonewall Creek, passing through chaparral, oaks, and pines, and finally across grassland, to a low saddle just east of the two equestrian campgrounds (a side trip to piped water sources is possible at this point).

Just beyond the low saddle is Soapstone Grade Road. Turn right (east) and skirt the edge of the broad, open valley containing Cuyamaca Reservoir. Trees stood in this valley in fair abundance before discovery of the nearby Stonewall Mine—afterward, the sudden demand for lumber caused a brief logging bonanza. The road is named for the soapstone, a talclike rock used commercially as a base for bath powders, exposed in the area.

After contouring for about one mile, the road turns sharply downhill along a scrubby hillside; in less than one more mile, it meets the Upper Green Valley Fire Road amid a fine canopy of spreading oaks. Now it's simply a matter of following the Sweetwater River downstream on the adjacent road. Your accompaniment is a riparian strip of oaks, pines, and willows, providing welcome shade on warm days, and shelter from the wind on blustery days. Stay with the Upper Green Valley Fire Road for 2.3 miles, pass the lower end of the Stonewall Creek Fire Road, and continue another 0.4 mile to a cutoff on the right. Go west on this cutoff trail for 0.4 mile, passing over a low ridge. Then merge into northbound Cold Stream Trail, and in just 0.6 mile you'll be back at your starting point.

Trip 10: Harper Creek

Distance	2.5 miles round trip
Total elevation gain/loss	200'/200'
Hiking time	1^1/2 hours (round trip)
Recommended map	Cuyamaca Rancho State Park map/brochure
Optional map	USGS 7.5-min *Cuyamaca Peak*
Best times	October through June
Agency	CRSP
Difficulty	★★

On a warm spring day, Harper Creek's shallow, jewel-like pools invite tactile exploration—with more than just the fingers. Slide into one of the pools, and let

On Harper Creek

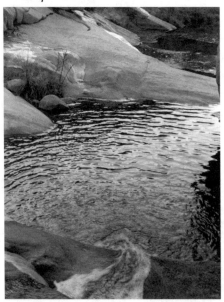

the involuntary scream rising from your lungs ease the shock of entry. Don't wait too long in the season, though; by late summer you might find only dry, sun-blasted slabs of water-polished rock here.

Harper Creek lies near the Cuyamaca Rancho State Park headquarters and museum, 8 miles north of Descanso on Highway 79. You can park your car for up to two hours there, or for a longer time in any of several turnouts along Highway 79 nearby.

From park headquarters walk east around the buildings of Camp Cuyamaca, a San Diego city and county school camp, and drop down to the sandy bank of the Sweetwater River. Find a place to cross over the shallow river, and pick up the East Side Trail on the far side. Follow the East Side Trail northeast across a grassy bluff overlooking the river. After about 0.7 mile, the trail turns briefly east and then crosses the Harper Creek. At this crossing, leave the trail and follow a side path along the left (north) bank of the creek. The trail soon peters out—but you can continue, with caution, by treading the rocky lower slopes of the narrowing canyon ahead.

The stream water flows over bedrock slabs, often streaked with mineral deposits, and collects in small pools, two to four feet deep, fed by mini-waterfalls. A gray-green mantle of lichens clings to the exposed rock above the creek. High on the slopes to either side are belts of chaparral, chiefly mountain mahogany, punctuated by the erect stalks of blooming yuccas. The best bathing pools are about 0.1 mile up from the point where you leave East Side Trail, but the creek remains interesting for another 0.2 mile up-canyon.

Trip 11: Dyar Spring/Juaquapin Loop

Distance	5.8 miles
Total elevation gain/loss	800'/800'
Hiking time	3 hours
Recommended map	Cuyamaca Rancho State Park map/brochure
Optional map	USGS 7.5-min *Cuyamaca Peak*
Best times	All year
Agency	CRSP
Difficulty	★★

If water is an element essential to your hiking pleasure, you won't want to miss this hike. Dyar Spring, midway along the route, gurgles from a pipe at head-high level, offering the possibility of a cool shower. Downstream, along Juaquapin Creek, you can sit in the shade and listen to the most peaceful of sounds—the gentle flow of water over stones.

The starting point is the large parking area at the Sweetwater River bridge, between mile 4.8 and 4.9 on Highway 79. From here, take the Harvey Moore Trail south and east across a hillside, passing first through a belt of oaks and pines, then later through chaparral.

After 2.4 miles, turn left (north) on the Dyar Spring Trail and enter the domain of East Mesa, an open, grassy expanse studded with oaks. Several shallow ravines, tributaries of Juaquapin Creek, indent the surface of the mesa. Most are outlined by clumps of wild rose, squaw bush, and (in the wettest areas) stinging nettles. At a point about 0.8 mile north of the Harvey Moore Trail, a sign directs you left (northwest) toward Dyar Spring. You'll find the spring somewhat hidden on the edge of a meadow among elderberry, wil-

Dyar Spring

low, live oak, and black oak trees.

The East Mesa area is excellent for spotting mule deer and coyotes. Station yourself on one of the knolls above Dyar Spring, enjoy a picnic, and watch the parade of wildlife below.

Back on the trail again, go northwest over a small rise and drop steeply down a slope densely covered by chaparral. Arriving at an oak-shaded saddle, turn left (south) on the Juaquapin Trail and continue downhill along a grassy draw that leads toward the west bank of Juaquapin Creek. Good displays of wildflowers are seen here in spring: forget-me-not, lupine, wallflower, checker, wild onion, and more.

The Juaquapin Trail stays on a bench above the creek, and finally turns northwest around the brow of a ridge. Look for several bedrock *morteros* in a clump of oak trees just south of the junction of the trail to Juaquapin Crossing. (This trail is a short cut to the Harvey Moore Trail.)

Upon reaching the next junction, turn left (the right fork goes toward park headquarters). Continue down along Juaquapin Creek and the Sweetwater River all the way back to your starting point.

Trip 12: Oakzanita Peak

Distance	4.6 miles round trip
Total elevation gain/loss	1200'/1200'
Hiking time	3 hours (round trip)
Recommended map	Cuyamaca Rancho State Park map/brochure
Optional map	USGS 7.5-min *Cuyamaca Peak*
Best times	October through June
Agency	CRSP
Difficulty	★★

Oakzanita Peak is one of only a handful of named peaks in the Cuyamaca Mountains, yet its humble appearance—at least on approach—would not inspire most hikers to climb it. Actually, the view from its rocky summit is quite impressive on a clear day, and well worth the long hike—if done during cool weather. Kids will enjoy scrambling over the rock outcrops near the top.

The new Descanso Creek Trail considerably shortens the formerly circuitous and tedious climb on fire roads. Begin at the parking turnout on the east side of Highway 79 at mile 3.1 (3.1 miles north of Old Highway 80 near Descanso). Follow the trail to the right (south) It quickly bends northeast, following oak-shaded Descanso Creek, and joins East Mesa Fire Road after 0.5 mile. Turn right, continue east up the fire road for just 0.1 mile, and then veer right on the Upper Descanso Creek Trail.

What follows in the next 1.1 miles is an almost perfectly constant and moderate uphill grade through dense, mature chaparral. The seed tufts of mountain mahogany shrubs, which resemble silvery pipe-cleaners, glisten in the sunlight alongside the trail. Here and there you pass under a live oak or a black oak tree; by late October, the leaves of the latter will have turned a distinctive yellow color. Red-barked manzanita shrubs show their colorful stuff all the time. The name "Oakzanita" was derived from the oaks and the manzanita hereabouts.

At the top of the grade, in a saddle, you meet the newly-cut Oakzanita Trail.

Head right (west) and climb a crooked 0.6 mile to the summit. A peak register lies at the top. The view includes most of the Cuyamacas' southern reaches: Pine, Airplane, and Arrowmakers ridges to the northwest, and the meadows of East Mesa to the northeast. In the distance lie the dark, wave-shaped form of Cuyamaca Peak and the pointed, alabaster summit of Stonewall Peak.

Trip 13: East Mesa Loop

Distance	10.5 miles
Total elevation gain/loss	1300'/1300'
Hiking time	5^1/$_2$ hours
Recommended map	Cuyamaca Rancho State Park map/brochure
Optional map	USGS 7.5-min *Cuyamaca Peak*
Best times	October through May
Agency	CRSP
Difficulty	★★★

This is what you could call a "grand tour" of the East Mesa area—and the state wilderness that encompasses it. Tracing a rough circle, you follow the route of the Harvey Moore Trail up and over the rolling meadows of East Mesa and down the canyon of Harper Creek. You complete the circuit on the East Side Trail along the Sweetwater River. There's enough scenic variety on this trip, as well as elevation change, to keep things interesting. If you plan to stay overnight at Granite Spring, you'll need to contact the park rangers for a permit and to make parking arrangements.

A good starting point is the Sweetwater River bridge parking area at mile 4.8–4.9 on Highway 79. Follow the Harvey Moore Trail south and east across a hillside, passing first through a band of oaks and pines, then through chaparral. After about 2 miles, oaks and

Live oak tree above Descanso Creek

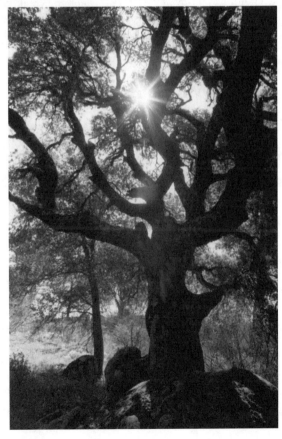

pines appear again. At the junction of the Dyar Spring Trail (2.4 miles), you'll have gained almost 800 feet, already the majority of the total elevation gain during the entire trip. East Mesa now lies ahead.

East Mesa isn't a mesa in the usual desert sense, but rather a gently inclined bench of broad grasslands interrupted by tree- and brush-covered promontories. The diversity of habitats in this area supports possibly the largest deer herd in the county.

After climbing over a low saddle you come to a junction (3.4 miles). Turn left and continue 0.6 mile to Granite Spring Primitive Camp, on the right. Of the two trail camps in the park designated for hikers and equestrians, this one is more remote from trailheads and therefore less popular. A hand pump dispenses potable, but somewhat unpleasant-tasting, iron-rich water.

From Granite Spring, return to the Harvey Moore Trail (which is now coincident with East Mesa Fire Road) and head north for another 1.0 mile to the next junction. Swing left and follow the Harvey Moore Trail north toward the canyon containing Harper Creek. The descent is gradual at first, then quite steep on many short switchbacks. A lush growth of oaks, pines, manzanita, and other head-high brush forms provides plenty of shade. After a loss of 700 feet, you reach Harper Creek.

The trail turns west and follows Harper Creek downstream; after three crossings, it climbs abruptly up the brushy north slope to a position about 100 feet above the creek to avoid the rocky gorge below. It then contours for about 0.4 mile and then drops sharply to the bank of the creek just below the gorge. Leave the Harvey Moore Trail at this point, cross the creek, and pick up the East Side Trail. It will take you directly back to the Sweetwater River bridge, about 3 miles away.

Trip 14: West Mesa Loop

Distance	7.2 miles
Total elevation gain/loss	1100'/1100'
Hiking time	3¹/2 hours
Recommended map	Cuyamaca Rancho State Park map/brochure
Optional map	USGS 7.5-min *Cuyamaca Peak*
Best times	All year
Agency	CRSP
Difficulty	★★★

The forest: you're never far from it on this hike. The fluttering of oak leaves, the soughing of pine needles in the breeze, the scurrying of gray squirrels, the pungent sweetness in the air—these you can enjoy any time of year. The best sights, sounds, and smells in this forest, however, are reserved for two special times of year—spring and fall.

The route is entirely on well-graded fire roads along the massive, but rather gently sloping, southeast flank of Cuyamaca Peak. There's more shade than sunshine along the way, and, if you're lucky, you'll see more deer than humans. Unfortunately, there's no dependable source of potable water.

Begin at the day-use parking area at mile 7.3 on Highway 79. Head west around a gate and continue up West Mesa Fire

Road through a forest of mostly oaks and pines. After 0.5 mile you come to a junction from where West Mesa Fire Road continues southwest toward Japacha Spring and the Fern Flat Fire Road branches right (northwest). Either direction you choose at the intersection is fine since this is a loop hike, but we'll assume you're going counterclockwise. Head northwest and ascend through stands of ponderosa and Coulter pine. Staying left at the next two trail junctions (following West Mesa Trail), you level off at about the 5200-foot contour and continue around several small ravines. These are carpeted with bracken fern and other shade-loving greenery. Elsewhere, ceanothus, ablaze with white blossoms in May, complements the various shades of arboreal foliage: these run the gamut from the light green of black oaks, to the dark green of incense cedars, to the curious dull reds and browns of flowering live oaks. You're in the middle of the biggest block of state wilderness within the park.

The Burnt Pine Trail (a disused fire road), intersecting from the right, can be used to reach Cuyamaca Peak, but it's a long and tedious haul. Beyond this intersection, the West Mesa Trail starts a gentle descent across a bald spot on the mountain slope. A beautiful vista of swaying grasses, rolling hills, and distant ridges lies before you.

The descent quickens and you soon come to the Arroyo Seco Trail (another former fire road) on the right. Stay left and continue along the top of Airplane Ridge. After 0.9 mile, round the hairpin turn (Monument Trail junction on the right) and notice the side trail on the left leading to the Airplane Monument (see Trip 15).

Continue descending, into and around the shady canyon of Japacha Creek, and in 1.2 miles from the hairpin turn come to the junction of Japacha Fire Road. Japacha Spring is nearby, accessible via a short spur trail.

Continue northeast along the edge of the broad meadow at the foot of Arrowmakers Ridge, and retrace your earlier steps on the West Mesa Fire Road back to your starting point.

Trip 15: Arroyo Seco/Monument Loop

Distance	7.2 miles
Total elevation gain/loss	1200'/1200'
Hiking time	4 hours
Recommended map	Cuyamaca Rancho State Park map/brochure
Optional map	USGS 7.5-min *Cuyamaca Peak*
Best times	September through May
Agency	CRSP
Difficulty	★★★

IN MEMORY OF COL. F. C. MARSHALL AND 1ST LT. C. L. WEBBER WHO FELL AT THIS SPOT DEC. 7, 1922. Without this inscription, the presence of an old 12-cylinder engine permanently mounted in stone atop remote Airplane Ridge wouldn't make much sense to a hiker passing by. The Airplane Monument is just one of several interesting sights along this loop hike.

One option is to carry your overnight gear along this route and stay at Arroyo Seco Primitive Camp; if so you must park your car overnight at Green Valley Campground. Day hikers can start from the

Sweetwater River bridge parking area at mile 4.8–4.9 on Highway 79.

From the bridge parking area, walk north over the Sweetwater River bridge and immediately turn left on a short spur trail that hooks up with the West Side Trail. Continue north about 0.4 mile, paralleling the highway, then bear left on Japacha Fire Road. You now wind uphill, following the south wall of the canyon containing Japacha Creek, and after about 0.8 mile cross the creek. Bracken fern, sword fern, thimbleberry, and wild strawberry thrive in the shade of oaks and sycamores along the creek bottom. Turning northeast to follow a shady draw, you soon come to a marked spur trail to Japacha Spring. The water merely dribbles from cracks in the bedrock, but nearby are some flat rocks to rest upon in a shady spot.

Go back down to Japacha Fire Road and follow it north to the West Mesa Trail, where you turn left (southwest). Climb gradually through a magnificent conifer and oak forest, and cross Japacha Creek once again. Now watch carefully for the small footpath—on the right about 0.2 mile past the creek crossing—that leads to the Airplane Monument. Here is another nice place for relaxation. You can sit in the shade on the stone bench, while the breeze fans

you, and look out through the trees toward Arrowmakers Ridge and Stonewall Peak.

Returning to the West Mesa Trail, you continue around a hairpin turn, doubling back to the northwest to follow the top of Airplane Ridge. (The Monument Trail branches south from the hairpin turn, providing a shortcut to Green Valley Campground for those who wish to bail out of this trip early.) Continue for 1 mile along the ridgetop, staying left at the next junction; then just afterward turn left on a narrow, poorly maintained segment of the California Riding and Hiking Trail. The trail descends quite rapidly on a series of long switchbacks through a dense forest of oaks (watch for poison oak here), passes an intermittent spring marked by an old water trough, and then favors a straight course through tall chaparral. Turn left at the bottom of the trail and continue downhill into Arroyo Seco Primitive Camp.

The camp lies at the south end of a wide meadow frequented by mule deer and other wildlife. To loop back toward your starting point, go downhill on Arroyo Seco Road toward Green Valley Campground, 1.5 miles away. Before you reach the campground take the cutoff trail on the left that slants over to West Side Trail. Then follow West Side Trail over to the Sweetwater bridge.

Trip 16: Pine Ridge Trail

Distance	3.3 miles
Total elevation gain/loss	600'/600'
Hiking time	2 hours
Recommended map	Cuyamaca Rancho State Park map/brochure
Optional map	USGS 7.5-min *Cuyamaca Peak*
Best times	All year
Agency	CRSP
Difficulty	★★

This hike is especially worthwhile during the winter months, when melting snow or soggy ground at higher eleva-

tions in the Cuyamacas can make hiking in those areas difficult. A good part of the route is open to the winter sun's southern rays, and the added warmth can be quite welcome and invigorating at that time. The hike is also short enough to be suitable for a sunrise or a sunset stroll, even during the hottest months of late spring and early summer.

Park in one of the day-use lots at Green Valley Campground, then head for campsite 38 at the southwest edge of the campground. The Pine Ridge Trail goes straight up the chaparral-covered ridge behind this site, and soon gains a foothold on a steep, south-facing slope overlooking the Sweetwater River canyon. Green Valley Falls lie below, unseen but often heard. Higher still, the trail swings to the north side of Pine Ridge and offers a spectacular view of West Mesa, Cuyamaca Peak, and the length of Green Valley. In the valley just below you can trace your return route,

Arroyo Seco Road.

In the first mile, the trail passes only through thick chaparral—mostly manzanita, chamise, and ceanothus. But some timber appears as you approach the topmost knoll of Pine Ridge. These trees—Coulter pines and black oaks —cling to the north slopes of the ridge, where less sunshine permits a greater retention of ground moisture.

Past the topmost knoll, the trail zigzags down to intersect the California Riding and Hiking Trail. Turn right (east) at this intersection, go 0.1 mile, and turn right again on Arroyo Seco Road. An easy return to Green Valley Campground follows. Mule deer, apparently accustomed to the human activity around the nearby campground, are often seen grazing in and around the meadow areas along this road.

Trip 17: Sweetwater River Loop

Distance	7.2 miles
Total elevation gain/loss	700'/700'
Hiking time	3¹/₂ hours
Recommended map	Cuyamaca Rancho State Park map/brochure
Optional map	USGS 7.5-min *Descanso, Cuyamaca Peak*
Best times	October through June
Agency	CRSP
Difficulty	★★★

Fed by countless ravines and rivulets on the slopes of the Cuyamaca Mountains, the Sweetwater River at last becomes a watercourse worthy of the name "river"—albeit sometimes a seasonal one. Below Green Valley Campground and Green Valley Falls, the sweet, bubbling liquid slides placidly down a pleasant little gorge shaded by alders and willows. For years there were sporadic attempts to introduce beaver along this stretch of the river, so look for evidence in the form of dams made from willow saplings and mud.

The obscurely marked trailhead and parking lot, next to a ranger residence, is located on Viejas Boulevard, 0.6 mile east of the main crossroads in Descanso. You can also reach it by going 1.1 miles west from Highway 79 along Viejas Boulevard.

From the lot, walk past a vehicle gate. The Merigan Fire Road takes you across a sunny meadow, then up onto a brushy slope. In springtime, the air rising along the slopes bears both the tangy fragrance of new growth in the chaparral and the humid scent of the stream-hugging wil-

Green Valley Falls

At 1.9 miles, you reach a junction of trails in flat area dotted with oaks and a few pines. Crossing the river there, you can pick up the Saddleback Trail, which takes you uphill and northwest to the California Riding and Hiking Trail (3.1 miles). During March this slope is alive with the drone of bees frantically gathering nectar from the blooming manzanitas.

Make a right turn onto the California Riding and Hiking Trail, a right on South Boundary Fire Road, another right to stay on South Boundary Fire Road, and a fourth right on the Sweetwater Trail (4.2 miles). Sweetwater Trail will take you down along the east wall of the Sweetwater gorge, at times almost 100 feet above the water. At 5.3 miles you'll arrive back at Merigan Fire Road; follow it back to the trailhead.

As an alternate to the loop described above, you can try this slightly longer loop with a little less elevation gain: At 1.9 miles, instead of crossing the river, continue on Merigan Fire Road as it turns east toward Highway 79. Just short of the vehicle gate near the highway, turn north and follow the Blue Ribbon Trail, going up a drainage toward South Boundary Fire Road. Take the latter down to the bank of the Sweetwater River and turn left on the trail going down the Sweetwater gorge.

lows just ahead. Blue ceanothus paints the brushy hillsides in April through early May. Mountain mahogany is conspicuous in late summer, sporting thousands of hairy seed tufts that resemble twisted pipe cleaners.

Just beyond the saddle, the Dead Horse Trail branches left, dipping to cross the river and its accompanying strip of riparian vegetation. Stay on the fire road. Another trail on the left, 0.4 mile farther, leads to an artificial waterfall—a silted-in diversion dam.

After some further climbing, the road enters a magnificent grove of live oak trees and sidles up against the high banks of the creek. Down below, through a screen of willows and alders, the ice-cold Sweetwater sparkles as it tumbles over the gravelly canyon floor.

Area M-8: Laguna Mountains

East of the Cuyamaca Mountains—the first great moisture-wringing barrier to Pacific storms—lies a second and slightly drier range, the Laguna Mountains. Here the storm clouds yield enough precipitation to support a patchwork forest of Jeffrey pines and black oaks. Farther east still, the land falls away abruptly. Below this escarpment lies the desert.

The human history of the Laguna Mountains closely parallels that of other mountain and foothill regions in southern California. The first peoples to arrive were bands of Kumeyaay Indians, who summered here to escape from the heat of the lowlands and gain sustenance from the natural resources of the forest. Bedrock *morteros*, commonly seen along the trails, are a reminder of this era.

The 1800s brought livestock ranching to the Lagunas, then mining for gold and other minerals. Mining activity peaked in the late 1800s, but continues on a very small scale today. Cattle grazing continues on private lands and on some national forest lands.

After the turn of the century, recreation played an increasingly dominant role. The Laguna Mountains were included within the boundaries of Cleveland National Forest in 1893, and one of the first ranger stations in California, El Prado Ranger Cabin, was constructed here in 1911. Summer homes were erected on private land within the national forest, and on certain parcels of forest land by lease arrangement.

In recent years, the emphasis has been on serving the public-at-large through recreation such as camping, hiking, and snow play. The Laguna crest, which includes elevations of about 6000 feet, is the highest place you can reach within the county by way of a public road. If winter snowfalls are heavy enough, the Laguna Meadow area becomes San Diego County's best playground for cross-country skiing. As the terrain here is mostly flat to gently sloping, there is probably no better area in San Diego County for easy skiing.

The higher Laguna Mountains have been placed administratively within a zone called the Laguna Mountain Recreation Area. The Forest Service—with volunteer assistance—is managing it as a heavy-use area, with campgrounds, picnic areas, and nature trails throughout. In recent years, several new trails have been added, mostly through the efforts of members of the Laguna Mountain Volunteer Association.

On summer weekends, rangers and volunteers offer interpretive walks, evening campfire programs, and other special events. On Friday and Saturday nights during the summer, San Diego State University's Mount Laguna Observatory offers visitors a chance to view various celestial objects through a 21-inch telescope and smaller instruments. Information about these and other events can be obtained at the visitor information office, mile 23.5 on Sunrise Highway, or by calling Cleveland National Forest's Descanso Ranger District office (see Appendix 4).

Currently, over 70 miles of hiking trails lace the Laguna Mountains. The biggest single share of this mileage is in the form of the Pacific Crest Trail, which passes north-south over the Laguna crest. For several miles the PCT edges close to the spectacular eastern escarpment—the "sunrise" side—of the Lagunas. Nowhere else in San Diego County can you experience so dramatically the interface between mountain and desert.

Most of the trips below traverse at least some part of the Laguna Mountain Recreation Area, where camping is allowed only in the developed campgrounds. Car

Area M-8: Laguna Mountains

Laguna Mountains Inset

camping and trail camping is allowed on most national forest lands outside the recreation area—but you must first obtain a remote camping permit from any Cleveland National Forest ranger station.

All of the trips below begin on national forest land, and all require a National Forest Adventure Pass for parking at trailheads. See the introductory section "Using This Book" for more information on this.

Trip 1: Kwaaymii Point

Distance	1.0 mile round trip
Total elevation gain/loss	150'/150'
Hiking time	30 minutes (round trip)
Optional map	USGS 7.5-min *Monument Peak*
Best times	All year
Agency	CNF/DD
Difficulty	★

If you have no than a half hour to spare during a cruise through the Laguna Mountains, at least stop at Kwaaymii Point and take this brief stroll along the eastern escarpment. Here, in the abbreviated transition zone between mountain and desert, you can peer down into the depths of the desert, almost 4000 feet below, and at the same time catch sight of cool forests on the Laguna rim.

You'll be walking on a segment of the Pacific Crest Trail incorporating an old roadbed literally chiseled into a cliff. Before 1975, this was a hair-raising part of Sunrise Highway; but it was bypassed by a newer, less spectacular, safer stretch of road to the west.

The starting point can be either Kwaaymii Point (turnoff at mile 30.3 on Sunrise Highway) or Pioneer Mail Picnic Ground (mile 29.3). The old roadbed between these two points skirts the lip of Cottonwood Canyon, a forbidding-looking abyss with just a hint of lushness in its deepest creases. In an effort to return the old roadbed to some semblance of naturalness, trail builders removed its macadam surface. The outer retaining walls are

Birding in the Laguna Mountains

holding firm, but tons of friable metamorphic rock have fallen from road cuts above the grade of the road.

From Kwaaymii Point, you can also walk north for less than a half mile on the PCT to the east shoulder of Garnet Mountain (distinct from Garnet Peak to the south), where the views of Cottonwood Canyon and the desert floor are even more panoramic.

Trip 2: Garnet Peak

Distance	2.4 miles round trip
Total elevation gain/loss	500'/500'
Hiking time	1$^1/_2$ hour (round trip)
Optional maps	Cleveland National Forest recreation map; USGS 7.5-min *Monument Peak*
Best times	All year
Agency	CNF/DD
Difficulty	★★

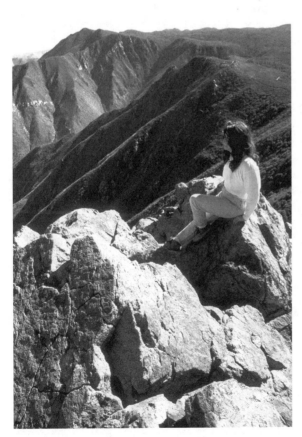

Atop Garnet Peak

Although Garnet Peak isn't the highest peaklet along the edge of the Lagunas' eastern escarpment, its exposed position makes it a good place to view both the pine-clad plateau and the raw desert below. Especially rewarding is a predawn pilgrimage to observe the sunrise from its summit. Around the time of the winter solstice, the sun's flattened disk peeps up over the desert wastes of northwestern Sonora, Mexico, some 150 miles away. On the clearest mornings at that time of year, you might witness the famed "green flash," an event occasionally seen on the horizon at sunset from San Diego's coast, but seldom seen at sunrise.

Park on the shoulder (but off the pavement) of Sunrise Highway near mile 27.8. Take the signed Garnet Peak Trail 0.5 mile north through Jeffrey-pine forest to where it crosses the Pacific Crest Trail.

Continue north, in open chaparral, on a rocky path that slants up along the shoulder of the peak. Lord's Candle yucca stalks, heavy with white flowers in the spring and early summer, poke through the ceanothus and manzanita brush along the trail.

The summit is crowned by a jagged cluster of layered, tan rock, the type seen along much of the Laguna escarpment. The peak falls away abruptly, revealing a vertiginous panorama of Storm Canyon and its distant alluvial fan. Along the horizon lie the Salton Sea and Baja's Laguna Salada, both desert sinks. To the south and west, the Laguna crest, dusky with oak and pine forests and patches of chaparral, seems to roll like a frozen wave to the edge of the escarpment.

Watch your step as you move around on the summit, and hang on to your hat. This must be one of the windiest places in the county.

Trip 3: Indian Creek Loop

Distance	8.0 miles
Total elevation gain/loss	1000'/1000'
Hiking time	5 hours
Recommended maps	Cleveland National Forest recreation map; USGS 7.5-min *Monument Peak*
Best times	March through June
Agency	CNF/DD
Difficulty	★★★

Here's a nice way to fit a scenic segment of the Pacific Crest Trail into a loop hike. You'll sample a variety of appealing environments—shady woodland, spice-scented chaparral, sage-dotted meadow—plus a bird's-eye view of the desert.

You may begin at the Penny Pines trailhead, mile 27.3 on Sunrise Highway, where parking is available along the highway's wide shoulder. Start by following the Noble Canyon Trail (see Trip 17 for more) west through Jeffrey-pine forest. After gaining the north slope of a hill, dropping to cross dirt roads three times, and ascending once again to circle around the north end of a ridge, you'll come to a junction with the Indian Creek Trail, 2.4 miles from the start. Turn right at this junction and descend about 0.8 mile through black oaks and chaparral to the grassy banks along trickling (or dry) Indian Creek.

You now leave the Indian Creek Trail and head north, upstream along Indian Creek, following the remnants of an old road on the left (west) bank. Keep going on what becomes a better dirt road until you reach Pioneer Mail Picnic Ground, 4.6 miles, on the far side of Sunrise Highway. Pick up the PCT, which passes downslope of the picnic tables, and head east.

After paralleling Sunrise Highway for a while, the PCT starts rising on oak- and pine-shaded hillsides often dotted with wallflowers, lupine, and paintbrush. Then, after contouring around a lilac-scented slope overlooking Cottonwood Canyon, you start trending south, intersect the trail to Garnet Peak, and maintain a course that takes you along the rim of the desert-facing escarpment. You can work your way east through some intervening chaparral growth to reach the very brink of the escarpment, or wait until you get to a stretch where you look straight down into the yawning depths of Storm Canyon. A final descent on the PCT, through oaks and pines, takes you back to the Penny Pines plantation and your car.

Jeffrey pine forest, Laguna Mountains

Trip 4: Cottonwood Canyon

Distance	3.2 miles round trip
Total elevation gain/loss	2000'/2000'
Hiking time	5 hours (round trip)
Recommended maps	Cleveland National Forest recreation map; USGS 7.5-min *Monument Peak*
Best times	October through June
Agency	CNF/DD, ABDSP
Difficulty	★★★★

V-shaped Cottonwood Canyon once provided Indians with a direct, but very steep, passage between the desert floor and the lush meadows of the Laguna Mountains. Springs and seasonal flows of water in the canyon undoubtedly served its travelers well. For a time Cottonwood Canyon was mistakenly believed to have been the route of the Jackass Mail (part of a pioneering mail route between San Antonio and San Diego)—hence the naming of Pioneer Mail Picnic Ground. Later research showed the true route of the Jackass Mail to be Oriflamme Canyon.

Like trips into the Grand Canyon, this is strictly a down-and-back-up affair.

Since private land lies on the desert floor below Cottonwood Canyon, you should retrace your path after descending. Unlike hiking the Grand Canyon trails, there's no established path, so even the downhill part is slow-going. There are lots of tricky little descents—especially if you're carrying extra gear—over small waterfalls. A 25-foot length of cord will serve you well for lowering or raising a heavy pack over the steepest precipices.

Start hiking at Pioneer Mail Picnic Area, mile 29.3 on Sunrise Highway. Follow the draw that descends northeast. At 0.4 mile, the "bottom drops out" and the canyon walls become steep—this first drop is a good example of what lies ahead. You won't find water here unless it's recently rained, but water usually runs at the surface farther down.

Down to about 1.4 miles, you'll stay mostly under a narrow, shade-giving cover of willows, live oaks, and bays. The cool pungency of the bay trees are rivaled by the equally sharp odors of white sage and stinging nettles. Here and there, the banks are loaded with Humboldt lilies (in bloom around May or June). Poison oak grows in fair abundance, too.

Unfortunately, a number of car bodies, tires, and various auto parts are wedged, probably permanently, in the canyon's deepest recesses. These vehicles were rolled down from the former Sunrise Highway (now Pacific Crest Trail) 25 or more years ago.

At 1.4 miles the canyon opens up, and it becomes possible to walk through the shrubbery well above the stream. You're in a chaparral belt here—a sort of transition to the desert vegetation below. You come upon a disused dirt road at 1.6 miles that could serve as space for setting up camp. According to your topographic map you've been in Section 21, a remote corner of Anza-Borrego Desert State Park, for the last mile. Private land lies ahead in Sections 15 and 16. If you follow the old road northeast and then southeast, you'll curl over into Section 22 (BLM land), where you'll come upon a spring tucked into the north flank of the Sawtooth Range.

Trip 5: Oasis Spring

Distance	2.0 miles round trip
Total elevation gain/loss	300'/300'
Hiking time	1 hour (round trip)
Optional maps	Cleveland National Forest recreation map; USGS 7.5-min *Monument Peak*
Best times	All year
Agency	CNF/DD
Difficulty	★

A more restful place could scarcely be imagined. A warm breeze from the desert below wafts up the shady canyon, bringing with it the scent of sage and California bay. A lone bigleaf maple tree shimmers in the sunlight. A sparkling stream gushes out of the ground and begins a headlong rush toward the dry desert sands a half mile below. "Oasis" is a perfectly apt description of this idyllic spot.

Oasis Spring lies only 200 yards from Sunrise Highway, but about 300 feet lower in elevation. The best way to reach it is by way of a gradually descending dirt road from the south. This gated road intersects Sunrise Highway at mile 26.7, but parking is very limited here. An east-side turnout at mile 26.5 offers more room. Just below this turnout, you may pick up the Pacific Crest Trail and follow it north. After about 300 yards, the PCT dips into a shallow ravine and briefly joins the road to Oasis Spring. Stay on the road and continue descending through an elfin forest of mostly mountain mahogany.

Curving left, the road leaves the ravine and briefly traverses the abrupt face of the Laguna escarpment. From the lip of the road there's a dramatic view of Storm Canyon and the distant alluvial fans and barren peaks of the desert.

From the road's end, a trail descends on tight switchbacks through a thick growth of live oak and bay to reach an old pumphouse. Nearby is the aforementioned bigleaf maple tree. This particular specimen was evidently planted here. The natural range of the bigleaf maple within the Pacific coast states extends no farther south than the Santa Ana and San Bernardino mountains.

Trip 6: Foster Point

Distance	1.4 miles round trip
Total elevation gain/loss	100'/100'
Hiking time	1 hour (round trip)
Recommended map	USGS 7.5-min *Monument Peak*
Best times	All year
Agency	CNF/DD
Difficulty	★

Come to Foster Point not only for the great view, but also for a chance to identify many of Southern California's highest mountains. A direction finder, constructed by the Sierra Club, shows 17 peaks, including the Southland's highest, San Gorgonio Mountain.

Park opposite the entrance to Horse Heaven Group Camp at mile 25.7 on Sunrise Highway. Walk up the hard-to-identify remnants of an old jeep road going east into a gently sloping forested area known as Flathead Flats. After about 0.2 mile, curve left (north) and you'll soon come upon the narrow but well-defined tread of the Pacific Crest Trail (remember this spot—you'll be returning the same way). Continue north on the PCT through oaks and pines another 0.2 mile.

At this point the forest cover abruptly ends, and dense chaparral begins. Walk 50 yards past the last of the small Jeffrey-pine trees, and you'll find a little trail to the right, marked by a FOSTER POINT sign. It goes about 100 yards through waist-high manzanita, ceanothus, and chamise to the direction-finder on top of a rounded knob.

Monument Peak and its supporting ridgeline cuts off the distant view to the east and the south, but the panorama from north to northeast is excellent. If you know the way well, try coming up here on a

Foster Point

moonlit night, when desert down below glows ghostly white.

Trip 7: Lightning Ridge Trail

Distance	1.5 miles
Total elevation gain/loss	250'/250'
Hiking time	1 hour
Optional map	USGS 7.5-min *Monument Peak*
Best times	All year
Agency	CNF/DD
Difficulty	★

You can reach this trail from either the amphitheater at Laguna Campground or the access road to Horse Heaven Group Camp intersecting Sunrise Highway at mile 25.7. To start from the latter place, park off the pavement, taking care not to block any gates. Head west down the road to Horse Heaven Group Camp. At a fork in 100 yards, take the dirt service road to the right. This goes to Chula Vista Reservoir, a water tank on top of the forested hill ahead of you. After another 0.2 mile,

go right on the unmarked footpath—the Lightning Ridge Trail. This will take you to the top of the hill in a more leisurely fashion.

The panoramic, tree-framed view from the reservoir includes Little Laguna Lake and a long stretch of Laguna Meadow. The water in the lake rises, falls, and vanishes according to the vagaries of the weather. In spring, the brimming surface can be like a mirror, reflecting the greens and blues of the surrounding for-

View of Laguna Lakes from Lightning Ridge Trail

est and sky. In the southwest, ridge after forested ridge leads the eye out to the distant, haze-shrouded coastal foothills.

Retrace your steps back down the trail to the lower end of the service road. There you can cross over to the other side and continue on downhill switchbacks toward Laguna Campground. When you strike a trail at the bottom, turn east, walk through the Horse Heaven equestrian/group camp and arrive back at Sunrise Highway.

Trip 8: Agua Dulce Loop

Distance	5.3 miles
Total elevation gain/loss	600'/600'
Hiking time	3 hours
Recommended map	USGS 7.5-min *Mount Laguna*
Best times	All year
Agency	CNF/DD
Difficulty	★★

By following the directions given here, you can piece together a rewarding loop hike along a long-forgotten alignment of a previous Sunrise Highway, into the shady canyon of Agua Dulce Creek, and through the south end of Laguna Meadow. Whenever several inches or more of snow arrive above the 5000-foot level (perhaps twice yearly), the same route becomes one of the best in San Diego County for cross-country skiing.

Park near the Meadows Information Station, mile 19.1 along Sunrise Highway, where plenty of parking space is available on the wide road shoulder. Proceed 0.2 mile uphill, off the road but parallel to it, to the second gated road intersecting Sunrise Highway on left (north). That road is a segment of the "Old County Road" which was replaced by the wider, straighter Sunrise Highway several decades ago.

Cross-country skiing in Laguna Meadow

Follow the crumbling macadam surface gradually uphill through serene oak and pine forest.

After 2.1 miles, where the old road reaches a crest and begins a slight descent, look for a gap in the barbed-wire fence on the left. Follow the dirt road going through that gap. You soon descend on that road into the upper ravine of Agua Dulce Creek. Enough moisture collects in this ravine to support incense-cedar trees in addition to the usual black oaks and Jeffrey pines found throughout the Laguna range.

Stay on the dirt road following the creek. At 3.6 miles, you come upon a disused pumphouse, part of the infrastructure for the abandoned Mount Laguna air force radar station on Stephenson Peak. Just beyond there, the road peters out. Push ahead through a meadow and bear left into Boiling Spring Ravine. Hook up with the well-worn Big Laguna Trail on the ravine's far side, and follow it westward toward the broad south arm of Laguna Meadow, a short distance away. After passing through a gate at the edge of the meadow, leave the main trail and stay to the left side of the meadow. Then bee-line it across the meadow, generally south or southwest, bypassing a cluster of buildings and corrals at the Laguna Ranch. Ahead and farther south lies Sunrise Highway and your starting point.

In summer or fall the passage across the dry-grass surface of the meadow is straightforward. In late winter or early spring the meadow is soggy, so you may want to travel along its east margin and eventually hook up with Old County Road. During the warmer months, several dozen head of cattle graze out in the meadow, but they seldom take much heed of passing hikers.

Trip 9: Sunset Trail

Distance	3.2 miles round trip (to Water of the Woods)
Total elevation gain/loss	400'/400'
Hiking time	2 hours (round trip)
Optional maps	Cleveland National Forest recreation map; USGS 7.5-min *Monument Peak, Mount Laguna*
Best times	All year
Agency	CNF/DD
Difficulty	★★

The Sunset Trail, opened in 1993, facilitates easy access by foot to the entire west rim of the high Laguna Mountain plateau. Like its analog to the east—the sunrise-facing Pacific Crest Trail—the Sunset Trail offers sweeping views, but on the "sunset" side. You'll almost invariably get the most out of this trail if you start early. As the sun rises unseen in the east, you can look down on either an immense "ocean" of low clouds hugging the coast and foothills, or the real ocean, tinted dark blue by the low angle of the sun's rays.

Park along Sunrise Highway at the Meadows Information Station, mile 19.1, about 5 miles uphill from Interstate 8 at Pine Valley. Walk a little way up the highway shoulder to reach the trailhead, marked by a wooden sign. The gradual climb up the trail takes you toward a gently undulating ridge crest dotted with vanilla-scented Jeffrey pines and black oaks. After nearly a mile, the trail suddenly veers left to circle a rocky outcrop. There, a view opens of velvet-smooth Crouch Valley, some 500 feet below, and much of coastal San Diego County whenever clear air prevails at lower altitudes. The view is worth the trivial effort invested so far.

Thereafter, the trail loses about 200 feet of elevation and draws near a tributary of Noble Canyon that drains Laguna Meadow. The water tumbling or trickling down this steep and densely overgrown ravine eventually reaches Pine Valley Creek, Barrett Reservoir, Cottonwood Creek, Rio Tijuana in Mexico, and finally the Tijuana River Estuary just north of the border. Much of the Laguna Mountain crest sheds water which, if not intercepted by aqueducts, flows through Mexico—a little-known fact.

Rising again briefly, you reach, at 1.5 miles, the lowermost edge of Laguna Meadow and a beautiful pond called "Water of the Woods." Veering left, the Sunset Trail follows the edge of the pond for a short while, then slants up the ridge to the left (northwest). By continuing on the Sun-set Trail you could travel to the north end of the Big Laguna Trail and make a long loop back to the start by way of that trail and Laguna Meadow. If it's spring and the lakes are brimming, try walking around the north edge of Water of the Woods and around the hill to the left. Big Laguna Lake, its half-mile long surface holding the reflection of the blue sky, spreads before you.

Since *laguna* means "lake" or "lagoon" in Spanish, the name "Laguna Lake" is redundant. The name seems to originate from the mountains, which were themselves so named because there were lakes (lagunas) on them. In an average rainy season, the Laguna lakes begin to fill with water or snow by December or January. Carpets of wildflowers—tidy tips, asters, buttercups, goldfields, dandelions, wild onions, and western irises—appear on the meadows surrounding the lakes in April and May. By June, however, the hot sun causes water levels in the lakes to decline rapidly, and the flowers quickly wither.

Trip 10: Big Laguna Trail

Distance	10.0 miles
Total elevation gain/loss	900'/900'
Hiking time	5$^{1}/2$ hours
Recommended maps	Cleveland National Forest recreation map; USGS 7.5-min *Monument Peak*
Best times	All year
Agency	CNF/DD
Difficulty	★★★

The 6-mile-long Big Laguna Trail, completed in 1991, wends its scenic way over gently rolling hills and grassy dales, never dipping below 5400 feet of elevation nor rising to more than 5900 feet. By combining the BLT with a 4-mile segment of the Pacific Crest Trail (PCT), as I describe here, you'll cover a relatively flat 10 miles with lots of varied scenery.

Mountain bikers can use the Big Laguna Trail portion of the route described below, but bikes are prohibited on all parts of the PCT, which is reserved for bipedal and quadrupedal creatures (humans, horses, and dogs). On a bike, however, you can close the loop by riding on Sunrise Highway.

The cool, dry days of autumn are a

On the Big Laguna Trail

perfect time to enjoy this loop hike. You'll walk under wind-battered, 200-year-old Jeffrey pines, and spreading black oaks whose golden yellow leaves shimmer in the breeze. Don't let Santa Ana conditions deter you. During strong Santa Anas, the Lagunas are an oasis of coolness, with average temperatures 25–30° less than in the coastal region. All traces of moisture and air pollution are swept away during these episodes, producing surrealistically blue skies that contrast nicely with the sunbronzed earth.

The Penny Pines parking area, at mile 27.3 on Sunrise Highway, is a good place to begin. Start by walking west on the Noble Canyon Trail. After 0.1 mile, there's a split: the signed Big Laguna Trail goes left. After another 0.8 mile through open pine and oak woods, the BLT turns south to skirt the margin of Laguna Meadow. By 2.5 miles into the hike, you'll be opposite Big Laguna Lake, which may or may not be filled with water, depending on the season.

Next, the trail turns east toward an arm of Laguna Meadow that contains Little Laguna Lake. When you reach a wire fence at 2.8 miles, don't go through the gap in the fence. Instead, turn abruptly right and follow the fenceline over to the wooded area on the meadow's east side. A spur trail branches left toward Laguna Campground, where water is available if you need it.

The main trail continues south along the meadow edge and then east to follow a shallow ravine. After a turn to the north and a short bit of steep climbing, you cross the graded Los Huecos Road (4.5 miles) and hook up with an old roadbed going east and later north. You ascend easily through chaparral—mostly ceanothus, which puts on a great floral show in the late spring. Look for the shiny-leafed chokecherry bushes, which may bear prodigious quantities of ripe red fruit in the fall.

When the roadbed makes a hairpin turn to right (at 5.0 miles), stay left on the footpath that continues through a gap in a wire fence. The path curls down through more pine and oak woods, crosses Sunrise Highway, and continues east, uphill, to join the PCT at 6.0 miles.

Turn left on the PCT and return to your starting point by way of a rambling but scenic stretch of the PCT. Along the way you'll pass several overlooks offering desert views, including Foster Point (see Trip 6 above).

Trip 11: Monument Peak

Distance	2.6 miles round trip
Total elevation gain/loss	550'/550'
Hiking time	$1^1/2$ hours (round trip)
Recommended map	USGS 7.5-min *Monument Peak*
Best times	All year
Agency	CNF/DD
Difficulty	★★

San Diego County is riddled with *ecotones*—boundaries between different geographic regions or ecological habitats. Ecotones harbor great biological diversity and often feature spectacular scenery, especially when the transition from one type of landscape to another is abrupt. Ecotones abound at the ocean's edge, where coastal sage scrub changes into coastal strand or rocky shore habitat and that in turn grades into the intertidal zone. Another major ecotone snakes its way along the top of the Laguna Mountains. In places, a strip of land just a few hundred feet wide separates cool plateau forests from steeply plunging slopes falling straightway to the desert floor.

This short hike through pine woods and windblown chaparral takes you to Monument Peak, smack-dab on the mountain-desert ecotone. A small cluster of communications antennae rests on the peak, a testament to its strategic geographic position. Few hikers come this way; as a result, the route is obscure and requires a bit of navigational attention.

Park off the pavement along Sunrise Highway at mile 25.2, and start walking uphill on the signed Big Laguna Trail. Continue 0.5 mile through a parklike forest of Jeffrey pines and black oaks to a junction with the Pacific Crest Trail. Turn left and continue moderately uphill, counting your paces as you go. After about 800 steps, you get a glimpse of microwave antennas ahead. This is an important clue. At the next sharp leftward bend in the trail, keep going straight (east) on an informal path through scattered manzanita and mountain mahogany brush. Soon, the path bends to the right and you clamber up to and around a fenced laser-research facility to join a paved access road (closed to public vehicle traffic).

Follow the road to Monument Peak's summit, where the vista of earth and sky spreads incredibly far and wide, particularly around the beginning and the end of each clear day. Early on, the sun vaults above a bluish horizon shaped by Arizona peaks. Late in the afternoon, Laguna Mountain shadows lengthen across the floor of the Anza-Borrego Desert, racing ever faster over sandy flats and badlands below.

Trip 12: Kwaaymii Trail

Distance	0.5 mile
Total elevation gain/loss	100'/100'
Hiking time	20 minutes
Optional map	USGS 7.5-min *Mount Laguna*
Best times	All year
Agency	CNF/DD
Difficulty	★

This walk begins at the visitor information office (mile 23.5 on Sunrise Highway) and loops over a small hill called Pinon Point (or Pinyon Point). The leaflet for this trail describes Indian uses of native plants for food, shelter, clothing, and medicine. Bedrock *morteros* (deep holes) and *metates* (shallow depressions) used for grinding acorns may be seen along the trail. The Kwaaymii, the most recent Native American inhabitants of the Laguna Mountains, were a subtribe of the Kumeyaay Indians.

The large pinyon pine on Pinon Point is a Sierra Juarez pinyon, with needles in clusters of five. Nearby is another smaller pinyon of the four-leafed variety. Pinyon pines with one, four, and five needles are distributed throughout the desert-facing slopes of San Diego and Riverside counties and the Sierra Juarez range of Baja California, but they are relatively rare here in the Lagunas.

Near the large pinyon on Pinon Point are a patch of prickly pear cactus and several holly-leafed cherry bushes. October brings a bountiful harvest of native fruit—a bit less than sweet to our pampered palates and full of seeds, but no doubt a fitting dessert after a meal of acorn and seed porridge.

Discovering **morteros** *on the Kwaaymii Trail*

Trip 13: Desert View Trail

Distance	1.3 miles
Total elevation gain/loss	150'/150'
Hiking time	1 hour
Optional map	USGS 7.5-min *Mount Laguna*
Best times	All year
Agency	CNF/DD
Difficulty	★

The Desert View Trail starts just inside Burnt Rancheria Campground at a lot signed NATURE TRAIL. The trail winds through vanilla-scented Jeffrey-pine forest and then joins the Pacific Crest Trail on a chaparral-covered ridge. As you head north along the ridge, there's a wide-open view of the La Posta Creek canyon, part of a remote southern area of the Lagunas that was swept by wildfire in July 1989. New growth, especially along the creek below, is softening the landscape.

Farther north, a view to the north and west opens: ahead are old radar domes at a former Air Force facility on Stephenson Peak; far off to the right is a slice of the brown desert floor. At a point 0.8 mile from the start, the signed Desert View Trail diverges left from the PCT, descends, and returns through the campground to the trailhead.

Trip 14: Wooded Hill Nature Trail

Distance	1.5 miles
Total elevation gain/loss	300'/300'
Hiking time	1 hour
Optional map	USGS 7.5-min *Mount Laguna*
Best times	All year
Agency	CNF/DD
Difficulty	★

The figure-8 path of the Wooded Hill Nature Trail will take you to the highest wooded summit in the Laguna Mountains. (Three slightly higher summits are nearby, but they're entirely brush-covered.) Atop Wooded Hill you can view a wide panorama that encompasses (when the air's very clear) San Diego, Point Loma, Santa Catalina Island, San Clemente Island, and the Coronado Islands. On the way up you'll catch sight of the white domes of Mount Laguna Observatory, San Diego State University's off-campus site for astronomical research and instruction.

Turn north from Sunrise Highway (mile 21.7) onto Wooded Hill Road, and drive 0.3 mile to the trailhead on the left. An interpretive booklet for the trail should be available either at the trailhead or at the nearby visitor information office.

Trip 15: Kitchen Creek Falls

Distance	4.5 miles round trip
Total elevation gain/loss	900'/900'
Hiking time	2 1/2 hours
Recommended map	USGS 7.5-min *Cameron Corners*
Best times	December through May
Agency	CNF/DD
Difficulty	★★

For the most part, San Diego County's section of the Pacific Crest Trail sticks to high and dry ridgelines and slopes, avoiding most canyon bottoms and streamcourses. On the southern slopes of the Laguna Mountains, however, the PCT passes just 200 yards above a hidden series of waterfalls on Kitchen Creek. Here, water from about 20 square miles of drainage flows through a narrow constriction in the bedrock, and tumbles about 150 vertical feet over water-polished slabs.

In the aftermath of major storms, the sound of the falling water gives away the location of the falls; at other times, finding them may be a bit difficult. A short stretch of moderate scrambling is required to reach them.

A convenient starting point is Boulder Oaks, a major access point along the PCT. Take the Buckman Springs Road turnoff from Interstate 8 and go south on the frontage road—Old Highway 80—two miles to the Boulder Oaks store and campground.

Across the old highway from Boulder Oaks is a broad pathway marked by a PCT post. Follow this as it meanders be-

Cottonwood Creek Falls

side oak-shaded Kitchen Creek and under the twin bridges of Interstate 8. Immediately past the second bridge, find the marked PCT, which abruptly ascends to the right. After a steep climb on tight switchbacks, you begin a gradual, winding ascent up along the brushy slopes above Kitchen Creek.

As the noise from the freeway recedes, you can concentrate on the pervading hum of countless bees and other insects drawn by the sweet fragrances of blue- and white-flowered ceanothus, manzanita, and many kinds of annual wildflowers. The most intense blooming usually occurs in April.

At a point just over 2 miles from Boulder Oaks, the PCT pulls close to the deeply creased canyon containing Kitchen Creek. Look for an obscure path through the low brush north of the trail. This path wanders past a couple of possible small campsites, then drops suddenly about 200 feet to the falls area, located (but not marked) on the topo map between the 3440-foot and 3600-foot contours.

The dry, water-polished rock on either side of the cascade provides fair traction, but beware of any wet streaks that may be slippery.

Trip 16: Cottonwood Creek Falls

Distance	1.8 miles round trip
Total elevation gain/loss	500'/500'
Hiking time	1 hour (round trip)
Optional map	USGS 7.5-min *Mount Laguna*
Best times	December through June
Agency	CNF/DD
Difficulty	★★

Yet another set of falls south of the Laguna Mountain crest invites your exploration. Although these falls on Cottonwood Creek are somewhat less spectacular than those on Kitchen Creek (above), they have the added attraction of swimmable pools.

Public access to the Cottonwood Creek falls is by way of a brushy draw which drains south from Sunrise Highway. Park in either of the two large turnouts between mile 15.3 and mile 15.4 on Sunrise Highway. From the top of the draw, where a utility pole stands, pick up a narrow trail that goes down to hook up with an old road following a small powerline. Along the way you'll find good springtime displays of white ceanothus, beard tongue, woolly blue curls, and yucca.

At the bottom of the draw, the powerline road intersects with another dirt road. Turn sharply left and go north to where Cottonwood Creek emerges from a narrow canyon. Clamber alongside several cascades to the upper and tallest one, where the stream drops 10 feet into a crystalline pool about 4 feet deep. The water warms to comfortable temperatures by May. By June or July, the flow in the creek slackens and algae takes over.

The oak-shaded, west bank of the creek just below the falls area provides some nice camping space—if you don't mind packing overnight gear and hauling it on such a short journey.

Trip 17: Noble Canyon Trail

Distance	10.0 miles
Total elevation gain/loss	650'/2400'
Hiking time	5 hours
Recommended maps	USGS 7.5-min *Monument Peak, Mount Laguna, Descanso*
Best times	October through May
Agency	CNF/DD
Difficulty	★★★

The Noble Canyon National Recreation Trail is an extension and reworking of an older trail built in the 1930s by the Civilian Conservation Corps. Since its completion in 1982, the trail has proven very popular among hikers, equestrians, and more recently mountain bikers.

With transportation arrangements set up in advance, you can travel one-way along this trail in the relatively easy downhill direction. You'll find the top end of the trail at the Penny Pines trailhead, mile 27.3 on Sunrise Highway, where parking space is plentiful along the highway shoulder. The bottom end is the developed Noble Canyon trailhead on Pine Creek Road near Pine Valley. Potable water is not available at either trailhead, so plan for your water needs in advance.

Good campsites are fairly abundant along the trail, particularly on shady terraces along the mid-portion of Noble Canyon (remember to establish your camp no less than 100 feet from water). Water flows in the canyon bottom year-round, though it slows to a trickle before the first rains of autumn. Purification is necessary if you intend to rely on it for your drinking or cooking needs.

From the starting point, head west along the marked Noble Canyon Trail. After passing through a park-like setting of Jeffrey pines, you rise a bit along the north slope of a steep hill. From there, the tree-framed view extends to the distant summits of San Jacinto Peak and San Gorgonio Mountain. Next, you descend to cross dirt roads three times, then climb and circle around the chaparral-clad north end of a north-south trending ridge. This seemingly out-of-the-way excursion avoids private inholdings in the national forest, but it opens up interesting vistas to the north and west. Three varieties of blooming ceanothus brighten the view in springtime.

Next, you descend on a long switchback into the upper reaches of Noble Canyon, where the grassy hillsides show off springtime blooms of blue-purple beard tongue, scarlet bugler, woolly blue curls, yellow monkeyflower, Indian paintbrush,

Lower Noble Canyon

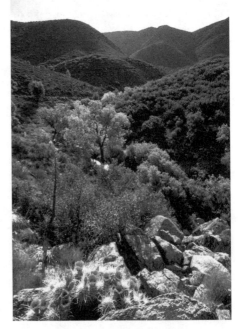

wallflower, white forget-me-not, wild hyacinth, yellow violet, phacelia, golden yarrow, checker, lupine, and blue flax.

The trail sidles up to the creek at about 3.0 miles, and stays beside it for the next 4 miles. Past a canopy of live oaks, black oaks, and Jeffrey pines, you emerge into an steep, sunlit section of canyon. The trail cuts through thick brush on the east wall, while on the west wall only a few hardy, drought-tolerant plants cling to the exposed metamorphic rock.

Back in the shade of oaks again, you soon cross a major tributary creek from the east. This drains the Laguna Lakes and Laguna Meadow. Pause for a while in this shady glen, where the water flows over somber, grayish granitic rock and gathers in languid pools bedecked by sword and bracken fern. Look for nodding yellow Humboldt lilies in the late spring or early summer.

You continue within a riparian area for some distance downstream. Mixed in with the oaks, you'll discover dozens of fine California bay trees and a few scattered incense-cedars. The creek lies mostly hidden by willows and sycamores, and dense thickets of poison oak, squaw bush, wild rose, wild strawberries, and other types of water-loving vegetation. The line of trees shading the trail is narrow enough that light from the sky is freely admitted. Greens and browns—and in fall, yellows and reds—glow intensely.

You'll pass some mining debris—the remains of a flume and the stones of a disassembled "arrastra" (a horse- or mule-drawn machine for crushing ore). This dates from gold mining activity in the late 1800s. Next, you'll come upon the foundations of two cabins, then two more cabins in disrepair. Someone long ago planted what is now a huge cypress tree in front of the larger cabin.

Crossing to the west side of the creek, you break out of the trees and into an open area with sage scrub and chaparral vegetation. The trail contours to a point about 100 feet above the creek, then maintains this position as it bends around several small tributaries. Midday temperatures, even in spring, can be uncomfortably warm along this stretch. Yucca, prickly-pear cactus, and even hedgehog cactus—normally a denizen of the desert—make appearances here. There are also excellent vernal displays of beard tongue, scarlet bugler, paintbrush, peony, wild pea, milkweed, wild onion, chia, and larkspur.

At about 7 miles, the trail switches back, crosses the Noble Canyon creek for the last time, and veers up a tributary canyon to the south. The trail joins the bed of an old jeep road, reaches a saddle after about 2 miles from Noble Canyon, then diverges from the road, going right (west) over another saddle. It then descends directly to the developed trailhead facility along Pine Creek Road.

Trip 18: Laguna to Cuyamaca

Distance	12.2 miles
Total elevation gain/loss	1250'/2700'
Hiking time	7 hours
Recommended maps	USGS 7.5-min *Monument Peak, Cuyamaca Peak*
Best times	October through May
Agency	CNF/DD, CRSP
Difficulty	★★★

This route, incorporating the new Indian Creek Trail (completed in 1989), provides a fairly direct and convenient connection between the Laguna Mountain

Recreation Area and Cuyamaca Rancho State Park. Only a small part of the route is shaded, so plan accordingly if the day is warm. The only potable water found near the route is at Granite Spring, near the end of the trip. It's best, then, to carry all the water you'll need.

Mountain bikers can use the route described below, except that they must finish on East Mesa Fire Road in Cuyamaca Rancho State Park and not use the west end of the Harvey Moore Trail, which is reserved for hikers and horses.

A car shuttle can be set up between the Penny Pines trailhead (mile 27.3 on Sunrise Highway) in the Laguna Mountains, and the Sweetwater River bridge parking area (mile 4.8–4.9 on Highway 79) in Cuyamaca Rancho State Park.

If you're going to backpack this route, you'll need to make parking arrangements with the state park, and also obtain a remote camping permit from the Forest Service for camping on national forest land. With prior arrangement, you could also camp at the state park's Granite Spring trail camp, just off the route.

The hike begins pleasantly with a scenic stretch of the upper Noble Canyon Trail (see start of Trip 17). After 2.4 miles, turn right on the Indian Creek Trail and descend 0.8 mile to the grassy banks along Indian Creek. After an indistinct crossing of the often soggy creekbed, the trail turns northwest to climb a chaparral-clothed hillside. After about 1.5 miles of steady climbing, the trail tops out at a summit (5440') dubbed Champagne Pass. On the clearest of days, your gaze takes in the western slope of the Lagunas, the eastern slopes of the Cuyamaca Mountains, and a slice of Pacific

Ocean freckled with the Coronado Islands.

Next you descend some 800 feet through chaparral and grassland to Deer Park Road in the upper reaches of Pine Valley Creek, 6 miles from the starting point. (An interesting diversion can be made from here: Walk south on Deer Park Road past an old stone house on the right. Next to the road a little farther on you'll find the remains of an arrastra, a circular ore-milling machine powered by horses or mules. Several mine shafts are located nearby, indicated on your topo map. These features date from the mining boom of the late 1800s.)

After crossing Deer Park Road, the Indian Creek Trail continues west 100 yards to join Deer Park Trail—an extension of the East Mesa Fire Road coming down from Cuyamaca Rancho State Park. Once inside the state park, you continue uphill along a sun-blasted, chaparral-covered slope. Near the top of the grade, some large black oak trees provide welcome shade and a good excuse to catch your breath.

East Mesa Fire Road tops out at about 5000 feet, then begins a long and gradual descent across an open meadow. On clear days, beyond the rolling and wind-rippled expanses of grass, Point Loma and the ocean horizon may be seen. Harvey Moore Trail soon joins from the right (north).

From now on, follow the route of the Harvey Moore Trail. After passing Granite Spring Primitive Camp, you'll have to veer right to remain on the hiker's route to the Sweetwater River bridge, which lies 3 downhill miles away. Mountain bikers must keep left here and follow East Mesa Fire Road to Highway 79.

Area M-9: Pine Creek

The Cleveland National Forest's Pine Creek Wilderness, created in 1984, encompasses more than 13,000 acres of chaparral-covered slopes and riparian woodland south and west of the Laguna Mountains. A 15-mile stretch of Pine Valley Creek (or "Pine Creek" as many people are referring to it now) meanders through the heart of the wilderness, flanked by sloping walls up to 1000 feet high. Motorists eastbound on Interstate 8 can catch a fleeting glimpse of this impressive gorge when crossing the Pine Valley Bridge, the highest bridge in the Interstate Highway System.

The Pine Creek Wilderness is among the most accessible wilderness areas in California, just 45 minutes east of downtown San Diego via Highway 94 through Jamul, and slightly less time via Interstate 8 through Alpine. If you plan to visit the wilderness area—either for day or for overnight use—don't forget to obtain the necessary wilderness permit from the Forest Service.

Trips 1, 2, 6, 7, and 8 below lie outside the Pine Creek Wilderness boundary, but still inside Cleveland National Forest. You do not need a wilderness permit for these, although a remote camping permit is required if you're going backpacking. All trips in this section are on national forest land, so they require a National Forest Adventure Pass for parking at the trailheads (see the introductory section "Using This Book").

Operation Gatekeeper, the federal government's recent attempt to stave off illegal immigration from Mexico into the United States, has resulted in an eastward shift in migration patterns (from Tijuana/San Ysidro to points well east of there) and a dramatic increase in migrant foot traffic northward across the mountains of San Diego County. Pine Valley Creek, along with other areas within 20 miles of the border, has been affected. Operation Gatekeeper involves the building of a sturdy fence many miles eastward along the international border. If and when this fence is extended as far east as the desert, the migration routes will likely shift into Imperial County. Since safety issues may be of special concern for anyone visiting the southern mountain region of San Diego County, it would be a good idea to contact Cleveland National Forest (Descanso Ranger District) for the latest update.

Trip 1: Roberts Ranch

Distance	2.0 miles round trip
Total elevation gain/loss	200'/200'
Hiking time	1 hour (round trip)
Optional map	USGS 7.5-min *Descanso*
Best times	All year
Agency	CNF/DD
Difficulty	★

Thanks to the crusading efforts of Descanso cabinet-maker Duncan McFetridge, affectionately known by some as the "Robin Hood of Cleveland Forest," two private inholdings near Descanso are being added to the Cleveland National

Area M-9: Pine Creek

Forest. The former Roberts and Ellis ranches, adjacent to Interstate 8 at Highway 79/Japatul Valley Road, were slated for subdivided housing until Duncan and his merry band of supporters (the Cleveland National Forest Foundation) helped raise money to finance their purchase.

To reach the Roberts Ranch, now open to the public, exit I-8 and drive south on Japatul Valley Road 0.2 mile to a pipe gate in the wire fence on the left, just short of a Caltrans maintenance station. Park on the road shoulder. Push through the gate and follow an old roadbed north across a

flat, then east up through dense oak woodland. After 0.5 mile, stay left and start bending north to enter an expansive meadow dotted with statuesque Engelmann oaks. The scene is quintessentially Old West, save for the slightly annoying hum of cars on the nearby freeway. If you walk all the way across the meadow, about half a mile farther east, you'll come upon the remnants of a century-old ditch designed (but never used) to shunt water from Pine Valley Creek into the San Diego River drainage. See Trip 4 below for more on this historic feature).

Engelmann oak, Roberts Ranch

Trip 2: Lawson Peak

Distance	4.5 miles round trip
Total elevation gain/loss	1600'/1600'
Hiking time	3 hours (round trip)
Optional maps	Cleveland National Forest recreation map; USGS 7.5-min *Barrett Lake*
Best times	November through May
Agency	CNF/DD
Difficulty	★★★

Lawson Peak is one of a triad of prominent, granite-topped peaks lying in the southwest corner of Cleveland National Forest. The others are Gaskill Peak and Lyons Peak. Lyons Peak, listed in the first edition of this guidebook, no longer has any legal access; Gaskill Peak, on the other hand, can be reached from Lawson Peak at the expense of an hour or two's extra effort, as noted below.

You begin at mile marker 13.0 on Lyons Valley Road (3 miles east of Honey Springs Road and Skyline Truck Trail), where there are two small turnouts for parking.

Start walking on the unsigned Carveacre Road, which is a challenge for off-road drivers, but relatively easy for hikers. The road crests in 1.9 miles, then descends slightly to meet Wisecarver Road. Mountain bikers would have to stash their bikes here. Lawson Peak lies straight ahead, a massive heap of granite slabs.

The fun begins as you plunge ahead through low brush and boulders east and north of the summit block. Just below the summit on the west side is a near-vertical fissure with abundant hand- and footholds. At the top of this is a narrow rock cave. By groping 15 feet or so into the darkness in back of the cave, you'll find an opening above. By mantling up onto a ledge, you'll reach a broad shelf (a nice picnic spot) with a view to the east. Nearby is an easy route to the topmost boulders on the peak.

Standing on the highest boulder is like being on top of the world. To the northwest is Lawson Valley, cut with new roads and dotted with ranches. In most other directions, the view is simply mile upon mile of sun-dappled chaparral and gleaming rock. Lyons Peak and Tecate Peak are prominent on the southwest and south horizons, while Barrett Lake nestles below an almost unbroken rim of mountains to the east. To the west, if the air's clear, the ocean spreads across the horizon.

If you haven't had your fill of peak bagging, return to Carveacre Road and turn north. After 0.5 mile of road walking, you can find and follow an obscure hikers' trail up the south ridge of Gaskill Peak. Attaining Gaskill's summit, which is slightly higher but less dramatic than Lawson's, requires in the end a short, but somewhat tricky bit of rock climbing. A large flat area of granite lies just northeast

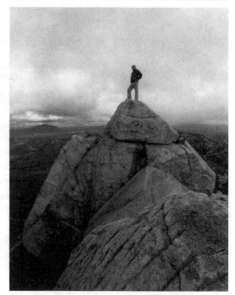

Summit block of Lawson Peak

of the summit—perfect as a "lunch rock" and suitable as a private, secluded campsite as well.

Trip 3: Horsethief Canyon

Distance	3.2 miles round trip
Total elevation gain/loss	500'/500'
Hiking time	2 hours (round trip)
Optional maps	USGS 7.5-min *Barrett Lake, Viejas Mountain*
Best times	November through June
Agency	CNF/DD
Difficulty	★★

The guttural croak of a soaring raven cracked the stillness as we sauntered down the dusty path. A groggy dragonfly flitted through a beam of morning sunlight. Cool air, slinking down the night-chilled slopes, caressed our faces and set aflutter the sycamore leaves overhead. Arriving at Pine Valley Creek, we felt puffs of warm, dry air pushing down the gorge—a Santa Ana wind flexing its muscles. We cupped the clear, cold water in our palms and dashed it across our heads.

If you want this kind of escape from the cares of the city, the Espinosa Trail down Horsethief Canyon is one place to find it. The trailhead, at mile 16.4 on Lyons Valley Road, is quick and easy to reach—either from the north (Japatul Road from Alpine) or from the south (Skyline Truck Trail) from Jamul. From the trailhead parking lot, a sign directs you north along a gated dirt road for about 300 yards. You then veer right down a ravine on the signed Espinosa Trail.

Pine Valley Creek

After a fast, 400-foot elevation loss, the path bends right (east) to follow live-oak- and sycamore-lined Horsethief Canyon. True to its name, this corral-like canyon was used in the late 1800s by horse thieves to stash stolen horses in preparation for their passage across the international border. The canyon bottom is dry most of the year, but agreeably shaded throughout.

After another mile and not much more descent, you reach the sandy bank of Pine Valley Creek, which in winter and early spring brims with runoff from the creek's headwaters in the Laguna Mountains.

If yours is a casual trip, this is as far as you should go. If the spirit moves you, you might wade across the creek and continue east on the Espinosa Trail toward higher ground (see Trip 5 below), or you could scramble up the Pine Valley Creek gorge as far as you like. Beyond the large pool just upstream from the trail crossing is a picturesque jumble of car-sized boulders and several mini-waterfalls. Watch your step on the slippery rock, and watch out for poison oak and rattlesnakes. If the water level is dangerously high, don't try following the creek upstream at all.

If you're hooked on loop hikes, you can try the following, less-scenic return route: Proceed downstream (south) on the west bank of Pine Valley Creek for 0.7 mile. At a point opposite the Espinosa Creek confluence, turn right (west) on an old roadbed paralleling a ravine. Follow its steep course upward through chaparral and over a summit to the trailhead parking lot.

Trip 4: Secret Canyon Trail

Distance	15.6 miles
Total elevation gain/loss	1200'/2300'
Hiking time	9 hours
Recommended maps	USGS 7.5-min *Descanso, Viejas Mountain, Barrett Lake*
Best times	November through April
Agency	CNF/DD
Difficulty	★★★★

This ambitiously constructed trail, through tough terrain and dense chaparral most of the way, takes you circuitously down the gorge of Pine Valley Creek. Completed in 1992, the trail takes advantage of an old, never-completed flume that would have shunted water from a proposed reservoir in Pine Valley over to King Creek (a tributary of the San Diego River) on the west side of the Cuyamaca Mountains. The Secret Canyon Trail follows some of the longest and best-preserved sections of this circa 1895 engineering effort. For several years in the mid-1990s, the remote middle section of the Secret Canyon Trail was severely overgrown—though now the Forest Service and volunteers seem to be getting the upper hand.

Begin at the Secret Canyon trailhead staging area (entrance at mile 3.5 on Old Highway 80, up the hill from the Pine Creek Road intersection). You'll end at the Espinosa trailhead on Lyons Valley Road.

For 2 miles, the trail follows the meandering Pine Valley Creek through a rather broad, but twisting gorge. At 1.8 miles you pass under the gargantuan Pine Valley Bridge. Its twin ribbons of interstate highway are held more than 400 feet above the canyon bottom by four massive pillars.

About 300 yards past the bridge, the trail gains a foothold on the brushy slope to the right and starts climbing in earnest to a point about 250 feet above the creek. There it joins the old flume ditch, which in places is accompanied on the down-slope side by remarkably intact walls of dry-laid stone. The latest (photorevised 1988) edition of the Descanso topo map shows the general course of both the trail and the

Canyon live oak and poison oak

flume bed over the next several miles. Since many of the side ravines were never bridged, the trail on occasion darts up and down to connect the nearly flat segments of the flume bed. At about 6.0 miles, there's a rough up-and-down stretch at the point where the topo map shows a nonexistent tunnel. Then it's easy going again until 6.9 miles, where the trail leaves the flume bed and abruptly descends into oak shaded Nelson Canyon. After rising slightly on the slope west of Nelson Canyon, the trail zigzags down and crosses Pine Valley Creek, 9.0 miles.

On the east side of the now-rather-wide Pine Valley Creek gorge, a gently inclined stretch of trail takes you through monotonous chaparral to a saddle overlooking Secret Canyon at 10.8 miles. You then descend and follow Secret Canyon's trickling creek downstream through grassy hollows where spreading oaks cast inviting pools of shade. The oaks are of two varieties—coast live oak and Engelmann oak.

At 12.5 miles, near Secret Canyon's confluence with Pine Valley Creek, the trail starts angling up a slope to the left. You meander along the east canyon wall of Pine Valley Creek and intersect the Espinosa Trail at 13.8 miles. Follow Espinosa Trail west across Pine Valley Creek and up Horsethief Canyon (see Trip 3) to the trailhead parking lot along Lyons Valley Road. The final stretch gains 400 feet quickly, so save some energy for it.

Here are some further suggestions if your tastes run to challenging cross-country travel, rather than long miles of trail walking: You're welcome to try boulder-hopping along all or part of the stretch of Pine Valley Creek paralleled by the Secret Canyon Trail. In addition to the spot where Secret Canyon switches from one side of the canyon to the other, there's access to the creek by way of the still-viable Horsethief Ridge Trail. It descends from the unpaved (and closed to motor vehicles)

Horsethief Ridge road.

Boulder hopping along Pine Valley Creek ranges from rather easy when the water level is low, to dicey and dangerous after major storms. In winter the water is achingly cold, for the creek carries snowmelt from the Laguna Mountains. In warm weather you'll probably want to wade right through the deepest pools.

The 4-mile stretch of the canyon between Horsethief Ridge and Espinosa trails is best. The creek flows over polished bedrock slabs and tumbles over several small waterfalls, accompanied most of the while by scattered willows, cottonwoods and sycamores.

If you decide to follow Pine Valley Creek south from the I-8 bridge, don't miss an interesting side trip up the short, steep canyon that drains Oak Valley. Floodwaters tearing through this mini-gorge have scoured out a number of huge "potholes" in the bedrock. The Forest Service is considering building a trail that would run along the side of this canyon and loop back under the I-8 bridge.

Trip 5: Espinosa Trail

Distance	7.8 miles
Total elevation gain/loss	1250'/2100'
Hiking time	4 hours
Recommended maps	USGS 7.5-min *Morena Reservoir, Descanso, Viejas Mountain*
Best times	November through May
Agency	CNF/DD
Difficulty	★★

If you can arrange to be dropped off at the east end of this route and picked up later at the west end, this can be an enjoyable and rather easy trip across the mountains. Do it in the early spring if possible, when the chaparral blooms and water bubbles down even the most insignificant ravines.

The east entry is approached by way of Interstate 8 and Buckman Springs Road. At mile 6.6 on Buckman Springs Road (3 miles south of I-8), turn west on Corral Canyon Road and proceed 4.8 miles on narrow pavement to a hairpin turn. The unsigned, gated Kernan Road goes northwest from the turn. Park nearby off the road. Your friends can drive around to Espinosa Trail's west terminus at mile 16.4 on Lyons Valley Road and meet you later.

Squeeze around the gate and walk 0.5 mile up Kernan Road along the Morena Creek drainage. Where the road bends right in a horseshoe curve, pick up the Espinosa Trail and continue northwest. After one more mile of climbing, you top a saddle and cross Los Pinos Road. Continue straight ahead (west) and begin a sharp descent toward Espinosa Creek. The next 3 miles of the Espinosa Trail are part of an approved off-road-vehicle route. In the wet season, Espinosa Creek trickles under a canopy of live oaks and splashes over at least one waterfall hidden in the brush. To the right, framed by twisted oaks, the sheer south face of Corte Madera Mountain thrusts skyward.

When you reach Corte Madera Road, jog north for 0.2 mile on it, then go west again on the continuation of the Espinosa Trail, now free of ORV's. (Note: mountain bikes are allowed on the route up to this point, but not beyond where the trail enters Pine Creek Wilderness.) The trail cuts across a chaparral-covered flat, and then descends viewfully into the Pine Valley Creek gorge.

Down at the bottom, cross the creek and continue west along the oak-shaded bottom of Horsethief Canyon for one mile. Then bend sharply left (south) to follow the steep path up to the trailhead parking lot along Lyons Valley Road.

Trip 6: Corte Madera Mountain

Distance	6.5 miles round trip
Total elevation gain/loss	1750'/1750'
Hiking time	4 hours (round trip)
Recommended maps	USGS 7.5-min *Morena Reservoir, Descanso*
Best times	November through May
Agency	CNF/DD
Difficulty	★★★

Here is one of San Diego County's prime view spots, affording a panorama that sometimes stretches from Santa Catalina and San Clemente islands to the Sierra Juarez plateau in Baja California. Corte Madera Mountain's sheer south face is noticeable as an abrupt drop in the mountain profile as seen from many parts of metropolitan San Diego; at one point there's a near-vertical dropoff of about 300 feet.

Begin along Corral Canyon Road—see Trip 5 above for directions. Upon reaching Los Pinos Road, on the saddle 1.0 mile up the Espinosa Trail, turn right and continue 0.3 mile to another saddle, this one a half mile southeast of boulder-studded, Coulter-pine-dotted peak 4588. Leave the road there and find and follow a path that works its way northwest up past peak 4588 and across another saddle just northwest of that peak.

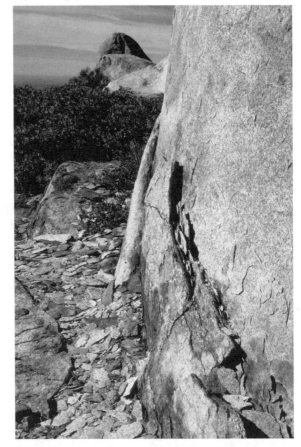

Exfoliating granite atop Corte Madera Mountain

Continue following the path northwest, then southwest along a crest to the gentle summit plateau of Corte Madera Mountain. The view north includes a fabulous vista, available nowhere else on public land, of the privately owned Corte Madera Valley. A beautiful lake and oak-studded meadows fill the valley. The name Corte Madera ("woodyard") apparently refers to the use of this area as a source of timber during the building of the San Diego area missions.

Corte Madera Mountain's summit plateau is covered by large sheets of granitic rock and patches of chaparral. From the southernmost point on the plateau you can peer over the abrupt face into the canyon drained by Espinosa Creek. To the southeast is Los Pinos Mountain, topped by a fire lookout—the last remaining active lookout in San Diego County.

If you care to do a little further exploring, try following the informal network of horse trails cut into the north slope of Corte Madera Mountain. These are most often used by riders who live in the private homes below. The trails meander down to the edge of the grassy Corte Madera Valley, where the private property begins.

Trip 7: Morena Butte

	Distance	8.0 miles
	Total elevation gain/loss	1500'/1500'
	Hiking time	5 hours
	Recommended map	USGS 7.5-min *Morena Reservoir*
	Best times	November through April
	Agency	CNF/DD
	Difficulty	★★★

Morena Butte's three-peaked summit plateau presides over a diverse landscape of V-shaped canyons, rock-strewn ridges, and grassy depressions known as *potreros* (pastures). All three peaks are attractive photographically, as they consist of great slabs and boulders of pink-tinted granitic rock weathered into sometimes-surreal forms.

The starting point for this hike (and for Trip 8 below) is Lake Morena County Park, 12 miles south of Pine Valley via Interstate 8, Buckman Springs Road, and Morena Village. Start hiking at the Pacific Crest Trail parking lot, at the entrance to the county campground.

Follow the PCT as it ascends west on the slope overlooking Morena Reservoir. During wet cycles, the lake expands to nearly fill this 2-square-mile former *potrero*; while in drought, the water surface shrinks to about one-tenth that size. Fine views of the blue water can be had for a while, but presently the trail swings away, generally south over and around several hilltops. Good displays of blooming ceanothus liven things up in the springtime, otherwise the chaparral-draped slopes can appear quite drab.

At 1.8 miles the trail starts descending generally west into a shallow tributary of Hauser Creek. You cross the ravine at 2.7 miles and gently ascend to a saddle on the southeast shoulder of Morena Butte (3.0 miles). From that point find and follow a rough and sketchy path going northwest up the ridge 1.0 mile to the summit area. Climb all three of the rocky peaklets

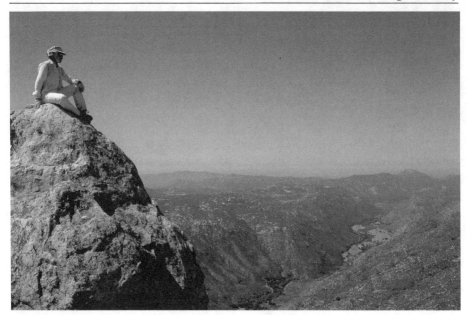

On Morena Butte

on top for great views in various directions.

Return to where you left the PCT, retrace your steps for 0.2 mile, then stay left on a path (old roadbed) that slants north, gains about 100 feet, and attains a broad divide. There you meet a dirt road that will take you northwest through a beautiful valley, graced with live oaks and Coulter pines, right beneath the stony gaze of Morena Butte. Continue to Morena Reservoir's shoreline road, and follow it 2.0 miles back to your starting point.

Trip 8: Hauser Canyon

Distance	13.5 miles round trip (to Marine Memorial)
Total elevation gain/loss	2000'/2000'
Hiking time	8 hours (round trip)
Recommended map	USGS 7.5-min *Morena Reservoir*
Best times	October through May
Agency	CNF/DD
Difficulty	★★★★

The linear, **V**-shaped gash of Hauser Canyon cuts across one of the really remote parts of the county. Years ago the public could descend into the canyon by way of a dirt road from Lake Morena Drive and reach a forest-service campground. Today, the east end of this road is blocked by a locked gate and the west end is washed out. Nowadays the canyon is visited only by hikers, undocumented migrants, and Border Patrol agents pursuing those migrants.

The stroll down oak- and sycamore-lined Hauser and Cottonwood creeks will be your reward for putting up with a long, somewhat uneventful approach (and return) on the Pacific Crest Trail. Begin by hiking the PCT, as in Trip 6 above, to the saddle southeast of Hauser Butte. From there you lose 900 feet of elevation as you zigzag down the north wall of Hauser Canyon (passing, incidentally, through a corner of the Hauser Wilderness). At 4.3 miles, the trail intersects Hauser Creek Road, down along the creek. Leave the PCT at this point and follow the road west, down-canyon.

At 5.8 miles Cottonwood Creek comes in from the north. Its flow depends almost solely upon releases at Morena Dam, about 2 miles upstream. A small waterfall and pool, sculpted into the bedrock, are just above the confluence. Nearby you'll find a pint-size rock cave.

Below the confluence, you must pick your way through a tangle of riparian vegetation. Just pick your way along the bank, or splash along through the shallow water. The site of the old Hauser Creek Campground is an oak-shaded bench along a bend in the creek at 6.3 miles. Nearby is a concrete dam and pond that once harbored bass (and perhaps still does). After another 0.4 mile, you'll come upon the Marine Memorial—a memorial to the nine Marine Corps fire fighters who perished at that spot during a 1943 wildfire. This is your turnaround point.

Beyond the memorial, the waters of Cottonwood Creek trickle down to Barrett Lake, a county reservoir closed to public use.

Yucca, Hauser Canyon

Area M-10: Border Ranges

Most admirers of San Diego's beautiful setting of mountain and sea are somewhat familiar with the long, pillowy range of mountains on the city's southeastern horizon. Rising from the flatlands of Otay Mesa, they are officially named the San Ysidro Mountains—but almost everyone knows of them as Otay Mountain, which is the name of the highest summit.

Otay Mountain's western slopes offer unexcelled views of San Diego, San Diego Bay, Point Loma, the Silver Strand, Tijuana, and Mexico's Coronado Islands. Seen on a clear winter morning, this wide-ranging panorama is almost aerial in perspective, and must be seen to be believed.

Otay Mountain lies within a large block of BLM-controlled land known as the Otay National Cooperative Land and Wildlife Management Area. The slopes are host to about two dozen rare or endangered plants, many of which are locally common, but found nowhere else in the United States or in the world. The most impressive of these is the Tecate cypress, which grows in scattered stands on the north slopes. Several species of rare wildlife, including the California gnatcatcher, make their home here, too.

The BLM has developed a comprehensive plan for its roughly 50,000 acres of land along the Mexican border, which include most of Otay Mountain, parts of Tecate Peak near Tecate, and parts of Hauser Mountain near Campo. Long forgotten by the public, these lands will increasingly be opened to recreational uses such as hiking, camping, horseback riding, mountain biking, and hunting. A trail to be called the Border Mountain Trail, separate from roads, may one day stretch from Tecate to Otay Mesa.

North of Otay Mountain, off Otay Lakes Road, 4800 acres of land at Rancho Jamul were put in trust for preservation in 1997 under the county's Multiple Species Conservation Program. This means that recreational opportunities will expand in this region over the next 10 years. For now, at least, you can enjoy the following three hikes—on unpaved roads—that lead to the summits of Otay Mountain and Tecate Peak.

Keep in mind that Operation Gatekeeper, a federal program designed to block illegal migration from Mexico (see Area M-9 introduction), is affecting migration patterns here and in the entire border region. It is probably safer to travel in a large group if you travel anywhere near the border.

Area M-10: Border Ranges

Trip 1: Otay Mountain—West Approach

	Distance	14 miles round trip
	Total elevation gain/loss	3100'/3100'
	Hiking time	7 hours (round trip)
	Optional maps	USGS 7.5-min *Otay Mesa, Otay Mountain*
	Best times	October through May
	Agency	BLM/PS
	Difficulty	★★★

Otay Mountain is penetrated by three graded dirt roads that join together at Doghouse Junction on the summit ridge. These roads serve communications installations on the mountain crest and provide access for fire-fighting equipment when needed. This trip describes the west approach up Otay Mountain Truck Trail; Trip 2 below covers the east approach.

Good timing can make this hike a memorable experience, rather than simply a long day's slog. Try to pick a crystal-clear morning following the passage of one of the bigger winter storms. On the clearest mornings the view from Otay Mountain stretches all the way to the snow-capped summits of the San Gabriel, San Bernardino, and San Jacinto mountains—all more than a hundred miles to the north.

To reach the starting point, take Interstate 905 east from either I-5 or I-805. It becomes Otay Mesa Road atop Otay Mesa. Just before the main road curves south to the Otay Mesa border crossing, turn left (continue east) on Otay Mesa Road. After 1.5 miles, turn north on Alta Road and continue 0.9 mile to an unmarked road on the right (0.1 mile past the entrance to the Donovan state prison). There's space to park ahead, before you reach a cluster of farm houses. The unpaved Otay Mountain Truck Trail begins at a gate just ahead, which may or may not be open to vehicular traffic.

The first couple of miles are uninspiring, but soon the first Tecate cy-

presses appear. The young cypresses are quite slender, while the more mature specimens, some more than 20 feet tall, assume a bushy form. Unfortunately, recent fires on the north slope have burned most of the mature cypress trees.

After about 4 miles (at roughly 2500 feet elevation) the road traverses a north slope, formerly thickly covered with cypress. At this level, the coastal stratus clouds often collect during the night and morning and give up some of their moisture.

The road continues up along the crest, swinging back and forth across a swath denuded of trees and large shrubs. This is the International Fuelbreak, created many years ago as a containment barrier for wildfires, particularly those sweeping north.

At 6 miles you come upon an old concrete structure and other remains nearby. During World War II, massive gun emplacements, ammunition batteries, and lookouts were established here to defend against an anticipated Japanese naval assault.

Finally, after about 7 miles, a paved spur road swings up the slope to the left, leading to an unsightly clutter of antennas on the summit ridge. Near the summit are some nice outcrops of grayish-green metavolcanic rock. A band of this metavolcanic rock stretches northwest from Otay Mountain to San Miguel Mountain and beyond. It is a remnant of the island-arc volcanoes that predated the rise of the Southern California batholith and the formation of the Peninsular Ranges.

Trip 2: Otay Mountain—East Approach

Distance	15 miles round trip
Total elevation gain/loss	2500'/2500'
Hiking time	7 hours (round trip)
Optional map	USGS 7.5-min *Otay Mountain*
Best times	October through May
Agency	BLM/PS
Difficulty	★★★

One of the most spectacular wildflower displays I have ever witnessed was found one April day along the northeast flank of Otay Mountain. The road to the summit was lined with a changing palette of blooming plants: yellow and red monkeyflower, morning glory, yerba santa, chaparral pea, wild pea, clematis, nightshade, mountain misery, and wild hyacinth. On one slope recently swept by wildfire, there were tens of thousands of bush poppy plants, each bearing hundreds of big, delicate, four-petaled flowers—millions of flowers in all, swaying in the breeze.

The eastern approach of Otay Mountain is slightly longer than the western approach, but it involves slightly less elevation gain and loss. To reach the starting point, drive 1.5 miles east of Dulzura on Highway 94 to Marron Valley Road. Proceed 2.1 miles south on a graded surface to a gate just beyond the South Bay Rod and Gun Club shooting range. Park here and begin the long trek.

Hike for 0.6 mile south of the gate, descending about 200 feet, then turn right (west) on Otay Mountain Truck Trail. At about 1.6 miles, pass through a wire gate (please keep closed). Bear left (west, up-

Climbing Otay Mountain

hill) at the next intersection. In the next 4.5 miles, you ascend along mostly north-facing slopes, partly in shadow during the cooler months. The Tecate cypress prefers these north slopes; not many big ones are seen, but large numbers of seedlings are naturally regenerating wherever fires have swept through. Scattered scrub oaks and a few large manzanitas intermix with the bigger cypress trees.

At Doghouse Junction (6.7 miles), bear left (south). The road traverses a steep, sunny slope providing views south into sparsely populated areas of Baja California between Tijuana and Tecate. After another 0.6 mile, turn right (north) on the road to the summit.

Trip 3: Tecate Peak

Distance	9.2 miles round trip
Total elevation gain/loss	1900'/1900'
Hiking time	5½ hours (round trip)
Optional map	USGS 7.5-min *Tecate*
Best times	November through May
Agency	BLM/PS
Difficulty	★★★

Tecate Peak straddles the US/Mexico border, overlooking the twin towns of Tecate, California, and Tecate, Baja California. Kumeyaay Indians called this peak "Kuchumaa," and believed that a holy power, for healing or harm, emanated from the mountain's granitic boulders. According to oral historical accounts, shamans from tribes involved in disputes would meet at the summit for peace conferences. Recent archaeological evidence suggests that the mountain was also used for fertility ceremonies. Even today, descendants of the Kumeyaay, who are allowed vehicle access to the upper slopes of the mountain, make periodic journeys to its summit.

The Tecate Peak slopes lie largely in the public domain, on lands under the jurisdiction of the BLM and the California Division of Forestry. In 1958 a dirt road was constructed on the eastern slope to serve an antenna site on the summit. A locked gate along this road normally bars vehicles, but not hikers, so you can enjoy a pleasant and usually traffic-free hike to the top. (The BLM advises that, notwithstanding any "no trespassing signs" posted on the gate, it is legal to walk on the road.)

To reach the starting point from San Diego, drive 35 miles east on Highway 94, then turn south on Highway 188 toward the Tecate border crossing. Turn west on an unnamed dirt road, just 0.4 mile shy of the border itself. The road swings south, hugs the border for a while, then turns northwest and starts climbing. A locked gate blocks the road 2.8 miles from Tecate, and you must find parking where you can below that.

At first you'll hike past chamise, ceanothus, laurel sumac, and yerba santa. Higher up, there's low-growing manzanita and a curious shrub called southern mountain misery. The sticky, fernlike foliage of the mountain misery exudes an aroma similar to witch hazel; clusters of white flowers, resembling strawberry blossoms, appear on it in early spring.

At a point 1 mile above the gate, you have the option of cutting off about 0.4 mile of tedious road walking by following the top edge of a huge, tilted granite slab bordering a ravine to the right. After about 100 yards of climbing, you can rejoin an upper level of the roadway. This is the most worthwhile of several possible short cuts on the way to the summit.

The commanding view from the summit includes most of San Diego County and vast stretches of northern Baja California. To the east there's an almost aerial view of the twin border towns. You can see the sharp delineation between Tecate, California (population about 100), and Tecate, Mexico, with a rapidly expanding population of over 100,000. The landmark Tecate brewery is visible near the center of the Mexican town.

Atop Tecate Peak

The Desert

Area D-1: Coyote Canyon

Coyote Canyon is the biggest rift between two major mountain complexes in the Peninsular Ranges—the San Ysidro Mountains and the Santa Rosa Mountains. The canyon is underlain by the San Jacinto Fault Zone, a splinter of the San Andreas Fault Zone. Being a natural passage through the mountains, it was for a time an important route of travel.

Pedro Fages was the first European to pass through; his 1772 trip in pursuit of deserters from the presidio at San Diego took him as far north as the San Joaquin Valley. In 1774, and again in 1775, Juan Bautista de Anza led parties of soldiers and settlers up the canyon while en route from Sonora, Mexico, to settlements in northern California.

Although many proposals for a paved highway through Coyote Canyon have been advanced, steadfast opposition has kept it free of pavement. A primitive jeep road down the canyon from Terwilliger Valley (near Anza in Riverside County) to the north edge of Borrego Valley remains the only vehicle access route. This road was built in the 1930s, and has not been maintained for more than two

Borrego Valley

Area D-1: Coyote Canyon

decades. It suits most users fine that Coyote Canyon remains a place difficult, but not impossible, to get into.

Because of its beauty and semi-isolation, Coyote Canyon has become one of the more popular destinations in Anza-Borrego Desert State Park. Coyote Creek's year-round flow supports three dense riparian areas: Upper Willows, Middle Willows, and Lower Willows. Formerly the Coyote Canyon road went right through the middle of the jungle-like Lower Willows. In 1988 the road was rerouted around Lower Willows, restoring quiet to the riparian strip there. Meanwhile, the rerouted section of the road has deteriorated so badly that some call it "Boulder Alley." Only the toughest 4-wheel-drive vehicles survive it without damage now.

Between Lower and Middle Willows, extending west to the base of the San Ysidro Mountains, is a broad alluvial basin called Collins Valley. Jeep roads and horse trails cross the valley floor, providing direct access to the major tributary canyons on the west side: Salvador Canyon, Sheep Canyon, South Fork Sheep Canyon, Cougar Canyon, and Indian Canyon. These canyons, along with several more to the south (see Area D-2) are part of a vast roadless area designated as state wilderness. Here, the intrepid hiker will find solitude, adventure, and rugged beauty.

Beyond Collins Valley, Coyote Canyon and its tributaries extend quite far into Riverside County. Information about the upper tributaries of Coyote Canyon can be found in Lowell and Diana Lindsay's guidebook, *The Anza-Borrego Desert Region.*

Even the lower end of Coyote Canyon's "road" can be tough on cars. Protruding rocks, soft sand, and stream crossings have conspired to render inoperative many an automobile driven too far. (It's worth noting that most towing insurance policies do not cover the rescue of vehicles from "off-highway" locales such as Coyote Canyon.) With care, you can usually cover the first few unpaved miles in a regular auto, but only sturdy, high-clearance, 4-wheel-drive vehicles are appropriate for travel beyond the first or second road crossing of Coyote Creek. In the trip descriptions to follow, it is assumed that you will start your hike at certain trailheads accessible by 4-wheel drive. If you have to park short of these trailheads, you may have to backpack in (or perhaps hitchhike) several miles to reach the starting points.

The sprawling desert town of Borrego Springs is the gateway to Coyote Canyon and most other areas in the northern part of Anza-Borrego Desert State Park. The town itself is about two hours' drive from most parts of coastal San Diego County by way of a variety of routes.

To reach Coyote Canyon from Christmas Circle in Borrego Springs, go east 0.5 mile on Palm Canyon Drive, then north on DiGiorgio Road 4.8 miles to the end of the pavement. Now set your odometer at 0.0 (all mileages below refer to this zero point), and proceed slowly on the upaved road ahead. You'll soon cross the Coyote Creek wash west to east—this usually dry crossing spot can become a muddy morass of wheel tracks after heavy rains. On the far side you continue northwest up alongside the base of Coyote Mountain.

At 3.2 miles there's a small parking turnout for Desert Gardens, a picnic spot in the midst of ocotillos and other low-desert flora. At 3.8 miles you'll come to the first (normally wet) crossing of Coyote Creek. There's plenty of parking space on hard-packed sand just before this crossing, and many choose to drive no farther than this.

The second crossing comes at 4.8 miles—often the limit for non-4-wheel-drive vehicles. At 5.6 miles the road veers sharply left (west), crosses the creek, and begins the short, steep stretch known as Boulder Alley (the Area D-1 map shows this crossing at the far right edge, which is the start of Trip 1 below.) Once over a 1420-foot pass, the road passes near a monument commemorating the passage of the Anza party in 1774, and descends to the margins of Santa Catarina Spring, where sandy roads branch west toward the primitive campground at the mouth of Sheep Canyon, and northwest toward Salvador Canyon and Middle Willows.

No permit is required for day or overnight use of the Coyote Canyon area or, for that matter, any other area, wilderness or otherwise, within Anza-Borrego Desert State Park. You will, however, have to display a parking permit on your car (see the section "Using This Book" for more information). The park has a unique open-camping policy that allows you to set up camp virtually anywhere (but not near remote springs and water holes—the wildlife depends on them). You can have campfires, as long as they're confined in metal containers and you bring your own wood. For your cooking needs, campstoves are the most practical.

Coyote Canyon and its tributaries are closed to all entry from June through September to protect the watering rights of bighorn sheep (check with the park for exact dates). No other area in the park is subject to this restriction.

Trip 1: Lower Willows

Distance	4.0 miles (to end of willows and back)
Optional maps	USGS 7.5-min *Borrego Palm Canyon*, *Collins Valley*
Best times	October through May
Agency	ABDSP
Difficulty	★★

Soggy Lower Willows, along with its primary source of water—Santa Catarina Spring—together comprise Anza-Borrego's richest riparian habitat. This short trip will introduce you to this surprisingly lush and jungle-like area. Don't forget your binoculars—the birding is excellent. You'll be tramping through some muddy areas and probably wading in the stream, so wear old shoes or boots and bring extra footwear to leave in the car.

Measured from the end of the pavement at DiGiorgio Road, the starting point for this hike is 5.6 miles northwest up the main Coyote Canyon jeep road. This is where the newer bypass road turns west to climb up a steep ravine. Park here and continue on foot up the main canyon on traces of the old jeep road—now a trail for hikers and equestrians. Where trucks and 4-wheel drives once waddled, wheezed, and snorted through the stream, there are now only the sounds of bubbling water, birds, and insects. The rampant growth of vegetation, largely willows, mesquite, tamarisk, and arrowweed, has obliterated most parts of the old road. Listen for the monosyllabic hoot of the phainopepla, a winter-resident bird that flits about with white wing patches flashing in the bright sunlight.

After about 1 mile Santa Catarina Spring, comprising several oozing acres, lies on the left. The air is heavy with humid odors, and colorful insects—grasshoppers, beetles, katydids, praying mantises—seem to be everywhere. Much of the canyon bottom here was blackened by

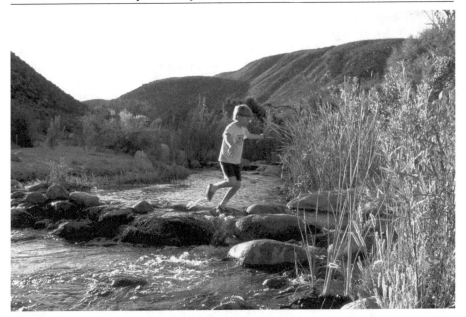

Fording Coyote Creek

wildfire in 1988. Since then, areas fed by surface water have experienced an amazing recovery. Cottonwoods and palms in the burned zone have sprouted new leaves and fronds, and tangles of wild grape vines once again drape many of the trees still standing.

After almost 2 miles, you come to the end of the dense willows. The open desert floor of Collins Valley lies ahead. A trail branches left (southwest), skirting the marshy Santa Catarina Spring and leading toward the nearest dirt road in the valley. You may turn back when you reach that trail, for a round trip of 4 miles—or, for a somewhat longer and drier looping return route, follow the trail and road south to a bluff overlooking Santa Catarina Spring, then east down the steep stretch of road nicknamed "Boulder Alley."

Trip 2: Sheep Canyon

Distance	4.0 miles round trip
Total elevation gain/loss	1200'/1200'
Hiking time	4 hours (round trip)
Recommended maps	USGS 7.5-min *Borrego Palm Canyon, Hot Springs Mtn.*
Best times	November through April
Agency	ABDSP
Difficulty	★★★

Each of Coyote Canyon's major tributaries has its own unique character, and Sheep Canyon is no exception. Palms are scarce here, but sycamores and cottonwoods thrive. Your footsteps will play counterpoint to the gurgle and spatter of water over polished boulders. Shady grottos provide coolness and shade at frequent intervals along the way. Depending on the current wet or dry cycle, the canyon's stream may or may not be flowing in the fall season, but there's almost always plenty of water in winter and spring.

Though parts of Sheep Canyon are rugged and overgrown with lush vegetation, foot traffic in the lower end has hewn out a followable, if primitive, footpath. From Sheep Canyon Primitive Camp it is only 2 miles—and a net gain of 900 feet— to a point where you enter a broad, bowl-shaped valley. This valley is a good destination for backpackers (there are plenty of campsites around), and also a good base camp for further exploration of points all around the compass. I'll mention several possible side trips in the narrative below.

For this trip and the next two trips, remember that the starting point is accessible only by the toughest kind of 4-wheel drive vehicle, by horse, or by foot.

From the primitive campground, go upstream along the banks of the wash (or stream as the case may be). Take care to bear right at the major canyon fork at 0.3 mile, staying in the main canyon. As the bed of the canyon twists and turns, you'll cross the shallow stream several times and climb up and over the rocky canyon walls in order to detour around several small waterfalls. Most of these detours are easier to make on one side of the canyon than the other, so look carefully for footprints or the rudiments of a trail to determine the best route.

At 1.2 miles (2250'), a small canyon leads north to a saddle: on its far side is the South Fork of Salvador Canyon. Continue straight ahead along the main canyon, where cottonwoods have begun to appear, gradually replacing the sycamores as you continue to climb. There's not much evidence of a trail now: you simply negotiate the easiest route across great slabs of fractured granitic rock.

Next, the canyon floor widens slightly, and you make your way directly through the streambed, or across grass- and shrub-covered flats to either side. At 1.5 miles the canyon turns abruptly to the right (west).

At 1.6 miles (2420'), a steep ravine climbs sharply south to a saddle between the two forks of Sheep Canyon. South of this saddle lies a broad valley at 3000 feet elevation in South Fork Sheep Canyon (see Trip 3). From the top of the saddle, two peak climbs are possible: The first is a boulder-strewn 3380-foot summit overlooking both forks, easily within reach to the northeast. The second is to the west—the massive, flat-topped 4649-foot promontory I'll call "Square Top," a conspicuous landmark seen from Collins Valley and points east. Square Top can be climbed from the east and possibly the south sides: attempts on the north and west sides will be doomed to failure by a combination of huge boulders and dense chaparral just below the summit.

At 1.9 miles, Sheep Canyon emerges into a broad bowl where two major and several minor tributaries come together. Possible campsites are abundant here. For dayhikers, it's a good place to enjoy the view of rugged peaks in every direction before turning around. Around the margins of the bowl, seasonal springs can be found in several of the small tributaries. They're often marked by small cottonwood trees or other riparian vegetation.

Trip 3: South Fork Sheep Canyon

Distance	3.0 miles round trip (to valley at 3000')
Total elevation gain/loss	1500'/1500'
Hiking time	4 hours (round trip)
Recommended maps	USGS 7.5-min *Borrego Palm Canyon, Hot Springs Mtn.*
Best times	November through April
Agency	ABDSP
Difficulty	★★★★

Mile for mile, the terrain covered on this hike is more technically difficult than that on any other trip described in this book. Skilled scramblers need not use ropes, but certain precautions must be observed.

Careful route-finding is the key to safe passage through this canyon. Some routes (especially going downhill) may look promising, but lead to steep rock exposures so that much time can be wasted in backtracking. Other routes can lead to deadends in the canyon bottom where it is difficult (or impossible) to climb out in the absence of outside help, so don't jump or slide down rocks if you can't determine the feasibility of the route ahead. Because of these difficulties, it is recommended that you don't backpack through this canyon without first having traveled it with a light day pack.

The rewards are a close-up view of an idyllic waterfall, glimpses of a half-dozen more, and the pleasure of exploring a hidden valley seldom visited by humans. Less water flows through the South Fork than the main fork of Sheep Canyon. Try to arrive here soon after the peak winter rains, when the stream bubbles with vigor and crashes over the falls.

Begin as in Trip 2, but stay to the left at 0.3 mile, entering South Fork. A well-beaten trail goes up along the bank, but peters out rapidly as boulders and underbrush become a hindrance. Find a way through the brush and climb over rounded

granite slabs, passing two palm groves, until you reach (at 0.6 mile, 2000') the base of a sublime 30-foot waterfall—arguably the most beautiful cascade in Anza-Borrego. Framed by full-skirted palms both top and bottom, and a lush carpet of grass below, this is a point of interest well worth reaching even if you don't intend to continue farther up the canyon.

From just below the waterfall, climb the steep, rocky slope to the right (north side of the canyon). Climb sharply upward

Grotto in South Fork Sheep Canyon

until you can traverse at an easier gradient, staying parallel to and about 200 feet above the canyon bottom. The slope is infested with cactus, agave, and sharp rocks, but if you stay at the right level, the footing is relatively stable. You'll hear the splashing of water in several hard-to-reach grottos below.

Continue along the north wall of the canyon for about 0.3 mile, then contour into the canyon bottom at about 2600 feet. Now thread your way around immense boulder complexes, staying generally close to the north wall. Note your route carefully so that you can retrace it when you return.

Turning south, you enter a valley at 3000 feet with several flat, sandy areas on the west side. This is a worthy enough destination for a dayhike: there are good views of distant peaks and ridges, and small pools in the stream to soak the feet in. Backpackers can reach this valley by way of a longer and less problematic route through the main Sheep Canyon and over a saddle between the two forks (see Trip 2 above).

Further exploration up South Fork is just as rewarding as it is challenging. Here are some highlights:

The canyon turns west at 3120 feet. Typical high-desert vegetation appears there—ribbonwood, scrub oak, and yucca on the slopes; palms, sycamores, cottonwoods, and alders along the stream. At 3250 feet, there's a narrow, grassy bench providing the last marginal campsites in this canyon. Amazingly, an incense-cedar grows here, miles away from its normal habitat high up in the mountains. Scattered palms extend several hundred feet upstream. This is truly an extraordinary overlap of mountain and desert flora.

Above 3400 feet there's a series of small falls, then huge boulder mazes and heavy brush. (Refer to Area M-3, Trip 2, for a route into this area from the Los Coyotes Indian Reservation.) From these upper reaches of South Fork, a very difficult, brushy traverse can be made into the main Sheep Canyon via the saddle west of Square Top.

Trip 4: Cougar Canyon

Distance	3.0 miles round trip (to pool at 2300')
Total elevation gain/loss	900'/900'
Hiking time	3 hours (round trip)
Recommended map	USGS 7.5-min *Borrego Palm Canyon*
Best times	November through April
Agency	ABDSP
Difficulty	★★★

Cougar Canyon is a place where new worlds open up at every turn. There are more beautiful sights to see along a half-mile of this canyon than in a full day's hiking in many other parts of Anza-Borrego.

Cahuilla Indians were using seasonal camps in the area around the mouth of the canyon as recently as about 150 years ago, and the evidence left behind in the form of bedrock *morteros* and ceremonial caves gives another interesting dimension to a hike here.

If you plan to stay overnight, the flat, open areas just below the mouth of the canyon make convenient campsites. A few marginal camping areas do exist in the canyon proper, but these have been overused and are really too close to the canyon stream to be considered appropriate places to set up camp.

Mileages in this description start from the road closure on the spur trail (the old Indian Canyon jeep road) going south from the mouth of Sheep Canyon. Begin by walking south on this eroded and partly overgrown jeep trail. After crossing Cougar Canyon's streambed three times, you'll reach a point a little beyond the mouth of Cougar Canyon (0.7 mile). Find the informal path that veers right (west) up Cougar's alluvial fan. A little northwest of this point, on a bench overlooking the stream, is a rock cave reputed to have been used as an Indian *temescal*, or sweathouse.

Follow the path west and cross the stream once more (0.9 mile). Now on the north bank, the path climbs to about 50 feet above the stream as the canyon walls close in rather tightly. Another rock cave yawns from the hillside.

Staying on the path well above the stream, it seems almost a shame to miss the beautiful scenery down below along the sycamore-shaded creek. But soon, steep walls of granite and gneiss force you to descend anyway. Go up the cobbled bed of the stream to the beginning of a palm grove, then climb up to a sandy, shaded bench on the left bank (1.3 miles). On a rock facing the bench is a huge psychedelic "eye"—rock art, circa 1970. Just beyond the eye, upstream, is a deep, shaded pool fed by a silvery waterfall.

The path, now obscure, continues up the south wall of the canyon to avoid a narrow section just beyond the eye. After climbing over a series of rock buttresses, you'll come to a point overlooking a feathery cascade of water flowing down a slab of banded rock in the canyon bottom. Just beyond this you can descend to the streambed again, and work your way up-can-

In Lower Cougar Canyon

yon to a large cottonwood tree nestled beside a sculpted granite wall. Using the limbs of this tree to hoist yourself up and over, you'll come upon the most beautiful spot of all—a clear, deep pool surrounded by sheer, polished granite walls, fed by a 20-foot waterfall.

This pool and waterfall (1.5 miles, 2300') mark the end of progress in Cougar Canyon proper without resorting to technical climbing aids. A long detour is necessary to bypass the next 0.6 mile. If you're interested, here's the way:

Back up to the point overlooking the feathery cascade. Now go straight up the south wall, dodging brush and boulders, until you reach a point on the ridgeline east of peak 3526. Here you have a bird's-eye view of palm groves in Bennis Bowl and Valley of the Thousand Springs, and a view of some nearly inaccessible palms in Cougar Canyon. Follow this jagged ridgeline west, pass over peak 3526, and traverse just south of two smaller peaklets. Then drop 250 feet northwest through a gully to reach the bed of Cougar Canyon at the 3080-foot contour. From there it's possible to continue up the stream banks for some distance. For more, see Area M-3, Trip 2.

Area D-2: San Ysidro Mountains

West of Borrego Springs, the fluted walls of the San Ysidro Mountains rise to a height of over one vertical mile. Slashing back from the edge of this escarpment are a number of beautiful canyon systems containing palms, sycamores, cottonwoods, and other riparian vegetation. Best known of these is Borrego Palm Canyon, first set aside as a park in the early 1930s. This was the small nucleus that eventually grew to encompass 600,000 acres—the Anza-Borrego Desert State Park. Today, tens of thousands of people every year hike up Borrego Palm Canyon to view the palms.

Borrego Palm Canyon may be the largest and most beautiful, but the other, less popular canyons nearby are worth visiting too—especially if crowds turn you off. Most of the hikes below start from either the state park visitor center or Borrego Palm Canyon Campground. The others begin along Montezuma Highway, no more than a few miles away.

A stop at the visitor center is highly recommended. Aside from the excellent interpretive displays, you can experience an audio-visual show that will surely whet your appetite for exploring the Anza-Borrego Desert region. During the springtime bloom, the visitor center can be jam-packed, so try to be there either at opening time, 9 A.M., or near closing time, 5 P.M.

Borrego Palm Canyon Campground is a good base camp for dayhiking the San Ysidro Mountains area, but be aware that camping reservations must be made weeks in advance during the busy winter and early spring seasons.

Trailhead parking for the trips below requires an Anza-Borrego Desert State Park parking pass. See the section "Using This Book" for more information.

Young antelope ground squirrel

Trip 1: Borrego Palm Canyon Nature Trail

Distance	3.0 miles
Total elevation gain/loss	450'/450'
Hiking time	1¹/₂ hours
Optional map	USGS 7.5-min *Borrego Palm Canyon*
Best times	October through May
Agency	ABDSP
Difficulty	★

In the first mile, there's nothing but sun-blasted vegetation, either thorny or low and prostrate. As you round a bend, you suddenly catch sight of a patch of iridescent green cradled in the yawning mouth of the canyon ahead. Hundreds of noble palms stand there, each holding high a crown of feathery, fan-shaped fronds.

TRIP 4: See Area D-1 Map

Area D-2: San Ysidro Mountains

Water splashes over boulders and gathers in pools, delighting all the senses. It's enough to make anyone as yet unimpressed with the desert an instant convert to the ranks of "desert rats"!

You can learn more about the Colorado Desert flora on this trail than anywhere else in the park. Be sure to pick up the interpretive leaflet at the visitor center, or upon entering Borrego Palm Canyon Campground. You begin hiking at the west end of the campground, where a special trailhead parking area has been established. A pond holding transplanted desert pupfish is nearby. The trail crosses the seasonal stream, and starts winding up the rocky alluvial fan toward the canyon's mouth. Along the lower part of the trail are various cacti, mesquite and catclaw (with the parasitic desert mistletoe), indigo bush, desert lavender, creosote bush, brittlebush, ocotillo, desert-willow, chuparosa, and sage. These may look drab most of the year, but they can really light up in a rainbow of colors by March or April of a wet year.

Soon after the palms first become visible, the trail enters the portals of the canyon. Desert-varnished rock walls soar 3000 feet up on both sides. After a second stream crossing, the trail goes up a series of steps hewn in the rock, passes a gauging station and a waterfall, crosses the stream once again, and enters the shade of the palms.

The palms are of one variety, *Washingtonia filifera*, the only palm indigenous to California. Although they are generally well-adapted to wildfire, several blackened and headless trunks in this grove show that some have failed to survive periodic fires. A few alders and sycamores struggle for light among the massive, straight trunks of the palms.

The trail terminates at a point just below a small waterfall and pool at the upper end of the palm grove, 1.5 miles from the trailhead. On the return leg, you can try the alternate trail that winds along the upper edge of the alluvial fan. Here you can study how plants are stratified according to habitat. Higher on the slope, less water is absorbed by the soil, so the drought-tolerant ocotillo dominates.

The so-called first grove at 1.5 miles is the starting point for boulderhopping journeys of any length into the remote recesses of upper Borrego Palm Canyon. Sturdy footwear and long pants are recommended for any such forays, as you'll be brushing past poison oak and spiny vegetation, and scrambling over potentially ankle-busting terrain.

One such extended trip could take you into the South Fork, wherein lies a 30-foot stair-step waterfall. At 3.0 miles (from the campground trailhead) and 2040 feet elevation, you'll find several flat areas above the canyon stream suitable for trail camping. At 3.3 miles, the South Fork branches obviously to the southwest, away from the main Middle Fork. After floundering around amid thorny mesquite and squishing through the swamp-like canyon bottom, it's possible to reach, at 3.7 miles, the base of the South Fork waterfall.

Upper canyon treks like this (and Trips 2, 3, and 4 below) are not to be taken lightly. The farther you venture up the canyon, the more rugged the terrain becomes and the more remote you are from any kind of help.

Palms in Borrego Palm Canyon

Trip 2: Indianhead Mountain

Distance	7.0 miles round trip
Total elevation gain/loss	3200'/3200'
Hiking time	7 hours (round trip)
Required maps	USGS 7.5-min *Borrego Palm Canyon*
Best times	November through April
Agency	ABDSP
Difficulty	★★★★

The north wall of Borrego Palm Canyon culminates in a spectacular, jagged promontory known as Indianhead. This is a conspicuous landmark seen and admired from most locations in Borrego Valley, and one of the few named summits in the San Ysidro Mountains. Map makers, it seems, haven't bothered to measure or estimate its height—its elevation is not recorded on topographic maps.

There are many ways to climb Indianhead, nearly all involving very steep ascents from the desert floor. My favorite route (detailed here) is somewhat longer,

Ocotillo blossoms

but safer. This can be a challenging dayhike, or involve a night's stay in Borrego Palm Canyon. With a base camp established well up in the canyon, you'll have the opportunity to do the climb in the early morning, when the air is clearest and the temperature moderate.

Begin as in Trip 1 above. Beyond the first grove (1.5 miles), but before the first major bend in the canyon (to the north), you'll scramble over some large, light-colored granitic boulders, soon picking up a fair trail on the south side of the creek. Mesquite, catclaw, willow, and desert-willow crowd in along the banks. Palm trees resume as you round the second bend (1.8 miles). Near this point there's a change in the exposed rock: the granitic rock is abruptly replaced by tan- and orange-tinted schist and gneiss. In several places, the creek flows over colorful slabs of this rock and collects in small pools shaded by palms both young and old. Small campsites are fairly abundant in the wider parts of the canyon, especially on the north side.

You reach the turnoff point for Indianhead at 2.5 miles (1800'), where a tributary canyon comes in from the north. Climb northeast straight up the ridge just east of this tributary. After about 0.7 mile, you'll reach a 3220-foot saddle northwest of Indianhead. From here make your way southeast around huge boulders and over slab rock to reach the highest point on Indianhead's flat summit.

Now the entire sweep of the San

Ysidro Mountains lies before you. In the north, beyond lesser ranges, the snow-capped San Jacinto Mountains float like a mirage. To obtain the best view of the bottom of Borrego Palm Canyon, scramble about 0.1 mile south of the high point, and work your way out to a jagged outcrop. You can sit there, legs dangling, and look almost straight down upon the crowns of hundreds of palms.

Trip 3: Middle Fork Borrego Palm Canyon Traverse

Distance	10.0 miles
Total elevation gain/loss	0'/4100'
Hiking time	12 hours
Required maps	USGS 7.5-min *Hot Springs Mtn., Borrego Palm Canyon*
Best times	November through April
Agency	LCIR, ABDSP
Difficulty	★★★★★

What dyed-in-the-wool hiker has hiked lower Borrego Palm Canyon and hasn't wondered what it would be like to explore the canyon in its entirety? Well, here's your chance. You'll experience Palm Canyon's main (middle) fork from top to bottom. But be forewarned: mile after mile of slippery rock, small waterfalls, and thickets of brush and alder will necessitate a very slow, painstaking, and difficult descent. Needless to say, this is for expert hikers only. Long pants and sturdy boots are essential. Also take along a 30-foot piece of cord to use for lowering your pack down one or more of the falls. Middle Fork is a perennial stream with fair-to-good water quality, depending upon the amount of grazing upstream on the Los Coyotes In-

Upper Middle Fork, Borrego Palm Canyon

dian Reservation.

You begin in the valley at the head of the Middle Fork on the Los Coyotes reservation (see the introductory text for Area M-3, and Trip 2 within that section for details on entry into the reservation). Walk southeast on a dirt road past some old buildings and a cemetery at San Ignacio (don't linger around these private sites). The pastoral valley on the right, lined with huge cottonwoods, is used for cattle grazing. Continue down the road under a canopy of live oaks, until you reach the point (1.3 miles) where the road swings south—away from the creek. You have two choices: leave the road to follow the creekbed to a confluence at 4070 feet, or stay on the road south about 0.2 mile, then drop southeast into a western tributary of Middle Fork and go down it to the confluence. The two alternatives are of equal length, and both involve some serious bushwhacking and awkward detours around waterfalls. Either way, this is the most difficult and hazardous stretch of the trip.

Below the confluence of the western tributary (2.0 miles, 4050') you enter a botanical transition zone of high-desert and mountain vegetation. The slopes are covered with ribbonwood, scrub oak, mountain mahogany, manzanita, chamise, ceanothus, and sugar bush. A few pinyon pines dot the north-facing slopes, wherever moisture can stay in the soil for long periods of time. In a narrow band along the stream, willows and cottonwoods thrive, along with moisture-loving shrubs and herbs such as wild rose, nettles, miner's lettuce, cattails, and wild peony.

The creek meanders on a gentle gradient for a mile below the confluence, with grassy campsites along the inner banks. You're now passing from a zone containing the common Cretaceous granitic rocks that make up the core of the Peninsular Ranges, to an area with older (pre-Cretaceous) granitic and metamorphic rocks exposed. You'll walk past colorful outcrops of orange-banded gneiss and other metamorphic rocks in the next 6 miles or so.

At 3.0 miles (3650'), the water shoots over a 15-foot vertical fall. Below this the creek drops steeply through a narrow gorge. Alder trees appear, and they conspire with the willows to impede your progress. It's easiest to walk right down the middle of the creek most of the time, underneath the tangle of tree limbs. Cottonwoods appear at about 3.8 miles (3300').

At 5.3 miles (2900'), just above the first palm tree, an easy traverse north over a ridge into the North Fork is possible. From here to the confluence of North Fork (5.7 miles, 2700'), both the creek and banks in Middle Fork are overgrown by a junglelike growth of vines that act like trip wires.

Below the confluence, the canyon becomes more open and less thickly vegetated. Slippery, water-polished rock is now the biggest difficulty. This can be a technically demanding and slow stretch during high water. At about 6.2 miles (2450') you'll traverse around two sets of falls.

By the time you reach the confluence of South Fork (6.7 miles, 2200'), the sparser vegetation of the low desert has begun to appear on the canyon walls, and palms line the canyon in greater numbers. The going gets progressively easier now (see Trips 1 and 2 above for more details).

At 8.5 miles (1300') you come upon the lowest grove of palms, where you pick up the Borrego Palm Canyon Nature Trail. Curiosity satisfied, you can saunter down this "tourist trail," smug in the knowledge that you, unlike the untold thousands who only glimpse the beauty of the canyon, have truly seen it all.

Trip 4: Indian Canyon/Borrego Palm Canyon Traverse

Distance	11.0 miles
Total elevation gain/loss	3100'/3900'
Hiking time	13 hours
Required map	USGS 7.5-min *Borrego Palm Canyon*
Best times	November through April
Agency	ABDSP
Difficulty	★★★★★

This is a grand tour of one of Anza-Borrego's most remote, rugged, and beautiful areas. In the midsection of this trip, you'll pass through a pristine wilderness where the tracks of a mountain lion are far more common than the impressions of a lug-soled boot.

The trip is best done as an ambitious (strenuous) two-day backpack. Lightly loaded internal-frame packs are recommended for ease of movement. A light rope will come in handy for lowering packs in a few places. Water may be scarce: plan on the possibility of a dry camp.

Transportation logistics are a bit problematical. The drive between the starting and end points is 15 miles, mostly on the rugged jeep road through Coyote Canyon. If your vehicle won't make it past Lower Willows, you'll have to walk at least four extra miles across Collins Valley.

Mileages in this description start from the Cougar Canyon trailhead (see directions in Area D-1, Trip 4). Follow the path south past Cougar Canyon and toward the wide mouth of Indian Canyon. At 1.3 miles, Indian Canyon bends right (southwest) and narrows. You pass a palm-studded bowl on

On the Indian Canyon traverse

the west side—Valley of the Thousand Springs—and an old tin mine near the mouth of Deering Canyon (2.0 miles).

By now the path has faded almost to insignificance. Follow the brush-choked streambed as it curves around in a gooseneck, and continue south to the point where two tributaries join from the southeast. Fill your water bottles here for a possible long, dry stretch ahead.

Climb steeply south up the ridge dividing the upper of the two tributaries from the main Indian Canyon. This ridge continues steadily uphill for 2000 vertical feet, with only moderate brush to contend with and good footing all the way. As you climb, hidden palms become visible in the tributary below, and the distant view expands to encompass Collins Valley and most of Coyote Canyon.

When the ridge tops out, traverse south, then climb slightly to a saddle (4.0 miles) just northwest of peak 4780. The remaining 7 miles to the mouth of Borrego Palm Canyon are all downhill, but more difficult than the 4 miles you've just covered.

Continue going south: descend obliquely down a brushy slope, and drop into the North Fork of Borrego Palm Canyon. The floor of the canyon is delightfully shaded by a dense growth of ribbonwood and scrub oak, which in places forms a canopy over the narrow, rocky bed.

After 0.3 mile in the canyon, you'll come to the top of a series of waterfalls (4150'). On the left (north) side, look for *morteros* and *metates* on several orange-colored metamorphic rock slabs. There are at least 45 of these, including two that are worn completely through the thinnest slab. This is one of the most impressive—and remote—old Indian milling sites in the county. Access into this area was by way

of a trail, now almost completely overgrown, west to San Ignacio on the Los Coyotes Indian Reservation. The remains of this trail, which is still shown on the *Borrego Palm Canyon* topo map, are occasionally used by hikers.

Bypass the waterfalls and continue down the gravel-and-bedrock floor of the canyon. After passing a major fork leading north toward Palm Mesa (no palms are there), the canyon trends south. There are several small (usually dry) falls to descend ahead. Flat deposits of sand become more abundant—but wait till you reach a wide, level patch of sand at about 3400 feet if you're looking for a good campsite.

At 3150 feet elevation, you must leave the canyon bottom and climb south up and over a low saddle. From the top of the saddle you descend 200 feet over a brush- and agave-strewn slope to return to the canyon bottom. This maneuver bypasses a gooseneck containing a 50-foot dry fall.

For the next 0.3 mile, the canyon floor is mostly bedrock, with potholes that may contain water. Just before the confluence of the Middle Fork of Borrego Palm Canyon, there's another set of dry falls—the "crux" of this challenging trip. You'll have to negotiate a route over the loose metamorphic slabs on the nose between the two forks. (A reasonable alternative is to backtrack about 0.1 mile, climb up and over the ridge to the west, and drop into Middle Fork at a point 0.5 mile above the confluence.)

Your water problems, if any, are solved now (assuming you have the means to purify the stream water), because the Middle Fork runs year round. See Trips 1, 2, and 3 above for the details on the last 4.3 miles down the canyon to Borrego Palm Canyon Campground.

Trip 5: Panorama Overlook

Distance	1.0 mile round trip
Total elevation gain/loss	300'/300'
Hiking time	40 minutes (round trip)
Optional map	USGS 7.5-min *Borrego Palm Canyon*
Best times	All year
Agency	ABDSP
Difficulty	★

Starting near campsite 71 in Borrego Palm Canyon Campground, this well-used trail climbs sharply up one of the ridge spurs of San Ysidro Mountain, offering a superb vista of Borrego Valley and its spectacular backdrop of mountains. The flat area at the top of the trail is called Panorama Overlook (or Panoramic Overlook on some maps). Any map of the Anza-Borrego region will help you identify the major topographical features visible along the horizon from northeast through the south: Coyote Mountain and the distant Santa Rosa Mountains; Fonts Point and the Borrego Badlands; Pinyon Ridge and a slice of the Vallecito Mountains. Facing west, you must crane your neck to follow the continuation of the rocky ridge you're standing upon. This culminates about 4000 feet higher, on the crest of San Ysidro Mountain (Trip 6 below gives further details if you want to climb higher).

Panorama Overlook is an excellent spot to witness the sunrise on the crisp mornings of fall and winter. Late afternoons are nice too: you can watch the mountain shadows slowly stretch across Borrego Valley as the sun sinks unseen.

This trail is one of the few in Anza-Borrego short enough for summer hiking. Summer afternoon thundershowers over the desert floor can be interesting to watch from here, but only if they're a safe distance away.

Barrel cactus above Panorama Overlook

Trip 6: San Ysidro Mountain

Distance	7.0 miles round trip
Total elevation gain/loss	4400'/4400'
Hiking time	8 hours (round trip)
Recommended map	USGS 7.5-min *Borrego Palm Canyon*
Best times	November through April
Agency	ABDSP
Difficulty	★★★★

The eastern brow of San Ysidro Mountain overlooks Borrego Valley from an elevation of nearly one mile. Here, in the cool pinyon-pine-and-juniper belt, you can experience a startling pseudo-aerial perspective of Anza-Borrego quite unlike that seen from any other land-based vantage point.

On this hike horizontal distance is trivial and vertical gain is everything. It's a taxing but immensely satisfying journey. Every step upward takes you closer to the heavens, and farther from the civilized world. The roads, dwellings, and wind-break-bordered fields etched on the floor of Borrego Valley always remain visible through the clear desert air, but they become more and more toylike and abstract—as if viewed from space—as you climb.

This is a tough hike, no matter how you do it. The gradient at times approaches 3000 feet of gain per mile of horizontal distance, often over a rugged landscape of weathered granitic boulders. No water is available anywhere along the route. Dayhikers should allow a full dawn-to-dusk day for the round trip. Backpackers need almost this much time for the ascent alone—especially in view of the amount of water that must be carried. Navigation is easy in the uphill direction, but a topo map and compass are useful for reference during the return leg, because it's possible to stray off the main ridge.

A convenient place to begin this trip is the visitor center—though if you are backpacking you may have to park your car somewhere else, as the visitor center parking lot may be closed at night. From the parking lot you can clearly see the route ahead. The transparent desert air compresses distance and height, and an illusion of perspective makes it appear as if the truck-sized boulders high on the ridge are really much smaller. The effort required to reach the top seems—well—trivial.

Head directly across the desert floor toward the spur ridge to the northwest 0.5 mile away (or use the Visitor Center Trail to angle over in that direction). Pick up the switchbacks of the Panorama Overlook Trail, then continue beyond the overlook using the narrower trail up the ridge. This trail peters out eventually.

You encounter a wide range of desert vegetation as you climb; first, the creosote bush/brittlebush/ocotillo/cactus community typical of the lower desert alluvial fans and slopes; then agave and widely scattered shrubs like sugarbush, scrub oak, and juniper; and finally pinyon pine.

Beyond Panorama Overlook, you're on metamorphic and later granitic rock, or on soils consisting of coarse rock fragments. Above a small flat on the ridge at 3100 feet, the slope becomes distinctly steeper. Large monoliths and stiff vegetation impede progress.

After topping out at 5200 feet, you'll

find some flat campsites nearby. It was here that I had a memorable experience: watching an orange-tinted full moon rise over the Salton Sea, awash in the purple glow of evening twilight.

Further exploration along the undulating ridgeline of San Ysidro Mountain is possible, but slow and difficult due to thick brush and boulders. To return the easy way, simply retrace your steps back down the ridge. More difficult return routes include those across Hellhole Flat and down either Flat Cat or Hellhole canyons.

View north from San Ysidro Mountain

Trip 7: Flat Cat Canyon

Distance	5.0 miles round trip (to palms at 2600')
Total elevation gain/loss	1800'/1800'
Hiking time	4^1/$_2$ hours (round trip)
Recommended map	USGS 7.5-min *Tubb Canyon*
Best times	December through March
Agency	ABDSP
Difficulty	★★★

Flat Cat Canyon is the curious name given to a rugged gorge just north of lower Hellhole Canyon. Anza-Borrego rangers found a dead bobcat (presumably *very* dead) in this canyon, and followed the honorable Western tradition of assigning colorful names to "colorful" places. As viewed from the alluvial fan below, Flat Cat Canyon looks like a boulder-choked ravine, seemingly unpromising. But its upper reaches hold a surprise or two.

Wear long pants and sturdy shoes; the canyon presents some serious bushwhacking and scrambling challenges. Begin at the large trailhead parking area near the foot of the Montezuma Grade (this is on the west side of Montezuma Highway, 0.7 mile south of Palm Canyon Drive, the main drag of Borrego Springs). From there, the gaping mouth of Hellhole Canyon lies just south of west, while Flat Cat Canyon is the next canyon to the right (north), and appears narrower and steeper.

Follow the trail leading straight toward Hellhole Canyon, but leave this trail and bend right toward Flat Cat Canyon after about a mile. Climb for about a mile in the canyon, gaining about 1000 feet. The sandy wash in the canyon bottom provides smooth going except when choked with vegetation—notably thorny desert apricot and catclaw bushes. Marginal trails of animals and occasional hikers thread the canyon walls, providing serviceable alternate routes. Flat Cat Canyon is hewn from gra-

nitic rock: note the contrast between the dark, desert-varnished rock high on the canyon walls, and the whitish, flood-scoured boulders on the lower slopes.

At 2100 feet elevation, your ears will discover a most welcome sound—the trickle of water. A little above this, you come upon a place where the water slides over a 20-foot precipice. Two hundred feet higher, you top a small rise and discover—palms!

Below the first group of palms is a flat little terrace suitable as a campsite for four or five people. Just above these palms, on the north side of the canyon, be sure to look for an unusual example of exfoliation. Frost wedging and other erosive forces have carved the rock on the canyon wall into concentric layers, resembling those of an onion. Higher still, where the canyon evenly divides (2600'), is the biggest grove—about two dozen palms.

Trip 8: Lower Hellhole Canyon

Distance	4.6 miles round trip (to falls)
Total elevation gain/loss	900'/900'
Hiking time	3 hours (round trip)
Optional map	USGS 7.5-min *Tubb Canyon*
Best times	December through April
Agency	ABDSP
Difficulty	★★★

In the midst of what is regarded as one of America's hottest and driest deserts, it seems a bit surprising to find a place where mosses, ferns, sycamores, and cottonwoods flourish around a sparkling waterfall. Maidenhair Falls is such a place, and it lies only 3 miles from Anza-Borrego's visitor center and the town of Borrego Springs.

Begin hiking at the large trailhead parking area on the west side of Montezuma Highway, 0.7 mile south of Palm Canyon Drive. Head west-southwest on a trail (formerly a dirt road) across the

upper (south) margin of Hellhole Canyon's broad alluvial fan. After 1.2 miles, the walls of the canyon begin to close in. You thread your way up the narrowing gorge, generally avoiding the vegetation-choked canyon bottom. On ahead you'll have to scramble over or around large boulders and fallen trees. Try to avoid encounters with the rose-bush-like thorns of the catclaw bushes. The remnants of fallen trees hereabouts are a result of a 1975 wildfire that burned the entire Hellhole Canyon drainage. Sycamores, cottonwoods, and scattered palms have returned since then.

About 200 yards past the densest cluster of palms, the canyon walls pinch in really tight. Tucked away in a corner of the canyon bottom—hard to find—you'll discover the grotto containing Maidenhair Falls. The falls plunge about 25 feet into a shallow pool. Tiers of maidenhair fern adorn the grotto, and sopping wet mosses cover the places the ferns don't.

Further travel up-canyon from Maidenhair Falls involves constant bush-whacking—slow going with a backpack. For a shorter, but not technically easier way into the upper reaches of Hellhole Canyon, see Trip 11 below.

Maidenhair Falls cool-off

Trip 9: Culp Valley Loop

Distance	1.7 miles
Total elevation gain/loss	300'/300'
Hiking time	1 hour
Optional map	USGS 7.5-min *Tubb Canyon*
Best times	September through June
Agency	ABDSP
Difficulty	★

While the low desert swelters, the temperature hovers in a more moderate register at Culp Valley, 3000 feet higher. This is the only designated camping area in Anza-Borrego where the heat on the cooler days of May, June, or September is quite bearable. July and August daytime temperatures are probably too warm for most people's tastes—typically the 90s and 100s.

Stark, gray boulders are piled up all around the floor of Culp Valley, sharply etching the horizon. The west wind blows capriciously, often whistling eerily through the rocks. Nearby, out of sight from the val-

ley, is a hillside spring surrounded by an oasis of green grass and small trees. It's this kind of contrast that makes hiking here especially rewarding.

To reach the starting point, drive to mile 9.2 on Montezuma Highway (2.8 miles east of the highway summit near Ranchita; 9.4 miles west of Borrego Springs) and turn north on the unpaved entrance road to Culp Valley Primitive Camp. The campground is truly no frills—just a few nooks and crannies where you can park your car overnight. Our little hike can start from the end of the road that forks west toward Pena Spring.

From the end of the road, walk downhill on the remnants of a jeep road that used to lead to Pena Spring. After 0.3 mile, you'll reach a thicket of large sugarbush shrubs. On the left, there's an obscure path through shoulder-high yerba santa and other shrubby vegetation. It leads 50 yards to the spring, which lies amid a soggy hillside meadow. Yerba mansa flowers poke up through the grass blades where the ground is saturated. Rabbits, coyotes, and other animals partake of the clear, cold water, which emerges from a small, raised pipe.

After visiting the spring, backtrack up the old roadbed 0.2 mile to the intersection of the California Riding and Hiking Trail, marked by a small wooden post. Go east on this, climbing up, then along, a rather flat-topped ridge that offers great views of Culp Valley, Pinyon Ridge, and San Ysidro Mountain, and tantalizing glimpses of the big gorge to the north—Hellhole Canyon. Here you'll find typical high-desert vegetation mixed with common chaparral: juniper, catclaw, desert apricot, various cacti, buckwheat, Mojave and Lord's candle yucca, and white sage.

After 0.5 mile on the CRHT, you'll come to the intersection of a trail going down to the campground, 0.3 mile south. About 100 feet north of this point are some rock outcrops offering a fine view of the Hellhole Canyon gorge, Borrego Valley, and the great wall of mountains beyond the valley. The pinyon-fringed, flattish summit of Rabbit Peak is conspicuous as the highest point visible on the long crest of the Santa Rosa Mountains.

East another 0.2 mile on the CRHT is the marked Vista Point ("Lookout" on some maps), offering a more panoramic but somewhat less spectacular view than you saw earlier. Northwest down the slope from the Lookout Point is a huge, weathered boulder split cleanly down the middle; it's fun to squeeze through the slot, or "chimney" up to the top.

Lastly, backtrack a little and follow the trail toward the campground, and dirt roads over to your parked car.

Trip 10: California Riding and Hiking Trail

Distance	8.0 miles
Total elevation gain/loss	500'/3700'
Hiking time	4^1/$_2$ hours
Recommended map	USGS 7.5-min *Tubb Canyon*
Best times	October through May
Agency	ABDSP
Difficulty	★★★

This delightful one-way (preferably downhill) route has a long and varied history. Originally a well-beaten Indian trail, it was used for many decades by cattlemen moving herds from the Mesa Grande area near Lake Henshaw to winter and spring grazing grounds at the mouths of Hellhole Canyon and Borrego Palm Canyon. After World War II the trail became a branch of the California Riding and Hiking Trail. Today, while the statewide CRHT has largely fallen into disrepair, this particular desert segment continues to be frequently used (if not maintained much).

Car shuttling is easy for this trip, as both ends of the trail intersect the same road—Montezuma Highway. The top of the trail is at mile 6.8, across the highway

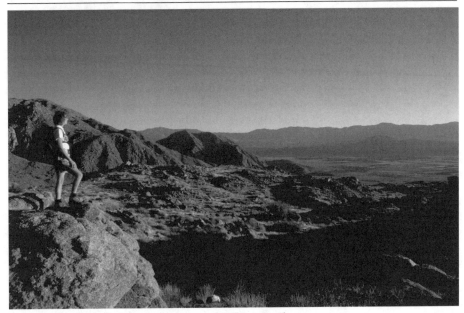

Sunrise along the California Riding and Hiking Trail

from the junction of the signed Jasper Trail. The bottom end is the large trailhead parking area on the west side of Montezuma Highway, 0.7 mile south of Palm Canyon Drive.

Topside, pick up the trail, marked by faded, yellow-topped posts, and follow it northeast over a low saddle. The vegetation here is mostly common chaparral—mountain mahogany, chamise, sugarbush, and scrub oak—but there are some high desert plants too, such as juniper, desert apricot, buckhorn cholla cactus, and beavertail cactus. After descending slightly to By Jim Spring, you'll find a trickle of water (in winter and spring) and the ruins of pipes and a tank. The trail continues on or close to a ridgeline for the next mile.

At about 2.0 miles the trail passes just below peak 4068, and a spectacular view of Culp Valley and the distant Borrego Valley opens up. From there the trail descends sharply, crosses the trail to Pena Spring (which offers the only dependable water near the route), and climbs toward the vista point, or "Lookout" at 3.5 miles.

From there on, the trail sticks mostly to the top of the ridge dividing Hellhole Canyon and Dry Canyon. You pass some flat, sandy areas—possible campsites—at 4.2 miles (3250'). Beyond, the trail descends sharply again, tending to the left (north) side of the ridge, with good views across Hellhole Canyon and out over Borrego Valley. At 5.5 miles (2500') you skirt a ravine that really comes alive with wildflowers in the early spring.

Toward the lower end of the trail, the vegetation grades into that of the low desert: ocotillo, creosote bush, and brittlebush. When in full bloom during March or April, the brittlebush spreads great patches of yellow color across the stony slopes. At 7.0 miles, there's a trail junction: the faint (original CRHT) goes east along a ridge and meets Montezuma Highway at mile 16.0, while a newer trail going north dives and zigzags down a steep slope. Take the latter trail and arrive, after one more mile, at the finish point near the foot of the Montezuma Grade.

Trip 11: Upper Hellhole Canyon

Distance	3.0 miles round trip (to waterfall)
Total elevation gain/loss	1600'/1600'
Hiking time	4 hours (round trip)
Recommended map	USGS 7.5-min *Tubb Canyon*
Best times	December through April
Agency	ABDSP
Difficulty	★★★★

The fastest entry into the upper reaches of Hellhole Canyon is not by simply going up from the mouth of the canyon past Maidenhair Falls. Nor is it by descending the South Fork below Pena Spring, though this is an interesting and challenging hike in its own right. Rather, it is by dropping down the ridge to the north of Pena Spring. This is a steep and at times slippery descent, but one accomplished in a fraction of the time required on the other routes. In this description, I will detail the way to a 30-foot waterfall in a northern tributary of Hellhole Canyon.

Begin this hike at the Pena Spring trailhead, as in Trip 9 above. Hike down to the spring first, then go north cross-country 0.4 mile, gaining almost 200 feet, to reach a flat part of the ridgeline overlooking Hellhole Canyon. Now head straight down (north) toward a large cottonwood tree in the canyon bottom ahead. In just over 0.2 mile of horizontal distance on the map, you lose 800 feet. If you choose your route carefully, the footing is quite stable on dirt and sparse grass, and over boulders. Be aware of the possibility of dislodging rocks, especially if traveling with others. Proceed very carefully if carrying a heavy backpack. In wetter years the stream down in the bottom carries water the whole year round.

Travel along the Hellhole Canyon bottom is very difficult due to vines, boulders, and fallen trees. About 100 yards downstream from the cottonwood tree, the canyon bends and widens, offering good camping possibilities. The tributary with the waterfall, however, lies upstream about 100 yards.

Go up the bottom of the tributary about 150 yards, passing several mini-waterfalls, until forced by dense vegetation to gain the slope on the right (east) side. Traverse for about 300 yards on the rocky slope until you can drop again into the canyon bottom at a point close to a multilevel cascade. Then make your way over large boulders and slabs to a grotto containing the 30-foot fall. The water shoots over in a thin stream, perfect for a shower on a warm day—but be careful of slippery rocks.

Further exploration beyond the waterfall is problematical if you remain in the canyon, but relatively easy if you gain the slopes and ridgelines. Hellhole Flat is one possible destination. So too are The Thimble (5779') and the highest summit on San Ysidro Mountain (6147').

Until the late 1980s, a herd of feral cattle flourished in the upper reaches of Hellhole Canyon and its tributaries. Because these cattle were competing for forage with the bighorn sheep and other native wildlife, many attempts were made to remove them—all unsuccessful until funds were made available for their evacuation by helicopter. This gave a modern dimension to the same predicament faced by old-time cattlemen a century ago: so many strays wandered into this canyon that it became known as a "hellish" place from which to retrieve cattle—hence the name "Hellhole."

Trip 12: Tubb Canyon

Distance	1.5 miles round trip
Total elevation gain/loss	200'/200'
Hiking time	1 hour (round trip)
Recommended map	USGS 7.5-min *Tubb Canyon*
Best times	October through May
Agency	ABDSP
Difficulty	★

Big Spring in a tributary of Tubb Canyon ("Tub" Canyon on some maps) is one of the more reliable water producers in the Anza-Borrego Desert. As such, it is an important watering hole for local wildlife. Tracks on the sandy pathways leading to the spring show evidence of visits by coyotes, mountain lions, and bighorn sheep.

Unknown to most park visitors, this isolated spring is actually very easy to reach on foot. The best place to begin is the small parking turnout on the north side of Montezuma Grade (Highway S-22) at mile 11.2. Walk due south across 400 yards of flat terrain, and cross over a gentle saddle. At this point you'll pick up a faint wildlife trail that descends into a sandy wash—the head of Tubb Canyon. After about 200 yards downstream the trail leaves this wash and passes over a low saddle to the south. Big Spring lies beyond, in the bottom of Tubb Canyon's south branch.

At the spring, the water gushes through tall thickets of seepwillow and thorny tangles of catclaw and mesquite—so it's hard to reach the water with one's hide intact. A few small willows and cottonwoods raise their crowns above it all. Enhancing the scene is the massive presence of Pinyon Ridge, rising to the south.

Before going back to the highway, climb the small hill (2720') east of the saddle you just passed over. This is one of the panoramic viewing sites used every summer by volunteers in the Anza-Borrego Desert bighorn-sheep-count program.

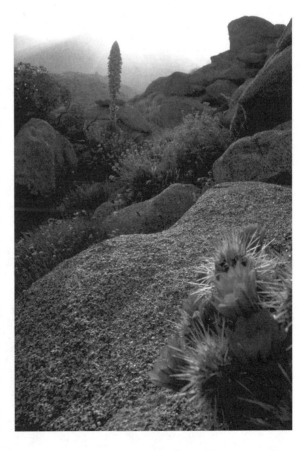

Hedgehog cactus and yucca flower stalk

Area D-3: Coyote Mountain/ Rockhouse Canyon

The Anza-Borrego Desert State Park extends over such a large area that duplication of place names is common. For example, the Rockhouse Canyon and Coyote Mountain in the north sector of the park are distinct from the Rockhouse Canyon (near Bow Willow) and the Coyote Mountains (near Ocotillo) that lie in the south sector.

The northern Coyote Mountain is a barren, brownish ridge separating lower Coyote Canyon from Clark Valley and Clark (dry) Lake. Geologically, it is a spur of the Santa Rosa Mountains which drifted away from the main crest by fault action. Coyote Mountain and its extension of lower hills to the northwest form a wedge between the San Jacinto Fault in Clark Valley and the Coyote Creek Fault in Coyote Canyon.

Rockhouse Canyon drains a large alluvial basin at the foot of the Santa Rosa Mountains. It meanders southwest between precipitous walls, then strikes a course southeast along the San Jacinto Fault. Clark Valley lies at the mouth of Rockhouse Canyon.

Trips 2, 4, and 5 below start along the only vehicle route penetrating Rockhouse Canyon. Standard passenger cars, if driven carefully, can usually maneuver up about 9 miles of this progressively more primitive unpaved road. Here's how to get to the starting points of these trips:

At mile 26.7 on Borrego-Salton Seaway (Highway S-22), just east of Pegleg Monument, turn north on Clark's Well Road. Pavement soon ends. Bear right, avoiding the spur road on the left to a highway-maintenance gravel pit. After 1.5 miles (from S-22), the road divides again. Take the left fork, the Rockhouse Truck Trail. In a short while it skirts the west edge of Clark Lake, which is where Trip 2 starts. (After heavy rains, a short section of the road ahead can become muddy and impassable.) Next, the road swings around a spur of Coyote Mountain, and continues toward the mouth of Rockhouse Canyon. At 9.2 miles from S-22, you come to the junction of jeep roads into Butler and Rockhouse canyons—starting point for Trips 4 and 5. Only high-clearance vehicles are suitable for further travel up either canyon.

Trailhead parking for the trips below requires an Anza-Borrego Desert State Park parking pass. See the section "Using This Book" for more information.

Clark Valley from Coyote Mountain

Area D-3: Coyote Mountain / Rockhouse Canyon

Trip 1: Coyote Mountain—South Spur

Distance	4.0 miles round trip (to viewpoint)
Total elevation gain/loss	750'/750'
Hiking time	2 hours (round trip)
Optional map	USGS 7.5-min *Clark Lake*
Best times	November through April
Agency	ABDSP
Difficulty	★★

A spectacular view of upper Borrego Valley—with its patchwork of tamarisk windbreaks, fields, citrus orchards, and palm nurseries—is the highlight of this hike. You begin at Pegleg Monument, nestled against the south spur of Coyote Mountain, and climb steadily on an old jeep road for two miles until you reach a point on the steep southwest escarpment offering the best view.

The monument, 7 miles northeast of Borrego Springs on Highway S-22, commemorates Pegleg Smith, a prospector and spinner of tall tales, and his famous lost gold. Adding stones to the big rock pile here, it is said, brings luck to the treasure hunter.

Vegetation along the way is sparse—mostly ocotillo, creosote bush, and brittlebush. When in bloom in the early spring, however, the brittlebush can create splashes of yellow color up and down the hillsides and ravines.

Beyond the viewpoint at 2.0 miles, the road continues winding up along ridges and through hidden valleys for another 2.5 miles until it fades out completely near peak 2589. The summit of Coyote Mountain (3192') lies another mile north. The route outlined in Trip 2 below is a faster and more direct route to that summit.

Trip 2: Coyote Mountain—East Approach

Distance	4.0 miles round trip (to summit)
Total elevation gain/loss	2600'/2600'
Hiking time	5 hours (round trip)
Recommended map	USGS 7.5-min *Clark Lake*
Best times	November through April
Agency	ABDSP
Difficulty	★★★

According to Coyote Mountain's informal summit register, relatively few people undertake the straightforward but somewhat arduous ascent. Many routes are possible, but most seem to climb the east slope. This is basically a walk-up ascent, though quite steep. Outcrops of solid, desert-varnished rock provide good footing on the lower slopes. Higher up, a veneer of small stones underfoot makes walking a little difficult.

To reach the starting point, drive 3.5 miles north of Highway S-22 on Clark's Well Road and Rockhouse Truck Trail. Park in a clearing on the left, near the foot of Coyote Mountain.

On foot, simply go straight up the steep slope to the west. Scattered shrubs and succulents—like brittlebush, cholla cactus, agave, and creosote bush—cling tenaciously to soil pockets amid the rocks.

As you climb, a pattern of lines becomes visible on the dry lake bed below, not unlike the famous intaglios of the Nazca Plain in Peru. These include the outlines of an antenna array of the defunct Clark Lake Radio Observatory, and a nearby landing field. Beyond the dry lake, the panorama of the west escarpment of the Santa Rosa Mountains, its rugged ravines, and classic (from a geologist's viewpoint) alluvial fans, is almost stupefying.

The broad, rounded summit at 3192 feet is topped by a surveyor's marker. The view is entirely panoramic, but it doesn't include much of the valleys below. You must move well away from the summit in order to look down. If you're looking for a place to bed down for the night, some small, possibly windswept campsites can be found 0.2 mile southwest of the summit.

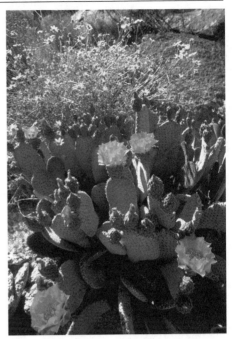

Beavertail cactus and brittlebush

Trip 3: Alcoholic Pass

Distance	2.0 miles round trip (to pass)
Total elevation gain/loss	650'/650'
Hiking time	1^1/2 hours (round trip)
Optional map	USGS 7.5-min *Borrego Palm Canyon*
Best times	November through April
Agency	ABDSP
Difficulty	★★

For centuries Indians used Alcoholic Pass as a convenient short cut between Coyote Canyon and Clark Valley. In time, a well-beaten trail was worn across the precipitous slopes west of the pass. Around the turn of the century, the Clark brothers, early cattlemen who homesteaded in Coy-

ote Canyon, used this trail to transport some primitive well-drilling equipment to the site now known as Clark Well in Clark Valley. Near the top of the pass, the old Indian trail squeezed between two boulders so closely spaced that the burros had to be unpacked before going through. Today, you can still follow the obvious trace of this historic pathway.

The starting point for this hike is along the main Coyote Canyon dirt road, 2.5 miles north of the end of the pavement at DiGiorgio Road. A small sign marks the start of the trail. East of here is a steep ravine leading up toward the pass. The old Indian trail does not ascend this ravine directly, but instead rises on the ridge immediately south of it.

You climb on a somewhat rough and rocky path, gaining altitude quickly. In a few places, foot travel and erosion have worn the bed of the trail to a depth of two feet. Looking behind you to gauge your progress as you climb, you'll be inspired by the ever-widening, almost aerial, view of Coyote Canyon and the surrounding mountains.

In the upper reaches of the pass, the trail levels somewhat and is a bit hard to follow. Just head for the pile of boulders at the top of the pass. There you'll catch sight of the massive wall of the Santa Rosa Mountains, topped by the dusky, pinyon-covered summit of Rabbit Peak.

The remainder of the old Alcoholic Pass route goes east along the sandy bed of a wide wash and eventually reaches the desolate floor of Clark Valley. The Rockhouse Truck Trail is 3 miles northeast of the pass; you could arrange for someone to meet you at some point on the truck trail if you wanted to hike one-way from Coyote Canyon to Clark Valley.

Trip 4: Jackass Flat/Butler Canyon

Distance	10.0 miles
Total elevation gain/loss	1000'/1000'
Hiking time	6 hours
Recommended maps	USGS 7.5-min *Clark Lake NE, Collins Valley*
Best times	November through April
Agency	ABDSP
Difficulty	★★★

A visit to an ancient Cahuilla Indian village site is the highlight on this long loop hike over mostly gentle terrain. Hidden Spring, about halfway around the loop, nearly always has some surface water, but cannot be considered a good source for drinking needs.

From Highway S-22 drive 9.2 miles up Clark's Well Road and the Rockhouse Truck Trail to the junction of roads into Rockhouse and Butler canyons. On foot follow the Rockhouse road north across a low bank and into the broad wash of Rockhouse Canyon. The next 4 miles are somewhat uneventful, though the canyon deepens impressively. The San Jacinto Fault parallels this section of canyon. At about 3 miles, there is a road closure sign.

Continue another mile to Hidden Spring, identified by a sign on the left. A small basin holds about two or three gallons of insect-infested water.

From the spring walk 150 feet back down along the canyon wall to a thicket of mesquite trees. A path through the mesquite will guide you to a deeply worn, eroded trail angling south and upward across a 200-foot bluff. Just over the top, on the eastern edge of Jackass Flat, are the remains of a Cahuilla Indian village occupied as recently as the late 1800s. You may chance upon some old fire pits, pieces of pottery, and flakes of a metamorphic rock known as wonderstone, which was once used for stone tools. (Remember that you must leave everything in place.)

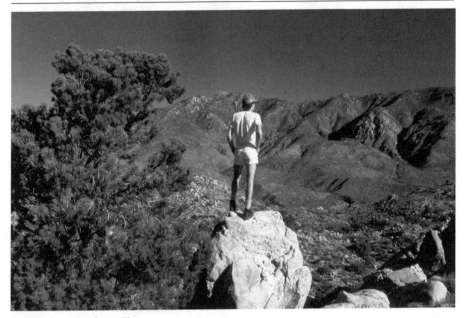

Ridge above Jackass Flat

Now head west about a mile to the uppermost reaches of Butler Canyon. You'll return by following this canyon, assisted by gravity all the way. As you descend and the canyon walls narrow, you may notice miniature pine cones lying about. These washed down from pinyon-dotted Buck Ridge, some 3 miles north and about 2000 feet higher. Buck Ridge and other mountains of similar height in the desert were important pinyon-nut-gathering areas for the Cahuilla Indians.

Follow the course of Butler Canyon as it descends gently for 4 miles through a spectacular serpentine gorge carved out of mostly granitic rock. Beyond the mouth of this gorge you'll pick up wheel tracks leading back to your car.

Trip 5: Rockhouse Canyon and Valley

Distance	25 miles
Total elevation gain/loss	4000'/4000'
Hiking time	16 hours
Required maps	USGS 7.5-min *Clark Lake NE, Collins Valley*
Best times	November through April
Agency	ABDSP, BLM/EC
Difficulty	★★★★

Rockhouse Canyon and the broad, sloping alluvial basin drained by it—informally known as Rockhouse Valley—constitute one of southern California's truly forgotten places. Not much more than a century ago, Indian villages thrived here. After the Indians moved to the nearby Santa Rosa Indian Reservation around 1900, a few hardy prospectors made forays into the area, traveling along the ancient footpaths, and in some cases living in the old rock houses built by the Indians. Today, there is still no road beyond the lower reaches of Rockhouse Canyon. The closest inhabited place is several miles away.

Although this grand tour of Rockhouse Canyon and Valley can be rushed through in a single, very long day, it's better to set aside two or three days to explore the area adequately and at a reasonable pace.

To reach the starting point, which is usually accessible by all but low-slung cars, drive 9.2 miles north from Highway S-22 on Clark's Well Road and Rockhouse Truck Trail. Park near the junction of roads into Butler and Rockhouse canyons (I'm assuming you'll start here—however a high-clearance, 4-wheel-drive car or truck might get you 3 miles farther on wheels).

On foot, walk 3 miles up Rockhouse Canyon to the road closure, and keep going another mile to Hidden Spring. Over the next 3.5 miles, Rockhouse Canyon is a narrow gorge flanked by soaring rock walls. You'll be on soft sand—alluvium washed down from the valley above—

most of the time.

At a point just south of the San Diego-Riverside county line, you'll come upon a granite dike forming a 20-foot dry fall. Well before this area was declared a state wilderness, jeep-club members built a road over this obstacle and used a winch to haul vehicles over it—though it's difficult to see how! Huge boulders litter the canyon floor now, a result of big flash floods in the late 1970s. Amateur road builders would need dynamite to clear a path today.

At the county line, you leave Anza-Borrego Desert State Park and enter BLM land. After you pass a major tributary to the east and a smaller tributary also to the east, the canyon broadens and you enter Rockhouse Valley. Here you'll spot some junipers, indicators of the high-desert realm.

Next stop is the hard-to-find lower rock-house ruins. Try this: follow the main wash up the west side of the valley until you reach the base of a boulder-strewn ridge 0.6 mile northwest of the valley en-

Rock-house ruins above Nicholias Canyon

trance; then go 0.2 mile due north to find the three rock houses, all of which are roofless. They're spaced along a low, elongated ridge with a view of the entire valley. Mud used as mortar still clings to some of the walls. Each house had a cozy fireplace inside.

The water source for this settlement was said to be a spring next to a lone cottonwood tree 0.5 mile east. Both the tree and the spring seem to have been victims of the tropical storms of the late 1970s; only a dry, sandy wash is in evidence there today. (The "Cottonwood Spring" indicated on USGS topo maps northwest of the ruins is apparently an error.)

From the lower rock houses, head cross-country due northwest through sparse vegetation (mostly catclaw, agave, and golden cholla cactus) toward a low, rounded hill spur at the upper end of the valley, 2.5 miles away. This spur forms the east wall of Nicholias Canyon, your next destination. When you reach the base of the spur, swing left (west) around it and pick up an informal trail that goes down to the creek in Nicholias Canyon. Plenty of water flows here during the winter and early spring. Follow either bank upstream, passing some old, rusted mining debris.

Up-canyon, after a bend to the right (northeast), you'll come upon a magnificent creek-hugging grove of alders and cottonwoods. These are beautiful in April when the new, delicate leaves shimmer in the breeze. Warm light floods in from the pinyon-studded, scrubby slopes surrounding the grove. This is an enchanting spot to camp—some brush-free campsites on sloping ground can be found on the west bank. Nearby you can explore the major source of the water, which is a spring 200 yards east of the main canyon in a tributary ravine. Good water may be obtained there.

Above and south of this spring are two more rock-house ruins, even more tumbledown than those seen earlier. You can also make camp on a nearby flat offering a commanding view of Rockhouse Valley, and the distant San Ysidro, Vallecito, and Laguna mountains. Massive Toro Peak, the crown summit of the Santa Rosa Mountains, looms in the north. (Adventurous climbers wishing to bag this peak can proceed up the ridge west of Nicholias Canyon. Nicholias Canyon itself, with its dry falls and boulder obstacles, is a slower and more technically difficult route. Plan on a full day's climb, with plenty of bushwhacking and talus scrambling.)

From the last rock-house ruins, go east to a sandy flat containing a scraggly row of cottonwoods (here's yet another possible camping spot). Follow the shallow drainage east of this flat; when it deepens, pick up the well-worn but partly overgrown trail on the left (north) side. The trail switchbacks downward, crosses a major southward-draining ravine, and then strikes a path southeast down a broad ridge. (This is one of several trails in Rockhouse Valley shown on circa-1900 topographic maps.)

A path straight ahead leads directly back to Rockhouse Canyon, but you can depart from it to make one more stop: the Old Santa Rosa Indian village. At about the 4000-foot contour, turn east and work your way over low ridges and sharp gullies toward the two "seeps" marked on the topo map in sections 17 and 18. The first, in a canyon at 4200 feet, has had evidence of Indian use—*morteros* and *ollas* (earthen jugs), the latter removed years ago. The second seep, backed up against the rocky slopes of the Santa Rosa Mountains at 3910 feet, is the site of the old village. Two rockhouse foundations are still intact here. It's hard to imagine a more wild and remote dwelling site. The seep is covered with a growth of mesquite, with no water on the surface.

Obscure trails radiate from the old village to all parts of the valley. At least two, still traceable, ascend ridgelines about 1 mile east-southeast of the village and connect with a trail into Martinez Canyon on the east slope of the Santa Rosas. There are springs at the mouths of two canyons near the base of these trails. Much time could be spent exploring this fascinating area—little changed over the last century.

From the old village site, the last leg of this trip is straight across the valley to the head of Rockhouse Canyon. From there you simply follow your footprints back to the starting point.

Trip 6: Box Canyon To Hidden Spring

Distance	12 miles round trip
Total elevation gain/loss	2500'/2500'
Hiking time	10 hours (round trip)
Required maps	USGS 7.5-min *Borrego Palm Canyon, Collins Valley, Clark Lake NE*
Best times	November through April
Agency	ABDSP
Difficulty	★★★★

Hidden Spring, according to Lester Reed, author of *Old Time Cattlemen and Other Pioneers of the Anza-Borrego Area*, served as a hub for Indian trails leading to at least half a dozen destinations. Among them was a route leading to the Lower Willows of Coyote Canyon via Box Canyon. Mr. Reed, himself an old cattleman, once followed this trail on horseback from Coyote Canyon to a tributary of Box Canyon, but apparently never returned to trace the entire route. Following general directions from his book, however, I have located significant parts of it.

The route traverses rough and isolated country, no less pristine than it was centuries ago when Cahuilla Indians passed this way on seasonal migration or food-gathering expeditions. If you haven't sharpened your skills at cross-country travel and trail-finding, you'll certainly have plenty of practice here.

It's possible to rush over this out-and-back trip in a single day, but a two-day backpack will allow you more time to look around. Campsites are abundant, but water is not. The meager supply at Hidden Spring cannot be counted on.

A one-way trip along this route is possible if you arrange to be picked up at the roadend in Rockhouse Canyon (a long, rugged drive by 4-wheel-drive vehicle). Another possibility is to continue hiking down Rockhouse Canyon and loop back through Alcoholic Pass (see Trip 3 above).

You begin the trek at the mouth of Box Canyon, just northwest of where the Coyote Canyon jeep road bypass turns west to avoid going through Lower Willows. This is 5.6 miles beyond the end of pavement at DiGiorgio Road (see Area D-1 introductory text). Bad road conditions and difficult fords may require that you park your car as much as two or three miles short of this point.

Follow the sandy, boulder-choked bed of Box Canyon northeast out of Coyote Canyon. After 0.8 mile, just beyond a narrow section of canyon where the walls pinch tightly, a tributary canyon branches to the right (east). Keep left, in the main canyon. After another 0.5 mile, a second tributary canyon branches right (east). Turn right, and in 100 yards go right again where this tributary divides. Proceed for another 0.3 mile, then leave the canyon bottom and climb to a low saddle on the ridge to the right (south).

Here you pick up a deeply worn trail, marked frequently by ducks (small piles of stones used as trail markers). Apparently disused in modern times, this trail is heavily encroached by desert vegetation, including formidable thickets of teddy-bear cholla cactus. In the manner of most Indian trails, this one strikes a path on the ridgeline above the canyon, rather than following the canyon itself. Since the Indians were master pathfinders and trail builders and keen observers of nature, they knew that flash floods would rearrange canyon bottoms, and that ridge trails would not be affected much by erosion. Having trails on ridges with clear lines of sight also facilitated easy route-finding in a world with no maps and direction-finding instruments.

Follow trail fragments up the ridge, bearing mostly left of the ridgeline, until you pass a 2720-foot knoll. Then bear right and cross a broad 2650-foot saddle, heading northeast. A playa (flat basin), several acres in extent, lies straight ahead. After heavy rains, a number of compact, shallow depressions (of mysterious origin) on the playa hold supplies of not-very-appealing-looking water. The playa is fringed by a dense growth of creosote bushes and surrounded by a low wall of hills. There's a splendid sense of isolation here, and it's no wonder—the nearest road or maintained pathway lies nearly 3 miles away.

Cross the playa and pass over a low spot in the hills to the northeast. Continue generally northeast, following occasional ducks and a hint of trail, and negotiate a steep descent into Butler Canyon. Avoid descending directly on the nose of the ridge that divides Butler Canyon and a deeply cut western tributary: the canyon wall is undercut below.

Once in Butler Canyon, follow it north onto the vast expanse of Jackass Flat. Then head for the Indian village site on its eastern lip, just above Hidden Spring (see Trip 4). Before you reach the main village site overlooking Rockhouse Canyon, you'll notice signs of former habitation—fire pits and potsherds—on the sandy areas of Jackass Flat. Within the main village area, you'll find the top of the steep, eroded trail leading down to Hidden Spring.

Ocotillo in Box Canyon

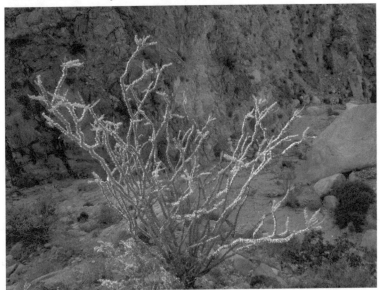

Area D-4: Santa Rosa Mountains

From the 8716-foot summit of Toro Peak in Riverside County, the main crest of the Santa Rosa Mountains undulates southeast past Rabbit and Villager peaks, then drops steadily to the desert floor at the edge of the Borrego Badlands. A complex of lesser ridges and promontories lies east of the main crest. Geologically, the Santa Rosas are identified as being an eastern arm of the Peninsular Ranges.

The northern summits of the Santa Rosa Mountains are high enough to support a variety of conifers, but the south half of the range—San Diego County's share—is quite desolate. The southern Santa Rosas are rugged, almost lacking in sources of water, virtually trail-less, seldom-visited, and (to the ill-prepared hiker) unforgiving. Yet it's here, more than almost any other place within the county, that you can really get away from it all. Perched on some high and dry peak, you can gaze out over hundreds of square miles of mountains and desert with a feeling that you own it all.

Other than Trip 1, which begins in Rockhouse Canyon, all hikes below start along the Borrego-Salton Seaway (County Highway S-22), northeast of Borrego Springs. Except for the area around the Calcite Mine (Trips 8 and 9), where vehicular traffic is allowed on certain roads and in certain washes, the southern Santa Rosas are classified as a state wilderness within Anza-Borrego Desert State Park. As elsewhere in the Anza-Borrego Desert area, you're on your own—no hiking or camping permits are required. Trailhead parking for the trips below, however, requires an Anza-Borrego Desert State Park parking pass. See the section "Using This Book" for more information. Also remember to observe the state park regulations, which are designed to protect all features within the park.

Refer to John Robinson's *San Bernardino Mountain Trails* for information about hikes in the northern part of the Santa Rosas, particularly the higher, forested areas within Riverside County.

Trip 1: Peak 6582

Distance	12 miles round trip
Total elevation gain/loss	5800'/5800'
Hiking time	13 hours (round trip)
Required map	USGS 7.5-min *Clark Lake NE*
Best times	November through April
Agency	ABDSP, BLM/EC
Difficulty	★★★★★

Peak 6582 (labeled "Dawns Peak" on some maps) is the highest point the main Santa Rosa crest between Toro Peak (8716') and Rabbit Peak (6666'). With one or two visits per year over the past two decades, it is one of the least climbed—and least accessible—peaks in the Anza-Borrego Desert. A few adventurers have passed

Area D-4: Santa Rosa Mountains

over its summit while traveling along the crest from Toro to Rabbit and beyond. Others have ascended from upper Clark Valley—my description below is one of several possible variations of that route.

It takes a strong sense of determination to withstand miles of waterless, rocky terrain and thousands of feet of steady elevation gain for the privilege of standing atop a bump on a ridge barely distinguishable from others of similar stature nearby.

But like many desert peaks, this one holds a special fascination. An elaborate pillar of stones, erected sometime before 1970, graces the summit—a monument to some unknown hiker or hikers who not only climbed the peak but also put in hours of skilled labor.

Although this trip can be done in one long, exhausting day, a two-day trip makes more sense. A base camp established halfway up, and a quick ascent of the peak

Climbing toward Peak 6582

using light packs, is a method that proved successful for every one of the ten people I once had the pleasure of leading on this route. The lack of water (except during rainfall or when snow is present at higher elevations) makes any trip longer than two days undesirable.

Refer to the Area D-3 introductory text for details on road access into upper Clark Valley (also note that this particular trip is plotted on the Area D-3 map). Find parking space along Rockhouse Truck Trail, somewhere between 6.8 and 7.3 miles north of Highway S-22. Don't forget to take a compass bearing of at least one nearby landmark to assist in finding your car later.

Start hiking north across the sandy floor of upper Clark Valley. Head for a broad ridge spur (with survey marker "Corp" noted on the topo map) that descends south to meet the floor of Clark Valley—about 1.5 miles away. Below the survey marker, some petroglyphs are inscribed on the jumbled, desert-varnished boulders.

From the petroglyphs, head north-east and gain the narrow, rocky ridge between two canyons that leads toward peak 2700. At about the 2200-foot contour on this ridge, drop into the canyon on the right (east). Follow the rock-strewn canyon bottom, bearing right at a major fork at 2380 feet, and continue about 0.3 mile to a large sandy flat ideally suited (except for lack of water) for camping. The wash and the rocky slopes surrounding this campsite show signs of both bighorn sheep and mountain lions.

Next morning, you can set out before sunrise to bag the peak, carrying light, dayhiking gear. Climb the steep ridge (with loose rocks and cactus) northeast of the campsite, topping out at or near peak 3489. Continue about 1 mile north over rolling terrain, dotted with agave and small shrubs, to the base of the ridge leading up to a point on the Santa Rosa crest 0.1 mile northwest of Peak 6582. In the last mile you gain nearly 3000 feet over jagged terrain. Luckily, scattered pinyon pines afford welcome shade on the way up.

The view from the rounded granite boulders at the summit is magnificent. You'll see most of the Santa Rosa crest, the dusky Palomar and San Ysidro mountains to the west, and long vistas south across Clark Valley to the middle and southern reaches of Anza-Borrego Desert State Park.

Don't forget to sign the register hidden beneath the towering cairn.

By noon at the latest, you ought to be off the peak and busy hightailing it back to the campsite. There you can hoist your backpack and start the long trudge to your car. With luck, you'll arrive before dusk.

Trip 2: Rabbit Peak via Villager Peak

Distance	20 miles round trip
Total elevation gain/loss	8300'/8300'
Hiking time	18 hours (round trip)
Required Maps	USGS 7.5-min *Fonts Point, Rabbit Peak*
Best times	November through April
Agency	ABDSP
Difficulty	★★★★★

Despite their remoteness, Villager and Rabbit peaks are among the most popular destinations for peak baggers in the Anza-Borrego Desert. Several dozen people per year attain the summits of these two peaks, and bottles and tin cans containing the peak registers are often overflowing with business cards and other mementos.

Rabbit Peak has two popular routes of approach. A steep, eastern approach from Coachella Valley, beginning near sea level, is described in John Robinson's *San Bernardino Mountain Trails*. Here, I will describe the southern route, up the main crest of the Santa Rosas via Villager Peak. This is longer, more gradual, and arguably more scenic (but overall more difficult) than the eastern approach; and it begins at a point closer to San Diego County residents. A minimum of two full days is needed, with the first night's camp on or near Villager Peak. Alternatively, you can set your sights on Villager Peak only—a hike of 13 miles (11 hours).

Park in the northside turnout at mile 31.8 on Highway S-22. Proceed north to-

ward the east end of a long, sandy ridge 0.5 mile away. The north face of this ridge is a huge scarp along the San Jacinto Fault—said to be one of the largest fault scarps in unconsolidated material in North America. North of this ridge, flash-floods exiting from Rattlesnake Canyon have cut a series of braided washes in a swath about 0.6 mile wide. A ducked trail takes you over this dissected terrain to the base of the long, ramp-like ridge leading to Villager and Rabbit peaks.

The initial climb is very steep, but the route soon levels off to a rather steady gradient averaging about 1000 feet per mile. Stay on the highest part of the ridge to remain on route. Here and there, you'll be on fragments of trail well worn by the passage of both bighorn sheep and hikers. Creosote bush, ocotillo, and glistening specimens of barrel cactus, hedgehog cactus, and silver, golden, and teddy-bear cholla cactus grace the slopes below 3000 feet. Dense thickets of agave at 3000 to 4000 feet may slow you down a bit.

Along the lower part of the ridge you'll come upon several Indian "sleeping circles," which may have been used as windbreaks or to anchor shelters made from local vegetation. At about the 3000-foot level (3.0 miles) a green patch marking Rattlesnake Spring comes into view in a tributary canyon of Rattlesnake Canyon about 1.5 miles east.

At 4100 feet (4.3 miles), you'll pass along the edge of a spectacular dropoff overlooking Clark Valley. The white band of rock prominently displayed along the face of this escarpment is marble. This is metamorphosed limestone predating the rise of the Southern California Batholith. Just beyond the 4800-foot contour (5.0 miles), the ridge descends a little to a small, exposed campsite with airy views both east and west.

In the next mile the ridgeline becomes quite jagged. Pinyon, juniper, and nolina (a relative of the yucca) now dominate. The rounded summit of Villager Peak (6.5 miles) offers good campsites amid spreading pinyons.

A predawn start is recommended if you plan to reach Rabbit Peak, return to your packs on Villager Peak, and make the long descent back to your car all in one day. Rabbit Peak is only 3.5 miles away and 900 feet higher than Villager Peak, but the undulating ridgeline between the two adds considerable elevation gains and losses both ways. The total gain/loss for the round trip between peaks is a surprising 3300'/3300'.

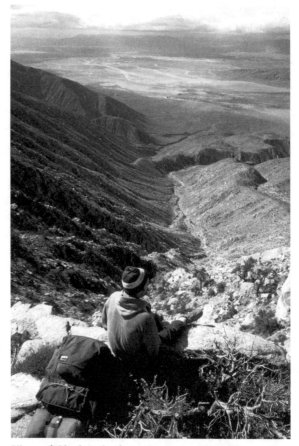

View of Clark Lake from the Santa Rosa Mountains

Rabbit Peak lies just 0.3 mile north of the San Diego-Riverside county line. If the county line were shifted just that far north, Rabbit Peak would be the highest elevation in San Diego County.

The flat summit of Rabbit Peak is dotted with pinyon pines, precluding the kind of panoramic views available from more angular peaks. Still, it's a delightful spot—a kind of sky island aloof from all the rest of Southern California.

Trip 3: Rattlesnake Spring

Distance	8.5 miles
Total elevation gain/loss	2500'/2500'
Hiking time	7 hours
Required map	USGS 7.5-min *Fonts Point*
Best times	November through April
Agency	ABDSP
Difficulty	★★★★

Rattlesnake Spring is one of the few reliable sources of water in the southern Santa Rosa Mountains. Several dozen bighorn sheep may depend on it for survival during periods of drought. The spring produces a low volume—it's more like a seep. You shouldn't count on it as a source for your own drinking needs.

On this loop hike, you'll approach the spring via one route and return via a second route comparable in difficulty. Both routes involve a substantial amount of scrambling. Feel free to reverse the direc-tion of travel from that described below.

As in Trip 2 above, park at the turn-out at mile 31.8 on Highway S-22. Proceed 1.1 mile north to the base of the broad ridge leading to Villager and Rabbit peaks. Bear right around this ridge and follow the main wash into Rattlesnake Canyon. At a point about 1.3 miles farther, a major tributary will be seen to the right (east). Climb the steep slope north of this tributary and gain the ridgeline containing survey point 2971. Continue north over the top of this ridge-line (3125'); bear northeast, avoiding some

Bighorn sheep at Rattlesnake Spring

steep terrain to the north, and then descend into the canyon containing Rattlesnake Spring.

Mesquite groves and a single large cottonwood tree grow in the moist area surrounding the spring. The chalky hillsides to the north of the spring have been stripped bare of vegetation by many a bighorn sheep hoof. Trails radiate in all directions to higher ridges where the bighorn spend their time when not in need of water. Do respect the watering rights of all kinds of wildlife by not camping close to the water.

You can now return by way of Rattlesnake Canyon. The tributary containing Rattlesnake Spring has a set of formidable dry falls at its mouth, so the following detour is recommended: Climb northwest from the spring over sloping terrain to a point in Rattlesnake Canyon below the 2960-foot contour. Then wend your way down-canyon, passing below the dry falls in the tributary.

Fallen rocks are common between the narrow walls of Rattlesnake Canyon, but several sandy stretches suitable for camping are here too. Just below the 2400-foot contour, you'll come to the top of a 20-foot dry fall—the biggest challenge on this trip. Lower your packs on a rope and down-climb directly; or detour around the fall on the rocky, cactus-infested slopes either left or right. The latter method is less elegant but probably safer. From this point on, the canyon widens, and the going is quite easy over small boulders and patches of sand.

Trip 4: Mile-High Mountain

Distance	13 miles round trip
Total elevation gain/loss	5500'/5500'
Hiking time	10 hours (round trip)
Required maps	USGS 7.5-min *Fonts Point, Rabbit Peak*
Best times	November through April
Agency	ABDSP
Difficulty	★★★★

This unnamed, tan-colored massif, which I have dubbed "Mile-High Mountain" for the elevation of its highest summits, rivals in prominence the main south ridge containing Villager and Rabbit peaks. The unobstructed eastern and southern view from its crest is probably unequaled anywhere in the Santa Rosas; it includes the entire shoreline of the Salton Sea and virtually all of the Coachella and Imperial valleys. From here I once spotted the summits of the Sierra San Pedro Martir, 180 miles away.

The most direct route up is by way of the ridge forming the west wall of Palo Verde Canyon. Park in the turnout at mile 31.8 on Highway S-22, and head northeast across the open desert for 1 mile to the mouth of Palo Verde Canyon. Follow the main wash up the canyon another 1.5 miles to a sharp bend at 1900 feet elevation. Now climb the steep slope to the left (west) and gain the ridgeline. (Palo Verde Canyon itself enters a steep bowl just below the usually dry Palo Verde Spring, where further progress is blocked.)

Simply follow this ridgeline north for the next 3 miles or so, gaining 3000 feet. The sequence of vegetation is similar to that on the Villager/Rabbit ridge to the west, described in Trip 2.

There are four distinct, rounded summits at the top, the highest of which is farthest north, elevation approximately 5340 feet. Peak 5300 is dotted with a few scraggly pinyons, and would accommodate perhaps two or three prone bodies.

Mile-High Mountain is a good hub for routes into many remote corners of the Santa Rosas. West of peak 5340 you can descend into Rattlesnake Canyon (where there are dry falls you must carefully climb around) or into the major unnamed drainage system to the north; or you can gain the Villager/Rabbit ridge. You can also visit survey marker "Rosa" (which has a climber's register) and descend from there into Wonderstone Wash.

Trip 5: Rock Tanks Loop

Distance	7.5 miles
Total elevation gain/loss	1300'/1300'
Hiking time	5 hours
Required map	USGS 7.5-min *Fonts Point*
Best times	November through April
Agency	ABDSP
Difficulty	★★★

Many experiences—some powerful and some merely annoying—await you on this hike: the palpable force of the desert sun's rays; the desiccated air, catching in the throat; the sharp prick of a cactus spine on the ankle, or the brittle scrape of an ocotillo wand on the elbow; the feeling of vertigo when you step to the edge of an abyss and view the shattered landscape below; and, most powerful of all, the sublime silence.

Here's how to get started with this quintessential desert experience: Park at mile 32.9 along Highway S-22, where a small wash crosses the road. This is Palo Verde Wash, named for the many palo verde trees along it. (These green-limbed, spindly trees are in glorious yellow bloom in April.) Begin hiking generally north along the braided wash, taking care not to stray into a smaller canyon that comes out of the mountains just east of Palo Verde Wash—this is an easy mistake to make. At about 1 mile you'll see a prominent cut in the mountains ahead—Palo Verde Canyon.

At this point it's possible to make a short side trip to see some cottontop cacti (*Echinocactus polycephalus*), which resemble small barrel cacti but grow in dome-shaped clusters. They're quite rare in the Anza-Borrego area. Look for them on the low ridge spurs west of Palo Verde Wash. One amazing specimen spans 5 feet.

At 1.3 miles the canyon walls begin to close in on both sides. Walk along the wall on the right side, and in another 0.2 mile, you'll spot an obscure trail going straight up the rocky slope to the right. The bottom of the trail should be marked by cairns. Ducks placed here and there alongside the trail will guide you over the next 1.3 miles. This trail is the beginning of an Indian route that goes over the Santa Rosa Mountains and down Wonderstone Wash to a spot where wonderstone (a raw material for stone tools) was quarried.

On your left, as you gain elevation, is an old mine tunnel sunk into a prominent vein. Woe to those who venture in more than a few feet: pack rats have se-

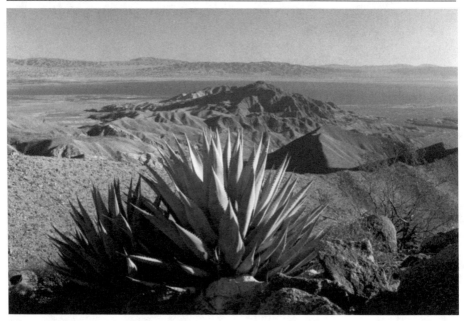

View of Salton Sea from Pyramid Peak

creted away a huge collection of cholla-cactus spines.

At 2.1 miles the trail crosses a divide and descends along a precipitous slope overlooking Smoke Tree Canyon. A rock slide has obliterated traces of the old trail, but hikers have forged a new trail. When you reach the canyon bottom, make a short side trip up the narrow tributary canyon to the northeast. Here, the scouring of flash floods has worn large depressions in the rock—the Natural Rock Tanks. Pockets like these, called *tinajas*, serve as natural reservoirs of water for weeks or months after major storms. If you're lucky, you may spot bighorn sheep in the area.

North of the tributary containing the rock tanks, remnants of the old Indian trail continue on the slope east of Smoke Tree Canyon all the way to a saddle at the head of Smoke Tree Canyon, just west of Pyramid Peak. You can also reach that saddle by following the canyon bottom all the way to its head. It's possible to make a long side trip up and over the saddle into the remote upper Wonderstone Wash drainage; for

detailed information on this, please see pages 207–09 in the first (1986) edition of this guidebook.

To continue our loop hike, head straight down Smoke Tree Canyon toward the highway, 3 miles away. The canyon becomes a narrow fissure in two places, where dark conglomerate cliffs hover menacingly overhead, seemingly subject to imminent collapse. (I once noticed, two days after a mild earthquake, numerous basketball-size rocks newly fallen and embedded in the sand just below these cliffs. If you're backpacking, choose a campsite well away from the cliffs.) There's a short scramble down a dry waterfall, followed by a mile or so of intermittent boulderhopping, and then it's smooth sailing on a nice bed of packed sand all the way to the highway.

Close the loop by walking along the wide shoulder of the highway. Or, if fatigued or just lazy, have one or more members of your party sprint over to pick up the car.

Trip 6: Coachwhip Canyon

Distance	1 to 4 miles
Optional map	USGS 7.5-min *Fonts Point*
Best times	October through June
Agency	ABDSP
Difficulty	★

Stark, dry, and almost barren, Coachwhip Canyon is somehow—despite these attributes—a very peaceful and appealing place. A beautiful forest of smoke trees, framed by sandstone formations, stands at the entrance. The wind, which can blow like the devil just outside, seldom seems to intrude within the confines of the canyon. Hidden nooks in the side canyons, each unique, invite you to pause, rest, and enjoy.

The wraithlike, gray-green smoke tree, a handsome shrub in any season, puts on quite a show in June, when it is festooned with thousands of indigo-colored blossoms. The smoke tree forest literally hums then with the wingbeats of bees gathering nectar. It is, of course, terrifically hot at that time of year, so you would want to do your hiking at dawn or dusk.

There are actually dozens of steep-walled ravines here, all draining into Ella Wash. The ravines twist and turn through soft sandstone, each one ending abruptly at the horseshoe-shaped headwall that surrounds the area.

Coachwhip Canyon lies along Highway S-22, 16 miles east of Borrego Springs. Turn north into a sandy wash at mile 34.8. The sandy wheel tracks can accommodate most ordinary passenger cars for some distance in, but turning your car around could be problematical without 4-wheel drive. Appropriate vehicles can make it 1.2 miles or more up either of two branches of the canyon. There are several good spots for car camping along the way.

By exploring some or all the tributaries, you'd walk anywhere from 1 to 4

View of Borrego Badlands from rim above Coachwhip Canyon

miles. In a few spots, you can climb high enough up the headwall to get a good view of both the Coachwhip area and the Borrego Badlands beyond. Once on top, you could continue to follow the main ridge 3 miles north to 3500-foot Pyramid Peak.

Smoke trees in Coachwhip Canyon

Trip 7: Truckhaven Rocks

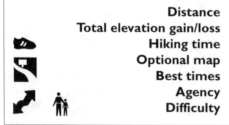

Distance	1.5 miles round trip
Total elevation gain/loss	200'/200'
Hiking time	40 minutes (round trip)
Optional map	USGS 7.5-min *Fonts Point*
Best times	October through May
Agency	ABDSP
Difficulty	★

The Truckhaven Rocks are some-what reminiscent of the outcrops of sandstone at Garden of the Gods in Colorado Springs, Colorado. The tilted slabs of orange-tinted sandstone, which can be plainly seen from Highway S-22, are a favorite haunt of photographers.

Park on the wide shoulder of Highway S-22 at mile 35.5, and head up the wash that leads toward a point a little east of the Truckhaven Rocks. Climbing out of this wash to reach the outcrops, you'll cross a boulder-strewn plain dotted with ocotillo. Here and there, in areas free of large rocks, are patches of "desert pavement," a common surface condition in which small pebbles of roughly uniform size form a flat mosaic. This is a result of fine particles being blown away, leaving the larger particles and pebbles to settle and pack together.

Trip 8: Calcite Mine

Distance	4.0 miles round trip
Total elevation gain/loss	800'/800'
Hiking time	2 hours (round trip)
Optional map	USGS 7.5-min *Seventeen Palms*
Best times	November through April
Agency	ABDSP
Difficulty	★★

Thousands of years of cutting and polishing by water and wind erosion have produced the chaotic rock formations and slotlike ravines you'll discover in the Calcite Mine area. The highlight of this hike is, of course, the mine itself. During World War II, this was an important site—indeed the only site in the United States—for the extraction of optical-grade calcite crystals for use in gunsights. Trench-mining operations throughout the area have left deep scars upon the earth, seemingly as fresh today as when they were made.

Park in the roadside turnout at mile 38.0 along Highway S-22; then walk 0.1 mile east to the Calcite jeep road intersection. An interpretive panel here gives some details about the history of the mine. Follow the jeep road as it dips into and out of South Fork Palm Wash, and continues northwest toward the southern spurs of the Santa Rosa Mountains. Ahead you will see an intricately honeycombed whitish slab of sandstone, called Locomotive Rock, which lies behind (northeast of) the mine area.

About 1.4 miles from S-22, the road dips sharply to cross a deep ravine. Poke into the upper (north) end of this ravine

Sedimentary formations, Calcite Mine

and you'll discover one of the best slot canyons in Anza-Borrego. (Skilled climbers can squeeze through the slot and go up a break on the right side to reach a point above and northwest of the mine area.)

At road's end calcite crystals lie strewn about on the ground, glittering in the sunlight. You could spend a lot of time exploring the mining trenches and the pocked slabs of sandstone nearby. Palm Wash, a frightening gash in the earth, precludes travel to the east.

On the return, try this alternate route: Backtrack 0.5 mile to the aforementioned slot ravine. Proceed downstream along its bottom. As you pass through deeper and deeper layers of sandstone strata, the ravine narrows until it allows the passage of only one person at a time. When you reach the jumbled blocks of sandstone in Palm Wash at the bottom of the ravine, turn right, walk 0.3 mile downstream, and exit the canyon via a short link of jeep trail that leads back to the Calcite road.

Trip 9: Palm Wash/Sheep Tanks

Distance	7.0 miles
Total elevation gain/loss	900'/900'
Hiking time	4 hours
Required map	USGS 7.5-min *Seventeen Palms*
Best times	November through April
Agency	ABDSP
Difficulty	★★★

Off the beaten track, this loop hike gives access to a labyrinth of deep gorges and a bench with clear traces of ancient Indian pathways. The upper end of North Fork Palm Wash, about halfway around the loop, offers good camping spots for backpackers.

Begin as in Trip 8 above. At 0.8 mile from Highway S-22, turn right leaving the Calcite Mine road and descending a jeep trail into Palm Wash. Head up-canyon (northwest) through the vertical-walled gorge, past fallen blocks of tan-colored sandstone. The walls of the canyon seem to be in a state of arrested collapse, with huge slices of rock fully separated from the walls, ready to surrender to gravity during the next earthquake or flash flood.

At a point 0.6 mile up Palm Wash, a major tributary enters from the left. (This tributary goes past peak 1122 toward the Calcite Mine, and can be used to combine

parts of Trip 8 with this trip. From this point you can also, if skilled at bouldering, continue up Palm Wash, climbing past sandstone blocks and huge granitic chockstones, to a point well above the Calcite Mine.) Opposite and a little beyond this tributary, on the right (east) side of Palm Wash, is an easy break through the sandstone wall. Climb this and head north along a sloping bench east of Palm Wash. You'll pick up an Indian trail that leads northwest, then northeast toward the Sheep Tanks in the North Fork of Palm Wash. (The south branch of this Indian trail approaches another break in the wall of Palm Wash about 1 mile south-southeast.)

Using map and compass, work your way overland to the Sheep Tanks, an important watering hole for bighorn sheep and other wildlife. These are located in a narrow, southern tributary of North Fork Palm Wash that joins North Fork at 700 feet elevation. From above you can look down (very cautiously) into the slot containing several deep tinajas. Their capacity is estimated at some 20,000 gallons—about as much as a backyard swimming pool.

A series of sloping sandstone ledges leads down the south wall of the slot to the lowest tank, then out to the North Fork, where you'll find wheel tracks. You may want to avoid the exposed bit of downclimbing by backtracking about 0.3 mile and going north into the upper end of the North Fork. Here, the North Fork has flat, sandy spots suitable for camping.

Close the loop by walking the North Fork jeep road to Palm Wash, and the Palm Wash jeep road back to the Calcite Mine road.

Moonscape above Palm Wash

Area D-5: Borrego Badlands

The Borrego Badlands consist of lake, stream, and alluvial-plain deposits that have been severely attacked by the erosive forces of water and wind. The clay soils are so weak, and the plants which might otherwise anchor the soil are so sparse, that flash floods have carved the land into a bewildering maze of sinuous channels, razorback ridges, and mud hills.

The most renowned point of interest here, and one of the best view spots in all of Anza-Borrego Desert State Park, is Fonts Point. Here you can stand on the edge of a receding cliff and look across many square miles of intricately carved landscape.

Relatively few plants thrive in the alkaline soil of the Borrego Badlands, but there are some surprises. Several groups of palms cling tenuously to life in areas where subsurface water is dependable; these may be the tiniest remnants of a much wider distribution of palms present during wetter periods of the past. Small trees—palo verde, desert-willow, and smoke tree—line some of the sandy washes where their roots can take advantage of ephemeral flows of water. The right combination of rainfall and sunshine occasionally brings forth a profusion of wildflowers, especially sand verbenas, desert asters, dune primroses, desert sunflowers, and desert lilies.

The Borrego Badlands are laced with approved jeep (street-legal) vehicle routes, and the passage of vehicles can be annoy-

Borrego Badlands

Area D-5: Borrego Badlands

ing if you're out hiking on a busy week-end. Nevertheless, there are several areas within the badlands where you can wander cross-country and find peace and quiet. Three such hikes are suggested below.

For any foot travel through the badlands, be sure to take along an adequate quantity of water and a topographic map and compass. While it is almost impossible to wander very far without running into a road, it's easy to lose track of your position and identifiable landmarks. Use the best maps available: the entire area is covered on USGS 7.5-minute quadrangles *Fonts Point, Borrego Mountain, Shell Reef*, and *Seventeen Palms*. These maps have a

contour interval ranging from 20 to 40 feet, which is enough to show a wealth of complex detail in the convoluted landscape.

Trailhead parking for the trips below requires an Anza-Borrego Desert State Park parking pass. See the section "Using This Book" for more information.

Trip 1: Fonts Point

Distance	1.0 mile round trip
Total elevation gain/loss	200'/200'
Hiking time	40 minutes (round trip)
Optional map	USGS 7.5-min *Fonts Point*
Best times	October through May
Agency	ABDSP
Difficulty	★

Sure, it's possible to drive to within a frisbee's throw of Fonts Point Overlook and take in the famous view of erosion-scarred mud hills and dry washes. But no, the overlook, per se, isn't really the best viewing place.

Try this: Starting from the Fonts Point parking area, walk east alongside (but not on the very brink of) the cliffs for about 0.5 mile. Here and there along this viewful stretch, you can walk (cautiously) over toward the cliff edge, where mile upon mile of convoluted landscape seems to unfold. Up to about one hour after sunrise and one hour before sunset, the razor-back ridges cast bold shadows across the honey-colored hills—perfect lighting for photography-minded visitors. Remember to approach the brink cautiously, especially if you have kids. In a couple of places, large blocks of the cliff face are beginning to cleave.

Driving to Fonts Point can be a bit of an adventure in itself. Ask about road conditions first if you'll be using a two-wheel drive vehicle. From Highway S-22 turn south at mile 29.3, and follow the signs to Fonts Point, 4 miles away. You may have traction problems on the first part of the road, which is sometimes dusted with soft sand.

Receding cliff near Fonts Point

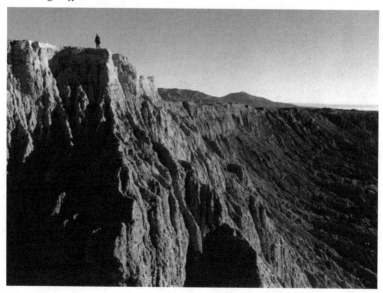

Trip 2: Seventeen Palms and Vicinity

Distance	2.0 miles
Total elevation gain/loss	200'/200'
Hiking time	1¹/2 hours
Recommended maps	USGS 7.5-min *Seventeen Palms, Shell Reef*
Best times	December through March
Agency	ABDSP
Difficulty	★★

Smack dab in the middle of the most desolate part of the Borrego Badlands stands a remarkable triad of palm oases. The best known of these, Seventeen Palms, is a popular destination for park visitors. The other two lie just a short distance away. They are accessible in a roundabout way via jeep trails, or overland on foot as described here.

The starting point for this hike is the Seventeen Palms parking area along Arroyo Salado. To get there, turn southeast from Highway S-22 at mile 34.9 onto the dirt road leading through Arroyo Salado Primitive Camp. The 3.5-mile-long unpaved stretch to Seventeen Palms is recommended for 4-wheel drives, but often it's in good enough shape for less rugged vehicles as well.

An interpretive leaflet available at the Seventeen Palms parking area recounts some of the old lore associated with this famous watering hole. Decades ago, prospectors and travelers used this oasis for relaying messages. The tradition continues today, and you'll probably find hundreds of notes and business cards in an old barrel beneath the palms. You'll also learn about the complex web of plant and animal life existing in this seemingly lifeless area. Because most animals that depend on the spring are nocturnal, you're asked not to camp in the area. Don't count on the water—if you can locate it—for your drinking needs; it is highly saline.

You start hiking cross-country at Seventeen Palms (410'). A hundred feet north of the northernmost cluster of palms, follow the small ravine that leads west into the mud hills. After about 100 yards, bear southwest across a low maze of washes. Continue southwest into a broad wash that bends southward toward a broad saddle. Topping this rise (510'), you'll have come about 0.5 mile from Seventeen Palms.

From the rise you can look south into a seemingly endless maze of dissected mud hills. Make an easy descent into any of the several small washes directly below. Continue downhill 0.3 mile to the Cut Across Trail (jeep trail) in Tule Wash. Turning left (east), you'll soon catch sight of Una

Prospectors' post office at Seventeen Palms

Palma (single palm), its forlorn crown peeping above the mudhills. Head directly for it, passing a clump of mesquite along the way. Una Palma does not appear on the USGS topographic map.

From Una Palma head northeast. Topping the first hill, you'll be able to see the only remaining large palm at Five Palms Spring, 0.5 mile away. Head directly for it east across the mud hills. If you have been scrutinizing your topo maps, you'll note a remarkable coincidence: all three oases lie at virtually the same elevation.

Complete the loop by following the Tule Wash and Arroyo Salado jeep trails back to Seventeen Palms.

Trip 3: West Butte Borrego Mountain

Distance	3.5 miles
Total elevation gain/loss	700'/700'
Hiking time	3 hours
Recommended map	USGS 7.5-min *Borrego Mountain*
Best times	November through April
Agency	ABDSP
Difficulty	★★

The twin peaks and eroded ravines of Borrego Mountain lie between the Borrego Badlands on the north and Lower Borrego Valley on the south. The area is laced with a network of unpaved roads of varying quality. In the adjacent Ocotillo Wells State Vehicular Recreation Area, any

Desert lily, Borrego Badlands

kind of vehicle may travel cross-country, but here (in Anza-Borrego Desert State Park) motorized travel is limited to street-legal vehicles which must stay on the designated roads.

The West Butte, with its sheer-cut ravines and slot canyons, is better for hiking than East Butte, which lies partly in the vehicular recreation area. Nestled against the southeast side of the West Butte is Hawk Canyon, the premier remote camping spot in this neck of the desert.

West Butte is a fun place to get slightly lost—fun, because all you have to do to recover your bearings is climb up to some higher vantage point. The most striking feature of the hike sketched here is called, ominously, The Slot. We'll save its exploration until the end of this hike.

To reach the starting point, turn north on unpaved Buttes Pass Road from State Highway 78 at mile 87.2. (This point is 1.5 miles east of Borrego Springs Road and 5.2 miles west of Split Mountain Road at Ocotillo Wells.) After 1.0 mile on the dirt road, stay left, following the sign to the

"Lookout." Drive another 0.9 mile over an increasingly rough road to a parking area overlooking The Slot.

On foot now, follow old wheel tracks 200 feet east until they end at the top of a ridge. Follow this ridge north, then northeast, directly to the summit of West Butte (1207'), the highest point within a radius of about 6 miles. You'll have excellent views of the Borrego Badlands and the Santa Rosa Mountains to the north, the Salton Sea to the east, and the Vallecito Mountains to the south.

The summit area is covered with crumbling piles of granitic rock, deeply stained by desert varnish, and there's lots of pegmatite too: thousands of white crystals glitter in the sun. Deep layers of soft sandstone, siltstone, and conglomerate lie to the west. These layers, pushed up long ago by the granitic mass now exposed at the summit, are in the throes of rapid erosion.

Backtrack about 300 yards on the same ridge used for the summit approach. Then turn west and find a faint trail leading west, then northwest, along the north wall of the deepest westward-draining ravine (try not to descend to the north, an easy mistake). This trail takes you down to a point where you can drop into the ravine at its lower end; from there you walk out to the jeep trail in Borrego Mountain Wash. (You could spend many fascinating hours exploring the maze of ravines in this area. If you do, be aware that the rock is absolutely untrustworthy, sometimes crumbling at the very touch.)

Turn south on the jeep trail following Borrego Mountain Wash and pass an area of wind caves and small arches on the left. On past some sandstone bluffs and colorful clay hills, you'll eventually spot a scarred hillside on your right. This is the "Dropoff," a one-way jeep route into Borrego Mountain Wash from the flatlands above. Keep following the canyon as it narrows and turns east.

You now enter the portals of The Slot. The walls are fashioned from multiple layers of dark gray siltstone, convoluted into bulbous parapets and spires. The Slot narrows as you move into it. Tilted parapets and giant chockstones lie wedged above you, seemingly subject to imminent collapse. The Slot narrows even more. You may have to remove your day pack in order to wedge through. When The Slot widens, there's a fork. Take the right branch, and in just 200 yards you'll be back at your car.

The Slot

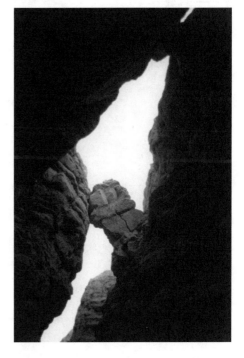

Area D-6: Grapevine Canyon/Pinyon Ridge

This sparsely vegetated area of rounded ridges and long, linear valleys lies between Montezuma Highway (Highway S-22) on the north, and State Highway 78 on the south. The highest elevations, about 4500 feet, feature the typical desert/mountain mix of pinyon, juniper, yucca, and chaparral shrubs; while the lower elevations, hillsides and washes around 2000 feet, exhibit the familiar creosote bush, cacti, agave, and desert-willow of the lower desert. In the few moist areas, willow, ironwood, and mesquite thrive.

Vehicle routes lace part of this area, but a large block centered around Pinyon Ridge is designated as state wilderness. As in all other parts of Anza-Borrego Desert State Park, wilderness or otherwise, you don't need a permit for either day or over-night use.

The longer hikes described below start and end along either Montezuma Highway or Highway 78. I've also included three of Anza-Borrego's very few maintained trails. All three are near Tamarisk Grove Campground at Highway 78 and Yaqui Pass Road (County Highway S-3).

Car-camping opportunities are abundant throughout the area, not only at the developed Tamarisk Grove Campground and two primitive campgrounds near it, but also along the several unpaved roads.

Trailhead parking for the trips below requires an Anza-Borrego Desert State Park parking pass. See the section "Using This Book" for more information.

Area D-6: Grapevine Canyon / Pinyon Ridge

Trip 1: Jasper Trail/Grapevine Canyon

Distance	11.0 miles
Total elevation gain/loss	500'/2900'
Hiking time	4¹/₂ hours
Recommended map	Anza-Borrego Desert State Park map/ brochure
Optional maps	USGS 7.5-min *Tubb Canyon, Ranchita*
Best times	November through April
Agency	ABDSP
Difficulty	★★★

This route, used by jeepers, motorcyclists, mountain bicyclists, and equestrians, is also a worthwhile one for hikers. Try it during off-days (weekdays) or during off-hours (early morning or evening) if you don't like the sound of groaning engines. Since the route is largely downhill, and almost entirely on soft sand or soft dirt, it's ideal for jogging too. A section of the old California Riding and Hiking Trail sometimes coincides with and sometimes parallels the route. The description below assumes that you stay (with a couple of exceptions) on the easier-to-follow roadways.

The starting point is the north terminus of the Jasper Trail (a jeep road), mile 6.8 on the Montezuma Highway east of Ranchita. In the first 2.4 miles, the road traverses rolling, brushy terrain, generally heading south. After passing over a rocky ridge at 2.4 miles, the road drops very sharply down a dry canyon for about 0.7 mile; then it turns north up a slope and briefly follows a ridge to avoid a narrow, rocky section of the canyon. On foot, it's easier to go down the bottom of the canyon and join the road again, saving 0.4 mile, not to mention needless elevation gain and loss.

In the next mile, the canyon is flanked by picturesque, near-vertical rock walls. After this stretch, the canyon widens, and the road swings right (west) to avoid another narrow chasm below. Don't make a short cut this time; follow the road as it crosses a flat and drops into the sandy bed of a draw leading to Grapevine Canyon.

Grapevine Canyon was one of the main routes of travel east from Warner Springs and Julian before the construction of Highway 78 through Sentenac Canyon. Several springs along the way served the needs of travelers in the early days of the automobile. Well before that, the canyon was a favorite camping area of aboriginal peoples. Bedrock *morteros* and other signs, especially around the springs, attest to many centuries of occupation.

Stuart Spring (0.4 mile east of the Jasper Trail junction in Grapevine Canyon) is the first source of water and a good place to fill up canteens. Angelina Spring, 1.3 miles farther, flows for several hundred feet through a tangle of willows. The road rises onto a bluff to the north; but it is more interesting to walk right along the riparian strip on a parallel horse trail.

At a point 2.3 miles beyond Angelina Spring (below the mouth of Bitter Creek Canyon), Grapevine Canyon Road bends left and then continues toward Yaqui Well and Tamarisk Grove Campground. Continue straight; Highway 78 lies ahead, 2 miles away. Arrange to be picked up here— mile 74.1 on Highway 78, just below the mouth of Sentenac Canyon.

Trip 2: Grapevine Mountain/Bitter Creek

	Distance	6.0 miles
	Total elevation gain/loss	2400'/2400'
	Hiking time	5 hours
	Recommended maps	USGS 7.5-min *Tubb Canyon, Earthquake Valley*
	Best times	November through April
	Agency	ABDSP
	Difficulty	★★★

This is a good hike to get acquainted with cross-country desert travel and "peak bagging." You'll make intimate visual contact (but I hope not physical contact) with cholla, hedgehog, beavertail, barrel, and fishhook cacti; in addition you'll see agave, catclaw, and mesquite—all thorny or prickly. There are boulders to scramble over on occasion and wildlife trails to follow through the low brush.

Winter months bring invigorating cool air to Grapevine Mountain, but the best months are March and April. This is the time to catch the cactus and the succulent blooms. You'll see everything from the pearl-like flower of the diminutive fishhook cactus to the showy magenta and red blossoms of the hedgehog and beavertail cacti.

A convenient starting point for this hike is along the dirt road connecting Highway 78 and Grapevine Canyon Road. This road intersects the highway at mile 74.1, just below the mouth of Sentenac Canyon. Drive 1.3 miles northwest on this road to reach a parking spur on the left. (Flowing water in San Felipe Creek may block the way; if so, you can park, ford the creek on foot, and walk the extra mile to the starting point.)

The parking spur is just east of a prominent unnamed canyon that leads southwest toward the highest slopes of Grapevine Mountain. Follow the sandy wash leading up to the mouth of this canyon. Around the corner is a formidable granite dike blocking direct progress up the canyon. Climb up and over on either the right or left side, through dense thickets of teddy-bear cholla.

Stay with the canyon for another 0.3 mile, then veer right toward a saddle just south of peak 2620. (If you continue in the canyon, you'll run into a second and more formidable dry fall.) The first twisted junipers appear on the saddle; junipers will be a familiar feature from now on.

From the saddle, head generally south along the ridge, up and over several small summits, all the way to the top of Grapevine Mountain. At one point you can look down into Bitter Creek Canyon and spot the lone cottonwood tree at Bitter Creek Spring.

Fallen survey stakes and ribbons mark the summit. Down below, the broad trough of the San Felipe and Earthquake valleys shimmers at the foot of a backdrop of dark ranges—the Volcan, Cuyamaca, and Laguna mountains.

Continue by descending west into Bitter Creek Canyon. In the first 300 vertical feet, the going is slippery on decomposed rock, with little worthwhile to hold on to other than a few small manzanita shrubs. Footing becomes easier as you take to a narrow ridge bearing northwest. Drop into Bitter Creek, and follow the sandy bed for as long as it stays open. Small pools of water may be found here

Running the Pacific Crest Trail near Grapevine Mountain

after rainy periods.

Soon you'll encounter a tangle of willow, mesquite, and tamarisk in the creek bed. Don't fight it. Instead climb up to the gentle slopes on the east side. Easy-to-follow animal trails will guide you for about a mile to a point where the creek bed is open again.

Near this point, look for the lone cottonwood, mentioned earlier, that marks Bitter Creek Spring. You'll find it in a nook about 100 feet above the creek bed. True to their names, both Bitter Creek and its nearby spring feature slightly bitter tasting, mineral-rich water. Old broken pipes lead from the spring to an empty bathtub downslope. The spring is a mecca for local wildlife; trails and tracks (including those of mountain lions and bighorn sheep) radiate from it in every direction.

All that remains is an easy stroll down the broad wash of Bitter Creek Canyon, and a short walk back to the starting point via the dirt road.

Trip 3: Yaqui Well Trail

Distance	1.5 miles
Total elevation gain/loss	100'/100'
Hiking time	45 minutes
Optional map	USGS 7.5-min *Tubb Canyon*
Best times	All year
Agency	ABDSP
Difficulty	★

Follow the yellow painted footprints from Tamarisk Grove Campground to the beginning of the Yaqui Well Trail, across Yaqui Pass Road. This is a self-guiding nature trail with interpretive signs posted beside several representative desert wash plants. The trail climbs slightly, skirts a hillside covered with dense growths of cholla cactus, and then descends to Yaqui Well, an important desert water hole.

Yaqui Well is one of the premier birdwatching sites in San Diego County. The presence of surface water and fine growths of ironwood, mesquite, and desert-willow have created a micro-environment cooler, more damp, and much richer in food sources than the surrounding arid hills. The well has been used by Indians, prospectors, and cattlemen, and is now surrounded by drive-in campsites. A fenced area keeps humans away from the seeps and allows wildlife undisturbed use of the water.

You can stroll back to Tamarisk Grove Campground by way of either Grapevine Canyon Road or the sandy bed of San Felipe Wash.

Trip 4: Cactus Loop Trail

Distance	1.0 mile
Total elevation gain/loss	200'/200'
Hiking time	40 minutes
Optional map	USGS 7.5-min *Tubb Canyon*
Best times	All year
Agency	ABDSP
Difficulty	★

The trailhead for this short but somewhat steep and rocky path is directly opposite the entrance to Tamarisk Grove Campground. On the first part of the trail, you'll find interpretive signs for a half dozen or so common desert plants. But the real story here concerns the ubiquitous teddy-bear cholla (also called Bigelow cholla and jumping cholla) cactus, which grows to exceptional size (up to 6 feet high) and density here.

The teddy-bear cholla has a well-deserved, fearsome reputation. Its thousands of glistening spines, like soft bristles, invite tactile exploration, but woe be to those who prick themselves even lightly with a single "bristle." Concealed beneath the straw-colored, innocent-looking papery sheath on each thorn is an incredibly sharp, barbed point. The spiny joints of the cholla can detach at the slightest brush by shoe or clothing, often seeming to jump at and "bite" unwary hikers.

E. Yale Dawson writes this about cholla cactus in his book *Cacti of California*:

> The vegetable kingdom has not produced anything else so fearfully armed. But in the desert one thing is worse than any pain of spine in the flesh. It is thirst. I have seen emaciated, dreadfully dehydrated cattle, deprived of water for months in the blistering heat, so mad from thirst that they eat the terrible cholla. They munch these awful morsels of moisture until their lips are pinned together with the spines, and their throats are a veritable pincushion. The spines eventually cause their death.

Incredible as it may seem in light of the above, there are reliable reports of bighorn sheep browsing on cholla cactus. On occasion you may come across a cholla,

Barrel and teddy-bear cholla cactus

hedgehog, or other similarly armed cactus plant broken open with fresh teeth marks in the green pulp.

Trip 5: Bill Kenyon Trail

Distance	1.0 mile round trip
Total elevation gain/loss	150'/150'
Hiking time	30 minutes
Optional map	USGS 7.5-min *Borrego Sink*
Best times	All year
Agency	ABDSP
Difficulty	★

Walk this easy trail in the early morning or late afternoon, when warm lighting and long shadows soften the landscape. You'll find the marked trailhead at the top of Yaqui Pass, the broad saddle in the mountains between Borrego Springs and Tamarisk Grove. The trail is named in honor of Bill Kenyon, a former Anza-Borrego park supervisor.

Vegetation is varied but sparse around the windswept pass area. Most varieties of indigenous cactus are represented. The best attraction, though, is the marvelous view from the two overlook points along the trail. Dominating the scene is Mescal Bajada, a vast, sloping sheet of alluvial deposits. The stark Pinyon Mountains, the source of the deposits, rise in the background.

You can easily imagine the processes that produced this landscape: Wind and water erosion, aided by alternating hot and cold temperatures, tear at the face of the Pinyon Mountains, opening up ravines and canyons. Great loads of sand and boulders wash out of these openings during floods and build alluvial fans. The fans coalesce to form a sloping skirt (or *bajada*) extending outward from the base of the mountains. Material on the lower edge of the bajada is picked up by flood waters in San Felipe Creek. This debris-laden water flows through one channel and then another, dropping its load gradually and creating a braided pattern of smooth, sandy washes and rubble-strewn "islands" in the bed of the creek.

Flat and uninteresting-looking at midday, Mescal Bajada comes alive with texture and color under the grazing illumination of the low sun. Gray-green seems to predominate, in part because of the dense growth of "mescal" (agave, or century plant) on its surface.

Trip 6: Pinyon Ridge

Distance	8.5 miles round trip
Total elevation gain/loss	1400'/1400'
Hiking time	4 hours (round trip)
Recommended map	USGS 7.5-min *Tubb Canyon*
Best times	November through May
Agency	ABDSP
Difficulty	★★★

Dry Pinyon Ridge stands just high enough on the desert rim to support a sparse growth of pinyon-pine trees. Like other similar "islands in the desert sky" such as the Pinyon Mountains and Whale Peak to the southeast, this ridge offers expansive views framed by picturesque foregrounds of eroded boulders and gnarled pinyons.

Happily, the Wilson Trail, an old jeep road along the crest of the ridge, has been converted to a hiking trail. The route leads to almost the exact center of a state wilderness area that is now completely free of motorized travel.

To reach the trailhead, turn west on Old Culp Valley Road from mile 10.4 on Montezuma Highway. The road becomes progressively more difficult to negotiate, especially if the surface has not been freshly graded. Bear right at the fork of a spur road after 0.4 mile. (The left branch leads to a pleasant picnic spot at the foot of Pinyon Ridge.) At 1.1 miles from Montezuma Highway, a turnout near Cottonwood Spring (easily identified by tall cottonwoods) offers the last easy place to turn around and park if you decide to drive no farther.

Whether you decide to drive or walk at this point, go another 1.9 miles to the intersection of the Wilson Trail, on the left. There's limited parking nearby.

The Wilson Trail's eroded track meanders south and east over and around a series of rocky knolls on the crest of Pinyon Ridge. Common vegetation seen along the way includes chamise, sage brush, mountain mahogany, scrub oak, sugar bush, manzanita, Mojave yucca, buckhorn cholla cactus, juniper, and, of course, pinyon pine. After 4 miles you'll pass north of "Wilson" peak (4573'). This is a good spot for a panoramic view. Scramble up over the rocks, discover the bench mark, and admire the view. Palomar Observatory's dome gleams on the dark Palomar ridge to the west. The broad sweep of the Santa Rosa Mountains in the northeast serves as a backdrop for Borrego Valley and Coyote Mountain. Far to the east are the Salton Sea and the Chocolate Mountains of Imperial County. The Pinyon Mountains and Whale Peak rise to the southeast; and the Laguna and Cuyamaca mountains stand to the south and southwest.

Sacred datura below Pinyon Ridge

If you're looking for a large, flat campsite, you'll find one 0.4 mile east-northeast of Wilson peak (at 4300'). Walk a short distance north from there for a great view of Borrego Valley.

Area D-7: Pinyon Mountains

The austere-looking Pinyon Mountains are the northwestern component of a large and complex range, the Vallecito Mountains, which lie across the geographic center of Anza-Borrego Desert State Park. (Trips in the Vallecito Mountains proper are covered in Areas D-8 and D-9.)

Although the Pinyon Mountains are largely within state wilderness boundaries, vehicle use is permitted for some distance up several of the sandy washes that drain from them. Most of these motor routes cross Mescal Bajada and intersect Highway 78. Beyond the upper ends of these roads, foot travel will take you into terrain that gets progressively rougher with higher elevation. Besides the hikes suggested below, there are plenty of other possibilities for exploration. Parts of the Pinyon Mountains have probably never felt the impact of boot or moccasin.

The existence of bighorn sheep in the Vallecito and Pinyon mountains is somewhat of mystery. In 1971 at Blue Spring, and again in 1983 near Harper Flat, water tanks and guzzlers were installed to enhance the bighorn habitat. Before these improvements were made, however, there were no known year-round sources of water. Perhaps in the course of your wandering about these mountains, you may stumble upon an unknown spring, solving this mystery.

Trailhead parking for the trips below requires an Anza-Borrego Desert State Park parking pass. See the section "Using This Book" for more information.

Trip 1: Narrows Earth Trail

Distance	0.3 mile
Total elevation gain/loss	50'/50'
Hiking time	15 minutes
Optional map	USGS 7.5-min *Borrego Sink*
Best times	All year
Agency	ABDSP
Difficulty	★

Stop at the Narrows Earth Trail for a brief lesson in geology. Most of the northern Vallecito Mountains consist of granitic rock pushed up fairly recently from the interior of the earth. But here, in an area fractured by faults, it is possible to view some much older metasedimentary rock in close proximity to the granitic rock. These metamorphosed layers of sand and mud represent the oldest kind of rock exposed in the Anza-Borrego Desert.

Area D-7: Pinyon Mountains

The interpretive leaflet for this trail is helpful, if not essential to the lesson. Leaflets may be present in a box at the trailhead (or available at the Tamarisk Grove Campground and the visitor center in Borrego Springs).

You'll find the trailhead at mile 81.6 on Highway 78, just above "The Narrows" of San Felipe Creek. The canyon behind the trail is designated Powder Dump Wash on topographic maps. For those interested in further exploring, nearby Quartz Vein Wash offers a direct way to climb into the Vallecito Mountains toward Sunset Mountain.

Trip 2: Sunset Mountain

Distance	6.0 miles round trip
Total elevation gain/loss	2200'/2200'
Hiking time	5 hours (round trip)
Recommended map	USGS 7.5-min *Whale Peak*
Best times	November through April
Agency	ABDSP
Difficulty	★★★

Sunset Mountain stands lofty and somewhat isolated from the main Vallecito mountain chain. Seen from Borrego Springs and other points in Borrego Valley, the desert-varnished rocks on its rounded flank glow warmly in the evening light. From the west and south the mountain appears more pyramidal and jagged, abruptly rising above the broad, sandy expanses of Mescal Bajada and Pinyon Wash.

The easiest and most direct way to climb Sunset Mountain is by way of Pinyon Wash. Four-wheel-drive vehicles can navigate to a point less than 2 miles south of the summit, but ordinary cars may get no farther than the intersection of Pinyon and Nolina washes—about 3 miles west of the summit. To reach this latter starting point, turn south at mile 81.0 on Highway 78 onto the Pinyon Wash jeep road and proceed 1.6 miles to the intersection of Nolina Wash. Park off the road on hard-packed sand.

On foot now, follow the Pinyon Wash jeep road east and southeast for about 1 mile. Soon the entire west slope of Sunset Mountain comes into view, and you can picture one or more routes to the top. Among the plethora of possibilities is the broad ridge west of the summit (marked on the topographic map as "Yak"—3657').

Cross the small *bajada* at the base of the mountain, and begin the route of your choice. In any event, it will be an arduous climb—a gain of almost 2,000 feet over desert-varnished boulders, loose pebbles, and sinister patches of agave and cactus.

The view from the top is worth the trouble, though. The Salton Sea is striking on a clear day—its surface mirroring the blue sky.

If you're going to combine an overnight backpack with a climb of Sunset Mountain, a good place to set up a dry camp is the small wash that passes south of the mountain and north of peak 2255. East of peak 2255 this wash broadens into a shallow, sandy bowl, marvelously insulated from the outside world and protected from the wind to boot. There are at least two obvious routes up Sunset Mountain from there.

The descent of Sunset Mountain

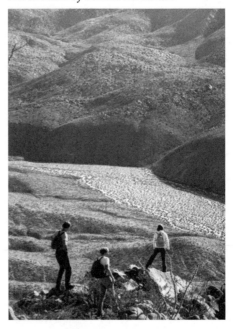

Trip 3: Pinyon Mountain—North Approach

Distance	14 miles
Total elevation gain/loss	3100'/3100'
Hiking time	10 hours
Required map	USGS 7.5-min *Whale Peak*
Best times	November through April
Agency	ABDSP
Difficulty	★★★★

Best done as a two-day backpack, this loop trip is still within the scope of an ambitious dayhike. Only about a tenth of the total distance covered involves difficult terrain, and most of that is in the first half. If you're backpacking, be sure to bring a 30-foot length of cord for lowering your pack down one or more dry falls.

Several dozen bighorn sheep make the Pinyon Mountains their home, and you may have a close encounter with one, as I did recently, in Bighorn Canyon. There being no easy escape route, the surprised ewe clawed her way up a sheer granite wall to reach a safer stance on the steep, rock-strewn slopes above. When threatened, bighorn sheep prefer this kind of "escape terrain," on which they're more nimble than any other large animal.

A good place to start this hike is along the Pinyon Wash jeep road. This road intersects Highway 78 at the 81.0 mile marker, and runs south across Mescal Bajada. Drive south 1.6 miles (ordinary cars will usually survive) to the intersection of the Nolina Wash jeep road. Park on hard-packed sand nearby.

Hike west about 0.3 mile to pick up one of the washes that drain Bighorn Canyon—the prominent cut in the mountains to the southwest. Don't confuse the mouth of Nolina Canyon, due south, with that of Bighorn Canyon. The going is easy over mostly hard-packed beds of sand for the next three miles; then the canyon steepens and there are some short scrambles over small boulder piles. Water may trickle

through this section of the canyon for several weeks following a heavy rain.

Blue Spring, 4.0 miles, is the site of a sophisticated water-delivery system for bighorn sheep and other wildlife in the area. Water is drawn from a silted-in catch basin and piped to a series of three 1600-gallon tanks. From there it flows to an open guzzler. Don't count on this as a source for your drinking needs, especially in a dry year.

Huge outcrops of quartz pegmatite surround and seem to hover menacingly over Blue Spring. Eroded into grotesque shapes by wind and water, they make a long stay here somewhat uncomfortable, particularly after the sun goes down. (In deference to the watering needs of the local wildlife, you should not camp here anyway.)

East of the spring there's a low pass with a tributary of Nolina Wash on the other side. You could use this route as a shortcut back to your car—about 5 miles away.

Our way continues south and much higher. The canyon above Blue Spring becomes very steep and rugged, so it's best to bypass it. From the spring, traverse east for about 100 yards, then go up the ridge leading to the Pinyon Mountain summit, a climb of 1700 feet. You'll be in the pinyon-juniper belt all the way, with plenty of shady spots for rest.

On and near the summit, there are many small, flat areas suitable as campsites, and enough pinyon, nolina, and other vegetation to cut the wind. At night, you can watch the twinkling lights in Borrego

Valley, gaze at the stars above, and truly feel as if you're "king (or queen) of the mountain."

From the summit, your return is entirely gravity assisted, though you will cover 9 miles instead of the 5 miles covered so far. Descend 500 vertical feet to the jeep road in Pinyon Mountain Valley and follow it eastward as it descends down the head of Pinyon Canyon. After about 2 miles, the road veers south out of the canyon, climbs a bit, and then descends east on a "dropoff" (one-way jeep route); it returns to the Pinyon Canyon wash after 1 mile, but then veers south toward Hapaha Flat and Fish Creek. If you don't mind some fun rock scrambling, don't take the road—simply stay in the Pinyon Canyon bottom and work your way down the narrow canyon bottom over water-polished slabs of rock. One exciting passage takes you down a sloping dry fall about 35 feet high.

After you reach the mouth of the narrow stretch of Pinyon Canyon, turn north and keep following Pinyon Canyon wash along the west edge of Harper Flat. Now classified as state wilderness, Harper Flat is closed to all motor vehicle use. At

Mountain lion tracks in Bighorn Canyon

the northwest corner of Harper Flat, you'll enter another narrow section of Pinyon Canyon. After a couple of twists and turns, and finally a hand-and-toe downclimb at a dry fall, you'll come upon the Pinyon Wash jeep road. Follow it an easy 4 miles back to the starting point.

Trip 4: Harper Canyon

Distance	9.0 miles round trip
Total elevation gain/loss	1500'/1500'
Hiking time	6 hours (round trip)
Recommended maps	USGS 7.5-min *Borrego Mountain, Harper Canyon*
Best times	November through April
Agency	ABDSP
Difficulty	★★★

Formerly accessible to off-road vehicles, the 4-square-mile expanse of Harper Flat now lies protected within a state wilderness area. Jeep roads approach it from the west and south, but a more interesting

route for foot travelers is by way of Harper Canyon on the north.

A patchwork of unmarked access roads at the mouth of Harper Canyon complicates things, so follow these directions carefully in order to avoid taking a wrong turn: Drive south from Highway 78 on the dirt road intersecting at mile 87.2. Go 1.6 miles south to a **T**-intersection with the old Kane Springs Road. Turn right, drive 0.2 mile west, then veer left on a dirt road trending southwest. (The "jeep trail" marked on the USGS topo maps no longer leads to the mouth of Harper Canyon; instead it leads to a small canyon a mile to the west.)

Those with ordinary cars should find a place to park no farther than 0.5 mile up this southwest-trending road, or back along Kane Springs Road. With 4-wheel-drive you can proceed 1.5 miles to the road's end at the mouth of Harper Canyon. Hiking mileages in this description refer to Kane Springs Road as the starting point.

In the first mile, you skirt the Cactus Garden, an area where most common species of cactus on the Colorado Desert are represented, but especially barrel cactus. Some specimens near the road are seven feet tall.

Beyond the roadend, the walls of Harper Canyon narrow, then widen again as tributary canyons split off on both sides. A better name for the canyon would be "Ironwood Canyon." Hundreds of these

slow-growing trees line it for 3 miles, providing welcome, if somewhat thin shade during the middle of the day. Desert lavender also grows quite abundantly here. Starting about February, its tiny purple blossoms exude a perfumelike aroma.

At about 3.5 miles the canyon narrows, and you climb over the bottoms of some sharply eroded fins of granitic rock that soar along the canyon wall. Smoke trees and desert-willow begin to appear. At 4.5 miles you reach the head of Harper Canyon, and come upon the broad expanse of Harper Flat. Curiously, Harper Canyon drains most, but not all of, Harper Flat.

If you're making camp here, there are several options for further exploration or travel. Peak 2628 lies directly to the north (scramble up 400 vertical feet), offering superb views of both Harper Flat and landmarks to the north, including the Santa Rosa Mountains and the Salton Sea. Harper Flat itself is rich in archaeological evidence of Indian use, and is easily investigated on foot. With prearranged transportation, you could devise point-to-point backpacking routes up Harper Canyon and out to points as far away as Blair Valley or Split Mountain.

Harper Flat

Area D-8: Blair Valley/Vallecito Mountains

Nestled between the rounded summits of Granite Mountain and Whale Peak is Blair Valley, a focal point of recreational activity in the south part of Anza-Borrego Desert State Park. Nooks in the rock-strewn ridges surrounding the valley serve as popular primitive campsites, and roads and trails radiate out to nearby attractions such as the Marshal South cabin and an Indian pictograph site. Motivated hikers can venture beyond these familiar points of interest and explore summits, such as Whale Peak, that afford some of the best views in Anza-Borrego.

At 2600 feet elevation, Blair Valley gives a taste of the transition zone between low and high desert. Creosote bushes and agave plants thrive in the valley itself, the latter sending up flower stalks by the thousands in April or May. A few hundred feet higher, in the bouldered canyons and on the ridges, juniper, Mojave yucca, ephedra (Mormon tea), jojoba, creosote bush, catclaw, desert apricot, cholla cactus, and white sage are common. Still higher, toward the summits of Granite Mountain and Whale Peak, pinyon pine, nolina, scrub oak, and manzanita flourish.

County Highway S-2, the long, lonely road through the southern half of Anza-Borrego Desert State Park, provides easy access for hikes starting in the Blair Valley area. Several dirt roads diverge from the highway and climb east into the Vallecito Mountains, where you can car camp or backpack in one of the most peaceful and remote areas of the county.

Another dirt road leads west from a point near Box Canyon historic site on Highway S-2 into Mason Valley and up through Oriflamme Canyon. Both Box Canyon and Oriflamme Canyon lie along important prehistoric and historic routes of travel.

Trailhead parking for the trips below requires an Anza-Borrego Desert State Park parking pass. See the section "Using This Book" for more information.

Area D-8: Blair Valley / Vallecito Mountains

Trip 1: Granite Mountain

Distance	6.5 miles round trip
Total elevation gain/loss	3200'/3200'
Hiking time	7 hours (round trip)
Required map	USGS 7.5-min *Earthquake Valley*
Best times	November through April
Agency	ABDSP
Difficulty	★★★★

Although there's no trail to Granite Mountain's summit, it is possible to climb the mountain from nearly every direction. The Pacific Crest Trail meanders around the mountain's north flank, but never approaches the summit close enough to be much good in facilitating a climb. The following route breathes some life into a task that, on most other routes up this mountain, is a bit of a bore. You'll multiply your satisfaction if you do this on a crystal-clear day—the summit view can be fantastic.

The starting point lies 1.1 miles down a sometimes-rutted dirt road going southwest from Highway S-2 at mile 21.5. From the end of the road, descend into the wash just north, and follow it west through a narrow portal. Complexes of granitic and metamorphic rock are seen along the walls and on the floor of this canyon. Thorny desert apricot bushes grow along the wash bottom, and the slopes are thickly covered with brittlebush, a big producer of yellow, daisylike flowers in early spring. After rains, mosses and green grass thrive in the shady spots.

After 0.2 mile the canyon divides. Take the left (major, south) fork, passing over several easy dry falls. At 0.9 mile the canyon splits into three forks. Go about 100 yards into the right (northwest) fork, and veer left to climb the ridge between the northwest and west forks. You climb moderately at first through sparse growths of cacti and small shrubs. Set your sights on the rocky shoulder 600 feet below and southeast of peak 4624. After attaining this shoulder, work your way steeply upward to peak 4624 over large boulders. Scattered pinyons and junipers appear now.

San Felipe Valley from Granite Mountain

You'll find flat campsites on the tablelike top of peak 4624, itself a worthy destination for those who don't wish to go on. Earthquake Valley and the Vallecitos lie before you.

Descend west a little to cross a saddle, and make your way up a difficult slope of brush and boulders to peak 5184. Then follow the easy ridgeline west toward peak 5633, where you may find yourself following deer and mountain lion tracks. After a short, brushy climb, you reach the topmost boulder pile—a truly panoramic view. On the far horizons are Old Baldy in the San Gabriel Mountains (seen just above the head of San Felipe Valley); San Jacinto Peak; a sliver of San Gorgonio Mountain; the Salton Sea; and, just beyond Julian in the mountains to the west, Santa Catalina and San Clemente islands!

Trip 2: Mason Valley Truck Trail

Distance	8.5 miles
Total elevation gain/loss	200'/2400'
Hiking time	4 hours
Recommended maps	USGS 7.5-min *Cuyamaca Peak, Julian, Earthquake Valley*
Best times	October through May
Agency	ABDSP
Difficulty	★★★

North of the Laguna Mountains and east of the green meadows rimming Cuyamaca Reservoir, Oriflamme Canyon cuts a curved gash in the mountain escarpment—a natural passage leading to the brown floor of the desert. Over many centuries, a well-beaten pathway through Oriflamme Canyon allowed local Indians to migrate easily between winter homes in the desert and summer encampments in the Cuyamaca Mountains. This pathway was also a part of the Yuma Trail, a main travelway between Indian settlements along the Colorado River and fishing villages at San Diego Bay.

In 1772 Pedro Fages, the Spanish military commander of California, led a detachment of three soldiers down Oriflamme Canyon in search of army deserters who had reportedly fled inland from San Diego. This was the first recorded passage by Europeans into California's interior desert. Fages and his men traveled as far east as the present-day shoreline of the Salton Sea, then turned northwest into Coyote Canyon—preceding the first of the famous Anza expeditions by two years.

Starting in 1854, horse and mule riders started carrying mail for the US Army through Oriflamme Canyon. By 1857 the so-called Jackass Mail, part of a mail route from San Antonio to San Diego, made use of the canyon as a shortcut. A short time later, the famed Butterfield Stage (St. Louis to California) took over the operation. Only mules could negotiate the Oriflamme shortcut toward San Diego; the stagecoaches had to use the much longer and more gradual wagon road up through Box Canyon and past Warner's Ranch (today's Highway S-2 route).

In the 1930s, an unpaved road was constructed on the north slope of Oriflamme Canyon by crews using little more than hand tools. Now known as the Mason Valley Truck Trail, it is currently closed to through auto traffic and serves as a link in the desert branch of the California Riding and Hiking Trail (CRHT). This is the route I describe here—the easiest and fastest way on foot to descend from mountain to desert anywhere in the county. (More difficult and obscure ways down the Oriflamme corridor are described in detail on pages 124–30 in the first [1986] edition of this book.)

Since this is a one-way trip, why not persuade your compatriots to drop you off at the starting point and later pick you up at Box Canyon down in the desert. While you hike, they can be sightseeing in the mountains—or feasting on apple pie in Julian.

Start at the Pedro Fages monument (mile 36.0 on Sunrise Highway—1.7 miles southeast of Highway 79), where a large turnout is available for overnight parking if needed. Walk 300 yards west along the highway to a cattle grate and find, on the north side, an unlocked gate in the barbed-wire fence. Pass through the gate (please close) and follow the CRHT which leads east and north into a broad, treeless valley.

At the north end of the valley, pass through a second gate, turn right (east) when you reach the Mason Valley Truck Trail, and proceed through a third gate. Just beyond, the Pacific Crest Trail comes in from the right. Just ahead there's an old water tank in a pleasant grove of planted

Fages Monument

pines. Springtime displays of blue ceanothus, bush poppies, and goldfields, and the white exclamation points of blooming Lord's Candle yucca brighten the otherwise drab slopes.

Now choose between two alternate routes: Our recommended route to the right (Mason Valley Truck Trail/CRHT) descends gradually to a broad saddle between Oriflamme and Chariot canyons. The old road on the left—the current PCT route—is more rugged and dips sharply into the upper reaches of Chariot Canyon; you'd have to climb about 300 vertical feet back up to reach the broad saddle.

At about 3.5 miles, just past the broad saddle, Mason Valley Truck Trail begins a sudden, zigzag plunge down the north wall of Oriflamme Canyon. The furnace breath of the desert is upon you now, but the sound of water rushing through the canyon bottom below atones for that. Down the road another mile or two you'll be able to reach the stream without difficulty. Tree-shaded campsites—and good picnic spots—are found in fair abundance alongside the stream.

Back on the road again, you'll bypass the scanty remains of a work camp used during construction of the truck trail. After that, you emerge onto a broad alluvial fan leading out to Mason Valley. Rodriguez Canyon's jeep trail joins from the left, and the road curves gently right (southeast) to skirt the base of massive Granite Mountain. Cacti of many species are represented here, including a peculiar hybrid resembling both the buckhorn cactus and teddybear cholla cactus.

About 0.6 mile past the Rodriguez Canyon junction, the main road is blocked by a gate (private property), but a lesser road continues east and southeast around this parcel and eventually joins Highway S-2 at mile 26.8. A more direct way to reach Highway S-2 is via a remnant of the seldom-maintained CRHT. It continues east along the base of Granite Mountain and strikes Highway S-2 at mile 26.5—a good pick-up point. This point is 0.8 mile west of the Box Canyon historical site.

Trip 3: Oriflamme Canyon

Distance	2.6 miles round trip (to waterfall)
Total elevation gain/loss	500'/500'
Hiking time	2¹/₂ hours (round trip)
Recommended maps	USGS 7.5-min *Earthquake Valley, Julian*
Best times	December through April
Agency	ABDSP
Difficulty	★★★

Oriflamme Canyon's gurgling waters are borne to the open air at a spring high on the east slope of the Laguna Mountains. For 5 miles or so they trickle over polished granite and schist, tumble over small waterfalls, and nourish a line of oaks, sycamores, willows, and cottonwoods. At Mason Valley they finally sink into porous sand.

A well-worn cow path, once used to move cattle back and forth between the Lagunas and the desert, threads through the bottom of the canyon. Currently, it is badly overgrown in the narrow, brushy upper canyon; though it probably remains a viable route for determined bushwhackers. On the other hand, it's not too hard to poke into the canyon's lower half, where the water at one point cascades over a 15-foot precipice. This is a beautiful hike when enough water is flowing—typically after winter rains, and sometimes after sufficiently heavy, late-summer thunderstorms. Be aware that this is prime rattlesnake habitat, so be especially alert and cautious during warm weather.

From mile 26.8 on Highway S-2, turn west on the road signed ORIFLAMME CANYON, which leads to Mason Valley Truck Trail. With the aid of a 4-wheel-drive vehicle, it's possible to navigate 2.9 miles to the site of a Depression-era road camp (this is 0.8 mile past the Rodriguez Canyon road split). Park off the road and walk down to the alder-shaded creek bank, where you'll discover some old concrete slabs.

From the old camp, find and follow the best path southwest up Oriflamme Canyon on the right bank. The canyon soon becomes narrow, and you'll be forced to walk along the bottom—back and forth across the bubbling stream and over crunchy leaf litter. Look for *morteros* ground into some of the streamside boulders.

After 1.3 miles (3120') a major tributary comes in from the right (west). Proceed another 0.1 mile south and you'll come upon the sublime, almost hidden 15-foot cataract and a shallow pool, framed by the twisted trunks of sycamores. Watch out for poison oak growing along the stream hereabouts.

Depending on the condition of the old cow path ahead, you could forge ahead to Oriflamme's source about 2 miles up-canyon, and from there ultimately reach Sunrise Highway. If you accept this challenge, you should have the 7.5-minute Cuyamaca Peak map for navigating beyond the 15-foot falls.

Trip 4: Marshal South Cabin

Distance	2.0 miles round trip
Total elevation gain/loss	400'/400'
Hiking time	1^1/$_2$ hours
Optional map	USGS 7.5-min *Earthquake Valley*
Best times	October through May
Agency	ABDSP
Difficulty	★★

The California desert has been home to many an eccentric, but possibly none so audacious as Marshal South. From 1931 until the mid-'40s. Marshal and his poetess wife, Tanya, lived atop what was then a very remote mountaintop in the Vallecito area, depending in large part on local resources for food, water, and shelter. Here, they built an adobe cabin, "Yaquitepec"; fashioned an ingenious rainwater collection system; raised three children; and tried to emulate, as completely as possible, the life of the prehistoric Indians.

The ruins of Yaquitepec are today one of Anza-Borrego's noted attractions—and quite easy to reach. At mile 22.9 on Highway S-2, turn east into Blair Valley. Follow the dirt road around the east edge of Blair Valley for 2.7 miles, then turn right (southwest) toward the foot of Ghost Mountain, site of the cabin. From the road-end parking area a trail climbs in switchbacks up the rocky slope, and turns east along the ridge to the Yaquitepec site. Little remains of the dwelling except some of the walls and the water cistern, but the view from the site is impressive.

South's writings on his family's experiment in primitive living appeared frequently in *Desert Magazine* during the 1940s. These articles are well worth looking up in the library.

Trip 5: Pictograph Trail

Distance	2.4 miles round trip (to overlook)
Total elevation gain/loss	500' / 500'
Hiking time	1¹/₂ hours (round trip)
Optional map	USGS 7.5-min *Whale Peak*
Best times	October through May
Agency	ABDSP
Difficulty	★★

The Kumeyaay Indians who made camp around Blair Valley well over a century ago left more than bedrock *morteros* and potsherds. They also left impressive pictographs—red and yellow painted designs—on the face of a large boulder in Smuggler Canyon. Generations of archaeologists have puzzled over the meaning of these and other pictographs and petroglyphs (etched designs) which appear not only in the Anza-Borrego region but throughout the Southwest. The diamond-chain motif at the Smuggler Canyon site has been linked to puberty rites, but the complete meaning of these rock inscriptions may never be known.

Drive into Blair Valley as described above in Trip 4, but make a left turn (northeast) at 2.7 miles. (At 3.5 miles, a fork goes right—southeast—toward a cluster of large boulders. Walk over, and you'll find Indian *morteros* on several of the flatter slabs. Note, also, how several of the tallest boulders are pocked with dozens of shallow depressions called cupules. Their use was associated with fertility ceremonies and puberty rites.)

At 3.6 miles, a road to Little Blair Valley branches to the left. Stay right (northeast)

and continue another 1.5 miles to the end (the topo map shows a nonexistent "petroglyphs" site here).

Continue on foot over the low pass to the east. Once over the top, bear right and stay near the west side of Smuggler

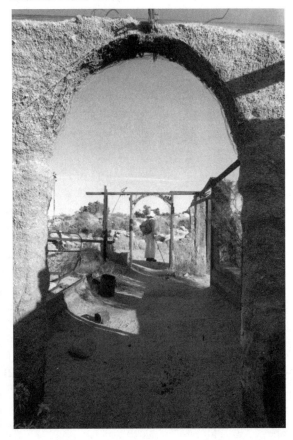

Marshal South cabin

Canyon—a wide, sandy wash at this point. You'll find the pictographs on the face of a very large boulder to your right, 0.8 mile from your starting point.

If it's a clear day, don't miss the spectacular view of the surrounding desert from a nearby overlook. Continue southeast down the wide bed of Smuggler Canyon another 0.4 mile to the lip of a dry waterfall. This frames a view of Vallecito Valley to the south. Climb the knoll east of you (peak 3237) for a more inclusive view.

Trip 6: Whale Peak—North Approach

Distance	4.0 miles round trip
Total elevation gain/loss	1500'/1500'
Hiking time	$3^1/_2$ hours (round trip)
Required map	USGS 7.5-min *Whale Peak*
Best times	October through May
Agency	ABDSP
Difficulty	★★★

Whale Peak is probably the most visited major summit in Anza-Borrego Desert State Park. Hundreds of people every year dayhike or backpack into this serene, wooded island in the desert sky. Like Granite Mountain, Whale Peak yields readily to approaches from nearly every direction. The area around it, however, can prove distressing from a navigational point of view. The peak lies within a complex of similar-looking hogback ridges and gentle valleys, and the peak itself remains hidden from view until you are almost upon it. Count on no sources of water along the way—even

Smuggler Canyon overlook

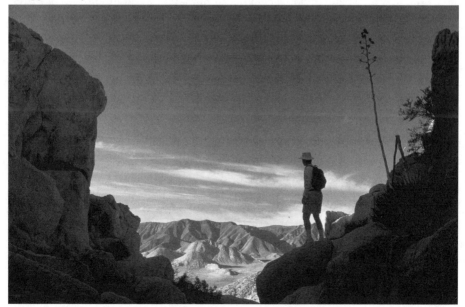

storm runoff sinks immediately into the porous, decomposed granite soil.

The easiest way to climb Whale Peak is from the north at Pinyon Mountain Valley (described here). A long drive on a primitive dirt road is required this way, however. See Trip 7 below for a longer hiking (but easier-on-the-car) approach.

At mile 21.4 on Highway S-2, turn east on the signed Pinyon Mountain Road (high clearance is recommended, 4-wheel drive helps). Stay right (east) at the fork in 0.1 mile, and continue up the alluvial fan. The road is never steep, but there are patches of soft sand and occasional protruding rocks. At 5.7 miles the road tops a watershed divide at 3980 feet in the middle of Pinyon Mountain Valley. Find a place to park in one of the turnouts or spur roads nearby. In his *Anza-Borrego Desert Guide Book*, Horace Parker describes Pinyon Mountain Valley as being "caressed by some of the most invigorating air found anywhere in the world . . . it has the tang and coolness of the high mountains and the warmth and dryness of the deserts."

Head directly up the small canyon to the south. A little hand-and-foot climbing is required to negotiate some large boulders. The canyon soon widens into a sandy flat just below 4400 feet. You can now pick up an informal trail trending southeast over and around several rocky summits. It's unreliable to focus only on following the trail, since thousands of hikers, taking different paths, have worn in a variety of routes. Keep track of your position by map and compass. Flat areas for trail camping are quite abundant along the way.

The mature pinyon pine, juniper, scrub oak, manzanita, yucca, and nolina on the north slopes of Whale Peak are San Diego County's best example of the pinyon-juniper woodland community. A similar, but much larger expanse exists on the Sierra Juarez plateau just below the Mexican border—some 30 to 60 miles south.

A little over a mile from the sandy flat, you come to a small valley west-north-west of Whale Peak. From this point scramble directly up the slope to the flattish 5349-foot summit.

Much time could be spent reading through the climbers' register, but don't ignore the view. In addition to the usual landmarks (the Santa Rosa Mountains, the Salton Sea, etc.), there's a good panorama to the south, including the Sierra Juarez, Signal Mountain, and Baja's Laguna Salada—a huge salt flat that occasionally gets covered by shallow water.

Trip 7: Whale Peak—West Approach

Distance	13 miles
Total elevation gain/loss	3200'/3200'
Hiking time	9 hours
Required maps	USGS 7.5-min *Earthquake Valley, Whale Peak*
Best times	November through April
Agency	ABDSP
Difficulty	★★★★

An interesting mix of experiences awaits you on this trek: a stroll down an old stagecoach path, meandering passages up and down boulder-strewn canyons, even the crossing of a dry lake. Don't forget to take along plenty of water.

You begin at Blair Valley (entrance at mile 22.9 on Highway S-2). Park in the camping area tucked up against a rocky ridge 0.5 mile east of Highway S-2. Walk north past outlying campsites and climb over the saddle ahead. This is Foot and Walker Pass, separating Blair Valley from Earthquake Valley. Passengers on the Butterfield Stage, which operated along this route in 1858-61, had to walk and sometimes help push the coaches over this rocky pass.

Just north of the pass pick up the dirt road to Little Blair Valley and go east. After 0.8 mile, bear left (east), while the main road swings south into Little Blair Valley. One mile farther, this spur road ends at the mouth of a small, rocky canyon.

Go up this canyon, taking care to bear right (southeast) at a fork just 0.1 mile ahead. Continue following the drainage up-canyon for another 0.4 mile, whereupon you emerge in a nearly flat valley. Bear east and a little south across the valley (staying with the same drainage), and continue going up a narrow gorge. After climbing about 1000 feet through this gorge, you'll reach a saddle at 4550 feet. This is a pleasant campsite if you're backpacking.

Continue northeast, dropping slightly, until you come to a sandy flat just below 4400 feet. Whale Peak lies 1.5 miles southeast of here—see Trip 6 for details on finding your way to the top.

The trip back to Blair Valley is an interesting variation on the approach route. Go back down the west slope of Whale Peak to a small valley that lies 0.3 mile west-northwest of the summit. Now head generally west, losing elevation steadily, until you drop abruptly into Smuggler Canyon. Follow the canyon out to a broad valley, and turn south toward the pictograph site. (Resist the temptation to continue toward Little Blair Valley by going north of peak 3777—you won't save time this way.) Swing west, picking up the Pictograph Trail and the dirt road leading to it. Once you're in the south end of Little Blair Valley, leave the road and cut straight across easy terrain to the valley's dry lakebed, over a mile away. This creosote-bush-fringed valley often comes alive with wildflowers in March and April. The lakebed itself can become a muddy morass after heavy rain.

Pass over a gap in the boulder-strewn ridge west of the dry lakebed, and *voila!*—Blair Valley and your starting point lie right below.

Summit of Whale Peak

Trip 8: Pinyon Mountain—South Approach

Distance	2.0 miles round trip
Total elevation gain/loss	500'/500'
Hiking time	1¹/₂ hours (round trip)
Optional map	USGS 7.5-min *Whale Peak*
Best times	October through May
Agency	ABDSP
Difficulty	★★

A long, bumpy drive up Pinyon Mountain Road puts you within easy hiking distance of the Pinyon Mountains' 4492-foot high point. The hike itself takes almost as long as the drive; it leads to one of the best and most easily reached view spots in the Anza-Borrego Desert.

See Trip 6 for details on the approach by way of Pinyon Mountain Road. From the road summit at 3980 feet in Pinyon Mountain Valley, simply head cross-country up the ridge to the north and west. The south slope is almost bald, but good growths of pinyon and nolina are found on the summit and on north-facing slopes, where the sun's drying effect is allayed.

Whale Peak swells across the southern horizon, blocking views in that direction. Opposite, however, is a sweeping vista of the San Ysidro and Santa Rosa mountains, Borrego Valley, the Borrego Badlands, and the Salton Sea.

Area D-9: Split Mountain/Fish Creek

This is the desert at its lowest, hottest, and—to the unappreciative eye—most unfriendly. To those who know it well, however, it is a fascinating labyrinth of rugged canyons, twisted arroyos, and mud hills, containing not only some of nature's best examples of earth sculpture, but also a complete sequence of animal fossils spanning a period of several million years. In truth, it's not unfriendly at all. Even the weather is beautiful—at least from late fall into early spring.

Fish Creek is the major drainage system of the area. Numerous washes feed into the upper end of Fish Creek from the south slopes of the Vallecito Mountains and the north edge of the Carrizo Badlands. For more than 2 miles, Fish Creek squeezes between the near-vertical walls of Split Mountain, which divides the rambling Vallecito Mountains on the west from the Fish Creek Mountains to the east. Fish Creek has maintained its course through this gap by cutting downward fast enough to compensate for the rise of the adjacent mountains. Split Mountain's canyon walls reveal layer-cake strata reflecting successive periods of invasion by the sea and reclamation by the land. Recent faulting has offset some of the layers, creating abrupt discontinuities.

Fish Creek was once a sluggish creek with large potholes in its sandstone and conglomerate floor, some containing desert pupfish. A huge flood in 1916, it is surmised, smothered the creekbed with a thick carpet of sand and destroyed the habitat for the fish. Today's Fish Creek supports only scattered smoke trees, desert lavender, mesquite, and other shrubs. A trademark of the area is the Orcutt aster, a plant whose purple-petaled, yellow-centered, daisylike flowers bloom profusely after the rains come.

Fish Creek and some of its tributaries are open to motor-vehicle use (by street-legal vehicles only). The more remote areas of the drainage system, especially on the north (Vallecito Mountains) side, are classified as state wilderness, and therefore accessible only by foot.

Paved Split Mountain Road leads south from State Highway 78 at Ocotillo Wells, passes the Elephant Trees Area (Trips 1 and 2), and continues south to a dirt road turnoff for Fish Creek Primitive Camp and Split Mountain. Passenger cars normally can make it to the entrance of Split Mountain (starting point for Trip 3). If road conditions allow, high-clearance vehicles usually have no problem on the passage through Split Mountain. Beyond the North Fork confluence (starting point for Trip 4), soft sand becomes more prevalent. Four-wheel drive may be needed to drive as far as Sandstone Canyon (Trip 5).

Trailhead parking for the trips below requires an Anza-Borrego Desert State Park parking pass. See the section "Using This Book" for more information.

Mud Hills off Fish Creek

Area D-9: Split Mountain / Fish Creek

Trip 1: Elephant Trees Discovery Trail

Distance	1.2 miles
Total elevation gain/loss	100'/100'
Hiking time	1 hour
Optional map	USGS 7.5-min *Borrego Mountain SE*
Best times	October through May
Agency	ABDSP
Difficulty	★

The elephant tree is one of Anza-Borrego's most unusual plants. This self-guiding nature trail winds through a small group of these trees and calls attention to 20 other plants indigenous to the low, hot, alluvial-fan environment. Numbered posts along the trail are keyed to a leaflet available at the trailhead.

Long considered to be rare north of the border, the few small elephant tree (*Bursera microphylla*) specimens you see here are only a part of a group that includes at least several hundred more to the west (see Trip 2). Elephant trees are also present in scattered numbers in the south end of the state park near Mountain Palm Springs, and at a small site high in the Santa Rosa Mountains.

The elephant tree is truly a botanical oddity. With a short, stubby trunk, puffy limbs, reddish twigs and sap, tiny green leaves, and purplish fruit, it is right at home with the weird types of vegetation found in Baja's central deserts. Like cacti and succulents, the elephant tree is able to store water internally.

Indians believed the plant was associated with a great power capable of curing many diseases, especially skin ailments. Shamans kept the sap from the plant hidden away, as it was considered too dangerous to keep openly around a household.

To reach the Elephant Trees Discovery Trail, drive 6 miles south of Highway 78 (at Ocotillo Wells) on the paved Split Mountain Road. A dirt road, negotiable with care by standard cars, goes 0.9 mile west to the trailhead.

Trip 2: Alma Wash to Starfish Cove

Distance	10.0 miles round trip
Total elevation gain/loss	1600'/1600'
Hiking time	7 hours (round trip)
Recommended maps	USGS 7.5-min *Borrego Mountain SE, Harper Canyon*
Best times	December through March
Agency	ABDSP
Difficulty	★★★

If it's solitude you want, this is your trip. Years ago, I hiked in on a cold, silent winter night, under the pale light of a first-quarter moon. I felt as if I were traveling a canyon no one had ever visited before—and that may have been close to the literal truth. In the flashlight's beam I discovered fresh, fist-sized tracks of a mountain lion.

By the light of dawn I discovered the densest population of elephant trees I'd ever seen in one spot. These trees grow on both sides of the canyon, but especially on the north wall, where the tiny leaves of the plants are exposed to the maximum amount of sunshine. Some stand upright 10 or more feet tall, while others, rooted to talus slopes, have limbs that slither along like stunted, bat-

Elephant tree and barrel cactus in Alma Wash

tered conifers at timberline. Once the wiry saplings gain a foothold in small pockets of soil, they survive by rolling with the punches: rockslides merely train the flexible limbs to grow in new directions.

Begin this trip on the Elephant Trees Discovery Trail (Trip 1 above). At post #6, leave the nature trail and bear left into one of the many channels of Alma Wash (which is labeled as such on the state park maps, but not on topographic maps). Follow the braided wash floor southwest around the left (south) side of a low dome, then continue west for about 2 miles up the alluvial fan that debouches from the mouth of a prominent, east-flowing canyon in the Vallecito Mountains. The wash bottom still shows evidence of floods during tropical storms Kathleen (September 1976) and Doreen (August 1977). Note the contrast between the desert-varnished rock on the higher areas of the fan and the gleaming white rock in the recently scoured flood channels. Desert varnish, a reddish or black patina of iron and manganese oxides, takes centuries or millennia to form on the surfaces of granitic rocks.

Scattered elephant trees appear on the fan as you approach the mouth of the canyon. Conglomerate rock is exposed at its portals, then big slabs of granitic rock—the bare bones of the Vallecito Mountains.

The going is relatively easy—mostly on flat sandy patches, but occasionally over small boulder piles. Creosote bushes intermix with elephant trees on the rocky slopes. From a distance the two plants look similar; the elephant tree foliage is a slightly darker or grayer shade of green.

After following the canyon for 3 miles, you'll come to junction of several tributaries. Because of its starfish shape on the topo map, I like to call it "Starfish Cove." Campsites on flat beds of sand are abundant here.

Starfish Cove is in the heart of one of the least visited areas of Anza-Borrego. There are numerous peaks and ridges to climb in every direction. On a warm winter day, however, you may be content just to vegetate in the sun and enjoy the splendid solitude.

Trip 3: Split Mountain/Lycium Wash Loop

Distance	12.5 miles
Total elevation gain/loss	1000'/1000'
Hiking time	8 hours
Recommended maps	USGS 7.5-min *Borrego Mtn. SE, Carrizo Mtn. NE, Arroyo Tapiado, Harper Canyon*
Best times	December through March
Agency	ABDSP
Difficulty	★★★

This long circle trip includes a passage through Split Mountain and a traverse over the arid, east extremity of the Vallecito Mountains. For a 3-mile stretch, you'll negotiate some semi-rugged terrain—a scramble through a narrow ravine and a descent along a rocky ridgeline. The rest involves easy walking on jeep roads and along a sandy wash.

Begin at the mouth of Split Mountain, roughly 2 miles south of paved Split Mountain Road. With an early start, you probably won't encounter many vehicles on the several miles of jeep road ahead. The walls of Split Mountain consist of two stacks of various sedimentary layers, including sandstones and a curious kind of conglomerate called "fanglomerate"—an aggregate of cobbles and sand that originated from deposits on ancient alluvial fans. In places, these layers are tilted or folded into spectacular synclines and anticlines.

Just past Split Mountain's entrance, look for evidence of landslides along the steep cliffs left and right. Notice also the series of vertical fault cracks in the west wall. The fresh debris at the bottom of the cliffs was the result of a 1968 earthquake centered near Ocotillo Wells. The visitor center in Borrego Springs has an interesting videotape of events immediately following this magnitude 6.4 quake.

At about 2.2 miles, just before the walls of Split Mountain begin to part, look for a spectacular anticline (an inverted **U**) of sandstone layers on the west side.

When the walls fully part, bear right (west) on the jeep road through North Fork Fish Creek. Continue 1 mile through a landscape dominated by clay hills (also called "mud hills" for their consistency when wet) strewn with sparkling chips of gypsum crystal.

Turn right (north) into Lycium Wash, named after the shrub *Lycium*, or boxthorn, which flourishes here and in other badlands washes. Follow Lycium Wash on a meandering course through more mud hills to the end of the jeep road, 2.5 miles past the turn into North Fork.

(Serious rock scramblers may want to investigate the fantastic passages through

Greatly folded anticline in sandstone wall of Spilt Mountain

nearby Stone Wash, a west tributary of Lycium Wash. Flood waters in this drainage have carved several steep chutes into layers of conglomerate or fanglomerate. The abundant protruding rocks provide enough handholds and footholds to facilitate a painstaking passage. It is also possible—actually faster—to follow the ridge between Lycium and Stone washes.)

From the road's end in Lycium Wash, continue up-canyon to the mouth of a narrow trench sometimes filled with *tinajas*. You can bypass the trench by climbing up and over on the right (east side). The fanglomerate rock soon yields to tilted sandstone layers sculpted by water into fantastic shapes. After scrambling over three low dry falls, you'll come to a big, boulder-choked defile that can be detoured by climbing up and over to the right.

Now make your way north over easier terrain, staying in the biggest drainage as tributaries separate left and right. You'll soon reach a high point along a rounded ridge frosted with darkly varnished granitic rocks. An old cairn of crumbling rocks marks the summit.

Go north from the summit, down along a rocky ridge dividing two north-flowing canyons that later join together. At any convenient place, make a steep descent over loose rocks into either of these, then proceed down the sandy wash ahead.

A shortcut across the rocky alluvial fan toward the mouth of Split Mountain is tempting, but not a time-saver, as the plain is cut by too many small washes and ravines. Instead simply follow the main wash as it curves east, then southeast toward the road that leads into Split Mountain.

Trip 4: Mud Hills Wash

Distance	5.0 miles round trip
Total elevation gain/loss	300'/300'
Hiking time	2 hours (round trip)
Recommended map	USGS 7.5-min *Carrizo Mtn. NE*
Best times	November through April
Agency	ABDSP
Difficulty	★★

This hike will put you within easy reach of ancient fossil shell reefs so dense that fossils and fossil fragments outweigh the very matrix in which they lie.

You can combine this walk with a stroll through Split Mountain if road conditions block passage by automobile through the Split itself. This would involve an additional 5 miles round trip. We'll assume you can start at the south end of Split Mountain, where parking is available on hard-packed sand.

Before or after your hike, be sure to check out the "wind caves" on the slope to

the east of Fish Creek—just past the south end of Split Mountain. At least three informal trails lead up to several sandstone outcrops, where sandblasting by the wind has hollowed out chambers and skylights. This type of formation is quite common in the Fish Creek watershed and elsewhere in parts of the Carrizo and Borrego badlands.

Just beyond (south of) the starting point, bear left, staying in the main Fish Creek Wash, as the North Fork veers to the right. In another 0.3 mile Mud Hills Wash comes in from the left (south). Walk south past the vehicle closure signs and make your way along the smooth bed of this wash. If the wash bottom is wet from rains, you'll accumulate about two inches of mud on your shoes, but that's all part of the fun.

On the right is a spectacular undulating landscape of mud hills, glistening with chips of gypsum. Above this you'll see a flat-topped butte with the formation known as Elephant Knees along its north flank.

About 1.5 miles up meandering Mud Hills Wash, there's a major split. Take the right (southwest) fork, and swing around the south side of the Elephant Knees butte. Here you'll find, scattered along the wash and imbedded within the butte, the fossilized remains of oysters and pectens (scallops) which thrived in a northern extension of today's Gulf of California several millions of years ago.

Further exploration in the immediate area is rewarding, but be sure to keep track of your bearings, especially if you travel overland into the mud hills. Take care not to stray into the Carrizo Impact Area, which is strictly off limits to the public.

Trip 5: Sandstone Canyon—East Approach

Distance	Up to 7 miles
Required maps	USGS 7.5-min *Arroyo Tapiado, Harper Canyon*
Best times	November through April
Agency	ABDSP
Difficulty	★ to ★★★

Sandstone Canyon has been called the most spectacular small wash in Anza-Borrego Desert State Park. After exploring the main canyon, and any of its many tributaries, it would be hard to argue with that assertion.

For the purposes of this description, a starting point at the mouth of Sandstone Canyon is assumed. Four-wheel drive is usually needed to reach this point, 10.5

Elephant Knees

miles up the main Fish Creek from Fish Creek Primitive Camp. Jeeps can navigate about two miles up Sandstone Canyon, but its tributaries can be explored only on foot. The uppermost reaches of Sandstone Canyon can be reached from the south via June Wash (see Trip 6).

The walls of Sandstone Canyon consist of horizontally stacked layers of tan and dark brown sandstone. In some places where the sheer walls soar almost 200 feet, there's not much room at the bottom for a car to get through. The canyon bottom is filled with granitic sand and boulders, washed down from the south slopes of the Vallecito Mountains (a largely granitic body). A few large smoke trees inhabit the canyon, along with catclaw, desert lavender, locoweed, and other small shrubs.

At a point 1.2 miles up from the confluence of Fish Creek, a major tributary enters Sandstone Canyon from the right (north). Up this canyon a short distance is a small *tinaja* below a narrow, almost unclimbable dry fall. In your wanderings about the area, take care not to descend this wash from above in the hopes of reaching Sandstone Canyon.

At 1.7 miles another major tributary enters from the left (west). This narrow slot canyon may be followed for 0.5 mile to the top of the gently sloping plateau above and to the south of Sandstone Canyon. A complex of Indian trails radiates into the Arroyo Tapiado and Arroyo Seco del Diablo drainages, and along the south wall of Sandstone Canyon. Excellent if somewhat frightening views of the bottom of Sandstone Canyon

can be seen along the latter trail. You could spend many hours tracing the upper tributaries of Arroyo Tapiado and Arroyo Seco del Diablo, discovering an array of bizarre landscapes strewn with sandstone concretions (erosion-resistant nodules).

At 2.1 miles a third major tributary enters from the right (north). This is an access to the top of the Mud Palisades overlooking Olla Wash. You can go up this canyon 1 mile, bearing right at all forks, and then climb the slope to the right. Technically, the Mud Palisades are a receding cliff, one of several similar features along the south flank of the Vallecito Mountains. The view from the brink encompasses most of the upper Fish Creek drainage and extends

Running Sandstone Canyon

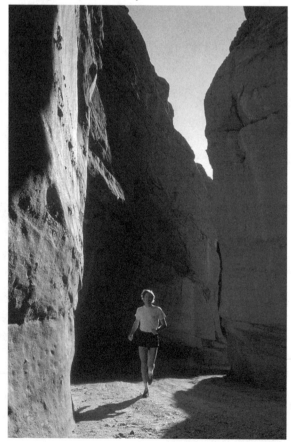

to the Imperial Valley and Mexico.

Past the third major tributary, you can go another 1.3 miles to reach the head of Sandstone Canyon—a saddle overlooking June Wash. From there you could scramble up the slope to the southeast to reach "Diablo" peak, where you'll get an inclusive view of nearly the entire Carrizo Badlands.

Trip 6: Sandstone Canyon—South Approach

Distance	6.2 miles round trip (to head of Sandstone Canyon)
Total elevation gain/loss	900'/900'
Hiking time	4 hours (round trip)
Required maps	USGS 7.5-min *Agua Caliente Springs, Arroyo Tapiado*
Best times	December through March
Agency	ABDSP
Difficulty	★★★

Many an early prospector or traveler tried to find a shortcut between the Vallecito Creek corridor (the Southern Emigrant Trail and Butterfield Stage route) and Lower Borrego Valley. Legend says that some of these travelers went "in" and failed to come "out." In the days before accurate maps were available, it was all too easy to become disoriented in the maze of washes within the Carrizo Badlands.

Today, it's not so hard to make a similar traverse, as long as you know how to locate yourself on a topographic map, and find and follow this route:

From mile 41.5 on Highway S-2, southeast of Agua Caliente Springs, turn east on the jeep road signed JUNE WASH (4-wheel drive recommended). A newer alignment of this route takes you north along the Vallecito Creek wash, then northeast into broad, sandy June Wash. After about 2 miles, the road veers imperceptibly to the right and follows a tributary wash another mile. There's parking for several cars at the road's end.

Walk over to the main June Wash by heading west for about 0.4 mile. Take note of your route so you can follow it back to your car when you return. Proceed up June Wash over sand and rocks for about 2 miles to just below the 1800-foot contour, where the canyon narrows and a small, south-flowing tributary joins on the left. Wind-sheltered campsites on flat sand can be found about 100 yards up the tributary.

Continue up June Wash, now over larger boulders, to where the canyon widens after another 0.5 mile. Leave the main wash there, and stay close to the base of "Diablo" peak, which rises on the right. After another 0.3 mile over rocky, cactus-studded terrain, you'll reach a broad saddle at the head of Sandstone Canyon, which lies to the northeast.

The saddle is a major divide between areas that shed water toward Vallecito and Carrizo creeks, and those that drain into Fish and San Felipe creeks. Runoff from the southeast slope of Diablo goes into Arroyo Tapiado and Arroyo Seco del Diablo. Diablo is thus a "triple divide peak." It's no wonder that early travelers were perplexed by the complexity of this landscape.

Your options are numerous now. You

could ascend Diablo to the southeast. You could descend into Sandstone Canyon and follow it all the way (13.7 miles) to the mouth of Split Mountain. With careful map and compass work, you could also enter one of the upper tributaries of Arroyo Seco del Diablo or Arroyo Tapiado, and follow either roughly 15 miles out to Vallecito Creek wash.

Wall of Split Mountain

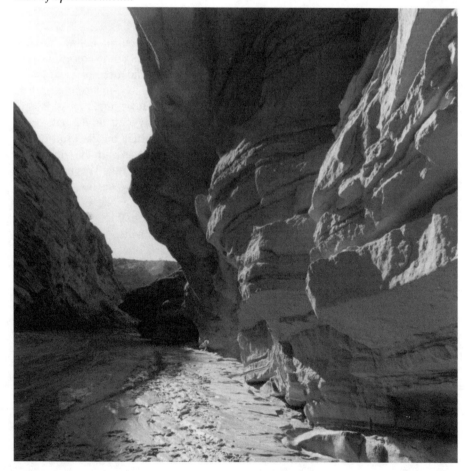

Area D-10: Agua Caliente Springs

Take in a deep breath of clean, dry air. Bask in the larger-than-life brilliance of the desert sun. Sink into the womblike comfort of warm spring water. At Agua Caliente Springs you can have your cake and eat it too—hike first, then enjoy a relaxing soak in the hot springs.

A county park has been established here in the midst of state park lands on the edge of the Tierra Blanca Mountains. The big campground and nearby store, along with the bathing pools, have made Agua Caliente Springs a focal point of activity in the southern Anza-Borrego area.

A splinter of the Elsinore Fault is responsible for the upwelling of 98°F, mineral-rich water. The Elsinore Fault passes through the Lake Elsinore area and Warner Springs, where hot springs are also found.

There are two options for hot-water soaking at Agua Caliente Springs: a large indoor jacuzzi (open 9–3), where the water temperature is boosted to more than 100°; and a shallow, outdoor pool (open daylight hours) at a temperature averaging a tepid 92°.

Two short trails out of Agua Caliente Springs, described below, penetrate the stark hills to the west and south. A third trip, for hardy hikers only, starts almost a mile higher in the Laguna Mountains. You will not need an Anza-Borrego Desert State Park parking pass for these trips, as their trailheads lie on county, not state, property.

Agua Caliente Springs lies off Highway S-2, 27 miles northwest of Interstate 8 at Ocotillo, and 22 miles southeast of Highway 78. Driving time is about the same along either route from the central San Diego and South County areas. The northern route (Highway 78) is faster from North County.

Area D-10: Agua Caliente Springs

321

Vallecito Mountains from Agua Caliente

Trip 1: Moonlight Trail

Distance	1.5 miles
Total elevation gain/loss	350'/350'
Hiking time	1 hour
Optional map	USGS 7.5-min *Agua Caliente Springs*
Best times	October through May
Agency	SDCP
Difficulty	★

This well-marked but somewhat steep and rugged trail climbs over a rock-strewn saddle, drops into a small wash mysteriously named Moonlight Canyon, descends past some seeps and a little oasis of willows in the wash bottom, and finally circles back to Agua Caliente Springs. You'll find the trailhead near the shuffleboard court at the south end of the campground. Although moonlight treks on this trail are possible, a good flashlight wouldn't hurt after dark.

True to their name, the Tierra Blanca ("white earth") Mountains are composed of light-colored granitic rock that tends not to develop desert varnish. The rock fractures easily, and its component mineral crystals break down into coarse sand.

From the high point on the trail, 300 feet above the campground, you can climb an additional 250 feet to reach Peak 1882, offering a superb view of Carrizo Valley and the Vallecito Mountains.

Another, much longer side trip may be made up-canyon (south) in Moonlight Canyon to a point overlooking the Inner Pasture, an isolated valley ringed by the Tierra Blanca and Sawtooth mountains.

This is one way to reach a big chunk of BLM-managed public land lying along the west edge of Anza-Borrego Desert State Park (see Area D-11, Trip 7 for more details).

Trip 2: Squaw Pond Trail

Distance	1.4 mile round trip (to spring)
Total elevation gain/loss	200'/200'
Hiking time	1 hour (round trip)
Optional map	USGS 7.5-min *Agua Caliente Springs*
Best times	October through May
Agency	SDCP
Difficulty	★

You can pick up this trail at the campfire circle near the county park's entrance. You wind over a low ridge, passing a spur trail leading to an overlook point a little higher on the ridge, then descend to a sandy wash in Squaw Canyon. Turn left and make your way past thickets of mesquite—vibrant green when leafing out in March, and festooned with creamy yellow-green flower spikes April through June.

The nutritious pealike pods of the mesquite ripen in September, and are eaten by various mammals. Ahead lies Squaw Pond—a marshy area with several large willow trees and some small palm trees. At least one diamondback rattlesnake makes a living on the small furry creatures that come here to drink. Coyotes and bobcats also frequent this little oasis. On the nearby hillsides you can admire the natural gardens of barrel and teddy-bear-cholla cactus.

Just beyond the spring, in a jagged ravine to the south (the main Squaw Canyon), is a tiny cave, a *tinaja*, and a usually dry waterfall. Further exploration is possible up any of the several branches of the canyon.

Trip 3: Mount Laguna to Agua Caliente

Distance	11.0 miles
Total elevation gain/loss	300'/5100'
Hiking time	9 hours
Required maps	USGS 7.5-min *Mount Laguna, Monument Peak, Agua Caliente Springs*
Best times	November through April
Agency	BLM/EC, ABDSP
Difficulty	★★★★

Get set for an incredible journey. Botanically and climatically, this is the equivalent of traveling from Canada to Mexico. From the edge of cool pine forest, you descend to a land desiccated by the hot sun and inhabited by austere-looking plants. Depending on the time of day, the temperature increases by perhaps 50°F and air you breathe becomes noticeably denser and drier.

This route offers the only relatively easy way to travel from the top of the Lagunas to the desert floor without trespassing on private property. You'll cross national forest land, a big parcel of BLM land, a strip of Anza-Borrego Desert State Park, and finally Agua Caliente County Park. The BLM land is part of the federal 35,000-acre Sawtooth Wilderness. The area is seldom visited, rugged in its upper reaches, and extremely remote from the usual pathways of travel.

This hike is strictly a one-way downhill affair, unless for some reason you have the desire (and stamina) to scramble up 3000 feet of loose rock and scree. Backpacking is an option, although dayhiking with light but sufficient gear is probably more rewarding and trouble-free. Plan your water needs carefully, as there is no guarantee of its availability. An early start is important if you're dayhiking; it's essential in November and December, when darkness falls by about 5 P.M.

Have someone (preferably with a good book to read) take you to the starting point (refer to Area M-8 map), and pick you up later at Agua Caliente Springs. The starting point is found by taking the vista point turnoff from Sunrise Highway at mile 23.8. (This turnoff is distinct from the turnoff to Desert View Picnic Area, 0.1 mile south.) Drive up the vista point road exactly 0.25 mile to the first parking area overlooking the desert. The continuation of this road leads to a telecommunications site (formerly an Air Force radar station) on Stephenson Peak. If your car remains parked here, you'll need a National Forest Adventure Pass to avoid getting a ticket.

At the vista point, you'll be able to see most of the route ahead. The green patch in the distance is the *cienaga* at Vallecito Valley. You will turn to the right before reaching Vallecito Valley and go over a divide into Agua Caliente Springs,

which is hidden from this vantage point by the Sawtooth Mountains.

The key to an easy descent on this cross-country route is to avoid going straight down. Instead, angle down and to the left (northeast) through low chaparral. Sooner or later you'll hook up with one or more deer trails lacing the brushy mountainside.

Resist the temptation to drop too fast. Stay generally about 300 or 400 feet lower than (south of) the ridgeline that is directly east of Stephenson Peak. You'll traverse slopes dotted with mountain mahogany, scrub oak, and ceanothus shrubs, and occasionally traipse through colorful patches of lupine.

After a total of about 1.5 miles, you'll have reached a point where it seems best to drop into the canyon below. If you're here in April, you'll be able to see, even from a distance, some large yellow-blossomed shrubs in the canyon bottom. This is a colony of fremontia, or flannel bush, one of the showiest of California native plants. Some of these spindly shrubs bear thousands of big, waxy, yellow flowers.

A small stream flows through the canyon at this point, flanked by dense clusters of California bay, willow, and scrub oak. Follow the water where convenient, or push through the vegetation on the banks. This vegetation includes white sage and desert apricot, typical inhabitants of the higher desert. At the 3160-foot contour, the canyon widens, and you'll pass under a broken plastic pipe suspended over the canyon by a barbed-wire strand. Follow this pipe north to a dry watering trough, and pick up a disused jeep road leading north into "The Potrero," the large scrub-covered alluvial basin that abuts both the Laguna and Sawtooth mountains. The Potrero was once known as Treasure Canyon, after a story about a cattle rustler and bandit who robbed miners from the rich

California gold fields and reportedly hid the loot there.

You now face a long and somewhat tedious march down the length of The Potrero. The disused road merges with a better road, and this road continues about 2 miles toward a prominent rocky hill. At 0.4 mile past the hill, bear right, and go about 0.3 mile to pick up a well-traveled dirt road aligned due north. After 0.5 mile, veer right at the fork and continue northeast about 1.5 miles to the point where the road swings abruptly left (northwest). Now you're beginning to see low-desert vegetation like creosote bush, indigo bush and ocotillo.

Where the road swings abruptly northwest, leave it and head cross-country east-northeast over an easy saddle into a tributary of Squaw Canyon. (Take care not to blunder into one of the drainages that go north into Vallecito Creek.) In Squaw Canyon you will pick up the Squaw Pond Trail, leading to the camping area at Agua Caliente County Park. In this last part of the hike, the only thing driving you on may be the thought of lounging in the infinitely relaxing, spring-fed pools.

The edge of the Carrizo Badlands, which includes some of the rawest desert anywhere, lies an easy 3 or 4 miles farther east from Agua Caliente Springs. This fact opens up the possibility of experiencing, in a single day's walk, environments ranging from cool pine forests to hot, barren badlands. There are few places in the world where such a trip is possible.

Ocotillo at sunset

Area D-11: Bow Willow/In-Ko-Pah Mountains

The area between County Highway S-2 in the south end of Anza-Borrego Desert State Park and the BLM's McCain Valley Cooperative Management Area constitutes some of the most wild, beautiful and serene territory in San Diego County. Here, the Tierra Blanca and In-Ko-Pah mountains serve as a bridge between the hot sands of the low desert and a vast stretch of chaparral-dotted tableland southwest of the Laguna Mountains. Amid the tortured folds of these mountains are fan-palm oases, hidden waterfalls, and many species of plants that would seem more at home in places hundreds of miles to the north or south. Here, for example, water-loving trees like cottonwood and bay are found only a few miles from stands of elephant trees, which are common in the most arid parts of Baja California.

Bow Willow Campground (entrance at mile 48.3 on Highway S-2), the only semideveloped camping area in Anza-Borrego's south end, is a good staging area for hikes into the Tierra Blancas and the eastern In-Ko-Pahs. There is ready access from here into Bow Willow and Rockhouse canyons. Dirt roads lead to Mountain Palm Springs (turnoff at mile 47.1) and Indian Gorge (turnoff at mile 46.1), which are starting points for trips to side canyons, desert valleys, and peaks.

Topside, there's McCain Valley Road, a well-graded dirt road that runs some 14 miles north and west from Old Highway 80 near the town of Boulevard. (To reach it, leave Interstate 8 at the Highway 94/Boulevard exit, go 0.5 mile south, then go 1.9 miles east on Old Highway 80.) This road is the only public access into the McCain Valley area, which is managed for multiple uses by the BLM. Most areas west of this road are open for restricted and unrestricted off-road vehicle use, while most areas east of the road are closed to all vehicle use in order to protect bighorn sheep habitat. With the exception of a few hunters chasing game in certain seasons, the east margins of the McCain Valley Cooperative Management Area are essentially hikers' domain. Cottonwood Campground is a good place for car camping, and serves as a jumping-off point for hikes into the wild areas lying north and east.

Several interesting but rugged one-way hikes may be undertaken between McCain Valley and the desert floor. One such hike is specifically described below in Trip 7, while others are suggested in Trips 5, 6, and 8.

Trips 1 through 5 require an Anza-Borrego Desert State Park parking pass—see the section "Using This Book" for more information. Trips 6 through 8 begin on BLM land and do not require any parking fee.

Area D-11: Bow Willow / In-Ko-Pah Mountains

Trip 1: Torote Canyon

Distance	4.0 miles round trip
Total elevation gain/loss	1000'/1000'
Hiking time	2^1/$_2$ hours (round trip)
Optional maps	USGS 7.5-min *Sweeney Pass, Arroyo Tapiado, Agua Caliente Springs*
Best times	November through April
Agency	ABDSP
Difficulty	★★

Dozens of elephant trees cling to the walls of this interesting canyon. In Mexico, this tree is called torote, which means "twisted," in reference to the haphazard way in which the limbs twine upward.

A series of secluded valleys, each seemingly cut off from the rest of the world, lie up-canyon a mile or two. A broad expanse of sand, a few sparse shrubs, cobbled walls in the distance, and the vault of sky overhead: an hour spent quietly contemplating such purity and simplicity can bring on a feeling of profound peace.

Drive up the road into Indian Gorge (turnoff at mile 46.1 on Highway S-2), and proceed 1.8 miles to the mouth of Torote Canyon on the right (north), where it is possible to pull off the road onto what is usually hard-packed sand. On foot, scramble up the rock-strewn bed of the canyon, passing the elephant trees that cling tenaciously to the steep walls.

After 0.8 mile you enter the first valley, an almost-flat, sand-drowned expanse stretching nearly half a mile. Within this valley the canyon divides, with the main branch (Torote Canyon) climbing sharply up a bouldered crease on the left (northwest). Keep right, in what seems to be the main part of the valley, and proceed north into a small, narrow canyon, a tributary of Torote Canyon. Within 200 yards this broadens into a second valley, similar to the first. Continue northwest to the second valley's end, and climb to the low pass that

appears straight ahead. Reaching it, you'll discover a canyon just below that drains east toward the desert floor. To your left (west) you can contour over rocks into this canyon, and within 200 yards reach the east end of still another sand-drowned valley. This one is richly endowed with desert vegetation, and hosts a lively population of jackrabbits.

Smoke tree in Torote Canyon

This is as good a place as any to turn back and retrace your steps. If you do go on, though, you can make your way west over a divide, descend a rocky canyon, and reach the big valley above Canebrake Canyon.

Trip 2: Sombrero Peak—East Approach

Distance	3.0 miles round trip
Total elevation gain/loss	1900'/1900'
Hiking time	3¹/₂ hours
Recommended map	USGS 7.5-min *Sombrero Peak*
Best times	November through April
Agency	ABDSP
Difficulty	★★★

Cone-shaped Sombrero Peak rises head and shoulders above the east lip of the McCain Valley plateau, overlooking a hundred-square-mile expanse of rock-strewn mountains and gorges, sun-baked valleys, and distant badlands. Conversely, the peak itself is a prominent and familiar landmark widely observed from the desert below.

There is but one relatively easy way to climb to the summit from the desert side, involving a rather long approach by car up Indian Gorge and Indian Valley. (Another way to climb this mountain is from the west—see Trip 6.)

From Highway S-2 at mile 46.1, turn west and drive through Indian Gorge. After 2.0 miles, the walls of the gorge part, and you enter Indian Valley. In another 0.7 mile, the road splits, with branches going into the north and south forks of Indian Valley. Keep left at this junction and drive into the south fork about 3 miles to the road's end near the mouth of a canyon dotted (higher up) with a few palms. On a slope above this drainage, archaeologists have identified an Indian ceremonial site keyed to the rising position of the sun at summer solstice.

From the road's end, climb straight up the ridge to the south until you reach a flat at elevation 3100 feet. (As a side trip from here, you could traverse over to Sombrero Peak Palm Grove, a dense cluster of palms with no surface water in evidence.) Continue west, then southwest up the ridgeline to Sombrero's boulder-studded summit—scrambling over modest-sized rocks all the way. On top, the best view is east, where Bow Willow Canyon and its tributaries yawn open in the blazing sun.

On your return to Indian Valley, don't be tempted to descend the east slope toward Sombrero Peak Palm Grove; house-sized boulders and scratchy thickets of scrub oak will stop you!

Fishhook cactus in bloom

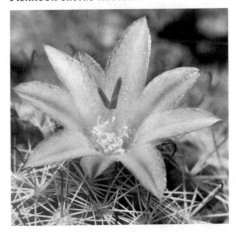

Trip 3: Mountain Palm Springs

Distance	2.5 miles
Total elevation gain/loss	350'/350'
Hiking time	1½ hours
Optional map	USGS 7.5-min *Sweeney Pass*
Best times	October through May
Agency	ABDSP
Difficulty	★

The Mountain Palm Springs area boasts, without a doubt, the most charming palm oases south of Borrego Palm Canyon. The palms here are gregarious, growing in dense clusters, often with pools of water at their feet. Many have never been burned: they still hold full skirts of dead fronds around their trunks, the better to serve the local population of rodents and snakes. In late fall and early winter, the sticky, sweet fruit of the palms hangs in great swaying clusters, sought after by birds and the sleek coyotes that prowl up and down the washes.

The palm groves are distributed along several small washes that drain roughly a square-mile area on the east side of the Tierra Blanca Mountains. Water lies close to the surface in several of the ravines. A primitive camping area sits on the alluvial fan just below the point where the washes come together. A short dirt road leads to this campground from mile 47.1 on Highway S-2.

Consider the loop hike described here as a fairly complete tour of the area; but do be enticed to extend your explorations in the form of side trips or extended loop trips if the spirit moves you.

Begin by walking up the small canyon southwest of the primitive camp. Past some small seeps you'll come upon the first groups of Pygmy Grove. Some of these small but statuesque palms grow out of nothing more than rock piles.

A long pause is in order at Southwest Grove, a restful retreat shaded by a vaulted canopy of shimmering fronds. A rock-lined catch basin fashioned for the benefit of the local wildlife mirrors the silhouettes of the palms. A couple of elephant trees cling to the slopes just above the grove, but for a better look at these curious plants, you can climb a spur trail to Torote Bowl, where a bigger group of elephant trees will be found. Further travel (cross-country over boulders) can take you to a single large specimen, perhaps 15 feet tall and 20 feet wide, 0.6 mile west-southwest of Torote Bowl, and 0.4 mile south of "Palm" peak.

From Southwest Grove, pick up the well-worn, but obscure trail that leads north over a rock-strewn ridge to Surprise Canyon Grove in Surprise Canyon. Up-

Palms at Surprise Canyon Grove

canyon from this small grove lies Palm Bowl, filled with tangled patches of mesquite and fringed on its western edge by more than a hundred palms. On warm winter days, the molasses-like odor of ripe palm fruit wafts upon the breeze, and phainopepla hoot and flit among the palm crowns, their white wing patches flashing.

Northwest of Palm Bowl Grove, an old Indian pathway leads over a low pass into Indian Gorge—another tempting diversion. To conclude the loop hike, however, you return to Surprise Canyon Grove and continue down-canyon to the campground. On the way, you pass North Grove, hidden in a side drainage on the left.

Spring at Southwest Grove

Trip 4: Bow Willow/Rockhouse Canyon Loop

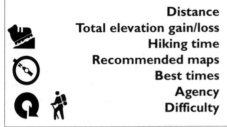

Distance	7.5 miles
Total elevation gain/loss	1100'/1100'
Hiking time	4$^{1}/_{2}$ hours
Recommended maps	USGS 7.5-min *Sweeney Pass, Sombrero Peak*
Best times	November through April
Agency	ABDSP, BLM/EC
Difficulty	★★★

A simple shack fashioned of rock, cement, and corrugated metal might be unremarkable anywhere else, but in the midst of thousands of acres of wild desert, it becomes a significant point of interest. The old cattlemen's line shack in Rockhouse Canyon is a case in point: hikers routinely travel miles overland to visit it.

This rather popular if somewhat rugged hike includes some stretches of well-worn but poorly marked trails. Ducks and wooden stake markers are of some help in following the route. Topo maps are very handy if you do go off course.

From the starting point, Bow Willow Campground, walk 0.5 mile up-canyon; on your left (south) is a small alluvial fan leading up to a rocky draw in the mountains. Clamber upward through this draw, passing a single palm tree (whose source of water is mysterious), gaining about 200 feet. You'll come up to a sandy wash that winds upward to a gently sloping plateau area of broken rock formations. Hardy desert plants, like cholla cactus, ocotillo, and creosote bush, cover the area. After you stay with the wash for about a mile, ducks and wooden markers guide the way

generally south-southwest over an almost imperceptible divide (1600'), then down more steeply onto the broad floor of Rockhouse Canyon.

The jeep road shown on the topo map is gone now; simply head up-canyon 0.5 mile to an elliptical valley thickly covered with cholla and ocotillo. Nestled against the rocky hillside on the south side of this valley is the line shack, which leans against the face of a large boulder. The decrepit interior of the shack houses the remains of a fireplace and the usual rusty bedsprings.

East of the shack, at the mouth of a canyon, is a watering trough and the remains of a pipeline to a seasonal spring and waterfall 0.4 mile up-canyon. A pleasant hour or two can be spent exploring this canyon and the next canyon to the west.

The line shack marks the halfway point of the hike. Return by going directly over the low pass to the north into Bow Willow Canyon. An old cattle trail—probably once an Indian trail—traverses this pass. Once in Bow Willow Canyon, the walking is very easy over open stretches of firm sand.

Trip 5: Bow Willow Canyon

Distance	7.5 miles round trip (to palms)
Total elevation gain/loss	750'/750'
Hiking time	4 hours (round trip)
Optional maps	USGS 7.5-min *Sweeney Pass, Sombrero Peak*
Best times	November through April
Agency	ABDSP
Difficulty	★★★

The intriguing name "Bow Willow" seems to be associated with the supple wood of the desert-willow, used by Indians to fashion hunting bows. Hundreds of these fragrant, bushy trees are scattered along Bow Willow Canyon's lower end. A small spring at the mouth of the canyon serves a modest campground and a seasonal ranger station.

Vehicles were allowed on the sandy bed of Bow Willow Canyon until the early 1980s, when flash flooding obliterated the road and half the campground. Thereafter, park officials decided to keep the canyon vehicle-free. In 1985 new campsites, replacing those washed away, were built on a gentle slope out of reach of floodwaters.

The now-silent lower canyon is perfect for cool-weather hiking. Its white ribbon of sand winds, fjordlike, some 3 miles between steep walls heaped with desert-varnished boulders. In the upper canyon, the terrain becomes more rugged: the canyon divides into several branches cut deeply into the In-Ko-Pah mountains.

A 1.5-mile-long graded dirt road, intersecting Highway S-2 at mile 48.5, leads in to Bow Willow Campground, where hiking begins. Walking in the wash is easy since the sand is made up of rather large crystals deriving from easily decomposed granitic rocks above. As you stroll along, look for elephant trees—a few cling inconspicuously to the south wall. The canyon bends abruptly south, then gradually resumes a western course. The massive east flank of Sombrero Peak can be seen ahead, resplendent in early morning sunshine.

After 2.7 miles, a low pass over the ridge to the south-southeast can be seen. This is the route from Rockhouse Canyon (see Trip 5). On the opposite (north) side, a faint trail up and over the north wall leads to the South Fork of Indian Valley—a vigorous climb for the adventurous.

Our way straight ahead (west) now becomes increasingly choked with obstacles—low brush, rocks, and, during most of the year, a bubbling stream. The first scraggly palms appear at about 3.0 miles; but much finer specimens are seen farther on. Year-round water in the upper canyon nourishes dense growths of mesquite, catclaw, willow, and tamarisk in or near the streamcourse. Detour around this tangle of vegetation by staying high on the banks.

At about 3.7 miles (1680'), a dry tributary comes in from the northwest. (This tributary can be used to reach Sombrero Peak Palm Grove, an enigmatic, solitary cluster of palms on the flank of Sombrero Peak.) This junction is as good a place as any to have lunch before returning. Listen for the sound of falling water, and you'll be drawn to one of the secret grottos found in the canyon.

A major fork lies upstream (1880'), with **V**-shaped branches going west and southwest. The right fork is steeper, with less water, while the left fork enjoys a nearly perennial flow of water over massive boulders. In both branches (which ultimately lead to more gentle terrain atop the McCain Valley plateau), scattered cottonwood and alder trees lend a touch of softness to the harsh glare of naked granite.

Trip 6: Sombrero Peak—West Approach

Distance	9.0 miles round trip
Total elevation gain/loss	1300'/1300'
Hiking time	6 hours (round trip)
Required map	USGS 7.5-min *Sombrero Peak*
Best times	October through May
Agency	BLM/EC
Difficulty	★★★

Dust off your map-and-compass skills—you'll really need them on this approach to Sombrero Peak via the rolling McCain Valley plateau. The peak stays largely hidden behind growths of chaparral and intervening ridges until you're practically upon it. To make matters more difficult, many of the roads and jeep trails shown on the most recent USGS topo map of the area are totally overgrown and some new roads have appeared in the interim.

A good place to begin is Cottonwood Campground, 12.7 miles northwest of the McCain Valley Road/Old Highway 80 intersection. It's nestled in a pleasant strip of oak woodland along an upper tributary of Bow Willow Creek. Bedrock *morteros* nearby show that the Indians liked this area too.

Pick up the hiking and horse trail (a disused dirt road) 0.1 mile north of the campground entrance. Heading east at first, the trail soon swings generally north, crossing two small tributaries of Bow Willow Canyon. After about a mile, a 0.3-mile-long public easement begins, taking you through a corner of a private inholding within the BLM lands.

At 2.0 miles from the campground you should leave this trail (which continues north into Pepperwood Canyon) and

swing east over a gentle divide north of peak 4553. Once over the divide, work your way entirely cross-country east-northeast across a shallow tributary of Bow Willow Canyon and up along an east-trending ridge. Try to choose an easy route

Sombrero Peak

through the maze of tall, widely spaced chaparral shrubs. From higher ground, the conical summit of Sombrero Peak may pop into view.

Eventually, you'll come to a SOMBRERO PEAK sign at the base of the last pitch. A short, tough scramble up a heap of huge boulders puts you on the summit. Your route-finding challenge is now only half

over; on the return you'll need to navigate back toward peak 4553 and find the trail leading back to Cottonwood Campground.

Using a variation of the approach described here, expert hikers can use Bow Willow Canyon to reach the desert floor. These canyons are boulder-strewn and rugged, graced with palms, cottonwoods, and semi-perennial streams.

Trip 7: Pepperwood Trail to Canebrake

Distance	14.0 miles (to Highway S-2)
Total elevation gain/loss	450'/3700'
Hiking time	8 hours
Required maps	USGS 7.5-min *Sombrero Peak*
Best times	November through April
Agency	BLM/EC
Difficulty	★★★★

On a cool day this is one of the most delightful downhill hikes in the county. Except for a 2-mile scramble down the eroded and overgrown remnants of the Pepperwood Trail in Pepperwood Canyon, not too much effort is required to keep moving. Below Pepperwood Canyon, the route traverses the lonely reaches of Canebrake Valley and the Inner Pasture; these two form a large, **U**-shaped alluvial plain surrounded by the stark, boulder-strewn slopes of the Tierra Blanca and Sawtooth mountains. Much of this area is encompassed within the BLM's Sawtooth Wilderness.

The riparian area along the upper part of Pepperwood Canyon is a worthy enough destination of itself, as a trail of footprints attests. Traffic down the lower end of the Pepperwood Trail is virtually nil, though. Few people visit Canebrake Valley and the Inner Pasture either, save for ranchers who have been granted grazing allotments. If the BLM ever acts on a long-standing proposal to reconstruct and extend the Pepperwood Trail and develop

a trail camp, more people will surely be drawn this way.

Begin, as in Trip 6 above, at Cottonwood Campground. Follow the obviously trodden trail, marked intermittently by semi-legible signs, northeast and north for 2.3 miles (4180 feet'). There, you come to a fork in the trail with another set of barely legible signs. Keep going north; don't veer left (west), even though many footprints might lead that way, going to the terminus of McCain Valley Road. After another mile, the trail bends northwest and starts descending into the canyon containing Pepperwood Spring. The trail becomes steeper and more obscure, until finally it is only a narrow path kept recognizable through occasional use by hikers and wildlife. The soil is a loose, decomposed granite that flows downslope with your every step.

Before long, there's a pungency in the air that brings a sense of *deja vu* to those familiar with the Coast Ranges of Northern California and Oregon: this is the unmistakable fragrance of the pepperwood tree (California bay, or bay laurel). When crushed and sniffed, the leaves give off an odor that is pleasant but, if overdone, the cause of a headache. The line between pleasure and pain is a fine one, yet who can resist going the limit?

Stumbling down past the first pepperwoods, you reach the canyon bottom and a stretch of flat sand (4 miles, 3720'). A seasonal waterfall is just upstream, shaded by pepperwoods and cottonwoods. Downstream about 200 yards is a year-round spring in the flat bed of the creek. This area is a good place to turn around if you wish to go no farther.

Beyond the spring, faint trails lead down the steep walls of both sides of the canyon. Try to follow the trace of the original foot trail (as plotted on the *Sombrero Peak* topo map) on the ridge east of the canyon bottom. This leads, after some moderate scrambling over loose rocks and through low brush, to the floor of Canebrake Valley.

A search of the south side of the valley might turn up, among the strangely eroded granitic rock formations, many Indian *morteros* and a ceremonial site related to fertility rites. Without lots of time to spare, however, you should continue north to pick up the dirt road that will take you, after several miles, to Inner Pasture.

Strangely enough, Inner Pasture is drained by two major washes—North Wash, which flows through Canebrake Canyon, and another, unnamed wash that cuts through the Tierra Blanca Mountains to the northeast. It seems only a matter of a short time, geologically, before one or the other wash captures the entire drainage.

This unnamed wash can be your exit. You'll reach mile marker 41.0 on Highway S-2 after a walk of about 3 miles. The easy stroll down this wash is a fitting climax to a long day's (or weekend's) hike. In the late afternoon sun, the shattered walls of granite on either side glow softly, offering a silent benediction.

There are at least three other ways to exit. From a south arm of Canebrake valley, it is possible to reach Indian Valley's north fork via a rocky pass; this is the BLM-proposed route for the lower end of the Pepperwood Trail. From Indian Valley one could walk out to S-2 or get a prearranged ride. Another, more obvious, route is right through Canebrake Canyon itself, but private lands within the canyon make this route inadvisable without permission. By finding a low gap in the ridge north of Inner Pasture, you could also exit by way of Moonlight Canyon into Agua Caliente Springs.

Trip 8: Four Frogs/Jacumba Jim Loop

Distance	9.0 miles
Total elevation gain/loss	3200'/3200'
Hiking time	8 hours
Required maps	USGS 7.5-min *Sombrero Peak, Sweeney Pass*
Best times	November through April
Agency	BLM/EC
Difficulty	★★★★

The palm-lined canyons known informally as "Four Frogs" and "Jacumba Jim" lie in the heart of the BLM's Carrizo Gorge Wilderness, a region whose east boundary abuts a large expanse of state wilderness in adjacent Anza-Borrego

Desert State Park. The area supports a sizable herd of bighorn sheep most of the year. During the springtime lambing season, the sheep cross Carrizo Gorge and take up residence in the Jacumba Mountains. The strenuous, cross-country loop hike described here touches both canyons and gives a good overview of this rugged area.

Unlike most long trips in this book, this one starts "at the top," with most of the work—a 2400-foot elevation gain over gut-wrenching terrain—at the end. You'll dip deeply into your energy reserves for this one. Do it in a single long day, or take your time and backpack in.

A good place to begin is the intersection of McCain Valley Road and the former Lost Valley Road. Drive 8.0 miles north of Old Highway 80 to reach this unmarked road/trail and find a place to park.

Past a steel gate, the abandoned road takes you 0.5 mile east to an overgrazed meadow and the eroded remnants of a cattle pond. Above it, cross a flood-torn gully, proceed north on traces of a jeep trail over a viewful summit (0.9 mile), and continue down a slope into a wide draw. Stay in the draw (northeast) as old roadbeds intersect from the left. At 1.9 miles a good trace of jeep road detours you up and across the slope to the north, avoiding a sharp dropoff. After returning to the draw, pick your way down along the bottom for another mile. A thin stream of water flows here about half the year.

At 3.5 miles easy walking ends as you come to a spectacular abyss at the head of Four Frogs canyon. Negotiate a route downward over the tops of the truck-sized boulders, and you will soon see clusters of palms below. Little or no surface water is present at the biggest grove (2200'), but it's nice to stop here for shade.

A good two thirds of the trip, in terms of effort, remains ahead. Head due east from the grove, first contouring, then climbing obliquely, to a small flat (2450')

on the ridgeline above. Now, taking the path of least resistance, proceed generally south-southeast 0.5 mile across the glaring slopes to a flattish area, again at 2450 feet, covered with scattered low shrubs. This can be used as an excellent dry campsite, with a panoramic view of Carrizo Canyon and its many tributaries. Bighorn sheep "beds" (scuffed areas) and scats are common in this area.

Next continue generally south-southeast, descending sharply into Jacumba Jim canyon. You may notice a low wall of stones, possibly an Indian hunting blind, on the way down. Upon reaching bottom, turn west and make your way up toward the first set of palms. The springs in this canyon are among the most dependable in the In-Ko-Pahs, and a vigorous supply of water cascades over the polished rock after rainfall. Above the first palms, however, the canyon becomes choked with vegetation, and it is necessary to clamber over the rocks on slopes north of the creek to make decent progress. Water trickling over numerous small falls can be heard below.

Many more palms are found above 2260 feet, where a tributary canyon comes in from the right (west). At this point it's time to begin climbing in earnest. Swing southwest onto the ridge between the two forks and climb up the sandy slope. Make your way through large and small semi-desert shrubs (scrub oak, juniper, sugarbush, mountain mahogany) and a few palms. After about 0.7 mile, past an obstacle course of large rocks, you'll reach an old jeep road that leads northwest and west toward the washed-out pond and the meadow east of your car.

Area D-12: Carrizo Badlands

Much of southern Anza-Borrego is blanketed by the low, hot, and intricately dissected terrain known as the Carrizo Badlands. Spectacular examples of erosion in soft claystones, mudstones, and sandstones are found throughout the area. You'll see clay hills, mud caves, small arches and windows, receding cliffs, sinuous washes, and deep-cut ravines.

Several million years ago, today's badlands were nothing but ooze at the bottom of a shallow sea that occupied the southeastern corner of California. The same geological forces that built up the Peninsular Ranges to the west raised and tilted these soft sedimentary deposits. Erosion has acted almost as quickly to tear them down. The forces of wind and gentle rainfall, acting slowly, have done their part to smooth a few rough edges; but it is the catastrophic events—the rare flash floods and earthquakes—that have played and will continue to play the major roles as shapers of this chaotic-looking landscape.

The Coyote Mountains, bordering the Carrizo Badlands on the south, have a core of ancient granitic and metamorphic rocks overlain by marine sediments. Erosion has cut down through the softest sediments, leaving harder sandstones and fossil-shell reefs exposed. Fossil Canyon, Painted Gorge, and other areas on the east end of the range in Imperial County (not covered in this book) are well worth exploring. On the west end of the range, much older metamorphic and granitic rocks are exposed in places such as Canyon Sin Nombre and Mine Peak.

In the western Carrizo Badlands, centered on Arroyo Tapiado, many fossils of land creatures dating back one to two million years have been found, including bones of mammoth, sabertooth cat, rhinoceros, camel, and dire wolf.

County Highway S-2, the road that finally opened up southern Anza-Borrego to easy access by conventional autos in the early '60s, is still the only way to reach the

Area D-12: Carrizo Badlands

338

areas described here. Most San Diego County residents will find it easier to come by way of the south end of Highway S-2—from Interstate 8 at Ocotillo.

As in the Borrego Badlands, most of the major Carrizo Badlands washes are open to street-legal vehicles. Hikers, how-ever, have exclusive access to the hundreds of miles of smaller drainages.

Trailhead parking for the trips below requires an Anza-Borrego Desert State Park parking pass. See the section "Using This Book" for more information.

Trip 1: Mine Peak

Distance	2.5 miles round trip
Total elevation gain/loss	700'/700'
Hiking time	2 hours (round trip)
Optional map	USGS 7.5-min *Sweeney Pass*
Best times	November through April
Agency	ABDSP
Difficulty	★★

Mine Peak (1850') is the highest point on the west end of the Coyote Mountains. On a clear day the view from the summit seems to go on forever, with the wrinkled Carrizo Badlands in the north, the cobbled Tierra Blanca, In-Ko-Pah, and Jacumba mountains to the west through south, and the flat, hazy Yuha Desert and Salton Sink to the southeast and northeast.

Turn east at mile 53.4 on Highway S-2 onto the West Dolomite Mine Trail. Drive 0.7 mile, then turn sharply left (north). Go 0.2 mile to a large parking area and stop. After this, the road deteriorates dramatically.

On foot now, cross a wash and con-tinue up the road 0.6 mile to an abandoned dolomite mine. From here it's a simple mat-ter of scrambling straight up the ridge, due north, to the rounded summit of Mine Peak.

Trip 2: Canyon Sin Nombre

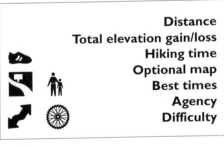

Distance	5.0 miles round trip
Total elevation gain/loss	550'/550'
Hiking time	3 hours (round trip)
Optional map	USGS 7.5-min *Sweeney Pass*
Best times	November through April
Agency	ABDSP
Difficulty	★★

One of the best examples of a slot canyon in Anza-Borrego's south end is off of Canyon Sin Nombre ("canyon without a name"). Canyon Sin Nombre serves as a rugged route for vehicle travel between Highway S-2 above Sweeney Pass and Carrizo Creek, but it's seldom busy. Hik-ing down this canyon, especially when a low sun brings out the variegated colors of its walls, is pure delight.

Park in the small turnout at mile 51.3 on Highway S-2, and begin by following the vehicle tracks that descend steeply down a sandy slope toward the head of Canyon Sin Nombre. As you approach the head of the canyon, admire the beautiful barrel cacti on the flats and slopes nearby: many grow to heights of 5 feet or more. Notice how they lean south—toward the sun at its brightest.

The entrance walls are only a fore-taste of the hodgepodge of shapes and colors to come. First, there are twisted, brown and gray layers of metamorphic rock, some shot through with narrow, light colored igneous dikes. Just beyond, more igneous (granitic) rock is exposed. On the right (east) wall, about 0.3 mile farther, notice the spectacular, crumpled swirl of sedimentary layers. Movements along the Elsinore Fault in this area have produced horizontal displacements of up to 3 miles.

On farther, the canyon broadens somewhat, and the walls are fashioned from a more uniform-textured mudstone and sandstone. At a point 1.3 miles into the canyon—at the 760-foot contour—a tributary cuts deeply into the clifflike left (west) wall. This becomes a narrow slot canyon, with walls perhaps 150 feet high. If you squeeze through the various narrow sections of this canyon, and climb out of the canyon on the left as soon as you can, you reach the brink of a cliff overlooking Canyon Sin Nombre.

The easiest way to return is the same

Concretions in tributary of Canyon Sin Nombre

way you came. Further exploration in this area might include a trek up the trace of an Indian trail running southwest along the hills west of Canyon Sin Nombre in the direction of Sweeney Pass; this trail can be picked up above the slot canyon. You might also try poking into one of the many concretion-littered tributaries east of Canyon Sin Nombre and north of Mine Peak.

Trip 3: Arroyo Tapiado/Arroyo Diablo Loop

Distance	16.5 miles
Total elevation gain/loss	600'/600'
Hiking time	8 hours
Recommended map	USGS 7.5-min *Arroyo Tapiado*
Best times	December through April
Agency	ABDSP
Difficulty	★★★★

This is one of the longest hikes described in this book, yet one of the flattest and most relaxing—relaxing, that is, if you pick the right day or days. Avoid weekends, particularly holiday weekends, if you can. Otherwise you'll share these arroyos with too many motor vehicles.

It's only by walking that the otherworldly beauty of this area can really be appreciated. Opportunities for side trips abound, so much so that you could easily spend two days on this circuit. If you're backpacking the route, secluded campsites well off the roads can be found in the upper reaches of both Arroyo Tapiado and Arroyo Seco del Diablo. The main route (not the side trips) is also suitable for mountain biking—though this method of traveling can in places be more tiring than walking because of soft sand.

The highlight of the trip comes early: the Arroyo Tapiado cave formations. Some of the caves are pitch dark; bring two flashlights (per person) and a hard hat or a rock-climbing helmet if you intend to explore them.

To reach the starting point, find the signed Palm Spring turnoff at mile 43.0 on County Highway S-2. This is opposite (east of) Canebrake Canyon. Go east, passing the spur road to Palm Spring, and continue (if road conditions allow) down Vallecito Creek wash. Park at the intersection of the road into Arroyo Tapiado, 4.5 miles from S-2.

On foot, proceed north in the wash of Arroyo Tapiado (meaning "mudwall wash"). After 2.0 miles you reach the beginning of a deep, twisting gorge. The next 2 miles will take you through what geologists call pseudokarst topography. Like the *karst* topography found in many parts of the world, *pseudokarst* contains caves, subterranean drainage systems, sinkholes, and blind valleys that end in swallow holes. Unlike karst, which results from the dissolution of limestone or similar material by water, this topography is the result of an unusual process: First, flood waters gouge out slotlike tributaries in the soft claystone walls of the main arroyo (Arroyo Tapiado). Second, landslides fill in the slots. Third, flood waters dig tunnels through the bottom levels of the landslide debris.

Some of the caves (subterranean stream channels) in the area are over 1000 feet long, with rooms up to 80 feet high and 30 feet wide. Others are tall and narrow, much like a meandering slot canyon with a roof overhead. Some have multiple levels, and one contains a 45-foot subterranean dry fall. Sinkholes (skylights) illuminate the interiors of some caves. Most cave passages eventually lead upstream through a swallow hole to a "blind" valley (a ravine having no exit for drainage except through a cave).

The bigger and more mature caves are quite stable, with ages on the order of thousands of years. Except during an earthquake or flood, the hard-packed floors of these caves should offer safe passage. It is very dangerous, however, to wander around topside in the pseudokarst valleys (those with sinkholes) and blind valleys (those ending in swallow holes). There would be no exit if one were to fall into some of these holes—or incipient holes. (This may explain the reported disappearance of travelers in the last century who tried various shortcuts across the Carrizo Badlands.)

Several tributaries on the left, just past 2.0 miles in Arroyo Tapiado, are worth investigating. Huge berms of slumped debris lie across most of them; climb these berms and cautiously peer into frighteningly deep pits that lie at the foot of dry falls.

A small grove of mesquite on the left at 2.7 miles is the clue to finding the entrance to one of the longer caves. Halfway through this cave is a tiny skylight, perhaps 50 feet up. Another cave entrance on the left at 2.9 miles offers an easy passage of several hundred feet to a wide swallow hole. This cave also features a large sinkhole in the roof of its midsection, and a curious oxbow, or alternate passage.

On the right at 3.1 miles you'll find the entrance to the "Big Mud Cave," the collapsed remnants of a former cave passage. It's an easy and worthwhile side trip, and you don't need a flashlight: Walk through the huge punctured cavern at the front and continue up the narrow wash bridged by many arches. After about 0.5 mile, on the left, you can climb out of the wash for a look at the mazelike terrain above. Stay on the ridgeline, don't wander through the valleys, and keep track of your footprints—you must reenter the same wash to get back safely!

Don't miss the slot-like passage just south of the Big Mud Cave entrance, on the same canyon wall. After squeezing through, let your eyes adjust to the dark

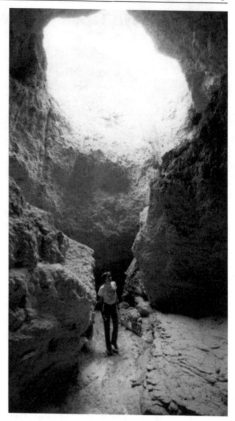

Big Mud Cave in Arroyo Tapiado

and behold an amazing sight.

Other passage entrances penetrate the walls of Arroyo Tapiado and some of its tributaries. So do "pipes," or upper-level conduits, which spew forth waterfalls during rare flash floods.

Arroyo Tapiado widens after 4.0 miles and sets a straighter course northwest. The canyon divides at 6.3 miles; take the right fork, following the sign indicating ARROYO DIABLO. At 6.7 miles, the road goes up the slope to the right and meanders southeast to join Arroyo Seco del Diablo at 9.0 miles. (A "dropoff" jeep route to Fish Creek intersects nearby, offering a direct connection to the Split Mountain area of the Carrizo Badlands.)

Shallow at first, Arroyo Diablo deepens steadily between golden-colored walls of sandstone—quite unlike the gray-green claystone walls you saw in Arroyo Tapiado.

Sandstone concretions, most shaped like balls or bullets, lie half-imbedded in the water-polished walls. Others have completely weathered out and lie on the ground. Between 11.0 and 13.0 miles, there are many interesting tributaries to explore if you have time. The one at 12.3 miles (west side) divides into a maze of narrow slot canyons chock-full of concretions, each one a unique sculpture. (Leave 'em as they lie— even rocks are protected in the state park.)

Down near the mouth of Arroyo Diablo are some mesquite groves, and a small seep in the floor of the canyon. When you emerge onto flat land just beyond the mouth, save some time and distance by leaving the wheel tracks and turning west to pick up the jeep road in Vallecito Creek wash.

Mud cracks in Arroyo Seco del Diablo

Area D-13: Carrizo Gorge

A north-south-trending fault zone is responsible for the series of ridges and canyons at Anza-Borrego's south end. Carrizo Gorge, the most dramatic of these, divides the Jacumba Mountains to the east from the In-Ko-Pah Mountains to the west. These mini-mountain ranges are links in the Peninsular Ranges from the Laguna Mountains in the northwest to the Sierra Juarez of Baja California.

Carrizo Gorge is best known for the railroad that threads along its eastern wall: the San Diego & Arizona Eastern. Built in 1907-1919, the railroad carried freight, and for a time passengers, between San Diego and the Imperial Valley. The gorge section features 11 miles of twisting track, 17 tunnels, and numerous wooden trestles. The spectacular Goat Canyon trestle, completed in 1933 as part of a realignment of the original route, is a noted county landmark. Hurricane Kathleen badly mangled the line in 1976, and cut off traffic through the gorge for five years. After reopening in 1981, the line was quickly severed again, this time by a fire that burned out several smaller trestles. Today the Carrizo Gorge section remains out of service, but there's never-ending speculation on its possible future uses. The tracks could someday carry sightseeing tourists through the gorge, or they might end up carrying cars filled with San Diego's solid waste destined for some future Imperial Valley landfill.

Hiking along the SD&AE tracks through Carrizo Gorge is expressly forbidden. The route is posted and sometimes patrolled. The railroad also owns a strip of land on either side of the tracks. It is the opinion of Anza-Borrego rangers, how-ever, that hikers are permitted to cross the tracks at right angles within the state park.

Trailhead parking for the trips below requires an Anza-Borrego Desert State Park parking pass. See the section "Using This Book" for more information.

Area D-13: Carrizo Gorge

344

Trip 1: Indian Hill/Carrizo Palms

Distance	6.5 miles
Total elevation gain/loss	900'/900'
Hiking time	4¹/₂ hours
Required map	USGS 7.5-min *Sweeney Pass*
Best times	November through April
Agency	ABDSP
Difficulty	★★★

A variety of interesting historical, botanical, and geological features are seen along this route. Even if you don't want to attempt this entire loop, you'll find much to fascinate you on an abbreviated hike.

You can begin at a point along the SD&AE tracks near Dos Cabezas siding. Do not take the Mortero Wash and Jojoba Wash jeep roads to reach this point in your standard auto! A route on much firmer ground, the so-called Dos Cabezas Road, is better. From Interstate 8, drive 4.1 miles up Highway S-2 to an unsigned dirt road on the left. Go south on this road and veer right after 1.1 miles. Continue another 6.1 miles, staying north of the tracks, to Dos Cabezas siding. From the siding, continue driving 2.2 miles on the north side of the tracks until you reach the road's end, which overlooks a wash.

On foot, backtrack about 200 yards, cross the tracks (west of here the tracks are posted against trespassing—don't walk along them or loiter around them), and head south-southwest across a broad alluvial plain dotted with cacti and small shrubs. Several rocky hills consisting of desert-varnished granitic boulders punctuate the surface of the plain. One of these is Indian Hill—which is incorrectly labeled on the *Sweeney Pass* topo map. The true Indian Hill, a site of former Indian occupation, has a fire-blackened cave and *morteros* on its northeast side.

Next point of interest is the remains of a circa-1912 railroad camp used during the construction of the railroad. The ruins are located 0.1 mile south of the center of section 20. Use your topo map as a guide. Here you'll find the walls of an old shed constructed of mortar and blasting-powder cans.

Back up about 0.1 mile and follow remnants of an old jeep road west toward a hillside overlooking the railroad tracks. Cross the tracks and descend over a rugged slope into a tributary of Carrizo Canyon; then go north in the sandy bed of the canyon past several seeps and small palm groves. There's good camping here and there in flat, sandy areas sheltered from the wind.

The seep and large grove of palms at the 1720-foot contour is one of the spots labeled "Carrizo Palms" on the topo map. During 1912 through 1919 railroad workers installed a pump here to boost water up to the camp.

After another mile, you'll come to a major confluence. Go right (east, upstream) into a narrow canyon with colorful rock formations, and scramble over a series of bedrock exposures and easy dry falls. After 0.5 mile the bed becomes sandy again; continue one more mile south to the tracks. Don't follow the tracks; instead cross them, continue south, and drop into an east-draining wash. Pass under the tracks and you'll soon arrive at a point just below your parked car.

*Ruins of powder-keg-
constructed shack*

Trip 2: Mortero Palms to Goat Canyon

Distance	4.0 miles round trip (to upper Goat Canyon)
Total elevation gain/loss	1500'/1500'
Hiking time	4 hours (round trip)
Required map	USGS 7.5-min *Jacumba*
Best times	November through April
Agency	ABDSP
Difficulty	★★★

Along the crest of the Jacumba Mountains lie several hidden bowls, surrounded by austere, rock-strewn peaks. To spend a night here on a bed of sand, immersed in an achingly profound silence, with nothing but a sky filled with stars overhead is to experience the desert in all its wonder and simplicity.

Not far away from one of these bowls is a landmark revered by railroad buffs the world over. This is the 200-foot-high, 600-foot-long trestle over Goat Canyon on the San Diego & Arizona Eastern line. It has been called the longest curved railroad trestle and one of the highest wooden trestles in the world.

You start this hike at the Mortero Palms trailhead, rather close to the rock formation known as Dos Cabezas ("two heads"). As in Trip 1, take the Dos Cabezas Road south and west from Highway S-2. At a point 5.7 miles from S-2, go south across the tracks on a paved crossover. Continue on the south side of the tracks for 0.1 mile, veer left (southeast, away from the tracks) and proceed 0.9 mile to a road fork. Bear left there, and stay left again after another 0.3 mile. Drive 0.4 mile farther (past an isolated, rocky hill on the left), and turn right toward Mortero Palms. Go 0.5 mile to the road's end overlooking a wide wash.

Take care to hike up the main (Mortero Palms) canyon to the west, not the tributary canyon to the south. A path follows the south bank for a while, avoiding the vegetation-choked streambed. Soon you begin climbing over granitic boulders. Look for a half-dozen *morteros*, namesakes of the palm grove, in the center of the drainage 100 yards below the beginning of the palms. A path also threads the north canyon wall—but you miss the *morteros* if you follow it.

The palm grove is one of the densest in Anza-Borrego, arising from seeps amid a jumble of huge boulders reminiscent of the rock formations at Joshua Tree National Monument. On warm days this is a seductively cool spot, and it takes some will power to get moving again to tackle the short but steep stretch of canyon ahead. Traverse left or right, or climb the water-polished rocks directly if you're a real daredevil.

At the 2440-foot contour it's easier to leave the canyon bottom temporarily and go up on the slope to the north through stands of teddy-bear cholla. Drop back in at about 2750 feet, but leave the canyon again at the 2840-foot contour. Proceed west and southwest across a small saddle and continue west over a divide into the Goat Canyon drainage.

Descend to a delightful, juniper-dotted bowl at about 3200 feet, a good place to spend the night. Further exploration in the area might include a visit to Jacumba peak (4512') south along the crest of the Jacumba Mountains, or a descent down Goat Canyon for a look at the famous trestle. At about 2700 feet in Goat Canyon, there's an excellent—if not close-up—view of the bridge, framed by the steep walls of the canyon.

Goat Canyon trestle

Trip 3: Carrizo Gorge

Distance	18 miles (I-8 to S-2)
Total elevation gain/loss	0'/2000'
Hiking time	14 hours
Required maps	USGS 7.5-min *Jacumba, Sweeney Pass*
Best times	November through April
Agency	ABDSP
Difficulty	★★★★★

The trek down the length of Carrizo Gorge is long, rugged, difficult, and memorable. It is one to be undertaken cautiously, with the right equipment and clothing. Essential are long pants and sturdy, waterproofed boots.

This trip is best done as a two-day backpack, though one very long day is sufficient for speed demons who travel lightly. The last 6 miles, on jeep tracks in the sand, can be done at night. If you're backpacking, keep the weight of your pack to a minimum. Consider leaving your stove, tent, and other luxury items behind. Several roomy rock caves may be used for shelter in the canyon's midsection. There's likely to be a fair amount of water in parts of the canyon, but carry drinking water anyway—or in lieu of that, a water-purification filter.

Although the SD&AE tracks along the east wall of Carrizo Gorge seem an easier alternative to the rugged, twisting bed of Carrizo Canyon, you're not allowed to walk them. Hikers who have been caught walking the tracks have had to pay heavy fines.

First, set up your car shuttle or drop-off/pick-up arrangement. The starting point is reached by taking the Jacumba exit off Interstate 8. Go west on the frontage road (Carrizo Gorge Road) to where it crosses under I-8. This is the assumed starting point. You might try getting permission to park at the nearby Thousand Trails

resort. The end point is mile 48.6 on Highway S-2.

Staying south of I-8, walk across the SD&AE tracks, and parallel the freeway for 200 yards until you reach the I-8 bridge over Carrizo Creek. Go north under the bridge and on down the broad drainage. Presently you enter a real canyon. The creek carries a respectable flow of water during the wet season, and you may be up on the banks most of the time in an effort to avoid having your boots fill with water. At 2.0 miles, the creek cascades over a tumble of car-sized boulders; you may have to detour over the jagged rocks on the left (west) side, a climb of 150 feet, class 3 rock climbing. This is the only really serious technical obstacle on the trip.

The next 10 miles offer bushwhacking, boulderhopping and mud-stomping in abundance. The sharp thorns of mesquite and catclaw; the needlelike tips of a particularly wicked type of bunch grass; dense thickets of carrizo, or cane, a bamboolike reed; and slippery rocks will all conspire to slow your progress. Feral cattle used to keep paths through the mesquite clear, but they were airlifted out of the canyon in the late 1980s. Mercifully, however, there are some easy stretches across sand and rock too.

The gorge has served as a trap for railroad debris which has tumbled off the slopes, and for flotsam and jetsam washed down from the Jacumba area during past floods. At about 4.0 miles, four sets of railroad wheels and axles lie in the canyon. You can look up to see rails drooping over two of the ravines like limp clotheslines, their underpinnings burned away.

At about 6.0 miles, above a landscape of rusted tin cans from a former railroad camp, there is a beautiful teddy-bear-cholla forest with specimens up to 10 feet tall. Barrel cacti up to 8 feet high are also seen a short distance down the gorge.

Goat Canyon, a tributary, enters from the right (east) at 8.5 miles. Climb 200 feet up the ridge to the north of this canyon for a great view of the famous curved trestle. Several rock caves are nearby, some with signs of Indian occupation, and nearly all with evidence of later visits by undocumented aliens (Carrizo Gorge is so overgrown now that few Mexican migrants use it anymore).

The gorge (now called Carrizo Canyon) widens past Goat Canyon, though it is not until about the 12-mile point that you can walk continuously on smooth sand. Four-wheel drives can sometimes make it up the canyon about 6 miles, but don't count on that for someone who might try to pick you up at the bottom. By walking all the way out, you end up at the Carrizo Creek crossing (mile 48.6) on Highway S-2.

Another possible endpoint for this trip is Bow Willow Campground. To reach it, leave Carrizo Canyon about one mile short of the highway and head directly northwest toward the dirt road into Bow Willow Canyon.

Giant cholla cactus

Area D-14: Jacumba Mountains

East of Jacumba, pressed against the California-Baja California border, is a series of scenic peaks and valleys in the Jacumba Mountains affording vistas of two counties and two nations. The BLM manages the area, which lies entirely south of Interstate 8, for wildlife protection and primitive recreation. Jeep roads penetrate its periphery, but the heart of it lies so untouched that it qualifies for consideration as a potential federal wilderness area.

Although American map makers consider this rugged area to be a part of the Jacumba Mountains, it is more closely associated with the 100-mile-long Sierra Juarez, Baja's northernmost link in the chain of Peninsular Ranges. As on the scenic Sierra Juarez crest to the south, you'll see great stacks of weathered boulders, with pinyon pines and other high-desert vegetation growing wherever sand or soil can collect.

Each of the three trips below is within Imperial County, just east of the San Diego County line. They are included in this book because they're so easily accessible from San Diego (about 90 minutes by car) and right next to Anza-Borrego Desert State Park.

To reach the starting point for Trips 1 and 2, exit Interstate 8 at In-Ko-Pah Park Road (east of Jacumba). Drive southwest 0.2 mile along the frontage road, Old Highway 80, then turn left on an unmarked dirt road. Ordinary cars should park no farther than 0.8 mile up this road, at a large turnout. Sturdy 4-wheel drives can continue farther, prudently, up the steep road to-

ward the patchwork of jeep roads and primitive campsites. The hiking descriptions below assume that you park in the large turnout.

A nice alternative (or complement) to the USGS topographic map listed below for Trips 1 and 2 is the Mexican government "La Rumorosa—I11D63," 1:50,000 scale map. Unlike the USGS map, which is blank below the border, the Mexican topo shows features on both sides. It is not legal, of course, to cross the border into Mexico except at official ports of entry.

Area D-14: Jacumba Mtns

Trip 1: Blue Angels Peak

Distance	5.0 miles round trip
Total elevation gain/loss	1300'/1300'
Hiking time	3 hours (round trip)
Recommended map	USGS 7.5-min *In-Koh-Pah Gorge*
Best times	October through May
Agency	BLM/EC
Difficulty	★★

Blue Angels Peak, one of several crags along a high north-south ridge spanning the two Californias, happens to be the highest point in "Alta" California within six miles of the international border. The peak is surely one of the windiest spots in southern California—especially in spring, when hot air rising up from the low desert to the east draws in a strong flow of cooler air from the coastal regions.

From the parking area 0.8 mile from Old Highway 80, walk up the road to a saddle at 3830 feet. A jeep road branches left to Smuggler's Cave, an old hideout of bandits and smugglers, now a fire-blackened, graffiti-emblazoned wreck. Proceed another 0.1 mile south and bear right (west). Continue south and finally east to the roadend, staying left at two road junctions at 1.1 and 1.4 miles. An old mining prospect lies at the end of the road.

Blue Angels Peak is to the southeast, hidden behind a false peak capped by a massive block of granite seemingly poised to roll. Scramble up over lichen-encrusted boulders and past scraggly pinyons to find the bench mark on the summit.

On the return trip, make a short detour to discover International Boundary Marker 231, a handsome 10-foot steel obelisk, in the middle of a flat south and a little west of the peak. These markers are numbered consecutively along the border from #1 at the Gulf of Mexico shoreline east of Brownsville-Matamoros to #258 at the Pacific shoreline.

Border marker south of Blue Angels Peak

Trip 2: Valley of the Moon

Distance	7.0 miles round trip
Total elevation gain/loss	900'/900'
Hiking time	4 hours (round trip)
Recommended map	USGS 7.5-min *In-Koh-Pah Gorge*
Best times	October through May
Agency	BLM/EC
Difficulty	★★

Strolling through the appropriately named Valley of the Moon, you would almost think that a square-mile chunk of Joshua Tree National Monument had been transported here—minus, of course, the famous Joshua trees. Huge granitic outcrops, seamed with horizontal and vertical cracks, ring the valley.

Begin this hike as in Trip 1 above, but bear left at the intersection 0.1 mile beyond the saddle. Descend sharply and bear southeast toward a small peak ("Tahe") containing the Elliot Mine, an abandoned amethyst mine. Keep straight, avoiding spur roads to campsites tucked up against coves in the rocks, but turn left (east) just before the main road continues sharply uphill to the mine. Bend east and south around the base of Tahe, then veer east and enter the Valley of the Moon.

The sandy floor of the valley is dotted with Mojave yucca, catclaw, Mormon tea, and buckwheat. You can continue toward an old water tank in the northeast corner of the valley, or follow any of the jeep roads that wind around the statuesque boulder heaps to the south. Photographers should be here early or late in the day, when the sun bathes the stone battlements in a warm light, and sharply defined shadows march across the valley.

In the Valley of the Moon

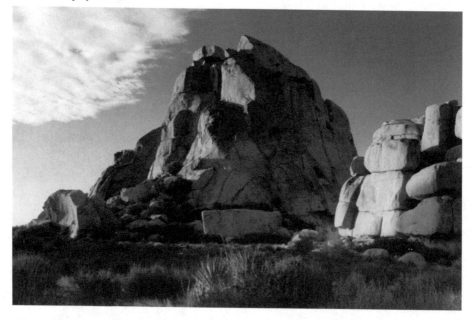

Trip 3: Myer Valley/Boulder Creek

Distance	4.0 miles
Total elevation gain/loss	1000'/1000'
Hiking time	3 hours
Required map	USGS 7.5-min *In-Koh-Pah Gorge*
Best times	November through April
Agency	BLM/EC
Difficulty	★★★

Have you ever driven down Interstate 8 east of Jacumba, and, eyeing the immense boulder piles that rise on both sides, wondered what it would be like to clamber over them? Here's your chance. Follow these directions, and in just a few minutes you can be parked off the freeway, and on your way into a primeval landscape visited only by an occasional adventurer like yourself.

Exit I-8 at Mountain Spring. At a point midway in the "island" between the eastbound and westbound lanes of the freeway, turn east on a rough dirt road. In 0.2 mile this road joins the abandoned concrete ribbon of old U.S. Highway 80. Drive east, dodging fallen boulders on the roadway, for an additional 1.3 miles and park near the road's end—just before the brink of a road cut made for the eastbound lanes of I-8.

Scramble down the slope (this is probably the most difficult part of the hike!) about 100 feet to the sandy bed of Myer Creek. Pass under the lanes of I-8 through the large culvert to the west and continue 0.1 mile in the wash until you come to the base of a rocky gully on the left (east). Scramble up the coarse-grained granitic boulders in this gully; after 400 feet of elevation gain you join a sandy wash. Continue east and top a saddle—this is 0.2 mile south of peak 2385. Pass over the saddle, and descend an easy drainage leading to Myer Valley. The half-square-mile valley gently slopes to the north. It is so thickly grown with creosote bush, ocotillo, and other plants whose color intensifies

after periods of rainfall that it can look from a distance as if it were covered by a verdant carpet. There is a maze of old jeep roads in the valley from the days when vehicles could navigate up Myer Creek from the Ocotillo area. Flash floods obliterated that route, and the valley has been closed to all vehicle use by the BLM.

Upon reaching the edge of the valley, you can turn south and skirt the west edge of the valley, following a minor wash. Pick up traces of an old jeep trail about 0.3 mile southwest of peaklet 2033. Follow this west-southwest to the top of a broad divide, then drop into a ravine that leads west into a north-flowing tributary of Boulder Creek. After some moderate scrambling, you'll arrive at a beautiful palm oasis, complete with a year-round spring. A sculpted dry fall and a nice set of Indian *morteros* are nearby.

From the palm oasis, it's an easy 1.2 miles back to the culvert under I-8, via Boulder and Myer creeks downhill in wash bottoms all the way. Several small groups of palms provide welcome shade if needed.

At 0.3–0.4 mile below the palm oasis, two canyons come in on the left, inviting side trips. The first of these, a rugged tributary to the south, is fascinating, with immense boulders, hidden cottonwoods and palms, and secluded campsites. Some difficult scrambling is required to fully explore it. The second of these, upper Boulder Creek canyon to the southwest, is vegetation-choked and unremarkable.

Appendix 1: Best Hikes

Best beach hike

La Jolla Shores to Torrey Pines Beach (Area B-2, Trip 1). Here the primeval Southern California coastline survives more or less intact.

Best suburban hikes

Torrey Pines State Reserve (Area B-2, Trip 3). Breathtaking views of the coastline, eroded landforms, and the rare Torrey Pine.

Daley Ranch—Tour of the Ponds (Area C-2, Trip 2). A rewarding springtime ramble through North County's newest open-space preserve.

Blue Sky Ecological Reserve (Area C-3, Trip 2). A quintessential example of riparian woodland and oak woodland.

Los Penasquitos Canyon (Area C-4, Trips 2 and 3). Largest undeveloped canyon bottom close to San Diego. Rolling hills, meadows, and a delightful, tree-lined stream.

Cowles Mountain (Area C-7, Trips 1 through 4). The summit has the best view of metropolitan San Diego.

Best mountain hikes

Lower Doane Valley/Lower French Valley (Area M-2, Trip 4). Trickling streams, dark forests, and sunny meadows.

Azalea Glen Trail (Area M-7, Trip 6). Oak and conifer forests and a trickling stream.

Sunset Trail (Area M-8, Trip 9). Visit Laguna Meadow and one or more of the ephemeral Laguna lakes.

Best desert hikes

Borrego Palm Canyon Nature Trail (Area D-2, Trip 1). Discover a fan palm oasis amid soaring canyon walls.

Calcite Mine (Area D-4, Trip 8). Discover how weathering and erosion carve the desert landscape.

Mountain Palm Springs (Area D-11, Trip 3). A half dozen palm groves secreted in boulder-strewn hills.

Canyon Sin Nombre (Area D-12, Trip 2). Tour a fault-churned landscape and squeeze through a slot canyon.

Best canyon hikes

Noble Canyon (Area M-8, Trip 17). A year-round mountain stream in a narrow, shaded canyon.

Horsethief Canyon (Area M-9, Trip 3). Use this tributary canyon to reach the bouldered bed of Pine Valley Creek—beautiful in the winter and spring.

Sheep Canyon (Area D-1, Trip 2). Palms, sycamores, lush vegetation, and waterfalls.

Best waterfalls and swimming holes

Cedar Creek Falls (Area M-5, Trip 3). San Diego County's most spectacular waterfall; deep "punchbowl" beneath.

Three Sisters Waterfalls (Area M-5, Trip 4). Three falls and three bathtub-like pools set amid a deep gorge.

Kitchen Creek Falls (Area M-8, Trip 15). A long series of steep cascades; spectacular when in flood.

Cottonwood Creek Falls (Area M-8, Trip 16). Easy-to-reach cascades with shallow pools.

Best peak climbs

Woodson Mountain (Area C-3, Trips 4 and 5). Giant boulder outcrops frame a coast-to-mountain view.

Stonewall Peak (Area M-7, Trip 8). Easy trail; good overview of Cuyamaca and Laguna mountains from the pointed summit.

Garnet Peak (Area M-8, Trip 2). Easy climb; fabulous view on the Laguna escarpment.

Villager and Rabbit peaks (Area D-4, Trip 2). Long, rugged, desert peak climb; views across half the width of California and deep into Mexico.

Best wildflowers

Torrey Pines State Reserve (Area B-2, Trip 3). Nearly all varieties of wildflowers common to the coastal region are represented here.

East Mesa Loop (Area M-7, Trip 13). Wildflowers of the mountain meadows and chaparral.

Big Laguna Trail (Area M-8, Trip 10). Wildflowers of the mountain meadows and pine forest.

Borrego Palm Canyon Nature Trail (Area D-2, Trip 1). Most common varieties of desert wildflowers bloom here.

Best autumn colors

Fry Creek Trail (Area M-2, Trip 6). Conifer and oak forest.

Kelly Ditch Trail (Area M-7, Trip 1). Conifer and oak forest; trickling streams.

West Mesa Loop (Area M-7, Trip 14). Conifer and oak forest; meadows.

Wooded Hill Nature Trail (Area M-8, Trip 14). Black oak and pine forest.

Best bird and wildlife watching

San Elijo Lagoon (Area B-1, Trip 3). Birds of shoreline and coastal lagoon habitats.

Tijuana River Estuary (Area B-4, Trip 1). Local and migrant bird life.

Guajome Regional Park (Area C-1, Trip 3). Excellent birding around the lake and marsh.

Wilderness Gardens Preserve (Area C-1, Trip 4). Chaparral, oak woodland, and riparian habitats, all within a small area.

Silverwood Wildlife Sanctuary (Area C-8, Trip 4). An Audubon preserve harboring birds and wildlife of the chaparral zone.

Barker Valley (Area M-2, Trip 11). Deer, bobcats, mountain lions, and eagles can be seen in this area.

Dyar Spring/Juaquapin Loop (Area M-7, Trip 11). One of the largest deer herds in San Diego County roams this area.

Lower Willows (Area D-1, Trip 1). Birds, small mammals, and insects thrive in the jungle-like growth.

Borrego Palm Canyon Nature Trail (Area D-2, Trip 1). Bighorn sheep are commonly seen here in summer.

Yaqui Well (Area D-6, Trip 3). Good birding in this small desert oasis.

Squaw Pond Trail (Area D-10, Trip 2). This desert oasis draws coyotes, bobcats, birds, bats, and rattlesnakes.

Best running trails

La Jolla Shores to Torrey Pines Beach (Area B-2, Trip 1). Beach all the way except for a few cobbled areas. Recommended during low tide only.

Daley Ranch—Jack Creek Meadow (Area C-2, Trip 3). Except for a steep pitch at the start, this is a gently rising and falling route following the margins of the beautiful meadow.

Lake Poway Loop (Area C-3, Trip 1). Pleasant loop around a small lake. One steep and several mild grades.

Iron Mountain Trail (Area C-3, Trip 6). Mostly moderate grade up the south side of this loop trail.

Los Penasquitos Canyon (Area C-4, Trips 2 and 3). Mostly flat dirt road. Pleasant scenery, cool breezes, peace and quiet.

Rose and San Clemente canyons (Area C-5, Trips 1 and 2). Wide trails shaded by oaks and sycamores.

Cowles Mountain (Area C-7, Trips 1 through 4). The quintessential mountain workout in the San Diego area. Superb views.

Sweetwater Trail (Area C-10, Trip 1). A classic California landscape of golden, rolling hills. Narrow trail with some short, steep grades.

Oak Grove to High Point (Area M-2, Trip 10). To the highest point on Palomar Mountain via road and trail. Experts only.

Cuyamaca Peak (Area M-7, Trip 7). Paved road all the way, but steep.

Stonewall Creek/Soapstone Grade Loop (Area M-7, Trip 9). Mostly gentle fire roads, some steep grades on trails.

West Mesa Loop (Area M-7, Trip 14). Pleasant, shady route on fire roads.

Noble Canyon Trail (Area M-8, Trip 17). Narrow, but mostly smooth trail. Downhill direction preferred. One long, steep stretch.

Otay Mountain (Area M-10, Trips 1 and 2). Steady ascent on good dirt roads. Unusual cypress groves, good views all the way.

Jasper Trail/Grapevine Canyon (Area D-6, Trip 1). High desert to low desert on mostly smooth, sandy jeep trails.

Mason Valley Truck Trail (Area D-8, Trip 2). Run from the mountains to the desert on an old dirt road.

Arroyo Tapiado/Arroyo Diablo Loop (Area D-12, Trip 3). Through the badlands washes on flat, smooth jeep trails.

Appendix 2: Recommended Reading

Hiking, Backpacking, and Mountaineering

Darvill, Fred, *Mountaineering Medicine*, 14th edition, Wilderness Press, 1998.

Ganci, David, *Desert Hiking*, 3rd edition, Wilderness Press, 1993.

Graydon, Don and Hanson, Kurt (eds.), *Mountaineering: The Freedom of the Hills*, 6th edition, The Mountaineers, 1998.

Manning, Harvey, *Backpacking One Step at a Time*, 4th edition, Vintage Books, 1986.

Moser, David and Schad, Jerry (eds.), *Wilderness Basics, The Complete Handbook for Hikers and Backpackers*, The Mountaineers, 1992.

Winnett, Thomas and Findling, Melanie, *Backpacking Basics*, Wilderness Press, 4th edition, 1994.

San Diego Area Guidebooks

Automobile Club of Southern California, *San Diego County* (guidebook), 1995.

Bringe, Scott, *Mountain Bike Guide, San Diego Region*, 3rd edition, Sunbelt Publications, 1993. (Out of print.)

California Coastal Commission, *California Coastal Access Guide*, 4th edition, University of California Press, 1991.

Greenstadt, Daniel, *San Diego Mountain Bike Guide*, Sunbelt Publications, 1998.

Hewitt, Lonnie and Moore, Barbara, *Walking San Diego*, The Mountaineers, 1989.

Johnson, Paul R., *Weekender's Guide (Anza-Borrego)*, Anza-Borrego Desert Natural History Association, 1987.

Knaak, Manfred, *The Forgotten Artist: Indians of Anza-Borrego and their Rock Art*, Anza-Borrego Desert Natural History Association, 1988.

Lindsay, Diana and Lowell, *The Anza-Borrego Desert Region*, 4th edition, Wilderness Press, 1998.

Mendel, Carol, *San Diego!. . . City and County*, Carol Mendel, 1985.

Mendel, Carol, *San Diego On Foot*, Carol Mendel, 1994.

Parker, Horace (G. Leetch, ed.), *Anza-Borrego Desert Guide Book*, revised edition, Anza-Borrego Desert Natural History Association, 1979.

Peik, L. and R., *Campers Guide to San Diego County Campgrounds*, Peik Enterprises, 1992.

Robinson, John W., *San Bernardino Mountain Trails*, 4th edition, Wilderness Press, 1986.

Ruland, Skip, *Backpacking Guide to San Diego County*, revised edition, Calif. Backpacking Co., 1984. (Out of print)

Schad, Jerry, *Backcountry Roads & Trails, San Diego County*, 4th edition, Centra Publications, 1993.

Schaffer, Jeffrey P., et al. *The Pacific Crest Trail, Volume 1: California*, Wilderness Press, 5th edition, 1995.

History and Natural History

Bailey, H. P., *The Climate of Southern California*, University of California Press, 1966.

Chase, J. Smeaton, *California Desert Trails*, Houghton Mifflin Co., 1919. (Out of print)

Ellsberg, Helen, *Mines of Julian*, La Siesta Press, 1972.

Evarts, Bill, *Torrey Pines: Landscape and Legacy*, Torrey Pines Association, 1994.

Gray, Gary and Havert, Bill, *Nature Guide to the Mountains of Southern California, by Car and on Foot*, Earth Trails Publications, 1996.

Jaeger, Edmond C. and Smith, Arthur C., *Introduction to the Natural History of Southern California*, University of California Press, 1971.

Lindsay, Diana E., *Our Historic Desert: The Story of the Anza-Borrego Desert*, Copley Books, 1973.

Pryde, Philip R., *San Diego: An Introduction to the Region*, 3rd ed., Kendall/Hunt Publishing Co., 1992.

Reed, Lester, *Old Time Cattlemen and Other Pioneers of the Anza-Borrego Desert Area*, Anza-Borrego Desert Natural History Association, 1986.

Stein, Lou, *San Diego County Place-Names*, Tofua Press, 1975.

Geology

Abbott, P. (ed.), *Geologic Studies of San Diego*, San Diego Association of Geologists, 1982.

Burns, Diane M.(ed.), *Geology of San Diego County*, Sunbelt Publications, 1997.

Kennedy, M. P., and Peterson, G. L., *Geology of the San Diego Metropolitan Area, California*, Bulletin 200, California Division of Mines and Geology, 1975.

Kern, Philip, *Earthquakes and Faults in San Diego County*, Pickle Press, 1989.

Kuhn, Gerald G. and Shepard, Francis P., *Sea Cliffs, Beaches, and Coastal Valleys of San Diego County*, University of California Press, 1984.

Remeika, Paul and Lindsay, Lowell, *Geology of Anza-Borrego: Edge of Creation*, Sunbelt Publications, 1992.

Sharp, Robert P., *Coastal Southern California* (geology guide), Kendall/Hunt Publishing Company, 1978.

Sharp, Robert P. and Glazner, Allen F., *Geology Underfoot in Southern California*, Mountain Press Publishing Company, 1993.

Weber, F. H., *Geology and Mineral Resources of San Diego County, California*, County Report 3, California Division of Mines and Geology, 1963. (Contains large-scale geological map of San Diego County.) (Out of print)

Biology

Bean, L. J. and Saubel, S. S., *Temalpakh: Cahuilla Indian Knowledge and Usage of Plants*, Malki Museum Press, 1972.

Beauchamp, R. Mitchel, *A Flora of San Diego County, California*, Sweetwater River Press, 1986.

Belzer, Thomas J., *Roadside Plants of Southern California*, Mountain Press Publishing Company, 1984.

Clarke, Herbert, *An Introduction to Southern California Birds*, Mountain Press Publishing Company, 1989.

Clemons, Duffie, *Plants of Anza-Borrego Desert State Park*, Anza-Borrego Desert Natural History Association, 1986.

Dawson, E. Yale, *Cacti of California*, University of California Press, 1971.

Jaeger, Edmond C., *Desert Wild Flowers*, revised edition, Stanford University Press, 1969.

Jaeger, Edmond C., *Desert Wildlife*, Stanford University Press, 1961.

Johnson, Paul, *Cacti, Shrubs and Trees of Anza-Borrego*, Anza-Borrego Desert Natural History Association, 1982.

Massey, Barbara W., *Guide to the Birds of the Anza-Borrego Desert*, Anza-Borrego Desert Natural History Association, 1998.

Munz, Philip A., *California Spring Wildflowers*, University of California Press, 1961.

Munz, Philip A., *California Desert Wildflowers*, University of California Press, 1962.

Munz, Philip A., *California Mountain Wildflowers*, University of California Press, 1963.

Peterson, P. Victor, *Native Trees of Southern California*, University of California Press, 1966.

Raven, Peter H., *Native Shrubs of Southern California*, University of California Press, 1966.

Unitt, Philip, *Birds of San Diego County*, San Diego Society of Natural History, 1984.

Appendix 3: Local Organizations

Anza-Borrego Desert Natural History Association
P.O. Box 311
Borrego Springs, CA 92004
(760) 767-3052
(Activities associated Anza-Borrego Desert State Park)

Anza-Borrego Foundation
P.O. Box 2001
Borrego Springs, CA 92004
(760) 767-0446
(Sponsors desert walks; raises funds to acquire additional park land)

Adventure 16 Wilderness Outings
4620 Alvarado Canyon Road
San Diego, CA 92120
(619) 283-2374
(Basic mountaineering instruction and backpacking trips in San Diego County)

Audubon Society of San Diego
2321 Morena Blvd., Suite D
San Diego, CA 92110
(619) 275-0557
(Nature and bird walks; also operates the Silverwood Wildlife Sanctuary)

California Native Plant Society, San Diego Chapter
P.O. Box 1390
San Diego, CA 92112
(619) 685-7321
(Offers outings to view native plants)

Cuyamaca Rancho State Park Interpretive Association
12551 Highway 79
Descanso, CA 91916
(760) 765-0755
(Activities associated with Cuyamaca Rancho State Park)

Cleveland National Forest Foundation
P.O. Box 779
Descanso, CA 91916
(619) 595-3693
(Seeks to preserve public land and purchase or acquire private land within the national forest boundary)

Laguna Mountain Volunteer Association
3348 Alpine Blvd.
Alpine, CA 91901
(619) 445-6235
(Activities associated with the Descanso Ranger District of Cleveland National Forest)

San Diego Hiking Club
P.O. Box 161068
San Diego, CA 92176
(Day hikes and backpacking trips throughout San Diego County; wilderness information)

San Diego Society of Natural History
(Natural History Museum, Balboa Park)
P.O. Box 1390
San Diego, CA 92112
(619) 232-3821
(Interpretive outings throughout San Diego County)

San Diego County Trails Council
P.O. Box 1969
El Cajon, CA 92020
(An affiliation of clubs and individuals interested in supporting trails for hikers, equestrians, and mountain bikers; helps to preserve and maintain existing trails)

Sierra Club, San Diego Chapter
3820 Ray St.
San Diego, CA 92104
(619) 299-1743
(Hiking and backpacking outings throughout the San Diego region; plus a wilderness basics training course in winter-spring)

Walkabout International
835 5th Ave.
San Diego, CA 92101
(619) 231-7463
(Sponsors mostly urban walks, but some hikes in San Diego's backcountry)

Appendix 4: Agencies and Information Sources

Parks and Agencies

Anza-Borrego Desert State Park (ABDSP)
P.O. Box 299
Borrego Springs, CA 92004
Recording: (760) 767-4684
Visitor Center: (760) 767-4205
Administration: (760) 767-5311

Balboa Park (BP)
(619) 235-1122

Batiquitos Lagoon (BL)
(760) 431-0240

Blue Sky Ecological Reserve (BSER)
(858) 679-5469

Bureau of Land Management (BLM/EC)
El Centro Resource Area
1661 South Fourth St.
El Centro, CA 92243
(760) 337-4400

Bureau of Land Management (BLM/PS)
Palm Springs-South Coast Resource Area
690 W. Garnet Ave.
North Palm Springs, CA 92258
(760) 251-4800

Cabrillo National Monument (CNM)
(619) 557-5450

California Department of Fish and Game (CDFG) (858) 467-4201

California Parks and Recreation Department
San Diego Coast District (CP/SDC)
(619) 642-4200

Cleveland National Forest
Supervisor's Office
10845 Rancho Bernardo Road, Suite 200
San 5Diego, CA 92127
(858) 673-6180

Cleveland National Forest
Palomar Ranger District (CNF/PD)
1634 Black Canyon Road
Ramona, CA 92065
(760) 788-0250

Cleveland National Forest
Descanso Ranger District (CNF/DD)
3348 Alpine Blvd.
Alpine, CA 91901
(619) 445-8341 or (619) 445-6235

Cuyamaca Rancho State Park (CRSP)
12551 Highway 79
Descanso, CA 92016
(760) 765-0755

Daley Ranch (DL)
(760) 839-4680

Dixon Lake Recreation Area (DLRA)
(760) 839-4680

Elfin Forest Recreational Reserve (EFRR)
(760) 753-6466

Fallbrook Land Conservancy (FLC)
(760) 728-0889

La Jolla Indian Reservation (LJIR)
(760) 742-1297

Lake Poway Recreation Area (LPRA)
(858) 679-5465 or (858) 679-5470
Recording: (858) 679-5466

Lake Wohlford (LW)
(760) 839-4346

Los Coyotes Indian Reservation (LCIR)
P.O. Box 248
Warner Springs, CA 92086
(760) 782-3269

Los Penasquitos Canyon Preserve (LPCP)
(858) 538-2480

McGinty Mountain Preserve (MMP)
c/o Santa Rosa Plateau Ecological Reserve
(Nature Conservancy)
(909) 677-6951

Marian Bear Park (MBP)
(858) 581-9952

Mission Trails Regional Park (MTRP)
(619) 668-3275

Palomar Mountain State Park (PMSP)
(760) 742-3462

San Diego City Lakes (SDCL)
(619) 465-3474

San Diego County Parks and Recreation Department (SDCP)
5201 Ruffin Road, Suite P
San Diego, CA 92123
Information: (858) 694-3049
Camping reservations: (858) 565-3600

San Diego (city of) Open Space Division (SDOS) (619) 685-1350

San Dieguito River Park (SDRP) (858) 674-2270

San Elijo Lagoon Regional Park (SEL) (760) 753-5091

San Pasqual Battlefield State Historic Park (SPBSP) (760) 489-0076

Silverwood Wildlife Sanctuary (SWS) (619) 443-2998

Tecolote Canyon Natural Park (TCNP) (858) 581-9952

Tijuana Estuary Visitor Center (TEVC) (619) 575-3613

Torrey Pines State Reserve (TPSR) (858) 755-2063

Map Sources

Most of the agencies listed above are good sources of maps and map/brochures for areas under their own jurisdiction. For general navigation and exploratory hiking in the Cleveland National Forest, you should have a copy of the Cleveland National Forest recreation map. This periodically updated map delineates public and private lands, and shows the locations of vehicle gates (either locked or subject to seasonal closures) on the forest-service road system.

Desert travelers should obtain the Anza-Borrego Desert State Park map/brochure for vehicle navigation. A nearly equivalent map of the Anza-Borrego region is bundled with the Lindsays' book, *The Anza-Borrego Desert Region.*

In addition, you can obtain a photocopied series of 15-minute USGS topographic maps of the Anza-Borrego desert region from the Anza-Borrego visitor center in Borrego Springs.

Tom Harrison publishes a shaded, topographic map of Cuyamaca Rancho State Park, and another map at a smaller scale covering most of the San Diego backcountry. In addition, CD-ROM versions of public-domain topographic maps covering various regions of California have begun to appear on the market.

For one-stop shopping for all kinds of local maps and guides, visit one of the following retail map stores. Each offers a complete selection of the USGS topographic maps referred to in this book.

Map World
123-D North El Camino Real
Encinitas, CA 92024
(760) 942-9642

Map Centre
3191 Sports Arena Blvd., Suite F
San Diego, CA 92110
(619) 291-3830

A good selection of maps and guidebooks are also available from the following outdoor equipment outfitters:

Adventure 16
4620 Alvarado Canyon Road
San Diego, CA 92120
(619) 283-2374

Adventure 16
143 S. Cedros Avenue
Solana Beach, CA 92075
(619) 755-7662

Recreational Equipment, Inc.
5556 Copley Drive
San Diego, CA 92111
(619) 279-4400

Miscellaneous

Project Hug-a-Tree
(send SASE)
6465 Lance Way
San Diego, CA 92120

San Diego County Sheriff
(Emergencies—dial 911)
(619) 565-5200

California Division of Forestry
To report fires: (619) 442-1615
(619) 588-0364

California Department of Transportation (CalTrans) Road condition hotline for all California state and interstate highways:
(800) 427-7623

Index

Author note

Jerry Schad is the author of nine books on outdoor recreation in Southern California, and is a recognized expert on its trails. Schad, a professor of physical science at San Diego Mesa College, writes a weekly column, "Roam-O-Rama," for the *San Diego Reader*, hosts the *Afoot and Afield in San Diego* series on KPBS-TV, and exhibits his astronomical photography at http://skyphoto.com.

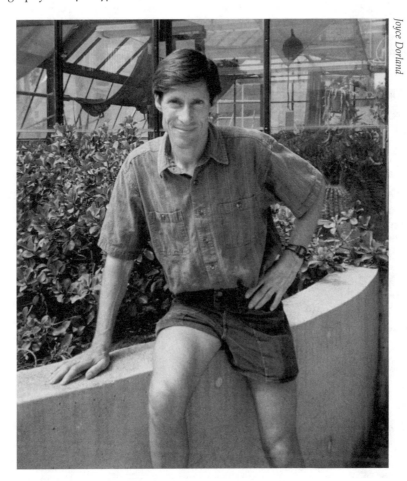

Joyce Dorland

Books by Jerry Schad

50 Southern California Bicycle Trips
Backcountry Roads and Trails, San Diego County
Back Roads and Hiking Trails, The Santa Cruz Mountains
Adventure Running
*Afoot and Afield in San Diego County

Cycling San Diego
California Deserts
*Afoot and Afield in Orange County
Cycling Orange County
*Afoot and Afield in Los Angeles County
Physical Science: A Unified Approach
*101 Hikes in Southern California

**Published by Wilderness Press

Other Jerry Schad Books from Wilderness Press

Afoot & Afield in Orange County

Whether you're up for exploring marine life at the Bolsa Chica Reserve or climbing Santiago Peak in the Santa Anas, or anything in between, this guide shows the way. Details 72 salubrious outings in every kind of natural environment, from teeming tidepools to windswept mountaintops.
ISBN 0-89997-206-3

Afoot & Afield in Los Angeles County

Covering all the best L.A. adventures, from strolling along at Malibu Lagoon State Beach to trekking up a mountain on Catalina Island. Close to 200 trips explore the City of Angels' own backyard, traveling through a variety of climate zones and revealing a remarkably diverse array of plant and animal life.
ISBN 0-89997-267-5

101 Hikes in Southern California

The book that proves there's more to SoCal than theme parks and strip malls. From the San Gabriel Mountains to the Anza-Borrego Desert and everywhere in between, this guide offers an incredible selection of exciting trips covering scores of hidden places just beyond the urban horizon.
ISBN 0-89997-193-8

Trail Runner's Guide San Diego

A comprehensive guide to running the myriad trails of sun-soaked San Diego, from the beach at La Jolla to the summit of Palomar Mountain. Runners and hikers alike will appreciate the detailed descriptions of 50 exhilarating routes. Includes climate and topography tips, maps, photos, and more.
ISBN 0-89997-308-6

Top Trails: Los Angeles

Highly visual guide to 48 of the Southland's best trails in the greater LA metro area, from Malibu to the Hollywood Hills, San Jacinto Peak to the San Fernando Valley. Includes trail feature tables, don't-get-lost milestones, maps for every trip, and more.
ISBN 0-89997-347-7